1750
+ /-
revchg

D1248639

The Library of Scandinavian Studies

THE IBSEN CYCLE

THE IBSEN CYCLE

The Design of the Plays from
Pillars of Society to *When We Dead Awaken*

Brian Johnston

TWAYNE PUBLISHERS

A DIVISION OF G. K. HALL & CO., BOSTON

The Library of Scandinavian Studies

Erik J. Friis, *General Editor*

Volume 2

The Ibsen Cycle, by Brian Johnston

Copyright © 1975 by G. K. Hall & Co.

Library of Congress Cataloging in Publication Data

Johnston, Brian, 1932–
    The Ibsen cycle.

    (The Library of Scandinavian studies, v. 2)
    Bibliography: pp. 369–71.
    1. Ibsen, Henrik, 1828–1906—Criticism and interpretation.
I. Title. II. Series.
PT8895.J58   839.8'2'26   74-12484
ISBN 0–8057–3313–2

MANUFACTURED IN THE UNITED STATES OF AMERICA

Contents

... except in directions in which we can go too far there is no interest in going at all: and only those who will risk going too far can possibly find out just how far one can go.

T. S. Eliot

Preface

Though the structure of this book consists of two parts, each a distinct unit, the reader is advised to read the chapters in the sequence in which they are set out. The book sets out an idea of Ibsen's theater, an idea that is incrementally amplified in the sequence of chapters, so that readers who might be lured to the analyses of individual plays (*Ghosts, Rosmersholm,* and *The Master Builder*) in the second part, before they have taken in the preparatory stages of the argument, will find themselves puzzled, baffled, and even somewhat outraged by the premises on which my analyses are based.

There is no point in my ignoring the fact that a thesis as novel as the present one is certain to encounter objections, and in the Introduction I envisage many of these objections and address myself to them. In the chapters that follow I gradually lead the reader to the central thesis: the account of the twelve plays, from *Pillars of Society* to *When We Dead Awaken,* as a single, Hegelian, cyclical, and evolutionary dramatic structure that might well come to be seen as the greatest single art work of the nineteenth century.

That this ambitious concept of literary and intellectual achievement *is* rooted in the cultural life of the nineteenth century—above all in post-Enlightenment Germany—is the theme of the first two chapters. Since the writing of these chapters I have read M. H. Abrams's definitive account of Romantic art and thought, *Natural Supernaturalism, Tradition and Revolution in Romantic Literature,* in which the reader will discover, greatly amplified by deep and wide-ranging scholarship, the main themes of my study, including the centrality of Hegel to Romantic art and thought. Abrams, of course, nowhere mentions Ibsen, whose art lies outside the province of his study; but it will not be difficult for the reader to see Ibsen as the heir to the intellectual world whose geography is so well described by Abrams. The Romantic movement, in Abrams's account, can stand with classical Greece and Renaissance Europe as one of the few cultural epochs in which the human condition was described and dramatized with such intensity, depth, and scale of exploration. Ibsen insisted that his art represented the end, not the beginning, of a cultural phase, and the great intensive power and extensive range of his drama, which the present study tries to indicate, depends to a great extent on the tremendous intellectual revolution that accompanied, and succeeded, the French Revolution: the first revolution in the history of the world, according to Hegel, which had as its aim the re-creation of mankind.

The idea of Ibsen that this book sets out is that of a post-Romantic artist who still remained loyal to Romantic aspirations: who, though he saw everywhere the betrayal of revolutionary and Romantic ideals, still held onto the impossible goal of "a revolution in the spirit of man." The famous Ibsen "realism" will be seen to be, not an abandonment of these ideals for the sadly pragmatic scrutiny of our everyday world in trouble, but the cunning tactics of a militant Romantic who is subversively smuggling the explosive Romantic powers into the pragmatic bourgeois world that had turned its back upon them. Nor does Ibsen stop short of infiltrating the most audacious, ambitious, and thoroughgoing of all Romantic forces—the philosophic vision of Hegel—into his unsuspecting bourgeois world, so that the work both of demolition and of re-creation, in the Cycle of twelve plays, is total.

The reader need not be alarmed that I have made this book the elaborate demonstration of an *idée fixe*. Ibsen's art is far too rich and complex for that, and a great deal that I admire in that art already was established for me before I decided to recover, for criticism and interpretation, the *idea of the world* (or world picture) that Ibsen is dramatizing. The Hegelian underpinning to the Cycle, as I hope to show, is not a mechanical strategy on Ibsen's part, but the starting point for the most boldly imaginative creativity, in which the artist is at no time subservient to the philosophical system.

Inevitably, such a demonstration raises questions and problems for Ibsen's art to which later Ibsen commentary should address itself: there is only so much that can be encompassed by the present study.

Though the central thesis of this study is new, my debt to previous Ibsen interpretation and criticism, even where, as often, I have disagreed with it, is extensive. Where I have agreed with previous interpretation I probably am far more indebted than I am aware, for there is a kind of innocent and unintentional plagiarism in all critical writing. To Rolf Fjelde, above all, I am indebted for inspiration, encouragement, and advice which were incalculably valuable in the early days when I was uncertain as to the destination—or even, sometimes, the direction—of my quest. His contributions of suggestion, correction, and requests for clarification have amounted to something like a collaboration. Another encouraging influence was G. Wilson Knight's admirable little book on Ibsen which manages, in its few packed pages, to suggest more than volumes of previous interpretation: the happy example of the imaginative response to imaginative literature. All students of Ibsen are by now aware of the great value of J. W. McFarlane's "Oxford" translations which, by virtue of their indispensable notes, early drafts, and supplementary material, have contributed immensely to Ibsen studies in the English-speaking world.

In addition I would like to extend special thanks to John D. Hurrell for pioneering my work in the unhappily defunct *Drama Survey* (perhaps the best drama magazine of its time) when such pioneering required taking an editorial risk. My thanks are due, also, to the editors of *The Drama Review, Comparative Drama, Scandinavian Studies* and *The Yale Review* for publishing articles which, in their very tentative and uncertain exploration of a newly evolving thesis, did not ingratiate themselves by any very obvious elegance of style or organization.

To Erik J. Friis, the General Editor of "The Library of Scandinavian Studies," the series in which this book appears, the expression of my gratitude can only seem like "a small payment on a boundless, incalculable debt." The coherence and order he has brought to a somewhat chaotic manuscript, all the time maintaining patience in the face of a barrage of revisions, deletions, additions, and corrections, are the result of a heroic effort at ridding the world of monsters.

Acknowledgments

Excerpts from *The Phenomenology of Mind*, translated and edited by J. B. Baillie (revised second edition 1949), by permission of George Allen & Unwin Ltd., London.

Excerpts from *The Oxford Ibsen*, Vols. IV–VII, edited and translated by J. W. McFarlane, the Oxford University Press, Oxford, England.

Excerpts from G. W. F. Hegel, *Lectures on the Philosophy of Fine Art*, translated by F. P. B. Osmaston, by permission of G. Bell & Sons, London.

Excerpts from Alexandre Kojeve, *Introduction to the Reading of Hegel*, edited and with an Introduction by Allen Bloom, translated by James H. Nichols, Jr., © 1969 by Basic Books Inc., Publishers, New York.

Excerpts from *Eros and Civilization* by Herbert Marcuse, by permission of Beacon Press, Boston, Mass.

Excerpts from *Religion and Philosophy in Germany* by Heinrich Heine, translated by John Snodgrass, Beacon Press, Boston, 1959.

Excerpt from G. W. F. Hegel, *Reason in History*, translated by Robert S. Hartman, copyright 1953, by The Liberal Arts Press, Inc., reprinted by permission of the Bobbs-Merrill Company, Inc.

Excerpt from *Ulysses* by James Joyce, Bodley Head, London, 1960, and Random House, Inc., New York.

Excerpt from *The Libation Bearers* by Aeschylus, translated by Richmond Lattimore, University of Chicago Press.

Excerpt from *The Philosophy of History* by G. W. F. Hegel, translated by J. Sibree with a new Introduction by Professor C. J. Friedrich, Dover Publications, Inc., New York, 1956.

Excerpt from *Wagner on Music and Drama*, ed. by Goldman and Sprinchorn, E. P. Dutton & Co., New York, 1964.

Excerpt from *Ibsen: Letters and Speeches*, ed. Evert Sprinchorn, Hill & Wang, 1964. (Farrar, Strauss & Giroux, Inc., New York.)

Excerpt from *The Poet in the Theatre* by Ronald Peacock, Hill & Wang, 1960 (Farrar, Strauss & Giroux, Inc., New York).

Excerpt from *The Three Ibsens* by Bergliot Ibsen, translated by Gerik Schjelderup, Hutchinson & Co., London, 1951.

Excerpt from *Plays and Controversies* by W. B. Yeats, reprinted by

Acknowledgments

permission of M. B. Yeats, The Macmillan Co. of London & Basingstoke, and Macmillan of Canada.

Excerpt from *The Flower and the Castle* by Maurice Valency, © Maurice Valency, 1963.

Excerpts from *Ibsen: Four Major Plays*, translated by Rolf Fjelde, The New American Library (Signet), New York, 1965.

Excerpt from *The Drama Review*, Volume 13, No. 2 (T-42), Winter 1968, © 1968 by *The Drama Review*, reprinted by permission. All rights reserved.

Excerpt from *Civilization and Its Discontents* by Sigmund Freud, translated from the German and edited by James Strachey. Copyright 1961 by James Strachey, W. W. Norton & Company, Inc., New York, N.Y.

Excerpts from *Hegel's Phenomenology*, by J. Loewenberg. Copyright 1965 by Open Court Publishing Company. Reprinted by permission of the publisher.

Excerpt from "Dimensions of Ibsen's Dramatic World" by Rolf Fjelde in *Contemporary Approaches to Ibsen*. Copyright Norwegian Research Council for Science and Humanities, 1971, Oslo, Norway.

Excerpt from G. W. F. Hegel, *The Philosophy of Mind*, translated by William Wallace and A. V. Miller, The Clarendon Press, Oxford, England.

Excerpt from J. N. Findlay, *Hegel: A Re-Examination*, Humanities Press, New York.

Excerpt from R. D. Laing, *The Politics of Experience*, copyright R. D. Laing, 1967. Reprinted by permission of Penguin Books Ltd.

Excerpt from Georg Brandes, *Inaugural Lecture*, translated by Evert Sprinchorn, reprinted with permission from Evert Sprinchorn.

Excerpt from *The Portable Nietzsche*, edited by Walter Kaufmann. Copyright 1954 by The Viking Press, Inc. Reprinted by permission of The Viking Press, Inc.

Excerpt from Friedrich Nietzsche, *The Birth of Tragedy*, translated by Francis Golffing, Doubleday & Co., Inc., New York.

Excerpt from Walter Kaufmann, *Hegel: A Re-Interpretation*, Doubleday & Co., Inc., New York, 1965.

Excerpt from Søren Kierkegaard, *Either/Or*, Vol. II, translated by Walter Lowrie with revisions and a foreword by Howard A. Johnson. Doubleday & Co., Inc. (Anchor), New York, 1959.

Explanation of Abbreviations

Phen. = G. W. F. Hegel: *The Phenomenology of Mind*
Phil. Hist. = G. W. F. Hegel: *Lectures on the Philosophy of History*

Phil. Fine Art = G. W. F. Hegel: *Lectures on the Philosophy of Fine Art*
Phil. Rel. = G. W. F. Hegel: *Lectures on the Philosophy of Religion*
Loew. = J. L. Loewenberg: *Hegel's Phenomenology: Dialogues on the Life of Mind*

Introduction

After a while Brandes got up and said: "The man who arrives at the eleventh hour is just as good as the one who comes at the seventh or the ninth; but there is a difference. Here in the North we have come in the seventh hour, we have understood Ibsen earlier than anyone." Here Ibsen began to shake that heavy grey head of his. Brandes was taken aback, and began a long explanation of how we had after all understood him before anybody else, but the more he explained, the more Ibsen shook his head; and when at last we all stood up to drink his health, he only half rose from his chair and said: "A great deal could be said about this speech," but he would not enlarge on it then.

Bergliot Ibsen, *The Three Ibsens*, p. 110

This book undertakes a complete revaluation and reinterpretation of Ibsen's methods and intentions as the dramatist of the twelve realistic plays from *The Pillars of Society* (1877) to *When We Dead Awaken* (1899). It follows Ibsen's description by seeing the plays as a single cycle "with mutual connections between the plays" and it demonstrates that this single cyclical structure is based upon the one great intellectual structure of reality available to Ibsen in the nineteenth century: the philosophical system of Hegel.

The novelty does not lie in attributing to Hegel a strong influence upon Ibsen's thought and art, for, though by no means generally accepted by interpreters of Ibsen, this has, at least, been recognized by a number of scholars and critics from the time of John C. Pearce's essay *Hegelian Ideas in Three Tragedies by Ibsen.*[1] What is new in the present study is the discovery that the realistic plays are structured directly upon Hegel's major philosophical work, *The Phenomenology of Mind*, and that the sequence of dialectical dramas in Hegel's account of the evolution of human consciousness is exactly paralleled in the sequence of dialectical dramas in Ibsen's Cycle. This argument is capable of proof, for the reader need only compare the dialectical actions of the two sequences to be convinced that a parallel of twelve matching actions, *in the same sequence*, is beyond the possibility of coincidence. As this

1

is the central argument of the book from which the rest of the interpretation of Ibsen's art follows, it is important that the reader understands the nature of the argument. The writer is not claiming merely that there are details in Hegel's text that can be found in Ibsen's text; he is claiming that the exact sequence in which these details occur is repeated in Ibsen's text.

This point is of the utmost importance. For it is quite possible that many of the themes of Hegel's work can be found, also, in other philosophers, particularly as Hegel is encyclopedic in scope and is quite avowedly incorporating all earlier systems into his system. Thus it could be asserted that Ibsen might well have got many of the themes of his Cycle from other philosophers. This is true, but he could not have got the most important thing of all: the manner in which these themes are linked together in an evolutionary advance of human consciousness. Nowhere, outside Hegel, do these themes appear in this way; nowhere, outside Hegel, could they serve as the basis for a dramatic cycle; nowhere, outside Hegel, could this account of human consciousness take on the *triadic* form that it takes, also, in Ibsen's Cycle. And, in fact, the desire to find some source other than Hegel is absurd. Ibsen professed his admiration for Hegel as he did for no other philosopher except, towards the end of his life, for Nietzsche.

This study, therefore, stands or falls upon the evidence it sets out that there is a direct correlation between the sequence of dialectical dramas set out by Hegel in the Second Part of *The Phenomenology of Mind*, and the sequence of dialectical dramas set out in Ibsen's realistic Cycle from *The Pillars of Society* to *When We Dead Awaken*, and the only valid negative judgment on the book's argument is one that considers the two sequences and then denies that they reveal any such correspondence. This book, therefore, hinges upon two basic premises:

(a) That Ibsen's twelve plays form a cycle, with mutual connections between the plays.

(b) That the sequence of dialectical actions of this cycle follows, in strict order, the sequence of dialectical actions set out in *The Phenomenology of Mind*.

I insist upon this point perhaps wearisomely because it is important that the reader sees that the nature of my argument is thoroughly objective, that it rests upon a presentation of evidence in the nature of scientific or mathematical proof, and that it must be met on these grounds. It is true that, after this demonstration, I then draw conclusions which are subject to the inevitable fallibility of all interpretive criticism; it is here that further interpretation and debate will be useful in refining and augmenting our idea of Ibsen's art. All the time, however, I have kept my eye on Ibsen's text, have related my interpretation to that text: to the words on the page and the actions on the stage. I am interested in Ibsen as a dramatic artist, not as a thinker; but, as Eric Bentley long ago pointed out, the adequate modern playwright is almost by necessity also a "thinker."

The idea that a dramatist might construct a great dramatic cycle based upon a highly complex account of the painful struggle of human consciousness to attain to truth and freedom (the theme of Hegel's text) probably will strike many readers as inherently implausible. It is therefore worthwhile to reflect that a contemporary of Ibsen's did just that! One of the major works of Hungarian drama is Imre Madách's *The Tragedy of Man* (1861) in which, according to Robert K. Sarlos, "the preoccupation with Hegelian dialectics is manifest in theme and structure. The battle and union of good and evil is a central issue, and successive scenes, as well as ideas, form dialectic triads."[2]

In twelve scenes (oddly paralleling Ibsen's twelve plays) the entire unfolding of the human spirit is revealed, from the Creation to the Future of a new Ice Age. "Adam dreams history. Egypt, Greece, Rome, Byzantium, Kepler's Prague, Paris 1789, and nineteenth-century London are his stations in the past." As Adam advances from one "age" to another, he accumulates within himself the spiritual history of this past, and his dialectical journey is one of repeated pain and suffering. At the end of this winding stairway of despair, and in spite of the doubts instilled by Lucifer, Adam senses the meaning of this spiritual labor and the spirit of the cosmos, the "Lord," enjoins: "O Man, strive on, strive on, have faith; and trust!"[3]

It is very unlikely that Ibsen knew of Madách's drama, which was first performed in Hamburg in 1892. In any case, for all the similarity of theme, there is a profound difference in method, for whereas Madách presents the audience with an evolutionary costume drama, each scene set in the appropriate historical period as Adam dreams the *future* history of Man, Ibsen's actions belong entirely to the nineteenth century and recollect the structure of the spiritual past beneath the everyday surface.

The great themes of Ibsen's Cycle, the recollection of the Past, the search for new spiritual direction in the Present, in which the entire spiritual history of humanity is resurrected for a judgment day upon the soul, are major Faustian themes of nineteenth-century literature. Flaubert's *The Temptation of St. Anthony*, Walter Pater's *Marius the Epicurean*, and Ibsen's *Emperor and Galilean* all, in their own way, take

up the theme of the ultimate meaning and direction of the human
spirit tackled by Hegel in *The Phenomenology of Mind.*

Of *Emperor and Galilean* Ibsen wrote that it was the *first* work of his
written under the direct influence of German thought. One of his biog-
raphers, Edmund Gosse, adds, "and the last," and Brian Downs, in his
influential *Ibsen: The Intellectual Background,* quotes Gosse's emenda-
tion with apparent approval. But Ibsen's statement that *Emperor and
Galilean* was the *first* work written under German influence *only* can
mean that other works, written under the influence of German thought,
followed this "first." These later works were the realistic plays of the
Cycle and, until very recently, it was accepted that we were not to look
at these admirably realistic plays for anything so alarmingly abstract as
German thought.

Obviously it was believed that the image of Ibsen the author of the
realistic plays, as the disenchanted pragmatist forsaking the great
visionary themes of his earlier writing (*Brand, Peer Gynt,* and *Emperor
and Galilean*), and, instead, submitting his age and himself to the closest
scrutiny, was more attractive. There probably are very deep and very
admirable reasons for this reaction against idealism and philosophical
abstractions; but it is a simplification of Ibsen's dramatic vision which
sees him, so late in life, performing some drastic lobotomy upon
himself whereby he truncates his imagination from the great universalizing vision of the earlier works.

One may wish Ibsen to be many things that he is not. It is the conviction of the present study, however, that its author's personal philosophy is irrelevant for the adequate interpretation of Ibsen. On the other
hand, I will admit having come greatly to admire Hegel's philosophical
vision and Ibsen's very imaginative adaptation of it to his own dramatic
vision. Because Ibsen employs the Hegelian world view, at least as a
structural principle for his Cycle, it is this world view that best can
clarify his art for us. This is not to say that the beginning and the end
of Ibsen criticism should be Hegelian—only that we cannot talk adequately about that art until we take account of the idea of reality from
which Ibsen proceeds to create his art. Many readers will detect an
analogous situation in the recovery of the Elizabethan world view for
Shakespeare interpretation in the present century.

This, then, is a book about the Hegelian structure of Ibsen's dramatic
vision, setting itself this limited purpose and no doubt open to the objection that it is not pursuing other purposes or taking account of other
aspects of Ibsen's art. Actually, however, the reader will discover that
my purpose is far from limiting and, though it must emphasize some

aspects of Ibsen's art at the expense of others, it is able to encompass more of Ibsen's total intention than previous accounts.

However, this study does not wish to turn Ibsen's great Cycle into "dramatized Hegel," for it is the present writer's belief that Ibsen's imagination was great and independent enough to absorb a complex philosophical interpretation of the world and yet create boldly original work that requires to be interpreted on its own terms. A contrast with Madách's *Tragedy of Man* is appropriate here for, to the present writer, at least, the major fault of the latter work is precisely that it far too rigorously (and, therefore, superficially) adapts the Hegelian system while at the same time employing an extremely conventional dramatic form. Ibsen's identity as an artist, for all its self-doubts (which were to be creative assets), was too strong not to transform utterly the ghostly conflicts of the *Phenomenology* into a vividly solid, complex, and original world of human drama.

In fact, I would advance the paradox that it was precisely because Ibsen was so consummate a man of the physical theater that he was attracted to such a spiritual odyssey as that which Hegel presents in the *Phenomenology*. For the theater's great strength is that it can present to our view a solidly constructed world of scenes and human actors, simulated passions and conflicts, and omnipresent "human interest." By means of this theater Ibsen could supply the human and realistic substance of his art; but if this art was not to expend itself merely in repetitive mimetic activity, if it was to be given some purpose and direction, it needed just such a dialectical and philospohical backbone as the Hegelian structure could supply. No other philosopher of the age could supply an equivalent structure; and no structure from the past would still be valid for a drama of the modern spirit. Ibsen assented to the Hegelian world view and employed it for his purposes, I believe, just as a modern dramatist might seriously employ Marx or Freud.

There is nothing new in this for literature, which, at its greatest, always has reflected a deep and wide-ranging interpretation of reality. The relationship between philosophy and poetry, after all, has been contentious but fruitful from the beginning. In the tenth book of *The Republic* Plato records the attacks upon philosophy by the poets and then returns the attack with interest; yet he envisions a union, with poetry purged and wise, readmitted to the ideal republic; and the tenth book itself, with its Myth of Er, offers a hint of what this new poetry might be.[4]

In the later literature of Europe, at least from Dante onward, major imaginative writing almost always has consciously reflected and adapted a philosophical world view and few critics today would attempt to interpret Dante, Chaucer, Shakespeare, Milton, Racine, or Pope without reference to the intellectual structures of reality within which these writers created their works. The Hegelian world view was the last great inclusive structure of reality, interpreting the cosmos in time and space, available to the European writer, and Ibsen's awareness of this, as well as his employment of the Hegelian world view, attests to his intelligence as a writer.

Matthew Arnold observed that the *discovery* of new ideas is the province of the philosopher, not the poet, but that the poet, nevertheless, to be fully effective must be in conscious contact with the best ideas current at the time:

> The grand work of literary genius is a work of synthesis and exposition, not of analysis and discovery; its gift lies in the faculty of being happily inspired by a certain intellectual and spiritual atmosphere, by a certain order of ideas, when it finds itself in them; of dealing divinely with these ideas, presenting them in the most effective and attractive combinations,—making beautiful works with them, in short.

In Periclean Athens or Elizabethan London, such a structure of ideas was "in the air," so to speak, and could supply the poet with a comprehensive and elaborate world view, a system of universals, to which he could give imaginative assent. With the late eighteenth century onwards, however, we come upon the modern phenomenon of the collision of mutually contradictory world views or systems, one idea of the cosmos being challenged or displaced by another, placing upon the imaginative writer the extraordinary dilemma of having to choose *which* cosmos he will inhabit. "I must create my own system or else be enslaved by another's," declared William Blake, taking, characteristically, the extreme view. A writer such as Goethe attempted to grasp the totality of all systems within the Second Part of his *Faust*, and it is precisely such an overweening endeavor that Hegel, with greater success, embarks upon in *The Phenomenology of Mind*.

The major cause of the breakdown of the tradional Christian-derived world view and its relegation to the status of merely one phase of the advance of human consciousness, was the newly developed sense of *history*, which accompanies the tremendous intellectual emergence of Germany into Europe in the late eighteenth century. We can trace the growth of the historical vision from Herder's *Reflections on the Philosophy of the History of Mankind* (1784–91) and its dynamic continuation through Schiller, Goethe, Hegel, Richard Wagner, and Friedrich Nietzsche, in all of whom the concept of a dynamic historical Time is paramount. Alexandre Kojève, in his brilliant study of Hegel, goes so far as to say that, for Hegel, Man *is* Time; that Time and human consciousness are the same thing:

...Nature is Space, whereas Time is History. In other words, there is no natural, cosmic Time; there is Time only to the extent that there is History, that is, *human* existence—that is, *speaking existence.* Man who, in the course of History, reveals Being by his Discourse, *is the* "empirically existing Concept" [*der daseiende Begriff*], and Time is nothing other than this Concept. Without Man, Nature would be *Space,* and only Space. Only Man is in Time, and Time does not exist outside of Man; therefore Man *is* Time, and Time *is* Man..."[5]

Such a radical change in concepts of reality and of the human condition within the cosmos was bound to change the very conventions of literature itself, and Ibsen's theater, I believe, is the culmination of a whole development in drama which begins with Schiller's historical dramas. The world of Ibsen's realistic dramas is, profoundly, a world subject to pressure and change, to the process of time, and to the "awakening" and evolving human consciousness within an historically created world. The Hegelian world view may not be that of the present reader, any more than the Elizabethan world view, but, in the hands of an Ibsen, as in the hands of a Shakespeare, such a structure of reality can be made to reveal its human, tragic, and dramatic possibilities.

A major emphasis of the present study is that in the Ibsen drama dialectical action and development takes precedence over character analysis; but there should be no quarrel between those for whom Ibsen's drama primarily is dialectical and those who prefer the older view that Ibsen's major gifts are those of penetrating psychological analysis and trenchant social criticism. The dialectic is Ibsen's strategy as the disruption of Order is Shakespeare's strategy, but this does not reduce his method to a mere formula, for the strategy is made to explore a world whose human implications are as rich as the world of Shakespeare.

The more one studies Hegel the less surprising it is that Ibsen should assent to and undertake to incorporate into his art the one great comprehensive world view still available to the nineteenth-century writer and to see in it a structure of ideas of immense advantage to the coherent shaping of his own art. The once fashionable denigration of Hegel beginning very early with Schopenhauer and Kierkegaard and being continued, in different terms, by modern positivism, is now giving way to the recognition that Hegel's "system" is not the enemy of individual existential experience, as Kierkegaard believed, nor the wildly unscientific and idealistic mysticism imagined by many positivists.[6] A number of excellent recent studies will establish this for the reader; he especially is recommended to consult Alexandre Kojève, Jean Hyppolite, J. Loewenberg, J. N. Findlay, and Walter Kaufmann, whose widely differing approaches will help to clear away many gross but still current prejudices as to the substance of Hegelian philosophy.

Of particular interest is Professor Loewenberg's study which insists that the method of the *Phenomenology* resembles that of drama, being mimetic; for Hegel *impersonates* each of the phases encompassed, and thus intellectually *lives through* each of the spiritual phases, errors, and conflicts in the same way that Madách and Ibsen impersonate and live through each of the phases of their cycles. Loewenberg's chapter by chapter or phase by phase explication of the difficult spiritual journey of the *Phenomenology* also will serve as a useful, though not always adequate, guide.

The reader will find in the following pages that not only do I find in Ibsen's drama a direct relation to Hegelian philosophy, but that I also insist that Ibsen's Cycle draws upon the whole rich storehouse of Western civilization. This can partly be explained by the fact that Hegel, too, is drawing upon this same storehouse so that to employ Hegel is to employ a multitude of sources. Ibsen, I believe, saw himself as coming at the end of a whole development of the European spirit, and, like Hegel, of summing up its entire content, but in the form of ambitious dramatic art works, from *Brand* onwards. Thus, the account of Ibsen that emerges from the following pages draws into the analysis of his art the entire intellectual heritage of the West—the entirety of human history—as far as the present writer is able to encompass this. This suggests that Ibsen's art is as rich in reference as that of Thomas Mann, James Joyce, T. S. Eliot, Ezra Pound, Samuel Beckett, and the many writers and artists of this tradition. The reader therefore must be warned that if he has an ingrained objection to the idea that Ibsen's art is richly responsive to and resonant of the cultural heritage of the West, there is much in the following pages that will alienate him.

Ibsen, I am suggesting, possessed a very definite *historical* imagination that could be satisfied in dramatic art only when it had found a place for the totality of his imaginatively apprehended cosmos; and that his obsession as artist was to express this totality even at the cost of the playgoer's or reader's intellectual comfort. Such an idea of Ibsen's art at least accords with his famous declaration to his sister Hedvig that he desired to achieve the greatest and most perfect that could be reached in power and clarity, and then to die.[7] Undoubtedly Ibsen also wished the result to be a dramatic art of absorbing interest and of formal beauty and these elements of his art will be kept in mind in the pages that follow.

It is precisely because the psychological and the technical interest is serving a universal vision, however, that it becomes so significant as art and as meaning. I believe that Ibsen saw his human and his esthetic problem with such urgency and clarity, forcing it to take on revolutionary artistic form, precisely because he was able to stand at a philosophical and historical distance from his own age. If this sounds too great a paradox, we can recall Ibsen's own words to Laura Kieler:

One must have something to create from, some life-experience. The author who does not have that does not create; he only writes books. Now I know very well that a life lived in solitude is not a life devoid of experience. But the human being is in the spiritual sense a long-sighted creature. We see most clearly at a distance; details confuse us; we must get away from what we desire to judge; summer is best described on a winter's day.[8]

The account of Ibsen's art that one only too frequently encounters in both his detractors and his advocates, is one that sees that art as, progressively, diminishing in range of interest. From the great middle period of *Brand, Peer Gynt,* and *Emperor and Galilean* in which Ibsen placed the human consciousness in great expanses of Time and Space, he retreated, so the accounts go, first into an examination of the conditions of public life in modern bourgeois Norwegian society, then retreated further to become the analyst of Interesting Individuals and their problems, and then, as if having nowhere further to retreat from the huge perspectives of the middle period, he entered the confines of his own private life, puzzling the world with riddling allegories of his career and his marital and emotional condition. In spite of much recent interpretation, such as that of Rolf Fjelde and G. Wilson Knight, which has brought to our attention the wider dimensions of Ibsen's later art, the above account is still the one we are most likely to encounter. It is the idea of Ibsen that one's students encounter, and it informs the idea of Ibsen's art in the latest biography of the dramatist.

That this is the exact opposite of the truth is the contention of the present study; it insists that Ibsen's realistic Cycle represents the most ambitious and extensive realization of his poetic vision, presenting us with an entire world for the unfolding of his great spiritual drama. I am suggesting, in fact, that the poet of the Cycle is the same man as the poet of *Emperor and Galilean* whose goal—"the third empire of spirit"—is the goal of the Cycle. This study, therefore, joins with those interpretations of Ibsen's later dramatic art that insist that, for all the change in dramatic method—dictated by a desire to find a *theatrical* expression of his philosophic and dramatic vision—that vision remained the shaping power of his art.

Though it is the purpose of the present study to demonstrate that the structure of Ibsen's Cycle, and the dialectical "stages of the Cross" that Spirit must undergo in its long pilgrimage to "the peak of Promise," are derived from Hegel, I would be the first to agree that Ibsen stands in a very independent relationship to Hegel's philosophy. The world

Ibsen has created in the Cycle, as well as his critical attitude towards it, derives from his own experience and observation. One might say that Ibsen has mastered the Hegelian argument and the dialectical method, as an artist might master a traditional technique; and that, to understand and appreciate Ibsen's daring and originality, it would be helpful for us to understand that technique. This will not endanger that aspect of Ibsen which has for so long been rightly admired: the admirable believability of his human drama of characters and conflicts. It merely adds to that art yet another important dimension—of a universal, as well as a particular, reality.

At first sight, no two figures would seem more incompatible than the Hegel of legend, the arch-apologist for the State for whom the Individual is utterly of no consequence, and Ibsen, the sturdy Individualist and exile who more than once pronounced the anarchist credo that the State must be abolished. Such an opposition, however, though effective for journalistic purposes, is misleading. Hegel did *not* set the State above the Individual *ultimately*: for Hegel the highest realm of reality, above that of the State, was the realm of Art, Religion, and Philosophy— spiritual realities that transcended the State; and Hegel's favorite work of art was the *Antigone* of Sophocles which, whatever else it teaches, does not advocate subservience to the State! And Ibsen's program of abolishing the State does not advocate primitive barbarism or a simple-minded return to Nature but, instead, the *surmounting* of the State by the spiritually awakened Individual—a goal not irreconcilable with Hegelian philosophy.

The precise nature of Ibsen's attitude to the whole realm of reality, analyzed in such great depth by Hegel in the *Phenomenology* must be gauged by each individual reader. I, for one, think it very possible that Ibsen saw the entire structure of given reality as analyzed by Hegel: the Objective world of evolved institutions, customs, and laws, and the Subjective world of psychological repression and conflict which also had evolved through centuries of dialectical development: as a structure of error, falsehood, injustice, and spiritual loss so massive that only the huge demolition effected by the entire Cycle of twelve plays was sufficient to clear it away and recover the foundations on which to build the "third empire" of the future. I believe that Ibsen saw the world of everyday reality in the way Plato saw it in his allegory of the cave: as a world of massive falsehood and illusion behind and beyond which essential and universal reality lay; I also believe that in each of the plays in the Cycle he removes one veil of illusion, infiltrates some of the essential reality into the stifling realm of falsehood until, by the end of the Cycle, the whole illusory fabric has dissolved and we come close to looking at the naked spirit. G. Wilson Knight put it well when he called Ibsen's method "spiritual strip-tease"; this, in fact, is also the method of Hegel in the sequence of dialectical dramas that occur in the second part of the *Phenomenology*.

For Hegel that which was essential for the human spirit in each phase or *gestalt* through which it passed, is that which has survived within the structure of Consciousness in the Objective and the Subjective worlds. That which is accidental, unessential, has dropped away, as if the human spirit continually is being refined in fire as it grows. To attain to authenticity and freedom in our consciousness, therefore, we must learn to come to terms with this essential content and to discard the unessential; we must, in fact, retrace the history of the origins and growth of human consciousness. But this journey inevitably is difficult and painful, for we must learn to reenact and relive past sorrow and loss within the present—as if undergoing a painful séance where *all* the spirits of the past continually must reassemble to reenact their pain, like the Book of the Dead in *The Odyssey* or as the reader is expected to reexperience the entire past of the race in Dante's *The Divine Comedy* (a work we know that Ibsen read). Hegel's "march of mind" is no simple paean to ruthless success, and though he quotes Schiller's apothegm, "the history of the world is the world's court of justice," Hegel is too honest and profound not to be aware of the appalling suffering and loss entailed by the history of the human spirit in the world as it advances, by means of dialectical conflict, to "higher" and freer phases. That the Spirit had passed through these phases was, to Hegel, the incontrovertible fact with which he had to reconcile his philosophy, and though he might feel disposed to lament the inevitability of conflict and destruction, the extinction of many superb or beautiful cultures—the Hellenic, for instance—he insisted that the life of the Present could not return to past forms except to acknowledge their necessary death. The strange text of the second part of the *Phenomenology* is filled with ghosts from the Past painfully resurrected, like the damned in the *Inferno*, to illustrate the errors and inadequacies of their spiritual convictions. And it is the novel theme of this study that Ibsen's Cycle is itself just such a succession of dialectical dramas in which, under the nineteenth-century surface, the ghosts of the Past, and the actions in which they lived and suffered, are reenacted.

As in the method of the *Phenomenology* Ibsen's "text" and his realistic dramaturgy create a texture in which we continually encounter echoes and quotations from the past of the race, as in the method of Ibsen's lifelong admirer James Joyce, suggesting that the greater part of reality, like the bulk of the iceberg, is beneath the conscious surface.

We might not consciously be aware of all the archetypal and historical memories that are being awakened by the modern actions, but these, nevertheless, are working upon us, controlling and guiding the nature of our responses in the theater, and creating that impression of richness we derive from Ibsen's plays, *when performed*, that contrasts with our immediate idea of the extreme economy of his form. The art of archetypal recollection continually is reactivating suppressed, tabooed, or forgotten areas of our consciousness and by thus resurrecting, reawakening, this submerged content of our consciousnesses the dramatic action can convert that content from a repressed and repressive to a liberating force; for what had been inhibiting, repressive, a structure of unrecognized habits and mechanical responses—the "ghosts" perceived by Mrs. Alving—now become disquieting, subversive. The awakened characters onstage, and the audience who comprehends their awakening, now move in a larger, more liberating, but more alarming cosmos.

The Past, thus awakened, can reveal values and possibilities we had allowed to be forgotten and which the structure of our given, immediate, and contemporary reality attempts to suppress, as the prisoners in the cave, according to Plato, will turn upon the philosopher who returns to liberate them. This conspiracy against truth and freedom, against the realization of our full human value, is all the more effective for not being, for the most part, conscious. Very much in the manner of psychoanalytic theory, this unawakened, suppressed content, like the traumata of childhood, creates the psychopathology of everyday life that inhibits the free functioning of a fully awakened consciousness.

This liberating function of the Past is the experience of anyone who enters into the spirit of a past culture and discovers in it values denied by the Present; the oppressive function of the Past is apparent to anyone who becomes conscious of how both the structure of his external world and the structure of his inner, individual world are the products of the total Past. In Hegel's profound vision man never can be the innocent consciousness awakening in a pristine world. That condition existed but once, in the myth of Adam in Eden; ever since man has to experience the Fall into Time. Ibsen agreed. He wrote to his friend Georg Brandes, "Raphael's art has never really moved me. His people belong to a period before the fall of man," and he advised a young would-be writer that a thorough knowledge of history was indispensable in order to judge one's own age and one's contemporaries at all adequately.

The world Ibsen presents to us in the Cycle is our normal, familiar world—familiar even to the point of banality. We are to know and feel this world intimately, share its confidence and its illusory sense of its own reality; we are to do this before we become aware of the way in which it is being disquietingly subverted by the pressure of a larger and more adequate reality emerging through unacknowledged conflicts or contradictions whose expression opens up huge historical perspectives. This is Ibsen's great contribution to the modern theater: a dialectical dramatic method that subverts the very image of reality it sets up, a reality which uses the very form and substance of the age to lead us to an awareness of realities that have existed before and will exist long after a particular moment in the late nineteenth century.

Ibsen chose the modern realistic method, I believe, because he felt that the "larger" gestures of Romantic drama, although they indicated the same realities he was determined to express, belonged to a condition of mind too innocent of the historical process. To retain the perspectives of man's spiritual history and identity within an art work speaking directly and powerfully to the modern consciousness, Ibsen was forced to create images of contemporary reality which, on close investigation, revealed the presence of that larger reality.

Paradoxically, this vast subject matter—the entire inheritance of the human spirit—could as well fit a modern provincial scene as the larger political, religious, and cosmopolitan scene of *Emperor and Galilean,* for the complex modern consciousness is the inheritance of every modern man and woman even if they are reluctant to acknowledge it. Ibsen's lonely fight against the trolls that infest the mind and heart could find its adequate expression in the little provincial community of Thomas Stockman or in Mrs. Alving's drawing room, as effectively as on the barricades of Paris in 1871. For were not the revolutionary heroes of modern consciousness such provincial figures as Kant in Koenigsberg or Hegel in Jena? In a century of great revolutionary conflict these provincial figures were greater forces for change than the heroes at the storm centers of Europe.[9] The historian Herder commented that

Men who succeed in removing wants from the creation, falsehoods from our memory, and disgraces from our nature, are to the realms of truth, what the heroes of mythology were to the primitive world; they lessen the number of monsters on the Earth.[10]

In *Emperor and Galilean* Julian had dreamed of just such an intellectual and spiritual combat where the battles would be bloodless and the contesting heroes "return to camp, arm in arm, harboring no ill will, their cheeks flushed, the blood pulsing through every vein, bearing the spoils of knowledge, and laurels on their brow." Julian's dream, however, is just that—a dream, which evaporates before the sheer complexity of the condition of consciousness that his endeavor uncovers. In the Cycle Ibsen examines more closely and delicately this condition of consciousness, for which his quiet method of concentrating, mostly, upon one or two people and the depths of their psyches is perfectly adapted.

Ibsen's Norway or James Joyce's Dublin can prove to be as consequential a confluence of spiritual currents (*aandelige strømninger*) as London or Paris; indeed, they are far less likely to be distracted by the accidental circumstances of human existence. Mrs. Alving's provincial drawing room where she marshals against the ghosts within and without the meager weaponry of a few modern and advanced books, is, as Eric Bentley has remarked, the perfect emblem of the modern condition.

This movement from the accidental to the essential accounts for an odd aspect of Ibsen's art: its tendency to be a *simplification* of the human surface situation, which is at the same time an increase of conceptual implication. His protagonists, shaken into a state of being awakened, find that the unessential aspects of their lives fall away as they move into a graver, more demanding reality; in much the same way, one imagines, that a modern rebel, through conscious or unconscious circumstances, finds himself for the first time participating at a higher level of conscious life whose issues become increasingly clarified and urgent.

For this reason, the openings of Ibsen's plays are almost always richer in small details than the condition of the endings (the development of *A Doll's House* is a perfect example of this movement from complexity to clarity). Against his little provincial scenes, initially so secure and confident, Ibsen brings the devastatingly clear requirements that emerge from this more essential reality, so that his bourgeois interiors are here shaken by a Greek action (*Ghosts*), there made to suffer the travail of a Christian consciousness (*The Wild Duck*) or, elsewhere, raised to a dialectical collision between enlightenment and repression (*Rosmersholm*) so that in the Cycle as a whole the entire structure of contemporary reality has recovered the very spiritual realities which everyday reality has contrived to shut out. Ibsen forces his audience to come to terms with its total identity, the total evolution of human consciousness from its prehistorical, mythopoeic origins up to the most advanced intellectual attitudes of the present day. This method is far more unsettling than that of *The Tragedy of Man* as it also is far more adequate as a portrait of "Man."

An action set in the Present, excluding the perspectives of the Past, plainly would be grossly inadequate, just as an action set in the Past, ignoring the consciousness of the Present, as in historical drama or Wagner's mythic art works, is inadequate. And this Past, too, is multidimensional. As merely rational history without the dimensions of myth and religion, as in much Naturalistic or Marxian literature, it would be an evasion of those potent spiritual realities that have helped to shape consciousness. As mythopoeic and spiritualist expression without the perspectives of rational history, as in much "ritualistic" theater, the portrait of consciousness would inexcusably leave out the whole realm of Reason that has created much of the world we inhabit. Either image of consciousness, the *Lehrstück* or the Dionysiac rite, is by itself drastically incomplete and the great merit of the artistry of the Cycle is just this adequacy, this complexity, of texture. Though we may miss the shock tactics of the savage theater, the brilliant didacticism of the theater of protest and commitment, the arcane mysteries of the esoteric theater or the pleasure of immediate and easy participation in a celebration of human warmth and sympathy of the theater of unforgettable characters, we are rewarded, by Ibsen as by all great artists, with a puzzling richness which does not exhaust itself on short acquaintance. His art rewards continual reexperience, continual meditation on its metaphors of scene, character, action, and dialogue, though undoubtedly this sets up those "difficulties" for his interpreters and his audiences of which the large public is far from being enamored. Henry James, long ago, noted this aspect of the dramatist:

Such a production as *The Pillars of Society* with its large, dense complexity of moral cross-references and its admirable definiteness as a picture of motive and temperament (the whole canvas charged, as it were, with moral colour), such a production asks the average moral man to see too many things at once. It will never help with the multitude that the multitude shall feel that the more they look the more intentions they shall see, for of such seeing of many intentions the multitude is but scantily desirous. It keeps, indeed, a positively alarmed and jealous watch in that direction; it smugly insists that intentions shall be rigidly limited.[11]

Apart from this richness of content each play's dialectical structure, while creating good theater, has the additional and higher interest of good logic, of a grave and difficult argument adequately concluded. This dialectical purpose impels Ibsen to an extreme economy of technique whose severity of purpose also can alienate the great public. A combination of moral complexity with the refusal to enter into expansive character studies or diverse and not always essential supplementary actions and details shows this art to be the result of a passionately logical nature (Ibsen called *Brand* a "syllogism") which, like Sophoclean drama, sees the greatest meaning in the ironic inevitability of events rather than in their rich and wonderful conglomeration.

Thus Ibsen does not "exploit" his situations: they are reined in, disciplined, not allowed a fraction of display more than is essential to the unfolding of the total idea. The richness of this art is the richness of good logic: of the immense implications of the frugal terms, terms which are reduced to their essentials. Ibsen is at his best when, wielding a dramatic Occam's Razor, he presents us with four or five people talking in a modern drawing room.

While watching an Ibsen play we are aware of a logic and a purpose driving the events, shaping its structure, and the gradual unfolding of an idea, inherent at the beginning, which the total action is bringing to light. There are, of course, many other dramatic methods, explored by other realists in the modern tradition, which are as satisfactory and even more appealing at first sight. It would be a mistake to claim that Ibsen, too, employs these methods, for this is bound to lead us to feel that he employs them less successfully than those dramatists who are not engaged with his artistic difficulties. The Ibsen method of the dialectical action and the recovery of the past is superbly successful in his hands once we thoroughly are aware of it.

To bring philosophical and historical perspectives to our interpretation of Ibsen's art does not take us away from dramatic criticism but brings us closer to it, for it means that we are concerned to fathom Ibsen's full intention—the complete Idea represented by each play and by the entire Cycle. Of all literary forms, drama is the one which is most resistant to the philosophical vision but, paradoxically, it is the one that perhaps best can express it. The dramatist needs to capture, and hold, his public and if, like Ibsen, as Robert Brustein has reminded us, he sees his function in somewhat messianic terms, he will attempt to capture the widest possible public, and not just a coterie of scholars. Furthermore, his dramas must be enacted vividly and with intense conviction by men and women who can identify in human terms with the roles they are called upon to embody. They cannot intimately identify with the Elizabethan world view or with the Evolution of Consciousness; so the dramatic poet, if he has the genius of a Shakespeare or an Ibsen, will give to even his most universal meanings palpability and vivid local life—"a local habitation and a name." The more seriously held the poet's philosophical convictions, in fact, the more likely they are to be rendered substantially in terms of realistic scene, character, action, and dialogue, for the philosophical vision will have permeated every area of the poet's experience of life. It is when the philosophical idea is a mere abstraction, is played with, merely, instead of having been absorbed as a profound commitment, that we get either obtrusively didactic writing or the insubstantial intellectualism of much Expressionist drama. In both cases, we find the Idea insufficiently *embodied*, not "proved upon the pulses."

The triumphant substantiality of Ibsen's visionary art, however, creates difficulty for those who insist that the universals of this art are at least as important as the vivid particulars; these particulars impose themselves so effectively upon his audiences, they feel so "in" in the worlds of Nora Helmer, Helene Alving, or Alfred Allmers (as Romantic critics felt so "in" in the world of Hamlet) that interpretation which insists on the importance of the universal intentions behind these particulars will seem cold, remote, abstract. In fact, however, the solidity and substantiality of a play is increased, not lessened, once we understand the universal ideas it is embodying. Interpretation of Shakespeare gained immensely in substantiality from our increased awareness of the universal purposes behind the conventions of his art. The older, character-interest school of Shakespearean criticism belonged to an age when only a handful of mutilated Shakespearean texts were considered suitable for production by actor-managers seeking prestige; with the more "intellectual" interpretation of Shakespeare which took into account the universal concepts of the Elizabethan world view, plays that once had been considered impossible on the stage (*Troilus and Cressida*, for example) are now considered full of dramatic interest. The reason is that Shakespeare's plays simply did not work according to the old character-interest view of them, so that their dramatic structures seemed inexplicably clumsy and incompetent (William Archer's demonstration of the superior dramatic skill of Arthur Wing Pinero is merely a more indiscreet expression of the general attitude). The new interpretation of Shakespeare showed that the plays worked admirably according to the new idea of their intentions, so that their conventions and details made great dramatic sense and could be successfully embodied in production by actors who were very far from sharing the Elizabethan idea of the cosmos and the human psyche. Once the director is aware of the underlying idea of the play, even if that idea is alien to him, or not of his own culture, he can work with it, get his audience to see it, or adapt it.

The actor, it is true, must believe in the "real life" nature of the dramatic character, whether it is Everyman or Willy Loman, and interpretation that concentrates upon character analysis obviously will be of great value to him just as purely technical criticism and interpretation will be of immense value to the director. But the interpreter has both the opportunity and the obligation to go beyond these terms when the author indicates, as strongly as does Ibsen, that his art contains far wider areas of significance. The technically adroit display of interesting characters in action, after all, hardly makes the poet a very significant event in the history of our culture, an event which justifies forcing our evolving theater to come to terms with him. The philosophical interpretation of an author or, rather, the demonstration of philosophical perspectives in his art, can be of real service to the actor, the director, and the audience by bringing into view the idea that the poet is embodying by means of the structure of his work and the particular details within it and so making the complete work a coherent intention. The entire texture of the play will then be seen to be explicable and rational and there will be no need, as in many productions of an Ibsen play—especially of the late plays—of hurrying over whole areas of the play in embarrassment, or even of pronouncing certain plays "failures." When a critical method pronounces a poet's work a failure it is very likely that the critical method, and not the work, is at fault, as H. D. F. Kitto has demonstrated in his reinterpretation of Greek drama.

If the actor and director can be assured that Ibsen's last plays, for example, for all the oddity of their method and subject matter, are rational and explicable structures, they will not find themselves forced to inject character-interest into parts, or lines, that seem impenetrably personal and eccentric, and that have nothing to do with the "'parts'" as they understand them. Interpretation that can demonstrate that each detail in the play contributes to an explicable overall meaning, however unwelcome that meaning might be, at least restores faith in the work as a coherent art form that can be enacted. Such interpretation will not be mere scholarship, detecting mythic patterns or historical correspondences as so much exotic addition to a basically "realistic" text: it will be concerned to demonstrate how such details are present as essential aspects of the movement and structure of the play.

By demonstrating that Ibsen's Cycle of realistic plays is a definite, objective, rational structure, highly dramatic in the dialectical development of its total intention, and capable, with effort, of precise analysis, I hope to show that the individual plays, too, are capable of rational analysis as objective dramatic structures, and that every detail in the play represents a discoverable intention.

Ibsen's language, for example, is neither an obscure cloud which we must penetrate in order to find a "character" nor a rather early attempt in the history of realistic theater to escape from the Romantic habits of metaphor and concept in order to depict the speech patterns of modern everyday life. It functions like good poetic and dramatic language, precisely and ambitiously relating the particulars of the play to its structure of universals. Ibsen wrote that it was much harder for him to write poetry in everyday modern language than to write verse. The important clause is that he is writing *poetry* in modern everyday speech, making modern everyday speech do the equivalent of poetry in verse form. The difficulty for Ibsen, therefore, was not to get Osvald Alving to talk like a modern young man, but to get him to talk poetry— that is, a language filled with universal implication. Translations that find Ibsen's original language rather "heavy" and stilted and so concentrate on giving it colloquial plausibility, are in danger of wiping away half of the language's intention, and so setting up an incongruous disparity between the language and the dramatic rhythm which was devised precisely to carry such a weight of implication.

A reexamination of the nature of Ibsen's dramatic language in terms of its universalizing intentions now is beginning to emerge which hopefully will restore faith in the esthetic sufficiency of Ibsen's texts. Analyses of *The Master Builder,* for instance, paid little attention to all that talk of three houses, three nurseries, nine dolls, a fire in winter, dead twins, music in the churchyard, harps in the air, trolls, vikings, princesses, castles in the air, and so on. This was seen merely as the rather extravagant way in which these real-life but slightly odd people happened to talk, and not the way in which Ibsen was structuring his poetic world of images and significations. The words on the page, however, are there to be analyzed as Ibsen's intentions, linked together in a pattern of meaning, and not as the odd verbal habits of real-life people who happen to be in a play. Psychological criticism, where it did not directly evade the text, went so far as to suggest that what the characters onstage said could not entirely be trusted, for, like people in real life, these characters were not in entire control of their world of meanings. When we find ourselves forced to discount the words of characters in a play, and to distrust their verbal habits, we hardly can function as an audience at all, for there is little for us to get hold of other than the rather miserable sense that we cannot get the information necessary to judge the characters as we would, after many years' acquaintance, begin to judge real-life characters; yet at the same time we are getting too much information to be able to settle down and enjoy a good story.

When, however, we see the details of scene, character, action, and language as functioning as the terms of a complex total intention, to be enjoyed in the way we can enjoy complex symphonic or chamber music or even a profound argument, though we still might be baffled by much of the play we will feel that a clear grasp of it is finally possible. The critic, then, must try to apprehend the idea that the poet is embodying by his work. Just as for Hegel the world of everyday human experience is to the awakened imagination the expression of universal forces—forces which can be apprehended, through the veil of Maya, by Reason—so for Ibsen what was engrossing to him in the world of contemporary reality was the configuration of the forces of a larger atemporal reality that could be detected behind it. His problem as an artist, the problem that spurred him to such rigorous feats of artistic discipline, was how to make his medium, the drama, mediate between the world of everyday appearance, and the world of universal reality—in other words, how to make his art reveal universal realities better than everyday life itself could do.

We can see the dramatic Cycle as an enchanted realm of dormant spirits waiting to be reawakened by actors and actresses who will take up the "roles" that cry out for expression. The realm of sleeping spirits, each locked in one phase of the Cycle, one phase of the Spirit's dialectical evolution, is resurrected when the old dramas are passionately taken up and embodied by new generations of men and women who find Ibsen's theater compelling enough to reawaken into life. Thus this theater is the perfect meeting ground of the universal and the particular, the abstract and the concrete.

The "double vision" of Ibsen's art, of looking closely and directly at the particular object, yet at the same time far beyond and above it, has been noted by some observers. The Cycle is a single, massive, complex concept, yet it is made up of innumerable passionately suffered moments. Henry James was fascinated by the fact that Ibsen's plays, when performed, have the strange quality of becoming at once more abstract and more humanly alive, and in this study I have tried to be faithful to both aspects of Ibsen's vision. Undoubtedly an easier, pleasanter, and simpler study would have resulted had I decided to stick to the human and particular details of the Cycle or if, on the other hand, I had discussed Ibsen's universal meanings with only occasional confirmations from the particulars of the text. Instead, I shall attempt the more complex problem of revealing the universal meanings *through* the details of the text and, in the second part of the book especially, this results in much very close, but also, I think, very exciting analysis. The idea of Ibsen's art that emerges will be unfamiliar to most readers, and unwelcome to some; but at least I hope it will be recognized that the writer refuses to impose his own ideas on Ibsen's art. As far as possible I have simply followed through the consequences of the discovery that the sequence of dialectical actions set out by the Cycle exactly corresponds to the sequence of dialectical actions set out in Hegel's account of the evolution of human consciousness in the second part of *The Phenomenology of Mind.*

Undoubtedly I would have made my task easier, and would have assured the book a more cordial reception, had I limited my project to such a topic as "Some Possible Mythopoeic Details in Ibsen's Realism" or "The Dialectical Structure of Ibsen's Realistic Plays" or "Literary Parallels to Some Details in Ibsen's Realism," and so on. Such projects represent the small-scaled and cautious approach that is considered good academic manners. This might be so, but it is not the way to approach a poet of the immensity of purpose of Ibsen. His plays, and the Cycle, are marvelous wholes which should not be dismembered into innumerable exercises, and I have felt it far more important to convey to the reader the immensity of Ibsen's total intention in the Cycle than to ingratiate myself by starting off a whole number of possible Ph.D. projects. My analysis, therefore, insists both upon a close analysis of Ibsen's *full* text, responding to it on all its levels of operation, and at the same time it insists upon our constant awareness of the overriding purpose and design of the Cycle as a total dramatic vision. Undoubtedly this involves discussing Ibsen's art in terms not usually associated with modern realism, and thus this disturbs that idea of Ibsen that can so conveniently place him in anthologies of modern drama as exemplary of some partial aspect of dramatic evolution. Nevertheless, I have found that these new terms make Ibsen, once again, exciting to young readers and make more convincing the claim that he ranks with the Greek dramatists and with Shakespeare.

PART I

CHAPTER 1

The "Dramatic" Content of Hegel's Philosophy

A drama is possible which pursues the stream of history to its most mysterious sources, the positive religions, and which—because it manifests in dialectic form all the consequences of the ideas that lie at the root of these religions for the Individual who is consciously or unconsciously affected by them—symbolizes all the historical and social conditions which would in the course of the centuries inevitably develop from all this.

Hebbel

. . . the individual must go through the evolutionary process of the race.

Ibsen, Note to *Emperor and Galilean*

"When philosophy paints its grey in grey, then has a shape of life grown old. By philosophy's grey in grey it cannot be rejuvenated but only understood. The owl of Minerva spreads its wings only with the falling of the dusk."[1] Thus, in 1820, Hegel virtually announced the closing of European intellectual and spiritual history and prepared the way for a multitude of prognostications of the decline of the West which were to become a *leitmotiv* of the cultural life of the nineteenth century. Nineteenth-century thinkers frequently saw themselves as conducting an inquest on the Western spirit, a judgment day upon its soul; and to these sessions the whole history of man was summoned. Hegel's own lectures on the philosophy of history, assembled and published after his death, were probably the major influence behind one of the most paradoxical aspects of the nineteenth century: the contrast between, on the one hand, the jubilant promise of the age of unparalleled technological and social progress and, on the other, the equally persistent assertions that, somehow, "all mankind was on the wrong track," as Ibsen sombrely observed in a note to *Ghosts*.

This contradiction is far more significant than a mere contrast between optimistic and pessimistic, radical and reactionary approaches to reality. Often it is the radical vision (as with Ibsen) that employs the idea of

man at the end of his tether in order to indict the present age and to call
upon a drastic "revolution within the spirit of man." At other times it
is the conservative and reactionary movement, concerned, as Herbert
Marcuse has pointed out in *Reason and Revolution,* to deny the validity
of critical reason, which casts a sardonic eye upon the pretensions of the
age as does Kierkegaard in the second volume of his *Either/Or*:

> Our age reminds one of the dissolution of the Greek city-state: everything
> goes on as usual and yet there is no longer anyone who believes in it. The
> invisible spiritual bond which gives it validity, no longer exists, and so the
> whole age is at once comic and tragic—tragic because it is perishing, comic
> because it goes on.[2]

Perhaps the most extreme example of this pessimism is Imre Madách's
The Tragedy of Man in which the entire history of mankind, past,
present and future, concludes in a new Ice Age where, in a cooling solar
system, Man expires as a spiritually feeble savage in a waste of snows,
losing his specifically human identity as he loses his historical memory.

Ibsen far from subscribes to Madách's somewhat naive pessimism nor
would he so facilely have reduced the complex Hegelian system to so
simple a schema; but an aspect of this vision is included in *Peer Gynt*
whose hero, tragic because he is perishing but comic because he goes on,
is in danger of forgetting and losing his specifically human attributes.
Far more philosophically, Ibsen presents Peer's world as a desert and
a waste-land that both reflects and is a result of Peer's spiritual sterility.
For Ibsen, the tragedy for Man would not be due to external natural
and cosmic causes but to internal failure, a spiritual decline that would
make Man a tragicomic figure in Kierkegaard's sense. This tragicomic
aspect of the age was exacerbated by its memories of its heroic and
hopeful origins in the French Revolution; since that time the life
of Europe seemed to have retreated into the condition so profoundly
depicted by Stendhal in *The Charterhouse of Parma*: intrigues without
dignity or purpose, the tragicomic loss of spiritual direction, and all
mankind being "on the wrong track." The end of the nineteenth century
is filled with the sense of *fin de siècle* so that it is with uncanny appropriateness that Ibsen's last play, with its theme of final resurrection from
the past, should appear in the last year of the century.

Praised as a harbinger of the new age, Ibsen, in 1887, suggested that
"the age in which we now stand could just as well be described as a
closure, and from it something new is in the process of being born."
Those living in the present cannot know the new form, that second
coming, its hour come round at last. They can, however, consummately
know, master, and, for the first time, transcend, all that *has* been as a

final disposal of the past and a preparation for the future. To summon the entirety of human history before the critical reason of the world would be a true judgment day upon the soul; and this is what Hegel sets out to do in *The Phenomenology of Mind*, a stupendously ambitious work in which "the individual must go through the evolutionary process of the race."

From *Brand* onwards, Ibsen's work moves beyond the imaginatively and deeply explored but limited historical perspectives of his earlier plays, to embrace the perspectives of world history. *Emperor and Galilean* is a "world-historical drama" involving no less than the entirety of human history, and this is world history of a thoroughly Hegelian nature—of a human world that has evolved dialectically in Time and is even yet existing as a dynamic complex of unresolved dialectical antinomies.

Modern readers are too ready to overlook the radical innovation in dramatic form and in concepts of reality represented by *Emperor and Galilean* and the plays that follow. Change, conflict, the subtle and complex interplay of subjective and objective realms of reality in Ibsen's plays are all taken by him to be the natural and normal condition of life and not the unnatural and terrifying disorder of the Shakespearean vision. Conversely, the static, fixed, traditional, and consecrated, all that the Shakespearean vision sets up as the natural, true, and good, is now seen as unnatural and unbearably constricting in its denial of the dynamics of evolutionary change. We are in danger of overlooking the immensity of perspective and the philosophical vision in Ibsen's drama if we fail to see that it is giving dramatic life to a world view as vast as Shakespeare's but diametrically opposed in its premises.

The world of the realistic Cycle, for example, is one very familiar to Ibsen's audience; it is meticulously detailed, highly plausible in its psychological motivation, its scene of action, its dialogues, and its dramatic rhythms. Its realism, by abandoning the older dramatic conventions of vague scenic location, implausible plotting, and even more implausible psychology, and by eliminating such convenient theatrical devices as impenetrable disguises, asides, soliloquies, onstage deaths-by-inches and long-armed coincidences, seems to be setting for itself nothing more ambitious than a faithful image of everyday surface reality, rather than, as is the case, raising itself to a discipline as severe and unobtrusively distinguished as that of Sophocles.

The consummately cunning plotting, the huge metaphoric "arguments" shaping the scenes, characters, actions, and speeches, are all too likely to be overlooked as we lose sight of the Ibsen poetic forest through our fascination with each detail of each tree. The problem in Ibsen interpretation is not that of keeping clear from abstraction and generalization in order to enter into the subtle local life of each play but, precisely, the opposite: of raising our vision beyond the poignantly presented particular details to the universal meanings which these particulars were designed to convey. While avoiding bloodless abstraction or the academic hobbies of symbol or myth hunting, we still must attempt to be faithful to the widest possible imaginative range of the play's meanings.

Many critics already have recorded their sense that Ibsen is doing something bigger than traditional accounts of Ibsen allow: something more than offering us trenchant social criticism, penetrating character analysis, and unsparing self-criticism together with consummate technical skill. These, undoubtedly, are virtues that would make the world reputation of any writer, but anyone who spends any time with the works of Ibsen is aware of something elusively present, something infinitely larger in intention.

It was in my search for some solid basis for my intimation of the scale of Ibsen's intention that I was led to study the spirit of Ibsen's age: its strong sense of history, of the presence of the Past, of the living reality of spiritual traditions from the first records and myths to the evolved consciousness of the modern world, of the dynamic and dialectical nature of human progress, yet of the Present as being made up of layer upon layer of past spiritual forms. Continually, it seemed to me, Ibsen's "realism" revealed the presence of these realities yet I could find no way of bringing them together as a consistent esthetic intention or as a consistent world view. For it would not be enough merely to keep to the traditional accounts of Ibsen's realistic intentions and then slightly confuse the picture by detecting mythic patterns in the realistic stories. This only would create an Ibsen of still modest intentions but irritating habits. I wrote a very tentative and clumsy account of *The Wild Duck* in terms of its Christian imagery and action, mentioning Hegel as a possible source for this idea of the recollection of the Past within the Present and suggesting the lines along which I believed future Ibsen interpretation should go.[3]

The more I read of the historical vision of the nineteenth century, the more I was led back to Hegel and, after following the ramifications of the Hegelian vision in nineteenth-century studies of myth, religion, art, and philosophy, I finally felt obliged to tackle the formidable thinker himself. Hegel's writings on the arts and on history continually threw brilliant light on aspects of Ibsen's plays (which I still did not see as a cycle). Here one saw human consciousness evolving events in the world and in art forms by which to express itself, one following the other, driven by an insatiable longing for greater and greater adequacy (truth and freedom) of self-expression; still, the correspondence, though close enough to convince me, was not exact. Finally I decided to take up Hegel's central and major but most difficult work, *The Phenomenology of Mind,* considered by many the key to his whole philosophy.

The experience was, initially, frustrating. The Preface, once one penetrated its density of texture, seemed to present a preview of all I had been looking for, but after this, the account of the evolution of consciousness from sense-certainty up to the fashionable philosophies and sciences of Hegel's own day seemed far less relevant than Hegel's writings on art and history.

It was when I came to the second section of the *Phenomenology,* the point where Hegel's dialectic takes up the history of the Western consciousness as the creator of a sequence of total world views or forms, that the light broke, for here Hegel sets out a sequence of dramas of consciousness exactly corresponding to the sequence of Ibsen's twelve plays. I will admit that this discovery was at first embarrassing as I did not quite know what to do with it. I certainly did not want to reduce Ibsen's rich art to dramatized Hegel, for this was totally false to my experience of that art; yet the Hegelian structure undoubtedly was built into the Ibsen structure as the dialectical core of the sequence of plays which I now came to see as a cycle.

Fortunately, my study of the spirit of Ibsen's age allowed me to see with what originality and variety the Hegelian vision was adapted by so many thinkers, and very soon my problem became, not how to avoid narrowing down Ibsen's intentions, but how to avoid allowing them audaciously to proliferate beyond my control. The relationship between Hegel's text and Ibsen's plays was similar, to adopt a Hegelian image, to that between an embryo and a fully adult human, so great a transformation had Ibsen worked upon his source material. There could be no more appalling a challenge than that of developing the human and esthetic implications of Hegel's text; the Greek dramatists' transformation of their mythic sources, or Shakespeare's transformations of his sources, required far less formidable feats of the creative imagination. The Hegelian world vision, it must be said, is itself a great and moving one and one that is inherently dramatic; but the conversion of its spiritual realities into an intimately felt and solidly substantial human world and, above all, into art forms of consummate esthetic discipline is an effort equally as astonishing and moving, in its way, as Hegel's. In every way it matches up to Ibsen's early resolution, confided to his sister, that he wished to create the greatest and most perfect that was possible in power and clarity, and then to die.

The problem for the poor interpreter, then, was how to take on the

painfully complex vision of Hegel's philosophy of consciousness, and
yet at the same time be as fully responsive as possible to the wealth
and immensity of Ibsen's own independent dramatic vision. This,
whatever the faults in the procedure of the present study, has been
my goal and it is for this reason that I continually draw attention not
just to the texts of Hegel and Ibsen but also to the ideas of Ibsen's
contemporaries and to that entire heritage of Western culture to which
I am firmly convinced Ibsen's imagination was so finely attuned.

Hegel's sequence of spiritual dramas, set out in the second part of
the *Phenomenology* as a dialectical and evolutionary advance (with
Consciousness discarding what is erroneous or inessential in each form
and taking up whatever is essential and true enough to survive the
activity of critical negation, so that the progress of Consciousness is
shown to be both cumulative and refining), also consists of three major
divisions of spiritual or mental activity: the objective world of social
and political life, the subjective world of the individual consciousness
alienated from the objective world, and, as a synthesis of these two,
the realm of ideologies—of art, religion, and philosophy at work in the
world. This, naturally, led me to examine Ibsen's twelve plays to see
if they revealed a similar tripartite cycle; and, in fact, the obviousness
and the appropriateness of the triadic division of the cycle was at
once apparent and thoroughly in accordance with Ibsen's own comments and later critical commentary upon the plays. Ibsen insisted
that his last four plays formed a distinct group or series; he announced
that *The Wild Duck* (the first play of the second group) marked a
new departure in his dramatic method, and it is a commonplace of
Ibsen criticism that the first plays form a distinct "didactic" (i.e., social
and political) group.

But, it may be protested, three groups do not necessarily form a
single cycle. It is therefore all the more useful to remember that on
more than one occasion Ibsen insisted upon the cyclical nature of the
plays. Near the end of his career, while at work on his "Epilogue,"
When We Dead Awaken, Ibsen informed his public:

Simultaneously with the production of my works another generation of
readers has grown up, and I often have noted with regret that their knowledge of my recent work was considerably more detailed than of my earlier
ones. Consequently these readers lack an awareness of the mutual connections
between the plays, and I attribute a not insignificant part of the strange,
imperfect and misleading interpretations that my later works have been
subjected to in so many quarters to this lack of awareness.

Only by grasping and comprehending my entire production as a continuous
and coherent whole will the reader be able to receive the precise impression
I sought to convey in the individual parts of it.[4]

It is Ibsen, we see, who is charging his interpreter with the formidable job of seeing his series of plays as a network of corresponding parts, so that any one part only can be understood as existing within a complex whole. Even more explicitly, in 1899, explaining the subtitle "Epilogue" to *When We Dead Awaken* Ibsen observed:

> . . . all I meant by "epilogue" in this context was that the play forms an epilogue to the series of plays that began with *A Doll's House* and which now ends with *When We Dead Awaken*. It completes the Cycle, and makes an entity of it, and now I am finished with it. If I write anything more, it will be in another context; perhaps, too, in another form.[5]

I admit that Ibsen's assertion that the Cycle began with *A Doll's House*, thus making it an awkward eleven-play entity, conflicts with my interpretation which sees the Cycle beginning with the play that precedes *A Doll's House*, *The Pillars of Society*. As I hope to show from the evidence of the Cycle itself, *The Pillars of Society* clearly inaugurates the Cycle and is built into its structural design. Ibsen may have made a slip of the tongue, or have been misquoted; but a possible explanation for his assertion does, in fact, lead straight back to the Hegelian source of the Cycle. *The Pillars of Society* stands somewhat apart, in method and subject matter, from the plays that follow; it is notably devoid of the quality of grave ethical argument that is typical of Ibsen's procedure from the last act of *A Doll's House* onward. And, in fact, the dialectical action of *The Pillars of Society* is, as I later will demonstrate, founded on a section of Hegel's *Phenomenology* that immediately precedes the creation of the "Ethical World" whose dialectical development is worked into the next three plays in Ibsen's Cycle: *A Doll's House*, *Ghosts* and *An Enemy of the People*. In my interpretation of the Cycle I see *The Pillars of Society* as the sub-ethical "ground" upon the crisis of which the dialectic of the ethical world is based.

If the plays form "a continuous and coherent whole," an "entity" in fact, then it no longer is possible to see the series of plays as a more or less random succession of gestures on Ibsen's part, dependent upon his reactions to events in the world or within himself. *Ghosts*, therefore, would not be a somewhat petulant demonstration to the critics of *A Doll's House* of the consequences of Nora's *not* leaving husband and children; after all, there is nothing in poor Torvald's character, deficient as it may be, that would lead to the appalling consequences of *Ghosts*. Nor is *An Enemy of the People* a reply to the critics of *Ghosts*, and *The Wild Duck* does not represent Ibsen's second thoughts (remarkably late in life) on making idealistic demands

upon life as in the preceding play, and so on. This reading of the
author's life in his works ignores Ibsen's protests on just this score
and also takes our attention away from the marvelous structure which,
like a great artist, Ibsen is consummately objectifying. It is far more
rewarding to see the Cycle as one single design, an entity, where each
play arrives to take its consciously planned place in the growing design.

If we look at the Cycle, for a moment, as a triadic structure, I think
it will be seen to make a great deal of sense. The first group of four
plays is concerned primarily with society and its laws and duties and
with the individual's attempt to liberate himself, painfully, within this
realm. The second group, on the other hand, is notably more "psychological" and its conflicts and tensions are located within the self-
divided psyche. In the third group there is a startling emergence of
directly symbolic and mythopoeic detail and action, a far more complex action of archetypal recollection, together with an emphatic
movement outwards and upwards to a recovery of the world of nature.
We do not need to agree upon the Hegelian underpinning to this
structure; nevertheless we must agree upon this already very radical
reinterpretation of Ibsen's methods and intentions. In other words, we
already have moved far from traditional interpretation of the twelve
realistic plays, and closer to Ibsen's own account of them. If we also
can agree that there is a dialectical development within the Cycle,
from the moral depths of *The Pillars of Society* to the somewhat
chilling spiritual heights of *When We Dead Awaken,* we have conceded
the major argument of this study: to discover exactly the same structure
in the second part of the *Phenomenology,* however great the difference
between the two works, is a relatively easy step to take after so consequential a journey from traditional interpretation of Ibsen.

Indeed, I am aware that at this point it would be more ingratiating
if I concealed the Hegelian parallel to the Cycle and merely offered
an interpretation, with a vaguely Hegelian reference, as if it were my
own entirely independent insight; but this would be dishonest, for
though the Cycle can stand as a great and independent work of the
poetic imagination (as much as Shakespeare's *Antony and Cleopatra*
is independent of its even closer source in Plutarch) we are in a far
better position precisely to appreciate Ibsen's boldness and independence of imagination by recognizing the source materials upon which
he has worked such a transformation. Anyone who understands the
nature of Hegel's vision in the *Phenomenology,* though he will understand the great appeal it would have to a poet of sufficiently bold and
ambitious imagination, will also be somewhat appalled at the challenge
which Ibsen has taken on: it is as if a dramatist of Athens were to

answer Plato's attack upon the poets by incorporating Plato's entire philosophy within his work.[6]

To facilitate the step from accepting that Ibsen's plays form a Cycle, with mutual connections between the parts, and which should, as Ibsen remarked on another occasion, be read in the order in which they were written, to an acceptance that this very bold conception originated in Ibsen's response to Hegel's philosophy, we might look first at the external evidence for Ibsen's Hegelianism. We have evidence that Ibsen knew of Hegel in his very earliest years as a poet, for it often has been noted that Hegelianism was dominant in the Scandinavia of Ibsen's early years. We have evidence from Ibsen himself that he still admired the German philosopher after the completion of the Hegelian *Emperor and Galilean*.[7] The editors of the Oxford edition of *Emperor and Galilean* note, with some astonishment, that that world-historical drama eminently fulfills the requirements of the Hegelian dramatist Friedrich Hebbel, who wrote:

A drama is possible which pursues the stream of history to its most mysterious sources, the positive religions, and which—because it manifests in dialectic form all the consequences of the ideas that lie at the root of these religions for the Individual who is consciously or unconsciously affected by them— symbolizes all the historical and social conditions which would in the course of the centuries develop from all this.

(This ambitious program, parenthetically, illustrates the dilemma of the nineteenth-century artist, so aware of the importance of historical evolution for the understanding of the present.) In fact, *Emperor and Galilean* fulfills Hebbel's dismaying demand less adequately than can the Cycle which, because of its greater scale and detail, better can trace the dialectical development of the human consciousness which emerged from the origins of Western spiritual life and discover their consequences within the rhythms and details of modern life. With this in mind, we can see Ibsen's entire career as that of a gradual liberation from the local and national preoccupations of his earlier writing to his eventual spiritual integration into the community of the total human consciousness: a program repeated by his great disciple, James Joyce.

Ibsen's youthful critical writings employ Hegelian arguments and terminology, as we later will see when considering an article Ibsen wrote defending the use of old mythopoeic material in modern writing— itself an Hegelian idea. *Emperor and Galilean* brilliantly dramatizes a Hegelian historical "moment": the point in history where the entire spiritual heritage of Western man—his pre-Christian and post-Christian ideologies—has developed into a crisis of world-shaking dimensions which will determine the course of succeeding centuries, the type of subject matter which Hegel himself praised in the historical dramas of Schiller and Goethe.

In 1873 Ibsen wrote to a friend, the Danish critic Georg Brandes, who had sent him Mill's *Utilitarianism*:

Now, as to Mill's pamphlet! I do not know whether I ought to express my opinion on a subject in which I am not an expert. Yet, when I remember that there are authors who write on philosophy without knowing Hegel, or without any knowledge of German scholarship in general, many things seem permissible. I must candidly confess that I cannot in the least conceive of any advancement or any future in the movement represented by Mill. I cannot understand your taking the trouble to translate this work, the sagelike philistinism of which reminds me of Seneca and Cicero.[8]

The conjunction of Hegel and John Stuart Mill in this passage is worth reflecting upon, because it represents the classic confrontation between Continental rational Idealism and Anglo-Saxon pragmatism, and very clearly indicates to which tradition Ibsen belonged. He cannot understand how anyone can write on philosophy *at all* without knowing Hegel; the tribute to the German thinker hardly could be stronger, and the reference to "German scholarship in general" supports the contention of this study that Ibsen was very deeply responsive to German intellectual life. The judgment on Mill, whatever its justice, must make us all the more reluctant to see Ibsen's art as predominantly concerned with political, social, or phychological issues. If one possessed a similar document by Aeschylus, for example, testifying to his admiration of Heraclitus, or from Shakespeare expressing his sense of the importance of a major Renaissance thinker, scholarship would attempt seriously to discover whether or not such a philosophic vision permeated the dramatist's art; it is thus no very outrageous step to examine Ibsen's art to discover whether it can, in fact, be illuminated by Hegelian philosophy.

The most important evidence for the Hegelian structure of the Cycle, of course, must be internal. We must see whether Ibsen's twelve plays, from *The Pillars of Society* to *When We Dead Awaken*, can be more adequately understood by employing Hegelian terms and implications.

In *The Phenomenology of Mind* Hegel sets out a dialectical sequence of conditions of consciousness, each a complete world view confident of its own total validity, and then proceeds to demonstrate the contradictions and conflicts inherent in each *gestalt* or shape of consciousness. The result of this undermining of each confident condition of consciousness is that each is forced to reveal its own inadequacy as a total world view and is forced to evolve into a more adequate, but equally contradictory, phase; that is, the condition of error becomes "higher" in the succeeding phase. The entire sequence is thus a tragicomedy of errors in which the human spirit moves on to higher and more adequate spiritual half-truths as the spirit of negation (a very rigid philosophical Mephistopheles) pits itself against the "positive" assertions of spirit. This whole program is present, in very simplified form, in *The Tragedy of Man.*

It is in the great second part of the *Phenomenology* that this painful spiritual progress becomes that of the human community on earth and through history: the evolution of the human collective consciousness through Time. According to Hegel's English translator and editor, this second part constitutes "the keystone of the whole arch of experience traversed in the *Phenomenology* for it is in this section that Spirit/Reason (*Geist*) makes its entrance upon Hegel's scene. *Geist* is the higher level of mind where "individuality is conscious of itself only in and with others, and conscious of the common life as its own."9 Until this point was reached, Hegel had been describing only the persuasions of the individual mind in isolation; in the succeeding pages Hegel recovers these isolated individual persuasions, but only as they are integrated into the life of the whole human consciousness. Nothing would be lost to the dramatist, therefore, who employs Hegel's scheme at this point, and, in fact, it is only from this point onwards that Hegel's procedure would be serviceable to the dramatist whose art depicts individuals only in relation to the consciousness of other individuals.10

An examination of Ibsen's twelve-play Cycle reveals that its sequence of actions exactly parallels the sequence of spiritual dramas set out by Hegel in the second part of the *Phenomenology,* suggesting that Ibsen's intention in the Cycle was less that of portraying various facets of his own times but rather, as with Hegel, portraying humanity itself, its full identity as it gradually has unfolded itself in Time. This, to be sure, is a very ambitious program for a poet, but it better fits the author of *Brand, Peer Gynt,* and *Emperor and Galilean* than the far more modest program usually ascribed to Ibsen.

In a form of Pilgrim's Progress of staggering dimensions Hegel charts the course of the human community, beginning in its attempt to live by purely selfish principles, then forced into ethical conduct and customs and, from the contradictions tragically inherent in these, forced to advance ever onwards to newer and higher and more deeply significant principles for living. The progress of Ibsen's Cycle, from *Pillars of*

Society to *When We Dead Awaken*, is, at least, similar in conception. But of far greater consequence for our interpretation of the Cycle is the fact that the sequence of dramas in the Cycle exactly corresponds to that of Hegel's sequence:

IBSEN'S TEXT *The Cycle*	HEGEL'S TEXT *The Phenomenology* *of Mind*	EDITION HOFFMEISTER	BAILLIE
The Pillars of Society	The sub-ethical society of individuals associated as "a community of animals," evolving into the realms of Reason as creator and critic of ethical principles.	258–309	419-49
	I OBJECTIVE SPIRIT (The ethical society of laws of family and of the community: archetype, the Greek *polis*.)		
A Doll's House	The law of Man vs. law of Woman. Family vs. State.	313–18	453–66
Ghosts	The Living vs. the Dead (Guilt and Suffering).	318–36	466–92
An Enemy of the People	Division of Community and of ethical individualism vs. communal conformism. Emblem: the contest between two *brothers*. The phase also of Socratic individualism and of Aristophanic Comedy.	337–42	492–99
	II SUBJECTIVE SPIRIT (Consciousness in self-estrangement. The divi-		

	sions within the Christian world from Antonine Rome to the nineteenth century.)		
The Wild Duck	Dualism within individual mind and within society. Loss of Nature, myths of fall and of self-sacrifice.	342–74	500–549
Rosmersholm	Conflict between enlightenment and autocracy and superstition.	376–413	549–98
The Lady from the Sea	Absolute freedom and terror vs. responsibility. (From revolution to categorical imperative. Romanticism.)	414–33	599–627
Hedda Gabler	Post-Napoleonic bourgeois culture and its frustrations.	434–72	629–79

III

THE RELIGIOUS CONSCIOUSNESS

	(Dialectic of historical ideologies: art, literature [including myth], and religion.)	473–564	683–808
The Master Builder	"God as Light"	483–564	689–808
Little Eyolf	Pantheistic "plant and animal" religion.	485–564	702–808
John Gabriel Borkman	Religious consciousness expressed through mineral forms. (The Artificer.)	486–564	704–808
When We Dead Awaken	The mineral form as the sacred human form—the Statue.	488–564	706–808

However sound the logic which Hegel claims for this extraordinary development of human consciousness in which each step is meant to be the inevitable dialectic result of the preceding, it at least sets out the drama of the human spirit in Time in terms sufficiently far-reaching and imaginative to be of great appeal to a poet such as Ibsen who was acutely conscious of the living presence of the Past. Hegel's anatomy of Man as a historical animal was as useful to Ibsen's intentions as Marx's anatomy of man as a social/class animal was to Brecht's. Such an objective account of the dramatist's subject—Man—would liberate the poet from a mere helpless subjectivity and better enable him to create, in T. S. Eliot's phrase, "objective correlatives" to his subjective condition.

If we describe, very summarily, the "plot" of the spiritual pilgrimage analyzed by Hegel and set out above, it will become more clear to what extent Ibsen's own Cycle—the spiritual odyssey from *The Pillars of Society* to *When We Dead Awaken*—resembles Hegel's. We must remember, also, that although Hegel's sequence very closely resembles the course of European history from the founding of the Greek city states to Hegel's own day, this evolution is intended to be logical rather than historical and entirely belongs to the Present so that, as in Ibsen's realistic Cycle, this painful odyssey must be undergone by any modern individual or society that seeks to attain to truth and freedom.

Before the fateful entry of Spirit upon Hegel's scene, we are given the sketch of a human community which it will be the task of Spirit to "awaken." This condition of consciousness oddly is termed "self-contained individuals associated as a community of animals" and describes a society in which the individuals profess concern for the common cause and for a realm of ethical principles, but actually act out of crass self-interest. In this society of cheats and hypocrites, one individual emerges of greater talent and compass than the others, whose actions and "work" help to beget a crisis which unmasks the deceptions of the hypocritical society and prepares the way for genuine ethical principles to emerge. This condition of consciousness, which serves as the ground, initiating Hegel's dialectical chain of actions, quite obviously is the condition of consciousness of *The Pillars of Society*, the play that inaugurates Ibsen's Cycle.

With the collapse of the hypocritical community, the community of animals now evolves into the ethical community which lives very genuinely by the seemingly complementary but inherently contradictory laws of the Individual, the Family, and the Community. The ethical community, because it genuinely holds by its ethical values (as far as it understands them) inevitably finds itself engaged in ethical conflict rather than in the sub-ethical conflicts of the previous phase, and this makes the ethical society vulnerable to Tragedy which, for Hegel, springs from ethical conflict. This ethical society discovers tragic conflict, Hegel demonstrates, first in the contradictory laws of Man and Woman (*A Doll's House*), then in the laws of the living against those of the dead (*Ghosts*), both of these conflicts also bringing into focus the contending claims of the Individual, the Family, and the Community. This dialectical development explodes into a conflict in which two brothers, members of the Family, fight for the control of the Community, bringing about the collapse of the claims of the Community as an absolute authority, leading to the emergence of a new ethical/spiritual Individualism—a development quite clearly repeated in Ibsen's *An Enemy of the People.*

With this collapse of the Objective world of the community of customary convention, the human spirit, in Hegel's account, seeks a more substantial basis of spiritual authority and now moves into the subjective, "self-estranged" world of alienation from Nature, Society, God, and the human community. This dialectical development begins with the portrait of a profoundly dualistic "fallen" world (the Christian world) divided between a foreground or "here-and-now" of work and unfreedom and a background or beyond (*jenseits*) of compensatory fantasy (*The Wild Duck*). With the destruction of this refuge of compensatory fantasy (Hegel has in mind the Lutheran attack upon Church superstition) the idealistic spirit now engages in a militant onslaught upon autocracy and superstition, producing a conflict between enlightenment and superstition, in which, however, both conflicting parties gradually discover that the identity of each has become inextricably that of the other (*Rosmersholm*). After this point, the two realms, the Idealistic and the Pragmatic realms of consciousness, divide into the extremes of the lure of a fearful and possibly deathly "absolute freedom" and an alternative realm of "spheres of duties" to which Spirit, after a struggle, finally retreats (*The Lady from the Sea*). Following this retreat of Spirit into the humdrum of everyday, non-idealistic bourgeois reality, Hegel concludes his account of the progress of Spirit in the human community with an account of various attitudes of the Romantic imagination intolerably confined (and therefore becoming malicious) within this reduced spiritual structure (*Hedda Gabler*). This is a world of "valets of the moral sphere" who deny the possibility of heroism (Hegel pithily remarks that the hero is not a hero to his valet, not because the hero is not a hero, but because the valet is a valet). At this point in the pilgrimage of Spirit set out by Hegel, we have arrived at an intolerable mediocrity and constriction which only can be overcome by the appearance of a new kind of consciousness—the religious consciousness with its reaching for the sublime.

The emergence of the religious consciousness in Hegel's text brings about the third new phase of Spirit. Spirit now undergoes an apotheosis in which it recollects and summons to its present life its primal myths, cults, religions, and arts. This higher phase of Spirit is an over-arching view of the whole realm of Spirit, taking up both Objective and Subjective roles into a new and higher synthesis. Not surprisingly, this is the most bewildering part of Hegel's text, and probably the most difficult writing in all of Hegel's difficult *oeuvre*; for the Spirit no longer progresses in a linear, chronological sequence, but, instead, seems to be continually circling, recapitulating its entire spiritual substance again and again, as it gradually ascends to the peaks of the Absolute Spirit.

The richly mythopoeic account of the human spirit struggling to evolve visionary truth and freedom opens with four spiritual movements— the positive religions from which, Hegel demonstrates, the spiritual life of the West to the present day has evolved. These four, which might strike us as arbitrary, are the religions of the Sun and Light; the pantheistic religion of the earth, plants, and animals; the worship of abstract mineral forms; and the worship of the sculpted human form, the Statue. Obviously, here, Hegel is tracing the general concretization and anthropomorphization of the religious consciousness from nebulous Light to Hellenic humanism. It is these four "areas" of religious consciousness—the cosmos, the earth, the abstract intelligence, and the fully developed human reason—that provide the essential basis for all subsequent higher spiritual life in art, religion, and philosophy, and in the pages that follow the introduction of these four religious modes, we will, like Hegel, return to each of them again and again, almost as if they were themes in a fugue or the *leitmotiv* of Wagner's *Götterdämmerung*. And Ibsen, too, sets out the same sequence of the Sun (*The Master Builder*), Plants and Animals (*Little Eyolf*), Mineral forms (*John Gabriel Borkman*), and the Statue (*When We Dead Awaken*).

The implications of this extraordinary odyssey of spirit seem to be that while the progress of human culture makes the older forms of heroism or spiritual extravagance non-viable, so that society *does* seem reduced to the intolerable condition dramatized by Ibsen in *Hedda Gabler*, this is just the point at which the entire realm of spirit can, with effort, be regained by the artist, mystic, and philosopher. This, in fact, *is* the development of modern culture, noted by Matthew Arnold and many others, in which the artist becomes the hierophant of the whole world of spirit, its priest whose artistic ritual helps to rejoin the entire human community to its spiritual sources, its total identity. The artists of this tradition are Goethe (*Faust, Part II*), Wagner, Ibsen, Thomas Mann, James Joyce, T. S. Eliot, Ezra Pound, and Samuel Beckett, all of whom, in their different ways, can be seen as direct heirs of Hegel.

I have, of course, greatly simplified the sequence of phases of human consciousness portrayed by Hegel and only in their full richness and complexity will their parallels with Ibsen's Cycle fully emerge. But even from the sketch given above I cannot see that it is possible to deny that Ibsen has incorporated Hegel's philosophical structure within the structure of his Cycle and that whatever his intentions in so doing, his final intentions as a dramatist can be understood only by taking into account Hegel's profound and imaginative account of the human spirit.

The transformation Ibsen has worked upon the Hegelian structure is so great that we are in no danger of reducing his great art to a mere schema. Like the Hegelian account of the structure of Consciousness, the structure of the Cycle is triadic. In each group of four plays, for example, we find a beautifully balanced development, with the two outer and the two inner plays in each group of four revealing parallels, giving the whole group a distinct shape even as its dialectic thrusts forward.

The first four plays, depicting the life of Objective Spirit—human consciousness as it expresses itself through the institutions of marriage, family, and society—is notably familial and civic in theme and atmosphere with the dramatic emphasis falling upon direct ethical and social confrontation and conflict and giving rise to a misleading idea of these plays as being more didactic in intention than the plays that follow. There is less direct Nature imagery (in the Romantic sense) in these plays, and where it does occur it takes the form of a dialectical opposition, such as the external winter weather against the internal domestic coziness of *A Doll's House,* or the metaphorically antithetical forces of rain and sun in *Ghosts,* or the cunningly hidden conflict between seemingly healthy external life and the invisible bacteria of *An Enemy of the People*—that is, "Nature" in these plays, as in Greek drama, is carefully subordinated to the terms of the ethical conflict. Nor is there much emphasis upon complex psychological conditions and motives, for here the human spirit gives itself over to objective laws and duties and seeks to liberate itself in these terms. In the greatest play of this group, *Ghosts,* the dramaturgy is very similar, in its grave and terrible ethical clarity, to that of Greek tragedy and, in fact, the ghosts of

Greek drama haunt these four plays as they haunt the section of the
Phenomenology upon which they are based.

In the second group, from *The Wild Duck* to *Hedda Gabler*, we
find an internalization of spiritual conflict and the action decisively
shifts from direct ethical confrontation to more indirect, psychologically
more complex situations. In these plays, too, there is a rich and omnipresent Nature imagery: of forest, mountain, sea depth, marshes, lakes,
the wild northern seas and distant peaks covered with snow. While
these plays lack the courageous ethical confrontations of the more
classical first group, they are notably more "romantic" in theme and
imagery: filled with such superstitions as the forests that take their
revenge, the flying Dutchman, the white horses that haunt Rosmersholm,
the mysterious sea life and the Stranger from *The Lady from the Sea*.
Even Hedda Gabler's veiled dream world in which she attempts to
force spiritual values upon the petty present are quite unlike anything
in the first group. These elements of folktale, superstition, and Romantic
longing are elements of the European imagination in its post-Christian
subjective and romantic development, in which the world of Nature,
so integrated in the life of Hellenic culture, is seen as a lost value to
be recovered by the human spirit.

In the last group of four plays the human consciousness recovers
this world of Nature from which it has so long been alienated, and, at
the same time, recovers long vistas and perspectives of the spiritual
past, so that these plays tend to be, as James Joyce noted, alfresco,
with *When We Dead Awaken* not only completely out-of-doors but
ambitiously scaling the same landscape as *Brand* and *Peer Gynt*. This
recovery of a lost natural world—the consciousness's spatial extension
into a more adequate *scene*—is accompanied by the gradual integration
of the human consciousness with its total spiritual identity—the temporal
extension into a more adequate spiritual history. In these last, difficult
plays, which expand so startlingly in time and space, the spiritual past
of the race is recollected by means of actions of passionate retrospection
and memory, where mythic patterns are woven into the realistic fabric
of family histories. This creates a very puzzling, multi-layered dramatic
texture which, however, compensates by its rich suggestivity for the
impression of obscurity it might create.

The *Phenomenology* is the philosophical dramatization of man painfully acquiring his full human identity and freedom. The course of
this development, as one commentator has observed, "is at once that
of the individual and of the race; it gives at the same time a psychology
and a history of culture."[11] Julian's injunction, in Ibsen's note to *Emperor
and Galilean*, that "the individual must go through the evolutionary

process of the race" is, for all its appearances of Darwinism, nothing but a reformulation of Hegel's own program for the individual and for the race, set out in the Preface to the *Phenomenology*:

> The individual, whose substance is mind at the higher level, passes through these past forms, much in the way that one who takes up a higher science goes through the preparatory forms of knowledge, which he has long made his own, in order to call up their content before him; he brings back the recollection of them without stopping to fix his interest upon them. The particular individual, so far as content is concerned, has also to go through the stages through which the general mind has passed, but as shapes assumed by mind and now laid aside, as stages of a road which has been worked over and levelled out.[12]

The single great theme of the *Phenomenology* is man's possible comprehension and mastery of his entire spiritual content—his total identity—the condition of his freedom. By means of a complex and laborious dialectical evolution, a series of conflicts and collisions in which defeat and death paradoxically are essential to the continuing life of the spirit, the total content of Spirit is re-experienced and comprehended. This is the task of the enlightened individual who would be free and of the world Spirit itself. The Absolute Spirit, writes J. B. Baillie, "takes upon itself and makes its own the stupendous labour of the world's history."[13] The stages of the journey, or "moments" that make up the total Concept (*Begriff*) of Spirit are distinct world views or shapes that have been established on earth by means of physical and spiritual battle. They have required pain and suffering and to recollect them requires courage and not the exercise of dry and dispassionate intellectuation. In fact, to Hegel's vision, so hideous and painful is the record of human history that only the conviction that behind this show Reason has established its Concept, can save the enlightened thinker from the pessimism later formulated by Schopenhauer. One might, indeed, say that Hegel's vision goes beyond Pessimism to Tragedy.

Man, as millions of individual men, heroes, thinkers, and nations, gradually has established through his actions, institutions, arts, sciences, cultures, religions, and philosophies the complete realm of Reason which modern man is capable, at great effort, of recovering. In this realm of Reason or total Concept, there is no *lost* past; what has been lost is only the unessential in past forms of consciousness; what was essential has been taken up into the continuing life of consciousness. In the structure of the human spirit, all that "is" includes all that "has been." This central theme of the *Phenomenology* is more clearly stated in the *Lectures on the Philosophy of History*:

While we thus are concerned exclusively with the Idea of Spirit, and in the History of the World regard everything as only its manifestation, we have, in traversing the past—however extensive its periods—only to do with what is *present*; Spirit is immortal; with it there is no past, no future, but an essential *now*. This necessarily implies that the present form of Spirit comprehends within it all earlier steps. These have indeed unfolded themselves in succession, independently; but what Spirit is it has always been essentially: distinctions are only the development of this essential nature. The life of the ever-present Spirit is a circle of progressive embodiments, which looked at in one aspect still exist beside each other, and only as looked at from another point of view appear as past. The grades which Spirit seems to have left behind it, it still possesses in the depths of its present.[14]

Memory, the recollection of the past, which readers will recognize as so important an element of Ibsen drama, is, in Hegel, paradoxically an instrument of liberation *from* the past. As in the Ibsen dramatic action, the Hegelian dialectical action enforces a serious life-and-death confrontation with the past, an "awakening" which, though it leaves behind it the demolition of a once complacently inhabited spiritual world, has impelled the consciousness toward *authentic* life. And, again, paralleling the Ibsen plot, even death, if it is an authentic act, is preferable to inauthentic life. Herbert Marcuse describes the important function of Memory as an instrument of liberation in Hegelian philosophy:

But the "end" of history recaptures its content; the force which accomplishes the conquest of time is remembrance (recollection). Absolute knowledge, in which the spirit attains its truth, is the spirit "entering into its real self, whereby it abandons its (extraneous) existence and entrusts its Gestalt to remembrance". Being is no longer the painful transcendence towards the future but the peaceful recapture of the past. Remembrance, which has preserved everything that was, is "the inner and the actually higher form of substance." . . . Hegel replaces the idea of progress by that of a cyclical development which moves, self-sufficient, in the reproduction and consummation of what *is*. This development presupposes the entire history of man (his subjective and objective world) and the comprehension of his history—the remembrance of his past. The past remains present; it is the very life of spirit; what has been decides on what is. Freedom implies reconciliation—redemption of the past. If the past is just left behind and forgotten, there will be no end to destructive transgression.[15]

The past, as the history of human consciousness, is also a record of spiritual error, pain, and injustice. The present cannot be allowed to forget this past of injustice, error, and pain, for:

To forget is also to forgive what should not be forgotten if justice and freedom are to prevail. Such forgiveness reproduces the conditions which reproduce injustice and enslavement: to forget past suffering is to forgive the forces that caused it—without defeating these forces. The wounds that heal in time are also the wounds that contain the poison. Against this surrender to time, the restoration of remembrance to its rights as a vehicle of liberation is one of the noblest tasks of thought. In this function remembrance (*Erinnerung*) appears at the conclusion of Hegel's *Phenomenology of the Spirit* (*Mind*); in this function it appears in Freud's theory. Like the ability to forget, the ability to remember is a product of civilization—perhaps its oldest and most fundamental psychological achievement.[16]

The Hegelian *temps retrouvé*, though depicting a dialectical process within the spirit of man, at the same time returns to events in the actual, historical world, the world created by man by the process of his Work. Hegel's dialectic completely covers the history, later elaborated by Marx, of man creating the condition of alienation, though Hegel's account of man alienated from the world of Nature, from society, his work, and his free self, is vastly more comprehensive. It would not be going too far to claim that Hegel's philosophy includes both the internal, psychological development of man described by Freud and Jung, and the external development of human society developed by Marx. This is an important point for our discussion of Ibsen, for if a dramatist's imagination were permeated with the Hegelian world view his drama would be neither purely psychological nor purely social and historical, but a dialectical interplay of both internal and external, subjective and objective realities. The individual "self" *would* be a social and historical product, but society and history themselves are products of the developing human spirit, of self-consciousness advancing and developing within the developing structure of the external world. This accounts for the uniquely powerful relationship between individual character and environment or scene that Ibsen creates in his modern drama, begetting a dynamic interplay between the external world on all its levels of historical reality, and the subjective world (itself historically evolved) of the individual self-consciousness. The external environment in an Ibsen play is both an extension of the human spirit and, in its invariably inadequate and often intolerable compromise with the absolutes of spiritual reality, a prison for the awakened consciousness. Just this dialectical interplay between the external and the internal and *vice versa*, makes the Ibsen scene, for all the economy of its terms, so powerfully explosive and subversive. It dramatizes the Hegelian idea of Man as Time, changing his world and being changed by it, both revealing himself and creating himself in his history.

There can be no greater disservice to Ibsen than the practice of truncating the modern actions and characters of his plays from the larger perspectives of natural and historical realities which, Ibsen saw, made of the modern situation only one moment (potentially decisive) in the life of consciousness. The invariable action in an Ibsen play is that of the spirit awakened from its spiritual sleep to a terrible awareness of the *unreality* of the world it finds itself in (a world from which it has derived its identity), and its unnerving exploration of dimensions of reality more authentic but more demanding. It is the Platonic parable of the prisoner who leaves the cave of illusions, or the Pauline insight that "it is a terrible thing to fall into the hands of the living God." After such an awakening, the once-sustaining scene, the world that had both created and imprisoned the psyche, vanishes into insignificance like the doll's house left behind by the awakened Nora Helmer.

In the larger drama of the totality of human history the human spirit similarly, by its actions and suffering, gradually establishes its true identity. Just as, in the Ibsen drama, we feel that there is a genuine identity, waiting at the end of the play, which the deluded character, at the opening of the play will, once awakened, journey towards and ultimately discover, so in Hegel's idea of the evolution of human consciousness man in Time (history) is consciously and unconsciously journeying towards the realization of his implicit identity. Hegel's illustration of this idea is the human development from embryo to the fully rational adult. The embryo is human "in itself" but not human "for itself"; it can become human "in and for itself" only as "the educated reason which has made itself that which it is in itself. Only this is its actuality."[17]

An important consequence of this is that one's human identity is not a "given" but a potentiality which each individual must struggle to attain. Walter Kaufmann recalls Pindar's "You shall become who you are," in this connection, and this idea that one's human identity is an ideal to be realized is, of course, at the heart of Ibsen's dramatic vision as such plays as *Brand, Peer Gynt*, and *Emperor and Galilean* clearly demonstrate. In Hegel's philosophy, therefore, we find two complementary concepts of human identity which, we believe, profoundly influenced Ibsen's concept of dramatic character: (i) the identity of the human race is a Concept painfully established in Time; (ii) this great evolution in History must be repeated in the life history of each individual who would attain to truth and freedom.[18]

If the individual's task on earth is to come to a full knowledge of his human identity as it has been revealed to the thinker by History (and by History we mean the entirety of human expression in all its forms), then it is obvious that the completely free individual must be a philosopher, a thinker—a conclusion from which existentialist thinking, beginning with Kierkegaard, not unnaturally recoiled. This would set the thinker, or the poet or artist, *above* the condition of his fellow men, as seer: and this, in fact, *does* become the condition of the modern thinker and artist. Though we find this condition to some extent anticipated by Dante and Milton, it is with the nineteenth century that the thinker and artist becomes detached from the human community as the Romantic mystic, seer, Wanderer, outcast, rebel, esthete, or dandy. Ibsen's Brand, Peer Gynt, and Julian explore among them almost all of the roles of the modern artist or thinker as we find such roles expressed from the time of William Blake to that of Samuel Beckett. Quite obviously, this sets up great difficulties for the dramatic artist who, as Ibsen himself noted after the reception given to *Ghosts*, should not be too far in advance of his public. If the artist is the omniscient seer, descending the mount to lead his public gradually to the peak of promise or promised land, he must be careful to keep that public and not, as with the example of Brand, become totally incomprehensible and hostile to it.

The problem becomes particularly acute when the dramatist must conceive his major dramatic character. Hegel, in his writings on drama, somewhere remarked that the modern hero must be an intellectual, like Hamlet. The reason for this is obvious. To act adequately and effectively, the hero must act from an understanding of (or a creditable attempt at understanding) the nature of reality. Yet this has developed into such a complex historical determinism that the hero, in order to think and act adequately, would need to be a combination of Hegel and Napoleon at once. This is the situation Ibsen faces in *Emperor and Galilean* where the riddles of the Objective Spirit (the course of history and the nature of the human and natural world) and the Subjective Spirit (the depths of Julian's and the human-archetypal psyche) make almost impossible any effective action. When Julian finally acts, his plausible misreading of subjective and objective "signs" giving him deluded confidence, he suffers tragic failure: a failure which, however, by the whole paradox of historical determinism, contributes to the inscrutable purposes of the *Weltgeist*.[19] It is obvious that tragedy, written on such a formidably complex and esoteric plane, would very soon lose the understanding and interest of that very public to which Ibsen was concerned to address his art.

In *Emperor and Galilean* Hegel's intellectual hero is given tragic definition by Ibsen. He is a figure of great mental endowments whose actions in the world, though they lead to a failure of himself and his cause, have impact upon the world. The alternative intellectual hero, he who succeeded, hardly would be tragic: the only variants on the situation of the intellectual hero would be the hero who died but

whose cause was to triumph, in which case the tragedy would not be
a tragedy of the intellect but only of the pathos of his human frailty;
or the hero whose personal success and the success of his cause required
the tragic sacrifice of others: a theme from which dramatists have
understandably shied away, for this would be to create the hero as
a god requiring sacrifice, chillingly remote from our human sympathies.
One only has to imagine Schiller's King Philip as receiving the endorse-
ment of the author and the audience for his cause, to understand the
ethical objections to this form of tragedy. And, in fact, just such
objections have been voiced against the argument of Brecht's *The
Measures Taken*, where the *ideological* justification for the sacrifice
of the Young Comrade is *ethically* unacceptable.

After *Emperor and Galilean*, therefore, if Ibsen was to create poignant
and tragic human drama, one cannot see an alternative to the path
he actually took: of creating a tragicomic drama of the human condition
in which the necessary "advances" of the human spirit were effected
by the conflicts, suffering, and deaths of characters who were unaware
of the ultimate justification for their suffering. We are not suggesting
that Ibsen consciously decided that this was his only alternative; but
it was a solution thoroughly in accord with the Hegelian idea of the
human condition.

For Hegel, the impulse behind Spirit's long and absurd odyssey of
pain, undergoing repeated suffering and death as gradually it ascends
to modes of spiritual life more adequate and more authentic, is the
impulse to truth and freedom. The experience of the greatest loss and
alienation may be the prerequisite for truth and freedom, and it is to
Hegel's credit that his philosophy engages directly with the existential
experiences of human pain and suffering. The whole tragicomedy of
mankind may, finally, be justified and reconciled with the Absolute,
but Hegel's Absolute, on the philosopher's own showing, is a somewhat savage god:

> It is not the universal idea [i.e. the Absolute] that incurs opposition and
> fight and danger: it keeps itself safe from attack and unharmed in the back-
> ground, while sending the particular of passion [i.e. the individual] into the
> fight to wear itself out. One can call it the cunning of Reason that it lets the
> passions do its work, while that through which it translates into existence
> loses and suffers harm . . . the individuals are sacrificed and surrendered. The
> idea pays the tribute of existence and transitoriness not out of itself but
> through the passions of individuals.[20]

Thus the passionately acting and suffering individuals, intensely caught
up in the world of particulars and totally unaware, perhaps, of any
justifying universal reality, are, nevertheless, fulfilling the purpose of

Spirit, much as the protagonists of Greek tragedy (at least of Aeschylus and Sophocles) reveal to the spectator, through their willful passions and errors, the supra-personal logic of the cosmos. Such a disparity between the passionately willed actions of the protagonists and the dispassionate logic of the cosmos is ironic in the manner of that masterpiece of irony, *Oedipus Tyrannos*. And this, I believe, is the situation of each play in Ibsen's Cycle. The total meaning and justification of the Cycle is the sum of all its parts; yet the parts are unaware of any universe, any sum or totality, other than their own.

Spirit (human consciousness), in the dialectical progress of the *Phenomenology*, gradually acquires an increasing content (wealth of spiritual detail), for all the "abandoned" phases of spirit are not left behind, but "sublimated"—that is, whatever is real in them survives destruction and contributes to the Whole. All that is lost is the unreal, the unessential. Another irony, therefore, is that the painful "deaths" in the *Phenomenology* are the conditions of spiritual life. "To be oneself is to slay oneself," the Button-Moulder tells the uncomprehending Peer Gynt. Just as the general mind, the mind of the race, by means of painful human history, has with difficulty abandoned tenaciously held false identities (concepts), so the individual mind, too, must learn dialectically to give up false "selves." Then, miraculously (the idea seems uncannily like Kierkegaard's concept of the "absurd" in *Fear and Trembling*), the tragic experience of loss will be a regaining of the "lost" self in its truer identity. Death, therefore, is the necessary condition of life—not just, obviously, in biological life, but also in the life of the spirit. On reflection we will find that this idea is not alien to our experience of life. In *Major Barbara*, at the moment when Barbara, seeing the terrible truth for the first time, painfully renounces her religion, Undershaft tells her, "You have just learned something; that always feels at first as if you have lost something."

Undershaft's comment puts the dialectical experience in the form of a brilliant epigram. It insists that the experience of learning, of spiritual growth, is painful and thus reserved for those spiritual aristocrats capable of risking and undergoing the deepest loss. It sets up truth and freedom as motives that imperiously override the claims of comfort and happiness. This idea is stated at greater length, but with equal force, by Hegel in the Preface to the *Phenomenology*, where Hegel likens the process of learning and of analysis to murder and dissection:

Death, if we care to call this unactuality by this name, is what is most terrible, and to hold on to what is dead requires the greatest strength. That beauty which lacks strength hates the understanding because it asks this of her and she cannot do it. But not the life that shrinks from death and keeps itself undefiled by devastation, but the life that endures, and preserves itself through, death is the life of the spirit. Spirit gains its truth only by finding itself in absolute dismemberment.[21]

The Hegelian dialectic, therefore, for all its unmerited reputation of insensitive systematizing, closely resembles our experience of life and, above all, the tragic experience. (It is not an accident that, as Walter Kaufmann observes, in that reference to "dismemberment" Hegel actually likens the dialectical experience to that of tragedy whose god is Dionysos Zagreus, the dismembered god.)

For all the forbidding toughness of its terminology, the *Phenomenology*'s attractions for a dramatic poet are not difficult to understand. It very profoundly engages with the major difficulty of the ambitious dramatist, of making the restricted time and space permitted by the conditions of the dramatic performance an intersection of time with eternity, the particular with the universal. Denied the flexible spatio-temporal resources of the epic poet or novelist, yet dealing, like them, with human characters and actions at a definite time and place, the dramatist needs conventions that enable his particular details to enact universal meanings. In earlier dramatic conditions, this extension of the plausible time and space of the performance was effected by the use of universal myth and the universalizing function of the traditional chorus or, as in the Elizabethan theater, by a highly flexible tolerance of spatio-temporal references beyond the given here-and-now of the dramatic story. (Hamlet is at once a contemporary Londoner, a prince of the old house of Denmark, and a royal member of a universal Christian kingdom.) The theatric structure of the Greek drama and, to a lesser extent, of the Elizabethan suburban theater, was itself a conventional mirror reflection of the prevalent world view, so that there was an immediately perceivable relation between theatric form and metaphysical content. The form of the nineteenth-century theater, especially that of the well-made-play or thesis-play, on the other hand, was specifically designed to *exclude* metaphysical content, to create the maximum theatric excitement with the minimum of conceptual risk, thus escaping the displeasure of the censor and of the very pragmatic bourgeois audience for whom ideological and metaphysical issues were either tiresomely irrelevant or directly threatening. (One can hardly imagine the sophisticated Parisian boulevard theater audiences tolerating Ibsen's *Brand*!) The world of the well-made-play is a doll's house designed to shut out those dimensions of reality that threatened to destroy the bourgeoisie's feeling of self-sufficiency, for even the thesis-plays of Dumas *fils* and Augier never stray from the complacent little realm of liberal values; the "abuses" they take note of are eminently correctible without any great fluttering of the dovecotes of the bourgeoisie.

The problem for a major poet forced to employ this theater and shake these audiences was, precisely, to reveal the manner in which this contrived stage-world was, like Plato's Cave of Illusions, a refuge from reality which, however, just because it had been so elaborately erected, was at least uneasily aware of the claims of that excluded reality.

Now the whole procedure of the *Phenomenology*, as we have noted, is to enter into, and enact, world views, conditions of consciousness, as if they were "theaters" of the human spirit which tenaciously insist on their self-sufficiency but which are, under unremitting analysis, provably inadequate. Hegel enters into each spiritual persuasion, makes it a compelling here-and-now, seems to share its errors and confusions, and undergoes with each world view the painful recognition of its inadequacy. Each spiritual drama is totally compelling as a vivid and particular human action; yet each of these seemingly isolated phases of spirit or world views is at the same time an eternally recurring drama of the absolute spirit and, even if unknown to itself, interwoven with the totality of spiritual reality. In the *Phenomenology* we encounter not abstract philosophic propositions but the drama of the mind actually bringing into being, then negating, world views. The conviction that knowledge, like life, is an organic *process* which changes even as one attempts to grasp it, dictates the profound and baffling methodology of Hegel and reveals his affinities with Romantic thought. This *mimetic* nature of the philosopher's method which would, one imagines, be of particular interest to a dramatist, has been noted by Professor J. Loewenberg who, in fact, likens the *Phenomenology* to a dramatic cycle. The dialectical dramas of the mind depicted by Hegel, where the protagonists are unaware of what is going on "behind their backs," resemble, Loewenberg notes, "a comedy of errors," while from another point of view Hegel's work can be seen as almost "unrelievable tragedy." We are reminded of Kierkegaard's description of his age which, precisely because it is undergoing dissolution as it continues, is comic and tragic at the same time. (This is not the only place where we find Kierkegaard reproducing the ideas of the philosopher he so elaborately affected to despise.)

Hegel's role in the *Phenomenology*, Loewenberg notes, "is comparable more to the actor's part of impersonation than to the laboratorial behavior of the scientist,"[22] for the dialectical method hinges "on two distinct kinds of illusion: the histrionic, in which the impersonator [Hegel] enters into his part; and the provably untrue nature of the persuasion imitated."[23]

In a work so mimetic and dramatic in nature, it probably is no accident that Hegel makes frequent references to Greek drama, and the dialectical method itself resembles the method of Greek tragedy; an example is the tragedy *Antigone* which Hegel never tires of quoting and of which he has provided a famous interpretation. And the dialectical method is the invariable method of Ibsen's Cycle. The reader will recognize how, in every play, we find a situation existing in untruth or in inadequate truth; how, under the impact of a shock (usually a sudden arrival from the past), the contradictory aspects of this given situation are brought into conflict, forced to reveal their inconsistencies; how, as the conflict progresses, a more and more adequate truth of the situation emerges—even if this proves a painful and destructive truth—until, at the end of the play, we have the complete and logical development of what was inherent but concealed at the beginning. The given reality of the beginning of the play is tested and found wanting by realities that both transcend and conflict with the given reality. Each play in the Cycle, like each episode in the *Phenomenology*, is a world view or state of mind which is explored and understood to the utmost and then, as it finally is exhausted, abandoned for a more adequate state of mind—the succeeding play. However, just because each play is a rich and complete world view, we are hardly aware of the inadequacy of its terms until we see them exposed.

It has become an almost canonical doctrine of Ibsen interpretation that the dramatist abandoned his idealism and his historical and universal themes, with which he had been preoccupied up to the completion of *Emperor and Galilean*, and, in the Cycle of realistic plays, confined himself to a pragmatic scrutiny of everyday reality and its problems—an idea of Ibsen that made him particularly congenial to the pragmatic tradition of Anglo-American culture.[24] It even has been possible to locate the moment of this drastic lobotomy of the imagination: Georg Brandes's Inaugural Lecture given at the University of Copenhagen on November 3, 1871. The Danish critic called upon writers of Scandinavia to join the main movement of modern European culture and thus to make their work relevant to the age. As Brian Downs observes, in many passages Brandes "virtually addresses Ibsen himself,"[25] and Ibsen wrote to Brandes that the lecture, which had given him a sleepless night, placed "a yawning gulf between yesterday and today," representing "a great shattering and emancipating outbreak of genius."

This praise must strike the modern reader as curiously excessive but it at least attests to the importance Ibsen attached to Brandes's lecture. We need, therefore, to understand just what Brandes is saying.

As Downs notes, Brandes contrasted the typical literature of the major Scandinavian authors, "remote from reality, or inimical to life"—idealistic works such as Ibsen's *Brand*—to the literature of the great European nations. "What keeps literature alive is that it submits problems to debate," Brandes declared, and this phrase has been seized upon to the exclusion of the main tenor of Brandes's argument to explain Ibsen's supposed abandoning of the wider dimensions of human reality in order to examine the problems of real people in real trouble. True, it sometimes is conceded that the lobotomy was not wholly successful— that old habits of poetic metaphor or idealist thought creep back into the modest new method, enriching or confusing that method according to one's preferences. It generally is conceded, however, that with *The Pillars of Society* and the plays that follow Ibsen's subject is the particular and not the universal: not the sweeping metaphysical and historical perspectives of *Brand, Peer Gynt,* and *Emperor and Galilean* but the close pragmatic scrutiny of life lived in late nineteenth-century Norway truncated from any larger concept of reality. These plays give us "life" and not "ideas" and their intention is to expose abuses and self-deceits. In the last plays, in fact, Ibsen's subject matter becomes even more confined and somewhat narcissistically and obsessively broods on the problems of the playwright himself.

That this is the very opposite of the truth is the whole contention of this study, and Brandes's Inaugural Lecture, rather than supporting traditional interpretation, actually opposes it. The lecture is a protest against the reactionary intellectual tradition of Scandinavia and a call to take up again the prematurely abandoned Hegelian school of thought which once enlivened Danish intellectual life. Discussing Paludan-Müller's *Adam Homo,* Brandes deplores that

at this time, the imported ideas in philosophy lose ground here, the newly started Hegelian schools suspend their activities, Heiberg gives way to Kierkegaard, and the passion for thought to the passion for faith. The philosophical movement ceases temporarily without having produced a single work, even a short work, while the ethical, religious movement that now begins does find a parallel and a continuation in literature.[26]

Quite clearly, Brandes, in calling for a literature that submits problems to debate, is not calling for the abandonment of that critical, rational attitude to reality represented by Hegel and his followers; on the contrary, this is the promising development that he sees prematurely abandoned. It therefore is quite erroneous to conclude, as does Downs, that the result of Brandes's challenge was Ibsen's conviction that "the world lay not now with Hegel any more than with the fathers of the

Christian Church."[27] This elegant formulation is misleading as to the substance of Brandes's lecture and of Hegel's philosophy. Reading the lecture we find it permeated by Hegelian thinking. Not only is Hegel and his philosophy invoked more than once, but the whole contention of the lecture—that Scandinavia had missed the experience of certain essential phases of European thought, missing the main action while experiencing, inadequately, only the later reaction—makes the Hegelian point that *all* of man's phases of consciousness must be undergone if the individual and the nation are to attain to adequate intellectual-spiritual identity:

> Not only are there periods in which we do not know how our people thought and felt, but there are periods in which our thoughts and feelings were more dull and feeble than those of other nations. Consequently, some important European movements reached us while others did not. Indeed it sometimes happened that, without having participated at all in the main action, whose broad waves were flat and spent before they reached our sandy beaches, we found ourselves participating in the reaction.[28]

There is nothing wrong in a nation experiencing a reaction. "Far from it ... a true, supplementary and corrective reaction constitutes progress."[29] But the reaction must be a relevant one, after a dialectically fully absorbed action, as in the method of the *Phenomenology*. Hegel has observed that it might be the duty of a poet of a backward nation to bring his people into the circle of fully civilized nations and, to effect this, it would be necessary for the backward people to experience the full spiritual development of these highly evolved nations. In *The Philosophy of Fine Art*, in fact, Hegel actually outlines the situation of the modern artist as being, for the first time, that in which he now has available for his purpose *all* the previous forms of artistic expression:

> ... Art is no longer under constraint to represent that, and only that, which is completely at home in one of its specific grades. Everything is now possible as its subject-matter, in which man, on whatever plane of life he may be, possesses either the need or the capacity of making his abode.[30]

The Philosophy of Fine Art, in fact, clearly sets out the artistic program followed by James Joyce and, we are claiming, by Ibsen in his Cycle.

Brandes's Inaugural Lecture, therefore, did have the impact upon Ibsen claimed by Downs, but this impact would have impelled Ibsen more in the direction of dealing with the totality of human experience than in the direction of retreating from this totality to a more local and confined subject matter. Creating a cycle of plays summing up the entire evolution of human consciousness, but in terms of the realities of modern Scandinavian life, was the fullest possible fulfillment of Brandes's requirement and, furthermore, completely consistent with Ibsen's own artistic evolution. (In fact, the play that followed Brandes's Inaugural Lecture, two years later, was the "world-historical drama" *Emperor and Galilean*. This work, I believe, can be seen as Ibsen's in-depth exploration of the central spiritual crisis in the life of the West before he applies its argument and vision to the realities of the contemporary world.)

The *Phenomenology* is Hegel's Judgment Day upon the soul of Western Man to which past spiritual forms are summoned. Walter Kaufmann draws attention to the literary or imaginative nature of Hegel's book, the way in which it as much resembles Dante's *Divine Comedy* or Goethe's *Faust* (and, for that matter, Milton's *Paradise Lost*) as it resembles traditional philosophical writing, for the *Phenomenology* sets itself the "Faustian undertaking" of summoning the entire drama of the human spirit to a present-day sessions:

> The Second Part of *Faust* and Hegel's *Phenomenology* are creations of men as lonely as the exiled poet of the *Divine Comedy*. Unable to settle down with any real contentment in this world as it is, and despairing both of changing it and of finding solace in human society, Hegel, like Goethe and Dante,[31] created a world of his own, and instead of peopling it with figments of his imagination, as many another writer has done, found place in it for the men and women and events he knew from history and literature as well as a very few of his contemporaries—and did not greatly care how much of all this would be recognized and understood. Of course, the reader is meant to grasp the structure of the whole, and the serious reader, who alone is of any interest to the author, is certain to recognize familiar faces at every turn, usually in unfamiliar surroundings: but not every detail is put in mainly for the reader's sake, for his instruction and the promotion of knowledge. A great deal is there because it happened just then to be of interest to the writer, and he was wondering where it belonged, how best to place it—how to fashion a cosmos of the totality of his cultural experience without suppressing anything that seemed to matter.[32]

This account of Hegel at least in great part fits the situation of Ibsen, self-exiled from his homeland and reconstructing, in his great Cycle, an alternative world with its own landscape, seasons, spiritual history, filled with enigmatic echoes from the European past, the whole endeavor being as much a difficult self-emancipation as a description of humanity.[33] This concept of the poet or artist in isolation discovering in himself the history of mankind, and in the history of mankind his own spiritual growth, can be traced back to the origins of Romanticism: to William Blake's ambitious pilgrimage from Innocence to Experience to Prophecy; to William Wordsworth's resolve, in *The Prelude*, to trace

"The Growth of the Poet's Mind" and to so much later literature where the expansion of the understanding of the world and its history is accompanied by the artist's own ambitious program of spiritual self-emancipation.

In the Cycle, as we demonstrate in Chapter III, Consciousness journeys through a Dantesque landscape from the sea level of *The Pillars of Society* to the peaks of *When We Dead Awaken.* In the last four plays we find an ascending action of increasing spiritual perception filled with the spirit forms of European history and, as with Dante, this great journey of the world soul is, at the same time, the artist's own effort at spiritual emancipation.[34] Ibsen's act of exiling himself from Norway was a rejection of his homeland as bitter as Dante's; yet Ibsen insisted that he could be understood only as a native of Norway. But it was only by emancipating his own spirit and his art, by attaining to freedom as an artist, that he could serve his country as well as humanity at large: and thus it was that he wrote to Brandes in 1871 that his friend should adopt "a thorough-going, full-blooded egoism, which will force you for a time to regard yourself and your work as the only things of consequence in this world, and everything else as simply non-existent."[35] Ibsen added the even more somber reflection: "there actually are moments when the whole history of the world reminds one of a sinking ship; the only thing to do is to save oneself."[36] It is not startling, therefore, that a poet with this vision of the actual world should construct an entire alternative cosmos and its history for his spirit to inhabit.

There is, therefore, no contradiction between the idea of Ibsen investigating in himself the universal history and identity of the race and his well-known statement:

Everything that I have written has the closest possible connection with what I have lived through even if it has not been my own personal experience; in every new poem or play I have aimed at my own spiritual emancipation and purification—for a man shares the responsibility and guilt of the society to which he belongs. Hence I once wrote the following dedicatory lines in a copy of one of my books:

> To live—is to war with fiends
> That infest the mind and heart;
> To write—is to summon oneself,
> And play the judge's part.[37]

The painful emancipation of the Spirit to truth and freedom and its purification from error and guilt is the subject and method of the *Phenomenology,* that huge judgment day upon the world soul, and many readers already may see how this Hegelian endeavor accords with our experience of Ibsen's great Cycle whose spiritual pilgrimage also involves a phase-by-phase journey to truth and freedom through error and guilt. Truth and freedom, which constitute "the one goal and basic drive" of Hegel's entire philosophy,[38] are the twin values, launched in the first play of the Cycle by Lona Hessel, Ibsen's first ambassador of spiritual emancipation. From this point on, truth and freedom will work devastatingly but liberatingly upon an immensely complex realm of error and guilt and of rich human detail. It is this rich human detail, together with a superb sense of formal beauty, which prevents Ibsen's dialectical method from being a mere stratagem and which makes of the Cycle one of the wonders of world drama.

Chapter 2

The Philosophical Content of Ibsen's Drama

Every art demands the whole of man, and the highest stage of art requires the whole of mankind.

Goethe, in the Introduction to *Die Propyläen*

A time comes . . . when Art has displayed, in all their many aspects, these fundamental views of the world, which are involved in its own notion, not less than every province of the content that is bound up with such world views: when that time arrives such art is necessarily cast loose of that which has been its previous specific content for any particular people or age; in such a case the renewed craving for material to work upon only fully awakes when it is accepted as inevitable that we must bid farewell to all that its activity has previously substantiated. . . .

. . . above all, is it indispensable that the spirit and mind of the great artist of today should have a liberal education, one in which every kind of superstition and belief which remains limited to circumscribed forms of outlook and presentment, should receive their proper subordination as merely aspects or phasal moments of a larger process; aspects which the free human spirit has already mastered when it once for all sees that they can furnish it with no conditions of exposition and creative effort which are, independently for their own sake, sacrosanct; and only ascribes to them value in virtue of the loftier content, which itself, as creator and worker, he reposes in them, making them thus what they ought to be.

Hegel, *Philosophy of Fine Art*, II, 391–92, 394

Our first impression of Ibsen's Cycle is of a world created with the most convincing solidity and attention to the minutest details. Nothing could be more remote from Hegel's shadowy dramatic Cycle of spirits; but what if, in Ibsen's Cycle, Hegel's drama of universals has taken on a vesture of human particulars? There would be a double gain in this: Hegel's abstract analysis of the advance of Human Reason in the world would become the vivid and poignant advance of particular human psyches within a distinct time and place; while, on the other hand, the

58

accidental surface particulars of individual and social life in nineteenth-century Norway would be raised to the level of universal actions involving the whole of mankind. If, as I believe, the theme of the Cycle is the possible transfiguration of *this* world, the "awakening" or "resurrecting" of worldly life to spiritual truth and freedom, then this world of stubborn particulars must be confronted and engaged with by the Spirit in complete and deadly earnestness. It is this continual struggle of spiritual reality and its army of universals against the stubborn resistance of the world of material particulars that sets up a dialectical tension within the very structure and texture of Ibsen's dramatic works. Scenes, characters, actions, dialogue, and stage objects all reveal this tug-of-war between the universal and the particular. So thoroughly *lived through* is each play, each world view in the Cycle, that it comes as something of a shock to find Ibsen able to set it aside as he advances to the succeeding phase.

It might be helpful if we put aside the usual assumptions about Ibsen's realistic method and, instead, were willing to see it as learned and mythopoeic work, closer to the realism of James Joyce or Thomas Mann than to the school of realist and naturalist dramatists for whose engendering Ibsen is so often held responsible. The Cycle, rather than being a rather dreary display of social abuses and neurotic individuals (a rather illegitimate branch of sociology and psychoanalysis) seems, rather, to be filled with a sense of history, with the accumulations of the human spirit—a vast séance of spirits crowding back into the conscious and unconscious life of the nineteenth century. This Past, however, is deeply buried in the fabric of the Cycle as it was deeply buried within the fabric of nineteenth-century life, so that the poet would have to be something of a miner if he were to retrieve this spiritual ore. In addition to a highly demanding dialectic structure the Cycle carries an enormous cargo of highly allusive, mythopoeic, literary, historical, and cultural references concealed beneath the metaphors of the realistic method. This is not an abstract academic game, for Ibsen really believes that we moderns *are* made up of the substance of the past, and that this anatomy of spirit is essential to an adequate modern portraiture.

Our awareness of the universals behind the particulars of the Cycle will better enable us to appreciate its subtlety and power. To deny the larger meaning for which the particular actions have been conceived is to deny Ibsen his major strength as an artist and to place him inappropriately and disadvantageously with the tradition of strictly realist writers who, not engaged with his difficulties, seem more immediately appealing. Ibsen's dialectical method, with its complex interplay of inward and outward spiritual and material forces, lacks the stark psychological immediacy of Strindberg, the choric ensemble richness of Chekhov, the brilliant propagandist force of Brecht, or the mythopoeic immediacy of the Wagnerian tradition in theater. Ibsen, desiring to combine all these areas of reality into a single complex action, cannot give any one area undue prominence.

Emperor and Galilean, the world-historical drama that immediately preceded the Cycle, must, I think, be considered the work in which Ibsen established for himself his idea of universal history and destiny. He declared that in that play could be found the "positive world philosophy" his critics had demanded of him. Just as in *Brand* and *Peer Gynt* Ibsen recovered for modern dramatic literature the great spatial metaphors of the Natural landscape and the cosmos as a human scene, so in *Emperor and Galilean* Ibsen creates for the first time in dramatic literature metaphors for the historical forces that are working upon the modern psyche. As I believe that the historical crisis presented in *Emperor and Galilean* is the crisis which also underlies the Cycle, it will pay to look, briefly, at the argument of the world-historical drama. The drama depicts the tragically unresolved conflict between the forces of paganism and Christianity within the mind of Julian the Apostate and within his empire, the Western world. The two terms, "emperor" and "Galilean," stand for two supreme but opposing life principles, and Ibsen's hero, Julian, is a Christian consciousness playing at paganism— futilely attempting to wipe away the inexpungible impress of Christianity upon the world and the human consciousness. The emperor's values are Hellenic, life-fulfilling, the exaltation of the human spirit through the raising of *this* world to beauty and power and glory. Against this Hellenic, objective spiritual quest (perfectly expressed in Aristotle's idea that the purpose of human life was "to seize hold of the beautiful"), the Galilean quest is, on the other hand, subjective, exalting the truth of the subjective spirit and its certainties against and above that of the world. In the very subtle argument of Ibsen's play, these forces are not merely locked in opposition, with pagans contending on one side and Christians on the other: a more complex condition has evolved in which both forces are at war in each individual with the parties *here* denying and uneasily suppressing their paganism, *there* as unsuccessfully attempting a supression of their Christian natures. Thus the Christians are convulsed with pagan passions which, just because they are suppressed, are distorted into ugliness and brutality; while such a would-be pagan as Julian, infected with Christian subjectivity and conscientiousness, distorts the once-living beauty of paganism into an artificial and academic charade. For the life of the ever-living Spirit, the *Weltgeist*, has passed from these past forms, and what clearly is required by the world is a creative union of these antinomies as we find envisaged in Blake's *The Marriage of Heaven and Hell*. If this program strikes us as being naive or eccentric, we should remember that the Romantic writers from Blake to Ibsen had to discover metaphors for the forces which we now designate by psychological terminology: the super-ego, the ego, the id, the unconscious, etc. It could well be that the Romantic terminology is at least as accurate and far more successful in maintaining the temporal perspectives behind the psychological forces it is analyzing. Certainly the psychological portraiture of *Emperor and Galilean* and the later Cycle is impressively capable of entering into the subtlest areas of human experience. Such a portrait is the emperor Constantius, conducting wars and ruthlessly maintaining his power like any pagan tyrant, yet, at the same time, tormented with guilt and fear and a sense of sin which only drives him to worse crimes as he restlessly moves from State action back to the Church, from his imperial ambitions back to his Galilean self-abasement. Julian's wife, Helene, as her name implies, is by nature passionately pagan, but her culture has made of her a fanatic Christian whose Christianity is only too obviously an unsuccessful sublimation of strong eroticism.

This study of inward division is brilliantly continued in the other characters in the play, above all in Julian himself, and it is extended and enlarged into the objective, external division in the empire itself where the inward psychological forces become externalized as opposing cultures, ceremonies, philosophies, and, finally, armies. This greatly underrated play is our indispensable guide to the objective and subjective conditions set out by the Cycle.

Only if the two great human tendencies: the pagan or Hellenic tendency to create heaven on earth, to objectify the deepest and highest human values and impulses in terms of a life of beautiful fulfillment; and the Christian tendency to hold onto inward truth and holiness against the corrupting influence of the world—only if these two tendencies could come together and fuse into one, Ibsen seems to say, can Western man escape the tragic impasse where these two tendencies infect and corrupt each other and lead to incessant futile conflict, endlessly swinging from one side to the other rather than advancing.

After the "world-historical drama" which had most clearly located the spiritual drama of Western man in its historical setting (and the choice of Julian and of Byzantium was perfect, for this was the last whole-hearted effort to undo the Christian revolution in terms of both intellectual and military-political power, after which the course of

Christian Europe decisively was confirmed), it then would be necessary for the playwright to work upon the substance of modern life and reveal the way in which the consequences of this history have shaped the life of the present, and to indicate how, in modern terms, these consequences might be acknowledged and then overcome. The whole substance of the present, therefore, both the Objective world of the first four plays in the Cycle, and the Subjective world of the second four, reveals itself to be a structure of imprisoned forms waiting to be liberated by the dialectical action of historical and archetypal recall, and the subversion of the repressive present. In the last four plays, with their emphatic movement from confining interiors to the open air and the heights, and with their younger generations escaping the past-imprisoned lives of their guilty elders, an energetic image of this liberation is at least tentatively offered.

With the completion of *Emperor and Galilean* Ibsen had formulated his "positive world philosophy" and now was free to apply this vision both to the world about him and to his dramatic art. It is for this reason, I think, that, while we find far more artistic assurance in the Cycle compared with the earlier plays, we miss that immediately creative and explorative power strenuously fashioning a symbolic cosmos that we find in *Brand, Peer Gynt,* and *Emperor and Galilean,* where, it seems to me, the philosophical and the esthetic problems are one and the same thing. In these plays one senses the tremendous difficulty with which the artistic conception at the same time labors to be a metaphysical conception producing a directly symbolic art very like that of Aeschylus. One remembers the concepts that inhere in such details in *Brand,* for instance, as the Gypsy girl, Gerd, or the Ice Church, or the hawk and dove metaphors, or the directly symbolic landscape of snow, ice, sea storm, and avalanche followed by the superhuman voice. This, like the scene of *Prometheus Bound,* is a world laboring to be an adequate spiritual concept, whereas the world of the Cycle, it seems to me, is the more artistically assured *embodiment* of a concept. If the art of the three great middle-period plays is Aeschylean, that of the Cycle is Sophoclean. Released from the necessity of having to discover and formulate his ideas of the cosmos, Ibsen now can channel his great vision and energies into the most consummate artistry. Unexpectedly, therefore, it is precisely with the so-called "problem plays" Ibsen is most free to be the artist and it is with these plays that *our* interest is esthetically most satisfied. Such consummately *shaped* structures as *A Doll's House* and *Ghosts, Rosmersholm,* and *Hedda Gabler* indicate on Ibsen's part a very firm sense of artistic purposes quite at variance with the image of the angry old polemicist or self-tortured narcissist given us by traditional Ibsen interpretation.

The structure of each play in the Cycle, as we have observed, is *dialectical*. The invariable pattern of action is a given situation existing in untruth or inadequate truth, concealing conflicts and contradictions from the past and the present which, when unmasked, will force an evolution to a new condition free of *these* contradictions but vulnerable to new and higher ones. An unexpected shock (a return from the concealed past or a sudden discovery) impels the contradictory situation into unwilling motion, setting up a sensitive network of painful resistances which themselves open up new perspectives of the concealed past or the contradictory present. The seemingly solid given situation is thus gradually undermined and subverted, not just in one or the other place, but throughout its entire structure of reality so that an entire world collapses with the collapse of the Helmer or the Alving household, as if the dialectical action were a Samson in the temple of the Philistines. The fall of each world of spiritual assumptions is necessary if truth and freedom are to prevail, and so the actions of the plays are ambiguous, being negative and positive at once.

The second major element of the Ibsen action, after the action of the dialectic, is that of the return of the past. This return of the past may recover tabooed values, as in *Ghosts* and *The Master Builder,* or it may reveal the history of deceit and injustice, as in *The Wild Duck,* or of old and unacknowledged transgressions, as in *Rosmersholm.* The past, thus recovered, opens old wounds, shows that they have not healed in time, and brings into focus perspectives that the present attempts to conceal. Just as the dialectical action is ambiguous, being destructive and creative at once, so the return of the past is ambiguous, for the past is both a source of repression, convention, inhibition, and dead habit, and, on the other hand, it is a source of liberation, of a release into larger terms of action and thought than those permitted by the present. If we wish to appreciate the controlled complexity of the Ibsen action we cannot do better than to see it as a fusion of the dialectic and of archetypal recollection. It would have been possible to have written effective drama with only one of these elements: it is their fusion into a single complex action that gives Ibsen's drama its peculiar richness and power.

Hegel's *Phenomenology* supplied Ibsen with the dialectic and with a wealth of recollected spiritual forms to which, I believe, Ibsen added his own not meager cultural experience. While acknowledging the obvious dangers of such an approach I would yet suggest that Ibsen can most rewardingly be understood if we see his art recollecting and recreating the entire cultural expression of European history: its events, literature, arts, philosophies, and religions.[1]

I believe that further investigation will reveal that the Cycle is filled with recollections of the arts of the Past. For example, each play in the first two groups seems to carry within it the ghosts of older theaters: Greek in *A Doll's House, Ghosts,* and *An Enemy of the People;* Shakespearean in *The Wild Duck;* Enlightenment theater in *Rosmersholm;* Romantic in *The Lady from the Sea;* and Scribean in *Hedda Gabler,* for as human consciousness evolves so it evolves new theaters and arts. Ibsen, who was himself a painter, seems also to draw upon the visual arts. The emphatic lighting effects of *The Wild Duck,* the humble Ekdal family in the foreground and the background of animals, the light streaming through the roof (the skylight) in a play that is recollecting the Christian spirit, seem to be recollecting, also, Christian iconography (the Holy Family and the stable of animals) and the chiaroscuro effects of Baroque painters and of Rembrandt. Such a method would make Ibsen's art a *Gesamtkunstwerk* of great subtlety and thoroughly in tune with much nineteenth-century art: not only that of Richard Wagner, but of Manet, for example, whose modern realistic pictures often are based on earlier masterpieces.

It would be much less unsettling if one suggested that these "quotations" in Ibsen merely were unconscious, unwitting repetitions of archetypes of which we (wiser than the artist) are impressively aware. This is the procedure of much archetypal and mythopoeic criticism which tends to take from the individual artist the credit for much of his creation and to give this credit to a collective unconscious of which the critic is a part. This, in a sense, even makes the critic the artist's superior. To suggest that Ibsen, too, is quite aware of the archetypal content of his art and that this content is a major part of his conscious intention dismayingly suggests that Ibsen's total intention still eludes us, that there are many more dimensions to his art than we have realized. This puts the artist back in his place as our superior, demanding the strictest vigilance and humility on the critic's part. The artist no longer serves as the convenient object for our urbane and self-congratulatory erudition. *Our* erudition, on the contrary, has to submit, humbly, to that of the author. To suggest that the mythopoeic, historical, and cultural overtones of Ibsen's art are accidental is to extend, alarmingly, the area of Ibsen's art over which he has no control—and everything we know of the poet insists that he had consummate Flaubertian control over his material. It is, indeed, with Flaubert that we come upon that phenomenon of modern realism, the discrepancy between the artist, with his awareness of the whole cultural tradition of Europe and its requirements for spiritual adequacy, and the nature of the artist's *subject*, modern bourgeois individuals with no knowledge of nor relish for the vast tradition with which the artist, ironically, surrounds them. That Ibsen *did* see the situation of the modern writer in such terms is confirmed by his advice to a young would-be writer:

... an extensive knowledge of history is indispensable to a modern author, for without it he is incapable of judging his age, his contemporaries and their motives and actions, except in the most incomplete and superficial manner.[2]

If an extensive knowledge of history is essential to the modern author, so must it be to the interpreter of that author. A knowledge of Ibsen's life and times, of theatrical conditions in the nineteenth century, and of a certain amount of individual psychology obviously is not sufficient, however indispensable we nevertheless allow these to be. These are the tools for exploring a smaller artistry than Ibsen's, and if we consider them sufficient, we will get hold of only a fraction of his intention.

Detecting the presence of historical and mythopoeic sources behind the details of many works of modern realism is not a novel endeavor and it may be that the human mind, constructed as it is, always will repeat such patterns however unconsciously and however disguised in form. Hegel, we remember, remarked that those who do not study history are doomed to repeat it. Nineteenth-century literature, which often set itself the task of breaking with the discredited past by demythologizing the imagination, presents us, also, with the odd spectacle of the ancient myths, returning like ghosts (*gengangere*), under the guise of the most rigorous-seeming scientific objectivity. Thomas Mann, from the Germanic tradition of letters which, as Edmund Wilson has noted, "retained and developed to an amazing degree the genius for creating myths,"[3] argues that the naturalism even of so determinedly scientific a writer as Emile Zola "amounts to the symbolical and mythical."[4] It seems, in fact, that the past cannot just be shaken off; that the living cling to the dead and the dead to the living and that our modern psyches, so confident of their limited autonomy, actually are shaped and fated by the past. Even if we deny history, we are doomed to repeat it, and so an art form like Zola's, proclaiming itself free from the past, merely is rediscovering the past by another path. Unlike Zola, however, Ibsen is consciously recollecting the past and so, like Prospero calling upon his spirits, he can control these powers rather than having his artistic imagination helplessly controlled by them.

German intellectual life in the late eighteenth and the nineteenth centuries not only retained the genius for generating such mythic forces as the *Weltgeist*, the *Zeitgeist*, the Dialectic: it was the culture in which the nature of man's spiritual origins and history was most profoundly explored and developed, from the immensely influential writings of Herder up to the sweeping apocalyptic visions of Nietzsche. Jacob Grimm's *Teutonic Mythology* (1844) fulfilled Hegel's prediction that Germanic (Scandinavian) mythology would assume central importance in modern education and, in the volumes of Grimm's great work, we watch the way in which this particular stream of the Western spirit evolves through centuries of European history, beginning in the far distance as vital cult and myth and, under Christianity, degenerating into nostalgic folklore—a submerged but still potent force which circumstances could cause to be resurrected.

Concern with the past of the race, with the history of a whole people and its discernible identity from its myths, legends, and folklore, increases greatly with the nationalist movements of liberation in the nineteenth century. There probably is a parallel, too complex to go into here, between the conditions of small nations and peoples in the nineteenth century shaking off foreign rule and entering the community of highly developed European nations, and the condition of Germany's belated explosion into French-dominated European culture in the eighteenth century.[5] The German rejection of the French-dominated culture, and the finding of its identity better in a recovery of and reinterpretation of European history that included the rediscovery of Hellenic culture, together with the installation of Shakespeare as the poetic genius of Europe, ended the reign of the Enlightenment and brought into focus forces (such as Time, ethnic identity, mythopoeic expression) which greatly deepened, and darkened, the idea of human history and identity.[6] This meant going *beneath* the given structure of reality and returning to origins: a process of recollection that has influenced modern culture from the time of Hegel to the time of Freud. Within Germany itself we find this astonishing change of outlook when we compare such Enlightenment works as *Nathan the Wise, The Magic Flute,* and *Iphigenia in Tauris* with Wagner's *Ring* cycle and the Second Part of Goethe's *Faust*. The earlier works are eminently rational, universalist, movingly portraying the overcoming of ignorance and evil and the creation of a community of Reason, of light succeeding darkness. The later works, especially Wagner's, present an image of the cosmos alarmingly unamenable to Reason and, in fact, finding its greatest consolation and value in the deeply irrational. Undoubtedly, Wagner's vision encompasses forces and energies within the human spirit and the cosmos which the Enlightenment artists refused to depict and we welcome this great expansion of their form even though we regret the loss of intellectual finesse. Ideally, art would follow Hegel's example and, while taking note of the inevitable expansion of human consciousness to include much that the Enlightenment excluded, nevertheless would reassert the primacy of Reason.

A common theme in the writings of the nineteenth century is that of the survival of the pagan gods, both of the northern peoples and the culturally richer peoples of the south.[7] The writings of P. A. Munch in Norway (an author Ibsen admired) and Viktor Rydberg in Sweden reflect this concern with the old spiritual forms of the Northern peoples which still refuse to be exorcised and whose survival, through generation after generation, maintains not only the identity but even much of the spiritual conflict of the life of the race. No one reading only a little of the literature of the nineteenth century can fail to be struck by the past-oriented nature of the age: above all, in the life of that Germanic culture of which Ibsen declared himself to be a product.

Richard Wagner and Friedrich Nietzsche, for example, both insisted that the modern imagination must return to its mythic origins because myth reveals the spiritual sources of the life of the race. Modern life itself has become deeply unsatisfactory in its inability to feed our hunger for those deeper layers of spiritual reality once expressed in myth, cult, and ritual. A return to spiritual health is possible, however, by means of the artist's and the thinker's recovery of the living reality of myth; this theme is as prevalent in the nineteenth century as it later became, in the Anglo-Saxon world, after *The Golden Bough*. Wagner argued that:

> The mythos is the poet's ideal stuff—that native nameless poem of the folk, which throughout the ages we ever meet new handled by the great poets of consummate culture: for in it there almost vanishes the conventional form of man's relations, merely explicable to abstract reason, to show, instead, the eternally intelligible, the purely human, but in just that inimitable concrete form which lends to every sterling myth an individual shape so swiftly cognizable.[8]

The myth, as the creation of the "folk," is an impersonal embodiment of the spiritual life of the race and is thus of far greater significance and power than either historical fact or the fictional invention of any particular writer. It is the job of the individual artist to return to this profounder and larger spiritual life in order to give his otherwise arbitrary art work genuine essential truth and universality and to speak to the deepest layers of the people's collective consciousness.

Wagner's whole endeavor to return, by means of myth, to the life-giving sources of the collective consciousness and to break free from the Waste Land of modern rational society was viewed sympathetically and taken up enthusiastically by the most profound thinker of the later nineteenth century, Friedrich Nietzsche, who eloquently opposed the growing tyranny of the factual, positivistic, and bourgeois culture, on behalf of a more adequate and satisfying spiritual reality. *The Birth of Tragedy* (1872) sets out an extraordinary and powerful analysis of the nature of Greek tragedy. On closer examination, however, it becomes obvious that Nietzsche's account of the origins of tragedy is as much a critical analysis of a whole culture and an account of the structure of the mind. In this account the basis of Greek tragedy is seen as the strange satyr chorus which, as ecstatic reveler, becomes the sympathetic beholder and companion of the suffering god, Dionysos. Dionysos symbolizes the energies within Nature and within man himself, a creative destructive Energy which precedes the "Apollonian" realm of individuation and of civilization. Individuation and civilization are merely a "dream" which man interposes between himself and the terror of reality; but in the ecstatic state this bulwark of beautiful illusion (Apollonian Civilization) is broken down and the collective consciousness becomes one with the satyr chorus beholding the creative-destructive suffering of the dismembered god, Dionysos Zagreus. The dismemberment of the god, Nietzsche claims, is an emblem of the dismemberment of consciousness from the primal unity or Oneness of reality into a multitude of separate individuals; thus, in the Dionysian rite we are able to put aside our petty individuality and once again approach the mystery of the life process itself.[9] As it is impossible to dwell long in this Dionysian state, and as the Apollonian condition is likely to grow stale without an infusion of Dionysian insights, so tragedy is evolved whereby the Dionysiac experience is transmuted into Apollonian dream and *vice versa*: a rare achievement, possible only in certain special cultural conditions, and one that easily can fall into disequilibrium. For Nietzsche, most art falls into one or the other extreme. The Nietzschean concept of Greek tragedy could be set out by means of the following diagram.

APOLLONIAN REALM	DIONYSIAN REALM
(Individuality and Civilization)	(Original Oneness)

Audience—Poet & Dramatic—Tragic Character—Satyr Chorus—Dionysos—Primal Reality.
(Polis)   Conventions   (Myth)   (Dithyramb)

Myth, in this structure, has extreme importance in providing a body of powerful and anonymous folk legends, *preceding* the conscious and individual creations of developed cultures, and therefore leading back, by means of archetypal characters and actions, to the perception of the nature of primal reality—what Nietzsche terms the "Original Oneness" that precedes dismemberment into separate self-existences. Because the civilized individual consciousness is far removed from this Original Oneness by the fragmentation of consciousness into individuation, tragedy performs the function of ritually shattering the individual and fusing him with this Original Oneness, yet in such a way (by means of perfect esthetic form) that the result is "an Apollonian embodiment of Dionysiac insights and powers."[10]

It soon becomes plain that, in *The Birth of Tragedy*, Nietzsche is seeking an answer to the modern cultural *malaise* and also is describing the structure of the human mind from unconscious energies to highly conscious censors in a way so anticipative of Freud that we would be astonished did we not remember how this same structure is, in fact, to be found in Hegel's *Phenomenology* and in the whole cultural life of Germany. Nietzsche merely has restated a common theme with the greatest brilliance and lucidity. His account of the mythopoeic mode of thought (and art) becomes a frontal attack upon the intellectual assumptions of his own age:

> The chances are that almost every one of us, upon close examination, will have to admit that he is able to approach the once living reality of myth only by intellectual constructs. Yet every culture that has lost myth has lost, by the same token, its natural, healthy creativity. Only a horizon ringed about with myth can unify a culture. The forces of imagination and of Apollonian dream are saved only by myth from indiscriminate rambling. . . . Over against this, let us consider abstract man stripped of myth, abstract education, abstract mores, abstract laws, abstract government; the random vagaries of the artistic imagination unchannelled by any native myth; a culture without any fixed or consecrated place of origin, condemned to exhaust all possibilities and feed miserably and parasitically on every culture under the sun. Here we have our present age, the result of a Socratism bent on the extermination of myth. Man today, stripped of myth, stands famished among all his pasts and must dig frantically for roots, be it among the most remote antiquities. What does our great historical hunger signify, our clutching about us for countless other cultures, our consuming desire for knowledge, if not the loss of myth, of a mythic home, the mythic womb.[11]

Nietzsche describes movingly a spiritual condition against which imaginative thinkers and artists of the nineteenth century rebelled, and it was the particular merit of the German intellectual tradition very early to have seen and clearly to have articulated that cultural condition that later became fashionable in the Anglo-Saxon world after T. S. Eliot's *The Waste Land*. If we are claiming an achievement for Ibsen startlingly similar to that of such poets as Wagner, T. S.

Eliot, James Joyce, Thomas Mann, and Ezra Pound, this claim at least
can point to the strongest evidence within German culture itself.

It was, in fact, long before Wagner and Nietzsche wrote the passages
quoted above that we find Ibsen, in 1851, rising to the defense of the
use of mythic archetypes in modern literature. In "Professor Welhaven
on Paludan-Müller's Mythological Poems" (an article recently translated into English by Rolf Fjelde who rightly has seen its significance)
Ibsen defends Paludan-Müller from the criticism of the Norwegian
poet and critic Welhaven, a writer towards whom Ibsen generally was
sympathetic. Welhaven deplored the tendency of modern poets to
gather their material "from old Hellenic gods and other ancient mythological figures" and called for a demythologized poetry more suitable
to the sensibility of the modern world. One is a little startled by the
earnestness of Ibsen's defense of the mythological poems of the Danish
poet, for it is not Ibsen's practice directly to employ mythological
figures in his poetry and drama; but the nature of Ibsen's defense and
the forbidding Hegelian terminology in which that defense is expressed,
open up perspectives on Ibsen's art that go beyond the immediate issue
of Welhaven's quarrel with Paludan-Müller. Rolf Fjelde's very illuminating commentary on this article describes the drift of its Hegelian
argument and the reader is referred to both.[12] For the purpose of the
present study it is necessary to take note of this argument only as it
has direct bearing upon the method of the realistic Cycle, a method
created many years after the article appeared.

Ibsen begins by conceding that the *original* creation of myth no
longer is possible for the modern writer for the very Hegelian reason
that human consciousness has advanced far beyond that phase when
myth was a viable mode of thought:

> The period of mythopoeic composition is well over with respect to the
> primitive (naive) creations; but since the myth contains the eternal in itself,
> its life in the imagination never will so end that one can no longer be per-
> mitted to lay a few more stones on the mythic foundation; one no longer sails
> across the seven seas like Columbus to discover new land, but rather to
> search into the nature of it now that its existence is known. So it is with the
> poetry of myth: the Idea as a mythic conception which the folk consciousness
> in its original condition once laid down as the foundation of its production
> must by no means be modified, and, in fact, cannot be so modified since it is
> the truth, objectivity itself: but to drag it up from its sea depths, to study it
> on the plane of speculation, is in no way the violation of a mythic poem's
> sanctity nor any betrayal of its basic nature; but, on the contrary, a necessary
> stage of its later development.[13]

This passage gives us a glimpse into the strangely conservative cast
of mind of a poet otherwise so radical. While still a very young poet,

at the threshold of his career, Ibsen nevertheless seems entirely to agree with Hegel's judgment upon the modern spirit: that it is the culmination and passing away of a whole development of human history, that the poet, following the thinker, should give himself up to searching into the nature of that which already is known rather than attempting to discover new territory. The images of sea voyage and sea depths look forward to Ibsen's most powerful metaphors in the later plays. Brand forgoes the sea voyage south and wrestles with the complex past at home; Peer Gynt travels across the seas and loses his identity and so must be shipwrecked at home to find his possible identity saved by a figure from the past. The world of the imagination is called "the depths of the sea" in *The Wild Duck,* and it is a figure from these sea depths that invades the Wangel household with the lure of absolute freedom in *The Lady from the Sea.*

The argument of the passage contrasts two phases of consciousness: one, in which the mind spontaneously conceived myths, creating that foundation from which all later conceptions would emerge. These conceptions undergo a later development in which the mythic foundation is retained within the more complex structure of consciousness. This later development of the life of the mythic conceptions—corresponding unmistakably to Hebbel's account of the development of the European spirit in history from the "positive religions"—will appear, writes Ibsen, as a "higher synthesis of reflection and that original spontaneity."[14] This "reflection"—deriving from man's historically developed consciousness—must, nevertheless, recognize the substratum of myth from which it has derived just as the audience in the Greek theater was brought to contemplate the primitive substructure, expressed in myth, of its own highly developed culture.

In a later passage in the same article Ibsen follows Hegel directly in distinguishing between epic, lyric, and dramatic poetry, and, like Hegel, sees the dramatic as the highest, a synthesis of the former two. The "higher synthesis" of reflection and spontaneity will be a poem of ideas and, as Rolf Fjelde comments:

When one recalls that for Hegel drama is the higher synthesis of epic and lyric, and that Ibsen was in the habit of calling his plays poems, it becomes apparent that Ibsen's "poem of ideas" must logically become (as it did) a drama utilizing a substructure of myth and presenting a "veil of symbols" within which rested its justifying idea (which could be understood as a Hegelian Notion or concept (*Begriff*).[15]

Ibsen's quite difficult argument might, for the sake of clarity, be set out in the following way:

(a) The creation of original myth no longer is possible

(b) but the modern poet can and indeed should build upon the mythopoeic foundation.

(c) This in no way will modify the myth but will represent the myth's continuously developing life in the imagination up to the present.

(d) The resulting work will be a synthesis of the primitive (naive) perception that created the original mythic concepts, and the more adult "reflection" that has derived from the later development of culture.

This, in fact, is a reformulation of the program set out by Hegel in the Preface to the *Phenomenology* and carried out by him, over a lifetime, through every realm of Objective and Subjective reality: a movement from origins to final results both within the microcosm of the dialectic method and in the macrocosm of the entire Hegelian system.

In modern education and culture, and, above all, in the study of philosophy, the advanced modern mind must retrace the whole development of mind from its origins in primitive sense perception to the totality of knowledge attainable in the present.

The individual, whose substance is mind at the higher level, passes through these past forms, much in the way that one who takes up a higher science goes through those preparatory forms of knowlege, which he has long made his own, in order to call up their content before him; he brings back the recollection of them without stopping to fix his interest upon them. The particular individual, so far as content is concerned, has also to go through the stages through which the general mind has passed, but as shapes once assumed by mind and now laid aside, as stages of a road which has been worked over and leveled out.[16]

This bygone mode of existence already has become an acquired possession of the general mind, which constitutes the substance of the individual, and, by thus appearing externally to him, furnishes his inorganic nature.[17]

The goal to be reached is the mind's insight into what knowing is. Impatience asks for the impossible, wants to reach the goal without the means of getting there. The length of the journey has to be borne with, for every moment is necessary; and again we must halt at every stage, for each is itself a complete individual form.[18]

... the content is one where reality is already canceled out for spiritual possibilities, where *immediacy* has been overcome and brought under the control of *reflection*, the various shapes and forms have been already reduced to their intellectual abbreviations, to determinations of thought [*Gedankenbestimmung*] pure and simple.[19]

The argument in each of the passages quoted above is that the modern, reflective consciousness is confronted with its entire substance, its identity unfolded in history; and to be educated into one's full humanity is once again to traverse this history. In *The Philosophy of Fine Art* (*Aesthetik*) Hegel suggests that a *nation*, if it is to outgrow barbarism, must go through the stages of poetic consciousness which the civilized world has undergone,[20] a requirement similar to that postulated by Georg Brandes for Scandinavia which, Brandes believed, still needed to undergo the full dialectical journey of thought undergone by the larger European nations, and this might supply us with the clue as to why Ibsen took upon himself so immensely demanding an undertaking—the self-analysis enjoined by the *Phenomenology*—for *his* painful progress to spiritual self-emancipation could be that of his people, too. We saw that the conclusion of *The Philosophy of Fine Art*, in fact, is that art itself, "is, and remains for us, on the side of its highest possibilities, a thing of the past,"[21] so that, at this late reflective phase of the spirit, all the previous art forms are available for the modern artist's recollection.

Hegel himself concludes that the modern artist now can draw upon the entire evolution of art through all its earlier forms:

> . . . Art is no longer under the constraint to represent that, and only that, which is completely at home in one of its specific grades. Everything now is possible as its subject matter, in which man, on whatever plane of life he may be, possesses either the need or the capacity of making his abode.[22]

The artist, however, cannot return to a past form. "Neither Homer, Sophocles, Dante, Ariosto, nor Shakespeare can reappear in our times. What has been sung so greatly, what has been expressed with such freedom, has been sung and expressed once for all. Only the present blows fresh; all else is faded and more faded." Hegel commends the French who, for all the defects of their art works, *did* translate the Past "into Art's present life"; for "all material whatsoever, it matters not from what age or nation it hails, only retains its truth for art as part of this vital and actual Present, in which it floods the human heart with the reflected image of its life, and brings truth home to man's senses and mind."

Not surprisingly, therefore, Hegel sees the task of the artist as resembling that of the philosopher: of having available the whole wealth of the past forms which he can transmute into an art answering the needs of the present. Such a recollective art inevitably must preside over the inquest of art itself, at least in its present form, and this, in fact, seems to be the meaning embodied by *When We Dead Awaken*, that "Epilogue" to more than the Cycle. A more explicit statement of this idea is found in Ibsen's speech given at a banquet in his honor in Stockholm in 1887 in which he declared, with customary contradictoriness:

It has been said that I too have been in the vanguard of things, and have helped to create a new age in the land. Against this, I believe that the age we now stand in could just as well be described as a closure, and that from it something new is in the process of being born. I believe that the scientific doctrine of evolution is valid also in respect of the spiritual elements of life. I believe that poetry, philosophy, and religion will fuse together to form a new category and a new power in life of which we who are now alive are incapable of forming any clear impression.[23]

"Poetry, philosophy, and religion"—that is, the great triad of art, religion, and philosophy which is the culmination of Hegel's entire system—are bewilderingly intertwined in the final pages of the *Phenomenology* and their fusion would, as Ibsen declared, "form a new category and a new power in life." Ibsen's speech in Stockholm indicates to what extent he endorsed Hegel's verdict, quoted in the first chapter, that the nineteenth century was the night of the old European spirit preceding that dawn of the twentieth century which, in fact, was to see a complete break with the artistic traditions of the European past.[24] Ibsen's "use of the past" stands in strong contrast to the more sentimental revivalisms of the Classical, Pre-Raphaelite, Viking, or Celtic twilights in being an investigation into the structure of the *modern* mind: a depiction of the inherited spiritual forces that make up the passions and prejudices, the limitations and the possibilities, of human consciousness within the Present.

In 1876, while at work on the first play in the Cycle, *The Pillars of Society*, Ibsen turned aside to write a preface to the German translation of *The Vikings at Helgeland*, in which he informed his readers that in the earlier play he had used the Sagas rather than the Nibelung sources for his plot because in the Sagas there already had taken place a humanization of the mythic figures that rendered them more suitable for dramatic art. The mythic figures are not, Ibsen insists, thereby degraded; but in idealized form they are unsuited to the stage, for the poet's task was to depict, not myth itself, but life in primitive times. We note the continuity of Ibsen's thinking, for the point he is making is exactly that of his article on Paludan-Müller's mythological poems: a later stage of the development of consciousness makes the original mythic conceptions unsuitable, but the later developments of the mythic conceptions *are* suitable.

In the Cycle, where the poet is depicting life in modern times, a further humanization of the mythic material, beyond the Saga level, would be necessary, this further humanization reflecting the historical development of man from the "positive religions" of which the myths were the first expressions. Just as modern man carries within his physical structure the history of his entire biological development, so, in Hegel's account, his spiritual structure contains the entire past through which it has evolved and (though Hegel is more ambiguous on this than Ibsen is in the Stockholm speech) a future of further spiritual evolution.

This is not to deny the admirable contemporaneity and modern relevance of Ibsen's actions whose details, undoubtedly, are taken from his own observation of the world around him. The realistic content of the Cycle exists convincingly in its own right as modern drama, for the dramatist has worked hard to create that illusion of reality which alone can "realize" (in the full meaning of that word) the spiritual subject matter. But, conversely, the world in which Ibsen found himself was only adequately experienced and understood when it was found to reveal its total, archetypal content. To insist upon the archetypal and mythopoeic content of the Cycle is not to threaten the existence of that grasp upon human realities for which Ibsen is so justly admired: on the contrary, it is to restore to Ibsen's realism the dimensions of a more adequate *reality*. For example, we would not dispute that the details of many of Ibsen's plays can be traced to events in Ibsen's own lifetime, such as the history of Laura Kieler's marital tragedy behind the marital tragedy of *A Doll's House*. But interpretation need not stop here; after all, many events occurred in the contemporary world that Ibsen inhabited. That he chose Laura Kieler's tragedy rather than these other events for the plot of *A Doll's House* is very likely for the reason that Laura Kieler's history best exemplified the universal themes which, at *that* particular stage of the Cycle, Ibsen was wrestling with.

We are suggesting that Ibsen saw his own age merely as one moment of the totality of human history, a part that could be understood only from an awareness of the whole. This, I believe, is where Ibsen became interested intensely in the bourgeois life he saw around him and which he made the subject of the Cycle. What rivets his attention is the half-conscious and unconscious resurrection of the archetypal substance of the human spirit within the reduced rhythms of the bourgeois world: in other words, the way in which the local and ephemeral identity of modern man, almost in spite of itself, comes to terms with its universal and essential identity. The structure of the individual mind, then, could become the microcosm in which the macrocosm of the world mind could be discovered, so that all human history is involved in the agony-in-the-drawing-room of *Ghosts, Rosmersholm,* and *The Master Builder.* A cycle of such microcosmic actions then could recover the total evolution of the human spirit that once required painful centuries to unfold. We can see, for instance, that the concept "modern European" presupposes the history of the world: of Persia, Israel, Greece, Rome, and medieval Europe. Any account of modern man, claiming to be adequate, which did not include this history, plainly would be inadequate and fraudulent—which no doubt is why Ibsen insisted that a thorough knowledge of history was indispensable to a modern author who was to judge his age correctly.

Until comparatively modern times the conviction was widespread at the higher levels of many cultures that the universal identity of humanity stood over and above any single identity or even any single world view. Are not the spiritual aristocrats of Ibsen's dramas those individuals who are shocked or lured into abandoning the comfortable "doll's house" world of everyday appearance and into moving toward the sometimes desolate, sometimes exhilarating realm of universal reality—the living God? The subject matter of his plays is always this—the ephemeral microcosmic world challenged by the eternally abiding macrocosm; and one can see in the tragic collision of these two structures the recovery of the Greek tragedy of fate. For the macrocosm, with its often fearful demands upon the individual, is waiting from the beginning for the daring spirit who, intentionally or not, finds himself launched upon this journey of larger self-discovery: a collision course towards his true spiritual identity. This "convergence of the twain" is, finally, necessitarian, fatalist, and it was with *Emperor and Galilean* that Ibsen declared he had become a "fatalist."

Lionel Abel, in his excellent book *Metatheatre*, argues that Ibsen gave a false fillip to the dead cause of tragedy when he "imposed a necessitarian structure on his realistic plays, a structure taken from Greek tragedy." This observation is correct except that Ibsen did not esthetically *impose* this structure upon a non-necessitarian subject; he actually viewed modern reality in such necessitarian (and Hegelian and Greek) terms.

The significant modern (and tragic) individual for Ibsen is he who, by accident or self-conscious design, is forced to respond to the "fate" that lies outside his local and temporal existence: a "fate" like that of Oedipus, which lies in the structure of reality itself for the awakened and fully human consciousness that is capable of tragedy. This fate can subtly be involved in the whole texture of the individual's life history, as with Helene Alving; or it can come blatantly knocking at the door, as with Halvard Solness. In both cases, the individual has come to live *essentially* (i.e., according to the essence and not the mere appearance) and so will take on, reluctantly, fearfully, painfully, the tragic gestures of the awakened spirit.[25]

The necessitarian, fatalistic content and structure of the plays (almost unique in modern theater until Samuel Beckett) sets them directly at odds with the optimistic philosophy of the positivist and technological modern age in much the same way, one imagines, that Sophocles opposed the confident rationalism of Athens with his fatalistic vision. The seeming contradiction in Ibsen's vision, giving his work its profound ambiguity, is the convergence of this fatalism with an equally "positive" program of spiritual evolution—an ambiguity also inherent in Hegel's philosophy, where the triumphs of the spirit are gained at the expense of appalling human suffering.

In the analyses of individual plays offered in the second part of this book we will detect archetypal scenes, characters, actions, and speeches behind the contemporary realism Ibsen so demurely and plausibly creates. It is as if the modern reality Ibsen is depicting continuously is discovering its universal *raison d'être*, and the archetypal identities beneath this modern realism enable Ibsen to capsule centuries of spiritual history and conflict within the restricted ritual of the modern theater. It is true that, compared with the theater of Dionysos, Ibsen's ritual of the thesis-play (the movement of the moral consciousness) is impoverished, but precisely this sense of the vast human spirit imprisoned unendurably within the confines of modern bourgeois life and its theater is one of the powerful metaphors of Ibsen's dramatic vision. It is a theater more of the mind than of the body, of memory rather than action, entailing a loss in rich externality of which Ibsen is not unaware. But his unique contribution to the theater precisely is this of creating dramatic intensity, poignancy, and terror out of the growth of the mind and the act of remembrance.

It was in the small pattern, in the withdrawn and secretive life of the soul, that the sunken reality had to be dragged up from its sea depths and brought back into the light of day. It is for this reason that Ibsen's drama of the mind, with its four or five characters within a drawing room, possesses a richness and depth unequaled in modern drama. The whole of reality, of time and space gradually is discerned in these plays, reminding one of Marvell's famous description of the mind:

> The Mind, that Ocean where each kind
> Does straight its own resemblance find;
> Yet it creates, transcending these,
> Far other Worlds, and other Seas . . .

Thus, behind the reduced little modern scene of Ibsen's plays we sense, not merely the exhilarating wastes of the uncharted future, what Francis Fergusson called "a blank check to the insatiate spirit . . . the uninhabited wilderness . . . the stage of Europe before human exploration, as it must have appeared to the first hunters," but also, as Fergusson surprisingly does not see (doubly surprising as he is discussing *Ghosts*), layer after layer of a richer past which, like the geological strata beneath the earth's surface, or the layers of oceanic water, not only is huger than the present but determines the very contours of the present.

It is a long way from the sunlit, richly elaborate, ceremonial theater of Dionysos to Ibsen's enclosed darkened auditorium, his artificially lit proscenium stage like the interior of a skull, and the intent stare of the middle-class audience at what seems to be the mere mirror reflection of its own surface identity; but if that audience stares hard enough it will detect, beneath the familiar-looking surface, layer after layer of reality stretching back to the origins of the race. And this, after all, is not so different from the subject matter of the Athenian audience's meditation in the theater. The nineteenth-century auditorium becomes a congregation of minds facing the image of its evolving universal mind; the world of images and lights and shadows behind the proscenium arch is the recesses of a mind, making Ibsen's theater as essentially that of the proscenium as Shakespeare's was of the apron stage. The foreground here-and-now of the room with the fourth wall removed, seemingly so solidly established at the beginning of each play, becomes, little by little, a transparent veil through which we detect the design of a universal reality.

This, naturally, calls to mind the theater of Richard Wagner which similarly was designed to translate the spectator from the here-and-now into the world of archetypal, mythopoeic reality. In 1876, after a brilliant campaign of self-advertisement, Wagner opened Bayreuth to be the stage for the unfolding of his visionary and mythopoeic *Ring* cycle. Only a year later Ibsen's more prosaic-looking *The Pillars of Society*, inaugurating his Cycle, had its first performance at the Royal Theater in Copenhagen. The conventional history of modern theater depicts the two artists as polar opposites, with Wagner and Ibsen as the mythopoeic and prosaic extremes of nineteenth-century theater. (Critics have not noticed the curious similarity of imagery, of sea, theft, guilt, and future redemption, in *Pillars* and *Das Rheingold*.) Ibsen's art, however, best can be seen as synthesizing the immediately mythopoeic art of Wagner and the uncompromisingly naturalistic art of, say, Emile Zola. If Wagner's art had too arrogantly dismissed as irrelevant the whole rational realm of historical process and experience of the modern world and its problematic details, Zola's art had so obsessively fastened on the present that its details, forced to carry Zola's extremely powerful poetic vision, became archetypal presences without benefit of historical perspective. Wagner's theater is inhabited by figures who are heroic and divine and monstrous before they are permitted to be human, as if two thousand years of subsequent history were of no account, whereas Zola's novels create a universe in which the gods of modern society (science, technology, capitalism, biological determinism) and the sufferings of their victims had totally taken over the universe, wiping out the past from the vision of humanity. In both cases the great power of the visions (strangely similar, as Thomas Mann noted) is gained at the expense of the truth of our deepest and most adequate reflection upon human reality. To use Matthew Arnold's expression in praise of Sophocles, they do not "see life steadily and see it whole." In contrast to the cyclical works of these two great artists, Ibsen's realistic Cycle, in order to see life steadily and see it whole, does not put aside the banality and complexity of modern life in order to attain to mythopoeic grandeur, nor does it truncate the modern moment in all its urgency from the shaping past in order to speak with immediate force to "the problems of the present." At its most Zolaesque, as when the offended Dionysian power, in *Ghosts*, strikes back in the form of syphilis, this still is an expression of Spirit;[26] and, even at its most Wagnerian, as in Solness's and Hilde's visionary "duets" in *The Master Builder,* the visionary dialogue is rooted in plausible human experience.

Ibsen's theater of the mind, of memory, gradually, throughout the progress of the Cycle, recovers the total past: the total spiritual identity underlying the disfigured and inadequate physiognomy of modern man. For only by this painful and laborious self-examination could modern man master his reality and thus attain freedom. From the moral depths of *The Pillars of Society* in which the human community seems to have turned its back completely on spiritual realities, to the forbidding heights of *When We Dead Awaken* in which, against the "silence" the characters have no time for anything but essential reality, Spirit, in the guise of a brilliantly variegated, individualized, and vivid procession of men and women (somewhat reminiscent of Chaucer's Canterbury pilgrims) has climbed the winding stairway of despair. At the end of this pilgrimage the last sound we hear in Ibsen's theater is Maia's song of *freedom* after the tortured dialectic of spirit has ended with the summit deaths of Rubek and Irene. Ibsen's dramatic method, which so rigorously had excluded verse for a quarter of a century, now breaks out into a tentative and primitive lyric:

> Jeg er fri! Jeg er fri! Jeg er fri!
> Mitt fangenskaps liv er forbi!
> Jeg er fri som en fugl! Jeg er fri!

(I am free! I am free! I am free!
My imprisoned life is put by!
I am free as a bird! I am free!)

The actors in this huge theater of memory are, paradoxically, most false and inadequate where they are most "realistic" in the conventional sense of that term, for the conventions of everyday realism create an uncomfortable gulf between the accidents of ordinary scene, character, action, and dialogue, and the spiritual realities that seek expression through them. Spirit, thus excluded, has to fight back and invade this reduced and pragmatic world somewhat violently, as in the "coffin ships" of *The Pillars of Society*, the "Capri dance" of *A Doll's House*, the burning orphanage and syphilis of *Ghosts*, and the polluted baths of *An Enemy of the People*. In the second group of plays there is a movement towards a closer integration of the two realms and reality becomes dual, double-natured, combining such half-real elements as the fantasy attic, the wild duck, the flying Dutchman, the white horses of Rosmersholm, the Stranger from *The Lady from the Sea*, and the veiled dream world of Hedda Gabler yearning for values prohibited by the reduced present.

The tragic gulf between the reduced reality presented on the realistic stage and the spiritual realities that must be reclaimed by the actors within the realistic convention is the major metaphor, and the major springboard of action, of Ibsen's theater of memory. Until this larger reality has been recovered in its totality, Spirit is imprisoned. Therefore, W. B. Yeats's horrified response to the notorious performance of *Ghosts* in London in 1891, which he records in *Plays and Controversies*, demonstrates how powerfully successful Ibsen's method was:

At the first performance of *Ghosts* I could not escape from an illusion unaccountable to me at the time. All the characters seemed to me less than life-size; the stage, though it was but the little Royalty stage, seemed larger than I had ever seen it. Little whimpering puppets moved here and there in the middle of that great abyss. Why did they not speak out with louder voices or move with freer gestures? What was it that weighed on their souls perpetually? Certainly they were all in prison, and yet there was no prison.[27]

Though this is recorded against Ibsen, as part of Yeats's attempt to recover poetry and ritual for the modern theater, it is an unwitting tribute to the truth and depth of Ibsen's method. "And yet there was no prison." It is odd that such an admirer of William Blake as Yeats was should not see that Ibsen could not hear the voices and see the gestures of his contemporaries without hearing, too, "the mind-forg'd manacles" that imprisoned modern man far more effectively than stone walls and iron bars. If the little Royalty stage seemed a great abyss, this was to a great extent due to Ibsen's art of careful and significant exclusion so that what is, shockingly, *not* present on the stage (in *Ghosts* that whole order of life associated with Eros and Dionysos) makes itself felt with more force than what is present. Ibsen would have been, I believe, the first to have approved of Yeats's dream of a recovered, vital, poetic, and ritualistic theater, only he would have insisted that such spiritual creativity and freedom only could arise from a community of free men, for life will not be redeemed by art, but art by life. Therefore, the burden of the past that still defines and limits us, setting a barrier between us and our possible freedom, must be painfully comprehended in order that it can be overcome.

It is in the third group of four plays in the Cycle, from *The Master Builder* to *When We Dead Awaken*, that we are given intimations that, beyond the dance of death of the European spirit, there lies the possibility of renewal. In these last plays in which the Cycle recollects all its spiritual forces, we are presented with the human spirit on the brink of apotheosis, recollecting "Resurrection Day" and looking upwards to the earth's summit, "the peak of Promise." *When We Dead Awaken*, however, remains within this world and so denies to the Cycle the culminating transcendental affirmations of Dante's *Commedia* or Goethe's *Faust*, or Wagner's *Parsifal*. The avalanche that sweeps Rubek and Irene to their deaths, denying them the final summit vision (as if the earth itself will not permit its creatures to transcend it) is, interestingly, Ibsen's second thoughts, for his first sketch of the play ended with their ascent to the peak. As it now stands, the affirmation of this epilogue to the Cycle is not of an earth-transcending value but, on the contrary, of "the love that belongs to the life of the earth—the beautiful miraculous earth-life."[28] Thus it is the animalic Ulfheim and Maia who survive as the ghostly, "higher" drama of Rubek and Irene plays itself out. Thus the Cycle seems to return to its beginnings, like Wagner's *Ring* cycle or Joyce's *Finnegans Wake*, for, beginning with the emergence from the "animal community," the Cycle ends with man becoming animalic again.[29]

Such Joycean ramifications to "the old masterbilker's" method, though at first alarming to those who have put their whole trust in the realistic solidity of Ibsen's plays, are really far less tortuous than psychological or autobiographical interpretations of the plays. These latter convert Ibsen's "judgment-day upon the soul," in which our whole collective spiritual inheritance should be shatteringly revalued, into a rather self-complacent holding court over the deficiencies of Other People. This Peeping Tom-ism is, needless to say, the very contrary of what Ibsen intends for us where it is ourselves who are on trial. The theme of *mea res agitur,* my own self is at stake, is more likely to represent the intention of the Cycle where "the individual must go through the evolutionary process of the race" than our role as spectators at a psychological gladiatorial show where, from our positions of safety, we can enjoy the suffering of the protagonists, smugly judge them, and doom or reprieve them according to our preferences. Ibsen is stalking much greater game than this. With his famously low opinion of the spiritual stature of his contemporaries he was not likely to be greatly agitated by their personal idiosyncrasies except where they helped him to see his world as still haunted by the ghosts of the past.

For the ghosts of the past are not harmless fancies. They not only everywhere prevent the human spirit from attaining freedom; by not being acknowledged and assimilated, they break out into the psychopathology of everyday life and into the dangerous currents that move whole nations. Heinrich Heine, who saw the full import of German intellectual life and the dangers of this tremendous stirring for the whole German nation and the world, prophesied with what now seems uncanny prescience, on the terrible potency of the old unsublimated gods and powers within the German spirit:

... the Philosopher of Nature will be terrible in this, that he has allied himself with the primitive powers of Nature, that he can conjure up the old demoniac forces of old German pantheism; and having done so, there is aroused in him that ancient German eagerness for battle which combats not for the sake of destroying, not even for the sake of victory, but merely for the sake of combat itself. Christianity—and this is its fairest merit—subdued to a certain extent the brutal warrior ardour of the Germans, but it could not entirely quench it; and when the cross, that restraining talisman, falls to pieces, then will break forth again the ferocity of the old combatants, the frantic berserker rage whereof the Northern poets have said and sung so much. The talisman has become rotten, and the day will come when it will pitifully crumble to dust. The old stone gods will then rise from the forgotten ruins and wipe from their eyes the dust of centuries, and Thor with his giant hammer will arise again, and he will shatter the Gothic cathedrals. . . . Smile not at my counsel, at the counsel of a dreamer, who warns you against Kantians, Fichteans, Philosophers of Nature. Smile not at the fantasy of one who foresees in the region of reality the same outburst of revolution that has taken place in the region of thought. The thought precedes the deed as the lightning the thunder. German thunder is of true German character: it is not very nimble, but rumbles along somewhat slowly. But come it will, and when ye hear a crashing such as never before has been heard in the world's history, then know at last that the German thunderbolt has fallen.[30]

This passage, with its grim warning, might provide a clue to understanding why Ibsen, following the example of Hegel, gave himself up to a lifelong wrestling with the primitive powers—the trolls that infest the mind and heart—not by ignoring them but by summoning them up for judgment day. At this sessions, not a speck of man's spiritual past was irrelevant or could be allowed to be left unexamined. Hegel's whole philosophic endeavor, too, had been a strenuous and noble commitment to creating "a community of consciousness" against the tendencies in his own age which, he saw, threatened to destroy the civilized fabric of centuries. Also attacking the "Kantians, Fichteans, philosophers of Nature," Hegel, in a moving paragraph in the Preface to the *Phenomenology,* provides a justification for the tremendously strenuous labor of Reason he expects the reader to undertake in the difficult pages that follow. The more alluring "intuitional" philosophers of his own times are dangerous siren voices for:

> Those who invoke feeling as their internal oracle are finished with any-one who does not agree: they have to own that they have nothing further to say to anyone who does not find and feel the same in his heart—in other words, they trample underfoot the roots of humanity. For it is the nature of humanity to struggle for agreement with others, and humanity exists only in the accomplished community of consciousness. The anti-human, the ani-malic, consists in remaining at the level of feeling and being able to com-municate only at the level of feeling.[31]

Following Hegel's example, Ibsen heroically made himself, in his art, the recorder of the world soul so that his arduous and imaginative self-examination would become that of his audience, too. Edmund Gosse pointed to "the intensity with which Ibsen pressed his moral quality, his virtù, upon the Norwegian conscience, not halting in his pursuit till he had captured it and banished from it all other ideals of conduct."[32] Gosse suggested that the "chivalric" and "gracious" attitude of the Norwegian nation in modern times was the result of a generation "nur-tured in that new temper of mind, that *spiritel nuovo d'amore* which was inculcated by the whole work of Ibsen."[33]

Such a new temper of mind was arrived at, we now can suggest, by a more arduous labor than Gosse suspected: a method resembling nothing so much as a psychoanalysis of the world soul. We hardly can say that we, now, need no longer battle with the ghosts of the past which Mrs. Alving saw as numerous as the grains of sand, but Ibsen's method, so unique in its time, and pursued with such lonely and reticent integrity, now is a recognized literary method—in fact *the* major literary method of modern times though, with ironic injustice, Ibsen is one of the last authors to be accredited with it. In the work of his lifelong and per-ceptive admirer James Joyce (whose admiration for Ibsen now will no longer surprise and embarrass his devotees), in the poetry and drama of T. S. Eliot, and the novels and plays of Samuel Beckett, it is just this awareness of the living presence of the past that is the major subject. Ronald Peacock, in his *The Poet in the Theatre*, a book in which Ibsen appears as a mainly baleful influence upon the modern drama, has written:

> Another aspect of intellectual life in this century showed itself unfavorable to dramatic art: the sense of history, the voracious extension of all historical knowledge regarding human civilization, primitive and advanced, the awareness of time's accumulations, of the past in the present. Eliot and Joyce are the two authors who have shown themselves most sensitive to these developments, most deliberately conscious of their importance, and most concerned that imaginative writing should adjust itself to them. Their writing is saturated with the historical and literary culture of Europe, it is allusive in the extreme, it postulates a similar culture in the reader. The verse of the one and the prose of the other, thus reacted quickly to the new intellectual climate. There is no drama that shows a similar reaction. The reason is obvious, for it is difficult to imagine a drama that would correspond to these two examples of modern writing and still be possible on the stage. The new development was essentially inimical to the acted drama.[34]

This admirably sets out the problem Ibsen faced—and solved. For Ibsen, too, was reacting to the "new intellectual climate" which, however, long had been established in German thought from Hegel and Hölderlin to Wagner, Nietzsche, and Thomas Mann. It is the complete, or relatively complete, isolation of the Anglo-Saxon world from this development that made it seem to burst with such sudden wonder in the twentieth century.

Ibsen belongs to the major poetic tradition of European letters, consciously takes his place within it, and does not deserve to be relegated to that rather unweeded area of the literary garden designated "modern realism." We already have suggested that in many ways Hegel's philosophic method, in the *Phenomenology*, is dramatic; at the same time it is true that German drama from Lessing onwards is distinctly philosophic in nature. That play which Ibsen claimed to be the first that he wrote under the influence of German thought, *Emperor and Galilean*, seems to derive equally from the dramatic nature of dialectical philosophy and the philosophic nature of German drama. Though the philosophic intention of the realistic Cycle is less overt as dramatic form and texture, it is all the more deeply engaged in the art.

It is obvious that this account of the Cycle opens up far more possibilities than can be pursued by the present study; they are possibilities which will, I hope, be pursued by others. Given the great length of time Ibsen spent on the Cycle, I do not think there are limits we easily can set to its encyclopedic wealth of recollected details from the whole cultural past of Europe. In the pages that follow we will attempt to give only the broadest outline of the structure of the Cycle and the nature of the human reality that it is shaping into such consummate dramatic art.

CHAPTER 3

The Structure of the Cycle

—History, Stephen said, is a nightmare from which I am trying to awake.
From the playfield the boys raised a shout. A whirring whistle: goal. What
if that nightmare gave you a back kick?
—The ways of the Creator are not our ways, Mr. Deasy said. All history
moves towards one great goal, the manifestation of God.
Stephen jerked his thumb towards the window, saying:—That is God.
Hooray! Ay! Whrrwhee!
—What? Mr. Deasy asked.
—A shout in the street, Stephen answered, shrugging his shoulders.

James Joyce, *Ulysses*, Bodley Head, 1960, p. 42.

When we approach Ibsen's realistic Cycle we are first and foremost
impressed, not by a great abstract plan or design clearly manifesting
universal themes and meanings, but by the vivid particularity and
solidity of its human and natural world. In spite of the fact that the
dramatist, riskily, maintains a single dramatic method—that of the
dialectical action within the realistic and domestic setting—we are aware,
at the conclusion, of the great richness and diversity of his character
types and the human histories and destinies they are made to enact. His
dramatic art which, in each play, had struck us as being so inward and
intensive proves to be, on a retrospective glance back along the whole
Cycle, astonishingly varied and extensive. And this is Ibsen's undeniable
and very great achievement: he has given us a world to inhabit in our
imaginations. We feel we can shake hands with his characters, enter
sympathetically into their situations, know his drawing rooms, sit on
his furniture, and look through the windows of these rooms towards a
real landscape with its seasons of the year, times of day, and changing
weather.[1] It is the art of the "shout in the street" and not, as in much
German Expressionist drama, of the philosophical or poetical abstraction.

These details are rendered with great meticulousness, for Ibsen wishes
us to inhabit and experience his imaginative world as thoroughly, if

86

possible, as he has done. But we also must see these plays *adequately*: not as social criticism, psychological analysis, psychological stratagems on the author's part (puzzles to be solved by the critic), but, instead, as complex and ambitious art works, objective and explicable metaphoric structures. From the solidly constructed theatric world of vivid characters and actions we should proceed to see esthetically shaped and balanced arguments beneath the surface details, setting the characters into clear and eventful conflict. These shaped arguments, in turn, will reveal by means of imagery, metaphor, symbol, and archetypal quotation, the presence of a larger argument in which the human spirit, no longer confined to one time and place, is placed in the greater temporal and spatial perspectives of history and Nature. The problem for the interpreter is to be true to all these dimensions—of the individual play and of the complete Cycle—and if the Hegelian world view enables us to see more dimensions than other ways of approaching the plays, we can use it, gratefully, without any fear of employing Ibsen's art merely to illustrate Hegel. The great advantage of employing the Hegelian philosophical vision is that that vision is itself too large and complex to encourage our turning Ibsen's plays into ludicrously modest strategies.

The great richness and variety of the theatrical world of the Cycle, therefore, is its main achievement, and if we keep one eye on the brilliant pilgrimage of characters and actions that lead from *The Pillars of Society* to *When We Dead Awaken* we already will gain some idea of the immensity of its intention. As we look over the whole series we also are astonished at the dramatist's ability to enter so profoundly into the actions, sufferings, and desires of such deeply rendered characters: the Cycle, that is, moves inwardly to depths beneath the surface, as well as outwardly, to a brilliant panorama of scenes and character types. (We must, however, be on our guard against seeing this drama as *too* inward: as psychologically secretive and mysterious and unfathomable, for this would merely be to say it is bad drama, insufficiently objectified into knowable art.) To go further, and claim that this rich and fascinating agglomeration of characters, conflicts, and scenes actually is organized into an evolutionary movement and structure (much in the way the multitude of characters in Dante's *Commedia* is so ordered) is not to endanger the Cycle's richness and variety, for an ordered system actually is richer and more complex than a chaotic mass of objects.

Few readers, for instance, would deny that the rich detail of each individual play in the Cycle is very carefully organized into a balanced esthetic structure and argument. The artist who created the supremely cunning structure of *Hedda Gabler*, with its exact balancing of outer Acts, I and IV, and of inner Acts, II and III, or the almost similar structure of *Rosmersholm*, is very likely to shape the larger structure of the Cycle itself in just such a careful way. The Cycle can, I think, profitably be seen as, play by play, building up one massive and complex structure, like the Aeschylean trilogy, the medieval Mystery Cycle, or the Shakespearean History Cycles. Thus each play in the Cycle pulses with the life of its own deep and complex drama, creates out of this life its own distinct "shape" and structure, yet at the same time is a "moment" or "stage" of the total structure of the Cycle.

To discern this larger structure made out of the series of smaller structures, our best principle will be to begin with the most obvious and explicable structural principle and, having established this, attempt to proceed to the more complex structuring. The basic structure of the Cycle is triadic—three groups of plays, with four plays to each group, though, at the same time, the Cycle is a continuously evolving whole. To state, so baldly, that the Cycle is triadic will no doubt evoke protest; yet, in fact, this idea of the Cycle has been accepted for some time, even if the implications have not been pondered. Ibsen is our first and best authority for this triadic division. Of *The Wild Duck*, the first play of the second group, he told his publisher that it "occupies a position by itself among my dramatic works, its plan and method differing in many respects from my former ones."[2] Similarly he confirmed that the plays from *The Master Builder* to *When We Dead Awaken* formed a distinct group.[3] We already have three groups in the Cycle, therefore, and Ibsen's hints as to this triadic division are supplemented by the many critics who have seen the first four plays as "didactic," the second four as "psychological," and the last four as either "confessional" or symbolical.

Now, once we accept the Cycle as divided into three distinct groups, it is not so great a critical leap to see each of these groups of four plays, in turn, as creating distinct structures. That is, investigation of each group seems to reveal that they contain two "outer" and two "inner" plays, the first and last plays of each group revealing strong parallels of scene, character, and action, and the two inner plays revealing a similar parallel to each other. If each group of four plays is a completed world view, a Concept, then there would be a dialectical movement within each group corresponding to the evolution of the Concept.[4] We already have suggested that the first group, from *The Pillars of Society* to *An Enemy of the People*, dramatizes the "Objective" of the ethical society, and that these plays are given over primarily to the mutually complementary and mutually opposing realms of the family and society. That is, the actions contained in this entire group are the actions appertaining to a particular (Objective) way in which the human mind structures the world and finds itself within it. In the following analyses of each of the three groups I hope to show how each group builds up a distinct mental (spiritual) world. The result of our "philosophic" analysis of Ibsen's art, therefore, should be a new awareness and appreciation of Ibsen's *artistry*, where the *meanings* of each play and of the whole Cycle cannot be separated from the dramatic structures.

THE FIRST GROUP

We will begin by claiming that the first four plays create a clear dialectical movement and then, in a closer analysis of this group, attempt to substantiate the claim. The dialectical movement within the group can be set out in the following way:

A	B	B	A-C-
The Pillars of Society	*A Doll's House*	*Ghosts*	*An Enemy of The People*
I		II	III

The crisis and climax of *The Pillars of Society* develops the dialectical situation of *A Doll's House* which resolves the earlier conflict but sets the stage for the dialectical conflict of *Ghosts* which, in turn, prepares the conditions for the action of *An Enemy of the People*. This last play returns to the themes and subject matter of the first (A), but now in a completely transfigured form and, at the same time, sets the conditions for the first play of the second group (C). The fact that a play does not complete a dialectical movement without setting up the conditions for the action of its successor, gives to the whole Cycle a single, evolutionary, and organic movement. I do not expect the reader to take this assertion at face value, and so, in the pages that follow, I will substantiate it by discovering the logical progression of the Cycle.[5]

The first four plays in the Cycle take, as their subject, the world of Objective Spirit creating and expressing itself through human institutions: the family, marriage, society, and institutionalized ethical and religious life. In this world the individual discovers his identity defined by the world of custom, rights, duties, and loyalties. This is not the whole of life: it leaves out of account the Subjective life of man, to be explored in the second group; but it is an important, necessary, and compelling part of the total human identity. The *basis* for a fully human identity, for Hegel as for Aristotle, is that of the free citizen of the state or *polis*, even though the fully human individual must transcend the state. Any portrait of the human condition that left out this area of his activity would be inadequate, for even as rebel, the rebel must define his rebellion within the context of his society.[6]

In his struggle to attain to full humanity man creates the ethical world of customary conventions, laws, and rights (the theme, for example, of Aeschylus's *The Oresteia*), and Hegel demonstrates how the ethical world inevitably evolves from the inescapable contradictions generated by a sub-ethical community—men as "a community of animals" who, whatever they may *profess*, recognize and live by no universal principles other than their own self-interests. This animal community is the pre-human world before the awakening of Spirit (Reason), and Hegel's analysis of this community of selfish hypocrites is highly satirical. The peculiar and difficult title of this portrait of sub-ethical humanity (on which *The Pillars of Society* is based) is *Das geistige Tierreich und der Betrug oder die Sache selbst* (The Intellectual Animal Realm and Its Deceit. The Actual Fact)—a good indication of the far from solemn nature of Hegel's writing. Royce's free translation, cited by Loewenberg, "The Intellectual Animals and their Humbug: or the Service of the Cause," better suggests the themes, actions, and general atmosphere of *The Pillars of Society* as well as of the spiritual world analyzed so satirically by Hegel. It is the purpose of Hegel's analysis to "unmask the deception" inevitable to a way of life not truly penetrated by universal values, so that the stage can be set for Spirit's entry and a truer union of particular and universal to take place. Hegel's account ruthlessly exposes the deceits practiced by a collection of individuals hiding their self-interests through a pretense of serving the good of society as a whole, and the dialectic is rich in comic detail as the human spirit displays its great capacity for various forms of hypocrisy.

Ironically, however, by acting and so making their actions and works objects for consciousness, these selfish individuals *are* unconsciously serving the cause of universal ends which will emerge from the contradictions and conflicts exposed by mutually hostile self-interests in opposition. Therefore, the title *Samfundets Støtter* (Society's Supports, or Pillars) is even more ironic than it seems, for these hypocrites are, as they profess, serving universal ends although in ways they cannot know.[7]

This society sees itself and discovers its true nature in "the work performed" (*Phen.*, 424), and there emerges from this an individual "of wider compass in his work, possessing stronger energy of will or richer nature," a figure obviously corresponding to Karsten Bernick. This is a merely quantitative judgment, however, for the individual is not ethically superior to his fellows. By acting upon the world, and transforming it, consciousness reveals itself to others and to itself and becomes aware of the contrast between "being and acting." The condition Hegel depicts, of multiple frauds perpetrated by self-serving individuals asserting (and perhaps partly believing) the virtuous and noble motives of their actions, declaring they are working for the common good (Society), yet furious when at last they are forced to do so, is, the reader will recognize, the whole moral situation of *The Pillars of Society*. Ibsen's vivid gallery of moral portraits, and the life histories he creates, is a complete transformation of Hegel's text and this will be true of the way Ibsen employs his sources throughout the Cycle. The plays are no more to be reduced to their source than *Macbeth* is to be reduced to the sources in Holinshed; the *Phenomenology* supplied Ibsen with the dialectical skeleton only for his flesh and blood drama: the transformation of the source material demanded far more imaginative creativity than Shakespeare's sources, with their given characters, required.

In this first play of the Cycle, aptly named *Samfundets Støtter*, for the rest of the Cycle is to be built on this foundation, we find the greatest discrepancy between the ethical protestations of the individuals and the ethical universals that their actions *should* express; and, as we travel through the Cycle, the gulf of this discrepancy is narrowed until, in the last four plays, the characters' actions and speeches are reintegrated with the full rich content of spiritual reality.

As with the opening plays of the second and third groups, *The Pillars of Society* opens with a fateful arrival which will trigger off the dialectical action of the whole group.[8] Each of these arriving figures, Lona Hessel, Gregers Werle, and Hilde Wangel, returning after a decade of absence, brings to the scene values and demands that have been lost sight of or evaded. The reappearance, in all three cases, is deeply disidealistic reality uncovers the truly subversive nature of the past and its requirements for the present. I further would suggest that these three arriving figures, returning into the world of the Cycle with such fateful results, bringing back the recollection of a forgotten or evaded Past, carry with them, respectively, the Hellenic, Christian, and Germanic traditions of the European spirit whose uncompromising resurrection in the present would be as alarming to the modern world as these three figures are to the households they invade. This tactless reappearance in a world that has made a decorous compromise with repression and unidealistic reality, uncovers the truly subversive nature of the past and its spiritual forces and, like the unwelcome return of repressed traumata in psychoanalysis, is, for all its alarming nature, essential to spiritual health.

Lona Hessel, arriving from America by sea, enters the Cycle from outside its geographical limits. Attacking its stifling life of conventions-gone-dead and empty of living universal reality, in a series of pregnant anticipations, she sees the charitable work of this society as "moral linen with a tainted smell—just like a shroud" and foretells, "we'll soon rise from the sepulchre" as she open this tomb to daylight and fresh air. Here we are looking across the whole Cycle to its conclusion more than twenty years later, to *When We Dead Awaken* whose central image is "Resurrection Day."

The subject of *The Pillars of Society* is nineteenth-century capitalist society launched upon life in a condition of drastic disrepair: its ethical life as rotten and as vulnerable to the first storm as the coffin ships that are at once a symbol and a symptom of this rottenness.[9] Every aspect of this society is shown to be rotten and concealed by mere patchwork; the relations of the sexes, of parents and children, of social class divisions, of the individual with his avowed ethical, esthetic, and religious values, so that this play passes in swift review the entire substance of the later plays in the Cycle. It is a sobering reflection that the spiritual condition analyzed by the play is that of our present-day capitalist society and its modes of operation (its practices belying its professed intentions), so that we members of this society still have to climb the painful stairway of authentic spiritual life which begins with *A Doll's House*. This journey, beginning with the ethical world of the Objective Spirit, is formidable both as an internal labyrinth of the mind and the memory within each one of us, and as an external world of deception and unfreedom to be overcome.

The selfish motives and actions of the individuals of the society of the play, we noted, ironically resulted in the gradual emergence of the essential principles that the individuals attempted to evade. As Hegel puts it: "The individuality of the world's process may doubtless think it acts merely for itself or selfishly; it is better than it thinks; its action is at the same time one that is universal and with an inherent being of its own." (*Phen.*, 410–11.) It is for this reason, I think, that Consul Bernick, in many ways the most complete "villain" in the Cycle, is "let off" so lightly. Ibsen is not concerned to satisfy his sense of justice with a moral parable of Good versus Evil but, instead, to trace the more interesting emergence of ethical consciousness itself out of the realm of selfish passions. Therefore the somewhat despicable actions of the characters of the play are to be welcomed for dialectically forcing the ethical world to be born.

The Pillars of Society, then, advances from the condition of selfish and hypocritical individualism and begins that transfiguration of the community into an ethical order which, however, will have its ironic culmination in the ethically motivated destruction of the ethical community. From the crisis in the "animal" community of *Pillars* emerges the change of heart that begets the realm of Reason as law *giver* and then of Reason as rebellious law *breaker* (the contrast between Aeschylus's *The Eumenides* and Sophocles' *Antigone*). Ibsen's *Pillars*, like *The Eumenides*, ends with a great civic torchlight procession (Ibsen ironically counterpoints our memory of the triumphant civic assertion of Aeschylus's play against our recognition of the collapse of a fraudulent civic order in his own play) and with an Athene (Lona Hessel) arriving from outside the little community to establish new principles (truth and freedom) for that community to live by.

When Karsten Bernick sees the flames of the torchlight procession, he shrinks back from them, exclaiming, in an image that draws directly upon Orestes's response to the Furies:

Take away all that! I don't want to see it! Put it out! Put it out! It's a mockery, I tell you! Don't you see that all these lights—they're flames, putting out their tongues at us. . . .

But Bernick, like Orestes, finally will reintegrate himself with the communal life, telling his fellow citizens, in a speech that obviously looks forward to the plays that follow:

Fellow citizens—your spokesman has said that we stand tonight on the threshold of a new era, and I hope that will turn out to be so. But if it *is* to, we must lay to heart the truth—truth which, until tonight, has been utterly and in every way alien to our community . . . I ask every one of you to go home, to collect himself—to look into himself.

When Bernick, deferring to the feminine world he had offended, concedes "it's you women who are the pillars of society," Lona Hessel, who formerly had seemed a pursuing Fury,[10] corrects him:

That's a pretty feeble piece of wisdom you've learned, Karsten. (*Lays her hand firmly on his shoulder*) No, no; the spirits of truth and freedom—these are the pillars of society.

This optimistic legislation for the new order to come will be modulated ironically in the plays that follow, where truth and freedom will engage upon a wholesale destruction of the whole repressive structure of reality; and here, the audience is being given the illusion it can handle such dangerous spiritual weapons without getting hurt. Truth and freedom constitute "the one goal and the basic drive" behind Hegel's *The Phennomenology of Mind*—indeed behind his entire system[11]—so that Ibsen's choice of just these two terms is significant. The conclusion of *The Pillars of Society* is, I think, deliberately unconvincing, for its too facile cutting of the Gordian knot of ethical complications warns us that the real work hardly has begun. We should be aware, I think, of the way in which the closing *tableau* of Bernick and his family circle is resting on extremely thin ice; and this scene very clearly is designed to contrast with the later *tableau,* at the end of this group of plays, of the rebel Thomas Stockmann and his family.

From the public and civic realm of *The Pillars of Society* with its bustling crowds, groups, processions, and public speeches, we move into the deeper and quieter rhythms of the two central plays, *A Doll's House* and *Ghosts,* whose actions take place entirely within the realm of the Family. For Hegel, the life of the ethical society is divided between the realm of the state and the realm of the family, the family constituting its own distinct community within the larger community. Whereas the two "outer" plays, *The Pillars of Society* and *An Enemy of the People,* are distinctly communal and civic in theme and atmosphere and so are dominated by the masculine figures Karsten Bernick and Thomas Stockmann, the two "inner" plays, being familial and "domestic" in theme and scale, are dominated by the feminine characters Nora Helmer and Helene Alving. In Hegel's account of the ethical society the masculine spirit rules over the realm of the state, the feminine over the realm of the family. The feminine realm is the realm of the Erinyes (Furies) and the nether world, while that of the state belongs to Apollo and the sun. These two ethical realms, man and woman, family and state, ideally complement each other to make up the total life of the *polis,* but their respective rights and duties are forced into collision from which emerges the spirit of Tragedy. Tragedy is not possible in the realm of the "animal community," for tragedy is the privilege of the fully human, and so the tragic spirit is not born in the Cycle until Nora Helmer abandons her animal and doll role to take on the same human attributes as her tragic precursor, Antigone. Hegel's own text, like Ibsen's, as it analyses the conflicts of the ethical society, is haunted by the ghosts of Greek tragedy: of the *Antigone,* the *Oresteia, Oedipus Tyrannos,* and so on: an incorporation of a wide spectrum of cultural phenomena within the analysis of a particular world view that is typical of Hegel's procedure throughout the *Phenomenology.*

The spiritual world now under analysis, and which has advanced out of the animal community of the previous phase, is one in which we find a society whose members "are conscious not of individual rights but rather of individual duties, to be performed in accordance with determinate laws" as certain as the laws of the sensory world.[12] The newly rational consciousness, advancing beyond the anarchic hypocrisy of the preceding phase (*Pillars*), now becomes first a law giver,[13] then a critical subverter of these given laws.[14] Human law and divine law delineate the spheres and duties of, e.g., man and woman,[15] the living and the dead,[16] the individual and society,[17] and with this last, and its attendant conflict, there emerges the wholly new concept of ethical individualism (Hegel obviously has in mind the Socratic challenge to Athenian society) which pronounces the death of the old Objective, ethical society and so prepares the way for the profoundly new Subjective phase of consciousness which found its most thorough expression in the experience of Christianity.

From *A Doll's House* to *An Enemy of the People* life lived in Objective ethical terms is profoundly and brilliantly investigated through testing the substance of Ibsen's own contemporary world. We better will be able to understand the artistry of these plays if we realize that Ibsen has not, so late in life, suddenly become "didactic" but that the consciousness of duties, rights, and institutions has become the subject of his art. For the goal of the Cycle—complete spiritual emancipation— freedom within the Objective world of social laws and customs is no less important than truth and freedom in the more Subjective world of the second group.

The dialectical action of *A Doll's House* quite clearly depicts that collision between the law of man and the law of woman described by Hegel as the first inevitable and fundamental conflict of the ethical society. Torvald's masculine and socially conventional concepts of right and wrong clearly contradict and come into conflict with Nora's values of feminine, instinctual loyalties and the action that brings this conflict out into the open is an act which Nora committed from love and the desire to save her husband's life but which, as in the *Antigone*, the state brands as a crime.

With *A Doll's House* a profound transformation of the human spirit depicted in the Cycle *begins*. The resurrection of the animal community into the emerging *human* spirit, in the form of the awakening young Nora, is remarkably close to Rubek's description of *his* masterpiece, "Resurrection Day," in *When We Dead Awaken*, where a young woman (Nora?) is seen to emerge from "a segment of the curving, bursting earth. And up from the fissures of the soil there now swarm men and women with dimly suggested animal faces...." The point in *A Doll's House* where the human identity emerges from the animal is signaled when Nora, after dancing the tarantella, retires to take off her masquerade Neapolitan dress. The tarantella is traditionally the dance which the victim of the bite of the tarantula spider dances until he dies, or the dance by which he expels the poison of the bite from his system. *Both* situations fit Nora, for at this time of the death of the old year (Christmas) and the birth of the new and of the Christmas rebirth of the human spirit, Nora will die and be reborn, will die from her old identity and will desperately attempt to expel the poison of the terrible new knowledge Krogstad has injected into her.

The animal associations of the tarantella are further reinforced when Nora tells Christine she learned the dance on Capri. Ibsen makes of this a Joycean pun, for as Torvald and Nora descend from the costume party and are about to have their tragic confrontation, Torvald, intoxicated and amorous, calls Nora "my Capri girl, my capricious little Capri girl." "Capra" means goat and tragedy is held to have evolved from a "goat song" or goat dance or dance of goatskin-clad dancers: a derivation built into the word "tragedy" itself and the cause of much critical speculation since Aristotle. It is a derivation, also, that luckily matches Hegel's account of the tragic consciousness's emergence from the "animal community." Any reader familiar with A Doll's House hardly needs to be reminded that Ibsen supplies a strong "animal" identity to Nora: of lark and squirrel, delightedly munching her macaroons, behaving like a clever pet to Torvald. Her first shock out of this animal identity occurs in Act I. Nora is playing "hide and seek" (the play opens with the word "hide" and the theme of hiding and concealment is dominant) with her children, scampering about the room like an animal, finally hiding under the table like an animal in its lair. As she crawls out, on all fours, from this lair, Krogstad, who has entered unnoticed, catches her attention and Nora answers him, first scrambling to her knees, then assuming the fully human, erect posture. Nora's actions, therefore, recapture, by analogy, the whole course of human development: its biological development from animal to human and its historical/cultural development to the condition of Hellenic freedom where the tragic vision becomes possible. If we are responsive to Ibsen's verbal and visual imagery a great deal of his intention will excitingly be revealed even if the full comprehension of the play will require a number of viewings and readings.

The tragic consciousness arises out of the experiences inevitable to a genuinely ethical society, producing that clash of Good versus Good that is the essence of Greek tragedy. Torvald Helmer, for example, is no tyrant or hypocrite; he genuinely is walking by the best light he has, and believes in the society of which he is an honest pillar. But, as Hegel demonstrates, the admirable-looking absolutes of ethical life cannot survive the activity of critical reason. Such a command as "everyone ought to speak the truth" or "one should love one's neighbor"—sound maxims of healthy natural reason—break down from the sheer difficulty of knowing the truth or knowing how to love intelligently. For example, "active love . . . aims at removing evil from someone and bringing him good,"[18] but to do this we need to know "what the evil is, what is the

appropriate good to meet this evil, what in general his well-being consists in; i.e., we have to love him intelligently."[19] Unintelligent love may
do more harm than hatred and may encroach upon that area of the
individual that belongs to the state—an area of far greater importance
than that of individual love or friendship.[20] Against the grave and universal rhythm of the state, the particular feelings and actions of an individual are not only trivial and dependent upon chance, but, also, for all
their intentions, liable to turn to evil. Such an action is Nora's unwitting
forgery, a trivial act which nevertheless turns to evil because it refused
to take the universal ethical realm into consideration at all, and therefore brought harm where it intended good. However, a fully conscious
ethical opposition to the universal, the state, and its laws, in the name
of laws equally sacred, is another thing altogether and marks the
difference between the criminal and the rebel. This higher level of revolt
is that of Antigone and of the fully awakened Nora who walks out of
her home and its duties in the name of equally sacred duties to herself.

Following Hegel, Ibsen sees this ethical collision first exemplified in
the conflict inherent between the law of man and the law of woman:
between the rational, communal realm of masculine customary convention, and the presocial, instinctual feminine and familial realm. Ibsen's
note to *A Doll's House*—"there are two kinds of spiritual law, two kinds
of conscience, one in man and another, altogether different, in woman.
They do not understand each other; but in practical life the woman is
judged by man's law, as though she were not a woman but a man"—
paraphrases Hegel's argument *and* adds the observation that a woman
today is judged as if she were a man, suggesting a radical flaw in the
structure of contemporary reality; a power or force which is being denied
but which will assert its right, as a Nemesis, against the *hubris* of the
masculine realm.

Though Hegel sees the conflicts inherent in the ethical society most
perfectly exemplified in Greek tragedy and the life of the Greek *polis*,
and though he resurrects the plots of Greek tragedy for his analysis, we
nevertheless are dealing with the life of the present. Professor Loewenberg observes, of Hegel's preoccupation with the *Antigone*:

... he sees in the tragedy an authentic expression of a universal theme. To
his dramatic vision society appears as if continually shaped and transformed
by ever-recurring Antigones. Are not the Antigones of this world the impas-
sioned champions of ideals running afoul of the established order? Such
individuals are not rebels who take the law into their own hands. They are
the very models of loyalty. But their loyalty is either to traditions from which
the present rules have swerved or to values of the future which those in
power abhor. The ethical persuasions of the Antigones are as compelling as

those actuating the Creons, the defenders of the existing state of affairs who regard as subversive all opposition to things as they are.[21]

The idea of the structure of reality that emerges from *A Doll's House* not only is repressive, but, anticipating the dialectic of *Ghosts*, also lethal. Nora's "crime" against society actually cheated Death of her husband and, like Alcestis, Nora in her "doll" identity will die for her husband. The imagery of Acts II and III is that of Nora's death by drowning and death by the tarantella which she dances "as if her life depended on it." But Nora (again like Alcestis) is brought back from death, while an aspect of her life, Dr. Rank, actually dies "like a wounded animal." Rank's hereditary disease functions, like Nora's earlier doll-like irresponsibility, to show how the spontaneous, instinctual, carefree way of living (joy-of-life) which might be seen as *one* escape from the ethical world, is invalidated because of the appalling and unforeseen consequences that spontaneous and carefree actions unwittingly engender (the judgment seems close to Socrates' refutation of Hedonism in both the *Gorgias* and *The Republic*). Rank is the victim of his father's "gay army days"—that combination of militarism and eroticism that we discover to be a pagan emblem in the figure of Captain Alving in *Ghosts*—and the hereditary syphilis of Rank, like that of Osvald in *Ghosts*, forcefully demonstrates that cultural and historical processes (the life of Spirit) can threaten the very basis of life itself.[22]

The result of the dialectical development of *A Doll's House* is that the fundamental assumptions of communal life and its consciousness are tested and found to be inadequate. The play is a perfect example of Ibsen's dialectical method. The theme of the play is that of the human spirit, here exemplified in the figure of Nora Helmer, being forced into an awareness of the unreality of its world and of its own identity taken from that world, and the painful but liberating movement of spirit towards a more adequate reality and more adequate identity. Nora, from the moment the play begins, gradually is moving towards an identity that is waiting for her at the end of the play: a greater but also potentially more tragic identity. This spiritual transformation is visualized onstage by the two changes of dress that Nora undergoes. It is important to understand this need for spiritual growth if we are to understand, also, the strange *hardness* of Nora's character at the end of the play when she walks out on, not a tyrant nor even a tiresome moralist but, finally, on a devastated human being looking for help as the world collapses about him. This strange hardness, which makes Nora "unsympathetic" and uncomfortable is due to the fact that underneath the doll identity there had been a repressed Greek or Saga heroine which now is beginning to emerge. We thus see that Ibsen's dialectical action is at the same time an action of archetypal recollection; the pressure exerted upon the structure of the present, uncovering its contradictions and conflicts, at the same time uncovers the fatefully shaping presence of the Past.[23] In the next play of this group, *Ghosts*, as its very title indicates, the shaping presence of the Past almost overwhelms the dialectical action of the Present.

The movement, in Hegel's text which now draws more fully upon the dialectical arguments of a number of Greek tragedies, is towards a more universal action and, by the same token, towards a more essential conflict where the individual, as enlightened self-consciousness acting consciously from universal principles, is brought to confront universal laws he has violated but whose validity he tragically comes to recognize. Nora, the belatedly awakened heroine of *A Doll's House*, her name a diminutive of Eleonora—a form of Helen—becomes the "Helene" of *Ghosts*, the discarding of the diminutive perhaps signaling the full maturing of the Hellenic tragic spirit. "After Nora Helene Alving had to follow," Ibsen commented and this necessity can be seen as the inevitable dialectical development out of the situation of *A Doll's House*—remembering, of course, that Ibsen's dialectic is a matter of flesh and blood, never merely abstract.[24]

In the dialectical opposition of the law of man versus the law of woman Hegel saw the classic collision between the state and the family. But the deepest level of this dialectical opposition, one which profoundly shakes the whole substance of the ethical society, is the dialectic which, for Hegel, emerges from the man-woman, state-individual opposition: the conflict between the law of the living versus the law of the dead. Just as, in a note to *A Doll's House*, Ibsen practically paraphrased Hegel's account of the dialectic between man and woman so, in this next play, a note paraphrases the next stage of Hegel's dialectic—that of the living versus the dead:

> Among us, monuments are erected to the *dead*, since we have a duty towards them; we allow lepers to marry; but their offspring—? The unborn—?

As we offer a lengthy analysis of *Ghosts* in the second part of this book we will, just now, touch on only a few aspects of the play as they continue the dialectical action of the first group as a whole. The carefully structured contrast between the "arguments" of *A Doll's House* and *Ghosts* seems clear. In the former play, an objective (masculine) social order was seen to have violated the very instinctual depths of the feminine consciousness as Creon's state edict violated Antigone's instinctual loyalties, and the play presented the rebellion of the feminine principle against the masculine, striking at the male roles of husband and master. In *Ghosts*, on the other hand, it is an alien moral order (allied with the feminine consciousness) that has violated the spontaneous, life-affirming instinctual life of the masculine consciousness, and the play demonstrates the terrible revenge of this violated masculine principle in the form of a struggle between the living and the dead where the offended masculine sexuality destroys the woman's role of mother. At least one implication of the play is that Mrs. Alving's very obvious inadequate sexuality is an offense against the very principle of life which, as mother, she should express.[25] While, in *A Doll's House*, it is an objective order of laws and duties that was revealed to have betrayed a primary duty-to-self, in *Ghosts* it is Mrs. Alving's willed choices of action that have betrayed essential objective duties and ethical principles (associated with joy-of-life), and which destroy her effort to remake the world in her own image. The *hubris* of daring to recreate the world from such a one-sided view of life (a *hubris* to which the Christian tradition particularly is prone) must be punished by the terrible manifestation of the excluded powers. This re-creation is an aberration, and therefore we move, in *Ghosts*, through a world of conventional communal pieties (marriage, the memorialized dead, the family), all of which represent gross distortions of the human and universal realities they are meant to express, until we come to the shattering emergence of the repressed forces of Alving's Dionysiac *livsglede*. Helene Alving, like Agave of *The Bacchae*, had offended Dionysos and this Dionysiac power turns against her and her son in the superbly appropriate symbol of poisoned sexuality. But, from the collapse of the false Alving household, with its grim memorial, chapel, and schoolhouse, the true Alving values of joy have been both exonerated and recovered in that image of the rising sun; an irresistible creativity within the cosmos itself, powerful enough to survive the degradation of this creativity in the world of the present. The dialectic which sees this creative eros or joy within human sexuality, but also throughout the whole structure of human and cosmic reality, is itself a powerfully Hellenic concept familiar to readers of Plato's *Symposium*.

It is something of this lost joy-of-life or *livsglede*, therefore, that we find in the last hero of this Hellenic group of plays, Thomas Stockmann, whose boyish and enthusiastic rebelliousness is turned upon the society that has wronged Nora and destroyed Alving. Ibsen ends this Greek tetralogy on an Aristophanic note of belligerent gaiety: a joyfully energetic note that will not return to the Cycle until another pagan, Hilde Wangel, knocks on the door of master builder Solness.

In the corresponding section in Hegel, after the exploration of the ethical world through the dialectic of the living versus the dead and the demolition of the ethical consciousness when it is forced to recognize as valid the law which it has violated, the ethical society now proceeds to open division and conflict, this division symbolized for Hegel by the conflict of two brothers, members of the family, who contest the control of the community. This development, where Hegel obviously is drawing upon the conflict between Eteocles and Polyneices, may strike the reader as somewhat arbitrary and fanciful, but it at least now draws together into a single conflict the two realms of the ethical community, the family and the society. And Ibsen quite obviously draws upon Hegel's emblem of this division, for the conflict of *An Enemy of the People* is one in which two brothers, Peter and Thomas Stockmann, fight for the ethical control of the community. This open division within the very structure of the objective society, in which the individual no longer can trust to customary conventions (these now being in open conflict) must lead to the emergence of an ethical individualism where the individual finds his absolute values within himself rather than outside in the community. Hegel, here, clearly is thinking of Socrates and his inner voice or *daimon*. This also is the phase of Aristophanic political comedy which depicts onstage the factions of the divisive ethical community.

An Enemy of the People, too, clearly depicts the inevitable dissolution of the ethical community and the emergence of a Socratic condition of ethical individualism where "the strongest man in the world is he who stands most alone." Quite apart from this Socratic discovery, Ibsen would seem to have given to Thomas Stockmann, in suitably reductive modern and Norwegian terms, many Socratic traits, for that original enemy of the people and Stockmann share the same wit and exuberance, the love of life and feasting, the famous abstraction of mind (as when Thomas repeatedly cannot remember the name of his own housemaid); and Stockmann's refusal to go into exile but, instead, to stay behind and attempt to transform his community, recollects the heroic Socratic action. Completely in the Socratic manner, too, is Stockmann's discovering in the most down-to-earth examples (the polluted pipelines feeding the baths) the most wide-ranging ethical and political implications. *An Enemy of the People*, the only straightforward political comedy in the Cycle, resurrects, also, the spirit of Aristophanes—appropriately for this conclusion to the Hellenic phase of consciousness. The public themes of the play, the crowd scenes and noisy debates erupting into physical violence, the collection of political schemers, demagogues, and even (at the great meeting) one Dionysiac drunkard who alone votes for Stockmann, conjure up much of the subject matter, artistry, and indignant zest of Aristophanic comedy. And there seems to be one conjunction of Socrates and Aristophanes at the end of the play in which the crowd has attacked Stockmann's house just as the crowd attacks Socrates' house at the end of *The Clouds.*

The symmetry of this group of four plays partly is indicated by the titles of the two outer plays: *The Pillars of Society—An Enemy of the People*, just as these two plays are very similar in atmosphere and details. The group had opened with a portrait of a whole society built upon lies, hypocrisy, selfish and sub-ethical individualism, and the first play ended with the resolution of its principal character, Bernick, genuinely to serve his community. The group closes, however, with the portrait of an ethical community organized into mutually exclusive and conflicting collectives (the ratepayers' association, and so on) afraid of a genuine ethical individualism, and with the emergence of a hero, a doctor whose vocation is ministering to his community, openly and honorably defying it. Thus the individualism with which the group closes is "higher" than the individualism-disguised-as-public-service with which it opened. The human spirit has tested itself against the objective world and has discovered that its essential truth is not adequately found within this world, and has now begun educating itself, and others, into searching for a more adequate truth and freedom.

A major metaphor of this Hellenic group of plays is the very Greek metaphor of *pollution*. It is a peripheral, background presence in *A Doll's House*, as Rank's hereditary disease (a dark subplot to Nora's agon), but moves into the foreground of *Ghosts* as Osvald's inherited syphilis, destroying the line of Alving, and in *An Enemy of the People* the pollution spreads through the whole community by means of the supposedly health-giving, but infected, streams feeding into the baths. In all cases, the pollution is associated with a source and is, I believe, Ibsen's image of the polluted past feeding into the present. There is nothing in this metaphor that is implausible in a scientific and positivistic age, but it is a metaphor, nevertheless, as much as the curse upon the house of Atreus or of Labdacus. In these three plays, that which should be life-giving destroys first the *body* of Rank, then the *brain* of Osvald, and, finally, the *ethical life* of a whole community and if we see these first four plays as given over to the recovery of the Hellenic, "emperor" and pagan values of Ibsen's third empire, then the implication of this pollution is that these Hellenic forces have become distorted and destructive and need to be restored to their old value: a restoration partially effected, perhaps, by the Hellenic artistry and courage of these plays. Thus the recollection of the Hellenic spirit in these plays (in terms of both form and content) identifies the spiritual and historical forces that have gone into shaping the ethical life of the present and at the same time serves to reproach the present for the way in which these elements of our inheritance have been debased: an intention we would expect of the author of *Brand, Peer Gynt* and *Emperor and Galilean.*

As the last play of the first group, *An Enemy of the People* prepares the dialectic for the first play of the second group in which the individual consciousness, severed from the sustaining ethical community, enters into the phase of subjective life, the phase, for Hegel, of the Christian spirit. *An Enemy of the People* seems to indicate this coming transition in a light way, for the Socratic Stockmann, exiled from his community, begins to assume a messianic role. In Act IV he declares, "I am not as sweet-tempered as a certain person I could mention. I'm not saying, 'I forgive you for you know not what you do'" (a phrase that Socrates himself, in fact, anticipates, insisting his foes are ignorant rather than evil), but, in spite of this refusal of the messianic identity he does resolve to gather about him "at least a dozen" boys as his students—again a nice combination of the Socratic and the messianic; and in the opening of Act V we find him resolving to save the stones thrown at him as "holy relics" (*helligdom*)—almost as if the veneration of martyrs was about to begin! These lightly stated themes will be taken up sombrely in *The Wild Duck* where Gregers Werle will humorlessly assume the messianic mantle and where the human spirit will begin its long and desolate trek through the phases of self-estrangement (alienation).

The transition from Aristophanic comedy to Christianity might seem a bizarre decision for the World Spirit to make but it is a decision we encounter both in the *Phenomenology* and in the *Philosophy of Fine Art* for, to Hegel, Aristophanic comedy was an expression of a new irreverent spirit that demolished (demythologized) the old Hellenic pantheon at the same time as the Socratic critical spirit destroyed the basis of the Objective spiritual life of the *polis*, thus preparing the way for the spiritual crisis which it was the mission of Christianity to overcome.

Let us recapitulate the dialectical development of the first four plays in terms which, while they are based on the Hegelian account of the dialectic of the Objective consciousness, do not, I believe, contradict our experience of the plays. The moral universe of *The Pillars of Society* is one in which the realm of individual action and motive is separated from a vitally active realm of universal ethical values so that this universal realm in no way effectively penetrates the world of individual, particular activities. Thus separated, genuine individuality, which, for Hegel, is the interpenetration of particular with universal, essence with appearance, cannot emerge and so this is a society of animals. The realm of universals is represented onstage by "Pastor" Rørlund, and, as Hegel

demonstrates, such an inactive consciousness of the universal, which refuses to commit itself to the particular actions out of which true universals will emerge, is helplessly forced to see universal providence in
actions mutually contradictory.[26] In such a world, the only means by
which the universal will appear is through the individual of superior
talent (Bernick) whose actions, however, must create a situation of
crisis the solution of which lies outside the realm of individual talent
and requires the genuine and active participation of universal ethical
principles.

It is from this crisis that the ethical world of A Doll's House is created.
Here, especially in the figure of Torvald Helmer, ethical principles are
genuine rules of conduct, honestly lived up to even though their implications and inherent contradictions are not comprehended. Torvald
Helmer is not a Bernick, both consciously and unconsciously masking
self-interest as ethical intention: on the contrary, his ethical principles
(e.g., not to borrow money) actually endangered his life which was
saved by Nora's instinctual criminal action which unwittingly violates
the ethical structure and will call it into question. Thus the dialectical
action of A Doll's House is "higher" than that of The Pillars of Society;
what is judged as spiritually/intellectually inadequate is not a mode of
life not guided by ethical principles but, instead, a mode of life whose
ethical principles reveal inherent contradictions. The play, therefore,
ends with an examination and questioning of these principles and with
an act of conscious rebellion.

Ghosts is one long examination and questioning of ethical principles
and one long, gradual rebellion. In this play we face the results of ethical
principles honorably pursued and firmly maintained, but, from the opening of the play, this entire ethical structure is undermined by the reality
that it has offended. Helene Alving and Pastor Manders have lived by
the principle of Duty at the cost of individual happiness and in so doing
have been forced heroically but perversely to engage against the opposing life values. The resulting tragedy reveals the structure of the ethical
consciousness to be helplessly inadequate to the reality revealed so that
by this action the limits of the ethical consciousness are reached and
consciousness is forced to advance beyond them.

From the failure of the ethical consciousness to be an *adequately*
rational and human consciousness emerges the individualism of *An
Enemy of the People*, in which the Objective ethical structure begins
to dissolve and the stage is set for the emergence of Subjectivity where
consciousness locates its values *not* within an Objective order (from
which it is banished) but within an inward order of reality or in a
"beyond" which compensates for loss of power and freedom within the

Objective world (*The Wild Duck*). In the figures both of Socrates and Christ history presents us with the human consciousness advancing beyond the Objective world and claiming to establish its values "within." This is a development within the history of the European consciousness and, for Hegel, logically inevitable and thus still to be undergone in the present.

Though the themes and archetypal actions of the Ethical Society were taken from the history of the Greek *polis* and especially from the theater and life of Athens, the subject matter, in Ibsen as in Hegel, is modern. In the *polis* the life of man as a political animal created and defined itself with classic clarity and so laid the foundation for the entire subsequent development of the Objective Spirit, but this spirit belongs just as vitally to the present (as the very word "democracy" attests). For example, the drama of Antigone is reenacted every time an individual, holding fast to laws violated by the state, is forced in turn to defy the state (as, for instance, if the state, by an unjust war, is guilty of crimes against humanity). The tragic pattern of the *Oresteia*, the Oedipal story, or of *The Bacchae* is repeated in the dialectical life of every modern family just as Freud discovered that the dark horrors of the Oedipal story are the inheritance of every modern man and woman. And the Socratic challenge to the whole universal realm of the state in terms of a hard-earned ethical individualism is still an altitude of spiritual courage attainable by a few.

In this first group the human world presented to us is one of humanity agitated by ethical conflict and therefore given to a decidedly "polemical" mode of action and speech. It was *this* phase of the Cycle that was to have such influence on the moralistic nineteenth century and which was to give rise to a very narrow idea of Ibsen as a dramatist of "thesis-plays." Matters are not much mended by Ibsen's later admirers who plead that he soon got over this phase and, with *The Wild Duck*, began to have second thoughts. Both accounts miss the very great artistry and the subtlety and complexity of these four plays which, for all their objective quality, are as fine as anything Ibsen has written. Today the so-called "psychological" plays of the second group hold the greater interest (though there are signs that the third "symbolical" group is beginning to find favor just as Shakespeare's last plays are now coming into their own) but this is based on an equally narrow idea of *their* content. The strong ethical shaping and "pointing," and the somewhat obtrusive ethical symbolism of the first group (a symbolism which is *theatrically* subtler and more effective than a mere *reading* of the plays would suggest) is a conscious part of Ibsen's intention to dramatize a world in which the ethical consciousness shapes the cosmos, and the final inadequacy of this compelling world view is acknowledged by Ibsen.

In this first group Ibsen has analyzed in depth the interaction of the individual with the Objective world of customs and institutions which man gradually has created from his own consciousness and which creates human consciousness in turn. If truth and freedom are to prevail, they must at some time come into conflict with the objective world, as much honorable modern rebellion and conflict reveal. Both Hegel and Ibsen are aware that there is more to the Hellenic spirit than this ethical (*sittliche*) world, and these other (higher) dimensions of the Hellenic spirit will be recovered in the last sections of the *Phenomenology* and of the Cycle; but it was the life of the *polis* that laid the foundation for our own ethical life and so it is in the archetypal conflicts of the *polis*, as expressed in dramatic art above all, that the *essential* structure and dialectic of the ethical world is best revealed. This recollection of the Hellenic world in terms of its dialectical creation and subversion of the world of customary convention is something far more serious than the nostalgic neoclassicism of Ibsen's age while at the same time it is truer than neoclassicism to the essential nature of the Greek world. Ibsen *did* make the Greek spirit live again (hence succeeding where his hero Julian had failed) as the outraged reaction to the plays (especially to the most Hellenic of the group, *Ghosts*) demonstrated. This Hellenism was not revived as an escapist fantasy of Greek columns, philosophic sages, and attractive students (as in the "School of Athens" scene in Act II of *Emperor and Galilean*) but as a resurgent, dynamic renascence coming into open attack upon the condition of unfreedom in the modern world. It is therefore most appropriate and most moving that, at a time when Ibsen was almost universally assailed for writing *Ghosts* it was a professor of Greek, P. O. Schjøtt, of Oslo (then Christiania) University, who stood in defense of the play, comparing it to Greek drama:

When the greatest tragic and comic poets of Athens presented the political, ethical and religious ideas of their age, and even their champions, on the stage, someone, no doubt denounced them and called their work tendentious. But posterity saw this as quite normal practice. When the art of dramatic writing stood at its zenith, in that golden age, it was this realism or, if you will, this tendentiousness, which gave it its vitality of characer. . . . We generalize thus with particular reference to Ibsen's play. . . . For of all the modern dramas we have read, *Ghosts* comes closest to classical tragedy. . . . When the dust of ignorant criticism has subsided, which we trust will happen soon, this play of Ibsen's with its pure bold contours, will stand not only as his noblest deed but as the greatest work of art which he, or indeed our whole dramatic literature has produced.[27]

THE SECOND GROUP

There is a very perceptible change in subject matter and method between the plays of the first group and those of the second: a change Ibsen himself pointed out to his publisher when describing the first play of this second group, *The Wild Duck*. The actions and the atmosphere of the first group are rendered with a forthrightness, clarity, and simplicity suitable to the Hellenic themes, the world of these plays being one of firmly distinguished ethical forces ranged in clear opposition one against the other. The translator of the Oxford edition of Ibsen notes that whereas in *An Enemy of the People* "truth is provable and demonstrable," in *Rosmersholm* "truth is an equivocal thing."[28] Not only truth but reality itself is equivocal, ambiguous in the second group as a whole, and this distinction is a useful starting point from which to understand the difference between the two groups. Much earlier criticism of Ibsen has had to postulate a radical internal change within Ibsen himself, impelling him to renounce the idealistic demands he so forcefully made upon life just two years prior to the completion of *The Wild Duck*; but a more interesting and a more admirable idea of the artist is that his art now is expressing a different form of consciousness, one which inevitably develops from the earlier form, and that the change of method is Ibsen's perfectly controlled response to a change in his subject matter. This is a less "romantic" idea of the artist, to be sure, but it at least places Ibsen among the "classic" tradition of writers in full control of their art, *and*, better still, it focuses our attention upon the art work itself and not upon the finally unknowable inner life of the artist.

If, as I hope to show, the second group is dramatizing the Christian consciousness or way of viewing the world, then we may gain some idea of the difference of method between the first and second groups if we consider the differences between Hellenic and Christian cultures. In a note to *The Wild Duck* Ibsen makes the observation that the advance of civilization is comparable to a child's growing up "whereby instinct is weakened, the power of logical thought is developed and the ability to play with dolls is lost."[29] Another note goes, "All existing things, art, poetry, etc., break down into new categories as does the mind of the child in the spirit of the adult." These notes imply that Ibsen was acutely conscious of the process of *transition* as he began work on this first play of the second group, and that this new group will mark a maturing and developing of spirit just as, for Hegel, the arrival of the Christian consciousness in the world is a tragic necessity similar to the loss of youth in the adult.

If we see the Cycle as retracing, in modern terms, the evolution of human consciousness ("the evolutionary process of the race"), then Ibsen's observation on the evolution of new categories of art, poetry, etc., *should* prepare us to see a marked change in dramatic method at this point in the Cycle. The change of method that is most marked is first and foremost from an "objective" to a "subjective" art; from a drama of clear ethical division to a more ambiguous drama of psychological self-division, from external to internal conflict. This is not to say, however, that Ibsen himself has become a subjective artist (which, as Nietzsche remarks in *The Birth of Tragedy*, is no artist at all) but that his art is taking for its subject matter the subjective phase of consciousness. This, in the *Phenomenology* and in the *Philosophy of Fine Art*, is a momentous change undergone by consciousness in the history of Europe, altering the very artistic expression of the race. *The Wild Duck*, I believe, is notably rich in both visual and verbal "quotations" or recollections from the art and literature of Christian Europe.

The Christian and post-Christian phase of spirit in this section of the *Phenomenology* is given the designation "Spirit in Self-estrangement" and describes human consciousness in profound and painful alienation from the world (Nature), society, and God—which, for Hegel, means an acute alienation from human consciousness itself. Man, tragically self-divided, inhabits a world itself divided between a foreground, fallen reality of prosaic work and a compensatory background or beyond (*jenseits*) of fantasy. The historical realities that Hegel draws upon to depict the full complex nature of this phase is the longest, most varied, and perhaps most difficult in the whole of the *Phenomenology*. The historical period covered (which Ibsen incorporates into this second group of plays) is no less than that between the Rome of the Antonines and the post-revolutionary Europe of Hegel's own day. Hegel's curious procedure of drawing upon historical archetypes to illustrate the spiritual evolution that he sees as a wholly *logical* development nowhere is more prominent than here where the densely packed pages continually are referring to unnamed historical and cultural characters and events, from the myth of the Fall at the beginning of this phase, to the various attitudes of the Romantic spirit of Hegel's contemporaries, at the end. The immense accumulation of detail and the richness and subtlety of Hegel's analysis of this phase of spirit make it far more difficult to summarize than that of the phase on which the first group is structured. And this richness finds a corresponding richness in the texture of the art of the second group, especially of the play based upon the richest of Hegel's dialectical sequences: *The Wild Duck*.

In the earlier phase, consciousness, expressing itself through ethical conflict in the Objective world, was less repressed, freer, more single-natured than in this later phase. At the same time it was more ignorant of its complete identity which its merely objective activity had failed to discover. In order to know this total identity, *implicit* only, in the ethical society, consciousness must undergo the most painful subjective experience—Alienation (*Entfremdung*) from the community, from Nature, from God, and from the self. For Hegel this self-estrangement or alienation, whose myth is the Fall, is the necessary condition for a true spiritual reintegration represented by the Christian myth of salvation.

Hegel's term for this phase, Spirit in self-estrangement, perfectly expresses the spiritual world of the second group. This self-estrangement is not a mere historical curiosity but, like every phase of consciousness in the *Phenomenology*, a condition that can be discovered within the mind of anyone who submits himself to philosophical self-analysis, just as the condition of consciousness of the ethical world can be discovered by anyone submitting his society and its assumptions to philosophical analysis; it is because Ibsen himself is conducting such a self-analyis, *living through* the phases he is dramatizing, that he is so intensely engaged in his art, so removed from that abstract Olympian detachment that might have been the danger of his whole procedure in the Cycle.

Self-estrangement originated in the discovery of the inadequacy of mere objective consciousness, a discovery signaled by the emergence of ethical individualism and the discrediting of the community as an absolute ethical value. In one of the most brilliant and profound analyses in the *Phenomenology* Hegel shows how consciousness, now denied the sensuous, esthetic, ethical freedom of the Greek *polis*, becomes *dualistic* in every aspect of its life. In compensation for this loss of objective freedom, consciousness, inhabiting a fallen world, now constructs an elaborate "other" world in the beyond (Augustine's duality of earthly city and city of God is a classic statement)—a realm of fantasy and spiritual consolation—and shuttles uneasily between this realm and the world of prosaic and repressive reality.[30] Hence the extraordinarily imaginative richness of this phase of consciousness with its quality of superstitions, miracles, dark folk tales and a whole fantastic subjectivity with, at the same time, an extreme ethical and political timidity compared with the Hellenic culture.[31] Hellenic culture, at its highest, had been integrated directly into, and was honestly reflective of, the ethical structure of the city state, to such a degree that, to adapt Shelley's phrase, the poets were the acknowledged legislators of their nation's spiritual life. It was a phase of consciousness in which the eccentric dualism of Don Quixote, the brooding subjectivity of Hamlet, the visionary rejection of the world of Dante, or the later histrionics of Romanticism would have appeared inexplicably aberrant. The division of the universe and of the human soul into higher and lower, good and evil, God and Devil, inward and outward realms of spiritual life, hero and villain, etc., all illustrate the fundamental dualism Hegel sees as characteristic of the Christian consciousness, and we will see that it is just this dualism that is profoundly characteristic of the second group.[32] The philosophic expression of this dualism is Cartesian philosophy with its tragicomic separation of mind and body, flesh and spirit, thinking individual and controlling God.

The dualism which shapes the world of Ibsen's second group of plays is *visually* apparent the moment the curtain goes up on the first play of this group, *The Wild Duck*, for we see the stage itself divided into two areas: a foreground room of dimmed lights and a background room, brilliantly lit, with a feast taking place. This division, in Werle's household, between foreground work and a background or "beyond" of pleasure, is repeated in transformed terms in the humble Ekdal home with *its* stage division of foreground photography studio and background fantasy loft. This should alert us to a dualism within the structure and very texture of the play. The world of *The Wild Duck* is one drastically split in two between the realm of the "ruler," Werle, and that of the "insulted and injured" Ekdals; between a realm of reluctant servitude and a realm of escapist fantasy; between a lost natural freedom (the forests and lakes of old Ekdal's imagination and of Werle's destructive hunting) and the compensating "heaven" (the loft) that is a non-subversive refuge from reality. Consciousness, then, has divided itself between a given repressive structure of everyday fact and a *jenseits* or "other" world which allows consciousness to accept repression by giving it the illusion of recovering its lost freedom. Within this static, dualistic scene by means of which Ibsen brilliantly recaptures the condition of the fallen consciousness, Gregers Werle erupts to "awaken" the potentially subversive, potentially critical nature of the "other" world, and, in Hedvig, who is in a tremulous phase of transition from childhood to adulthood, the dormant energies of the other world explode into disastrous but, I think, challenging reality, giving us our first intimation of the power latent in the "other" world.[33]

In *Rosmersholm* there is a distinct progression of the dualistic consciousness. The "other" world now has become openly critical and subversive, its enlightened and idealistic nature taking up arms against what it conceives to be repressive reality—the traditional order of established injustice and error in the actual world. The "other" world now actually seeks to transform the actual world, to remake it in terms of the enlightened consciousness, as in Rosmer's and Rebekka's campaign to "ennoble" humanity. The fact that the enlightened spirit is not as enlightened as it appears is the main point of Hegel's analysis of this next stage of the self-estranged consciousness.

The Lady from the Sea brings out most fully the development of this dualism into a hostile gulf between the "other" and the actual worlds and of the contradictory realities they represent. The "other" world now has developed into a destructive but also a challenging "absolute freedom" which refuses any compromise with the actual world, demanding, instead, that the actual world surrender itself entirely to the claim of the "other." So openly extreme has the conflict now become—represented by the extremes of the anarchic world of the Stranger and the ordered, decorous world of Dr. Wangel—that consciousness undergoes a drastic fission and the everyday world decisively renounces the claims of the "other" world. (Ellida renounces her anarchic lover and takes up the responsibilities and duties of the Wangel household.)

This, however, only can be a disastrous decision for consciousness to make (as Hegel demonstrates)[34] and, in the next play, *Hedda Gabler*, we find consciousness inhabiting a world view in which the subversive, alien and transcendent has been renounced and in which consciousness is stifling in its own staleness and boredom. Maurice Valency has pointed out the similarity between Hedda and Ellida, each banally married to a staid husband, each with the memory of a renounced "wild" lover in the background. In *Hedda Gabler* we live with the unlovely consequences of consciousness so drastically having separated itself from the "other" world. The given, actual, everyday world is stale, academic, respectable, and timid; the "other" world has become "bohemian," irresponsible, ineffective, and even squalid. Of all of Ibsen's plays, *Hedda Gabler*, for all its wit and sophistication, most creates the condition of Hell: of the human spirit denied the sight of the divine, that is, of the human consciousness severed from its own transcendent possibilities.

This is a condition of mind that can be rescued and uplifted only by some force entering from outside its present terms of existence, a force from consciousness's forgotten past, rousing it to a memory of greater possibilities. This help is absent from *Hedda Gabler* but it arrives buoyantly, mysteriously, and fatefully in *The Master Builder* when Hilde Wangel returns from the renounced "other" realm of *The Lady from the Sea* and enters the hell of the Solness household, claiming payment on a promise made far back in a fabulous past.

The artistic and thematic unity of the second group, forming a symmetrical design, resembles that of the first four plays, containing two outer and two inner plays and a developing dialectic. If we can avoid seeing this unity as merely mechanical and formal, recognizing that the

actual *life* of the plays escapes such convenient structuring, it nevertheless may help us to look for a moment at the design of the second group:

A	B	B	A
The Wild Duck	*Rosmersholm*	*The Lady from the Sea*	*Hedda Gabler*

I	II	III
(Idealism aroused to renounce given [fallen] actuality)	(Idealism openly challenges and engages with given reality)	(Idealism renounced: consciousness returns to given world of repressive actuality)

This, admittedly, very inadequately indicates the complex and rich
life of these four plays; we are not reducing the plays to the above
formula, merely indicating the presence of such structuring *within* the
rich artistry, making it even richer by adding the intellectual and philosophical intention to the human and esthetic intention. Ibsen's drafts and
preliminary sketches almost always indicate how he starts from a more
abstract dialectic, rather than from a sense of "character," and how the
"more delicate elaboration, the more energetic individualization of the
characters and their methods of expression" (as Ibsen explained this
later stage of his composition to Brandes) begin only after the plot of the
play has been created. Like all major dramatists, Ibsen's primary dramatic emphasis is, as Aristotle commended, plot, not character: a major
dialectical action for which the appropriate characters are conceived.

In the "outer" plays, *The Wild Duck* and *Hedda Gabler*, we find the
stage divided between a foreground room associated with everyday
and prosaic reality and, in the background, an inner room, more escapist
and secretive, suggestive of the inner recesses of the consciousness, a
visual dualism which, supplemented as it is by an omnipresent social,
political, and spiritual dualism, helps to establish a world reflecting the
condition of consciousness of Christian Europe. There are a number of
curious little minor parallels between the two outer plays: both are
punctuated by pistol shots and in both, the heroines (somewhat similarly
named) Hedvig-Hedda retreat to the inner room to die by shooting
themselves. Lieutenant Ekdal dons full-dress uniform for the catastrophe
of *The Wild Duck* and Hedda is found stretched out on the sofa beneath
the portrait of her uniformed father like a sacrifice upon an altar. In
both plays the somewhat similar Hjalmar Ekdal and Jørgen Tesman
have been brought up by two maiden aunts, in both households there is
a somewhat similar controlling and cynical "friend of the family" (Rell-

ing and Judge Brack) and there are many other similarly curious parallels between the two plays. Just what these parallels imply I will leave to the individual reader, but they are so obviously a part of Ibsen's total intention that any adequate account of that intention must at least take account of them and not proceed serenely as if they did not exist, or as if all this artistry were merely a "front" disguising a much more modest psychological strategy. Nor are these parallels mechanical, for the seeds sown in one play blossom into major themes in a later one, so that we even find character sketches in the first drafts of a play which are abandoned, the characters then turning up in the immediately succeeding play, another indication that the Cycle is a continuous evolving structure.

While the two "outer" plays are spatially constricted and divided, the two inner plays are freer. The room in which most of the action of *Rosmersholm* takes place is spacious and elegant, its doors and windows opening out onto an estate with "its avenues of ancient trees." Most of the action of *The Lady from the Sea* takes place in the open air. In *Rosmersholm* the vistas are of the past; in *The Lady from the Sea* the Prospect (Utsikten) scene suggests an as yet uncharted future and looks forward towards the spatial extensions of the last four plays. These two inner plays also are connected in theme and character. In an early draft of the play Rosmer was given the two daughters now transferred to Wangel; both characters have a dead wife in the background and a wayward and somewhat mysterious partner in the present. Rebekka West, from northern Finnmark (which, as Weigand notes, was long a surviving outpost of paganism), is termed a "mermaid," "sea-troll," and "witch" while the mermaid-like Ellida, that strange outcast in Wangel's bourgeois world, was called "the pagan" by "an old priest" at Skioldviken.

In the second group the Past functions in a wholly different way than in the first group; in the latter group the Past was directly and openly subversive of the Present, its disclosed error or injustice serving to break up the repressive Present. In the second group, however, the Past represents not so much a violated ethical principle as a lost spiritual value for which the Present mourns. The fantasy attic of the Ekdals attempts to recapture in imagination a whole lost world of pre-lapsarian natural man as the inhabitant and the fellow of forests, lake, sky, mountain, sea, and animal life, and this fantasy attic with its "depths of the sea" where "time has stood still" has shapes and shadows, echoes and intimations unlike anything in the first group. In *Rosmersholm* the past comes to dominate the brooding consciousness of Rosmer and Rebekka and the ghost of Beate, "greatly missed and greatly mourned," haunts the play in a manner wholly different from that of the ghost of the equally wronged

Alving in *Ghosts*. In *The Lady from the Sea* Ellida's allegiance to a romantic and mysterious sea-stranger who represents an "absolute freedom" from the conditions of the given world is a lure and a demand upon her consciousness, like the ebb and flow of the sea, a freedom that is as destructive as death itself. Even in *Hedda Gabler*, the most "prosaic" of this second group, Hedda romantically invokes, against the stifling bourgeois reality of the modern world, phrases and values from a dream of Hellenism which, in its poignant ineffectuality, is totally unlike the subversive Hellenism of the first group.

The world of the second group is divided drastically between inner and outer, higher and lower, and the predominantly "civic" world of the first group now gives way to an emphatically vertical landscape that gradually infiltrates the little stage. In *The Wild Duck* an immense world of Nature gradually invades the domestic scene through a commonplace language of factual description; it is an astonishing achievement of creating an ambitious imagery out of the very language that would deny the possibility of imagery: a dualism within the language where the language of parable, fantasy, allegory, and symbol struggles to emerge through a dialogue of seemingly pure factual description.

The psychological dualism of this group is equally drastic; it is a dualism unknown to the first group of plays. One only has to compare two somewhat similar plays, *Ghosts* and *Rosmersholm*, to see the great difference in dramatic psychology. In *Ghosts* Mrs. Alving gradually is brought to face the fact that a life honorably given over to one idea of life (Duty) entirely has betrayed an equally sacred idea of life. If Helene Alving finally stands self-condemned, this "self" is associated completely with the ethical value she represented and we are impelled to look beyond the tragedy to an objective awareness of the nature of that reality which the human spirit, with such *hubris,* presumed to re-create. In *Rosmersholm*, on the other hand, what stands self-condemned in the great judgment day of the last act is not an ethical power (enlightenment) but, instead, a complex of motives, intentions, responsibilities, and inadequacies which perplex and paralyze the protagonists. This is not to say that *Rosmersholm* is that very defective form, a mere study of particular psychological situations; the "psyche" analyzed by Ibsen is a generic one, something in which we all have a vital share. But the spiritual condition of the play refuses to shape itself into the clear, bold, pure contours of a Hellenic conflict. The positive ending of *Ghosts* was the exoneration of Alving and the life principle he stood for, signaled by the rising of the sun, that universal, life-renewing power that cannot be refuted by any human attitude. The positive ending of *Rosmersholm* is not such an objective force coming into its own but, more inwardly, a hard-won attitude of mind: the lofty aristocracy of spirit that, in the high Roman fashion, passes judgment upon itself and executes the sentence. Totally missing from the second group are such positive chords as Lona Hessel's confident law-giving, Nora Helmer's resolute leaving of her home, and Thomas Stockmann's boyishly jaunty defiance of his society and its hatred.

In Hegel's analysis, the collapse of the Hellenic world of Objective spirit, in which the individual was expected to discover his identity and his proper sphere of activity within the state, is succeeded by the Roman world of merely "legally defined persons" ruled over by a single "lord and master of the world" where the bond between the individual and the universal, so painfully achieved in the development of the *polis*, is severed. (In the modern world, this experience would be repeated by anyone discovering the ultimately inadequate absolutes of his objective world—its attempt totally to define the individual's identity and activity —and his subsequent exploration of his inward world.) This Roman world, says Hegel, is one of prosaic work, of art that has degenerated into mere "copying," of religion that has become a set of frigid allegories, of a language of tiresomely double meaning (such verbal tricks as finding significance in the fact that Roma, in reverse, is Amor and thus appropriately the city of Venus,[35] and so on), and of a complete loss of the creative joy and spontaneity Hegel sees as the characteristic of Hellenic life.

It is to this condition of consciousness that the Judaic myth of the Fall particularly speaks, for this tells of a tragic alienation of man from God and the world and of the longing for a reconciliation. It is into this somewhat fantastic, somewhat mournful condition that Christianity so fatefully erupts with its requirements first of the sacrifice of *natural* life (the world and its beauty) then of self-sacrifice, the sacrifice of life itself in martyrdom.[36] From the drastic dualism in the Roman and Judeo-Christian worlds, Hegel, in perhaps his most brilliant and sustained dialectical exposition, traces the complex and manifold manifestation of this dualism and alienation through *all* areas of conscious life from the beginning of Christianity up to the time of the "sun king" who is the final development of the Roman "lord and master of the world." It is impossible to summarize the rich dialectical analysis here; that must wait for a later independent study. Instead we will set out the stages of this dialectical development, to which the action of *The Wild Duck* corresponds, and then demonstrate the presence of these stages in Ibsen's play.

Details of Hegel's Analysis of the Self-estranged Spirit	*Corresponding Details in Ibsen's* The Wild Duck
Creation of a world of *legally* defined persons, in contrast to the political/ethical identities of the Hellenic phase.	*Legal* definition creates the social dualism of the "acquitted" and powerful Werle and the guilty and disgraced Ekdals.
The emergence of a "lord and master" of this realm: the Roman Caesar and Pope.	Grosserer (merchant) Werle is the complete lord and master of the world of the play.
The once creative spirit of Hellenism now declines into the *prosaic* and *copying* arts of Rome.	The Ekdal home is given over to the prosaic and copying art of photography. Old Ekdal is given "copying" work.
Language develops into a "frigid" riddling, ambiguous (dualistic) form of allegory and parable.	With entry of Gregers Werle the language of the play shifts from the prosaic to riddling double-meaning, allegory, *overt* symbolism.
Spirit experiences the Fall, of loss of Nature, the Objective world, of God.	The Ekdals have complexly "fallen" and have lost Nature (the forests), social position, and spiritual truth and freedom (God).
The Fall can be undone only by a supreme act of sacrifice: first of the natural world, then of *Self*. Christ's descent to save mankind from the judgment of his Father. The Christian community established, and its traditions of martyrs, of confessions, forgiveness of sins, etc.	Gregers's messianic descent from Høydal (High dale) to save the fallen Ekdals from his father's power requires confession, forgiveness of sins, and sacrifice; the sacrifice of the "natural" wild duck which Hedvig transforms into sacrifice of self.
The dualism of this consciousness now splits into a prosaic here-and-now of work and despiritualized fact on the one side and, in compensation, a "beyond" or other world: the Christian paradise, the literature of fable, romance, miracle, and martyrdoms.	The Ekdals, in reaction to the prosaic reality of the photographic studio and to their own fallen reality, create a complex fantasy world (the loft) in which the lost world of Nature is recovered in imagination.

The literature of this phase is darkly dualistic as in *Don Quixote* (chivalry versus practical reality), *Hamlet* (the inner versus the outer man).

The Wild Duck contains quotations and parodies of this literature and presents such dualities as Gregers and Hjalmar (Quixote and Sancho Panza) and Gregers and Relling (truth-teller versus therapeutic deceiver).

This dualism continued in terms of "higher" and "lower" realms of reality and inner and outer realms of conscious life. The appearance of Subjectivity.

The play is cunningly divided between outward appearance and inward reality: Hjalmar's rhetorical profession of inward suffering behind the outward well-being. Gregers's perception of concealed realities behind deceptive appearances; Relling's "life-lies" which serve Werle's ends and dress sordid reality in false finery.

The imagination of this phase of consciousness is entranced with mysticism, marvels, ritual.

The loft, with its "flying Dutchman," its "time that has stood still," and its sea chest of treasures, is thought of as mysterious and miraculous (Gregers asks Hedvig if she is sure the loft really *is* a loft).

The lord and master of the world finally develops into the sun king surrounded by flatering courtiers.

Grosserer Werle is surrounded by "court chamberlains" (kammerherrer) who need, Mrs. Sørby reminds them, "the sunshine of the court." Ibsen's "sun king" is nearly blind!

The Lutheran challenge to this whole spiritual tradition which resembles Christ's challenge to the Roman world.

Gregers's challenge to Werle's world, and his own character, have much of the Lutheran quality, as we will see.

Inevitably, we distort and grossly simplify the marvelous subtlety and fluidity with which these details of Hegel's analysis dialectically emerge and develop in his argument, and we need hardly point out that there is a great deal more to Ibsen's play than the details I have set out. But I think it also will be seen that Hegel's analysis presents a superb "subject" for the playwright: an extremely rich, strange, and profound condition of consciousness which will require the greatest imaginative power to render in terms of poignant human drama. The

major theme of the analysis is *dualism* which, beginning with the
relatively simple dualism of the individual versus the objective society,
organically grows into an immensely complex condition of the mind.
Hegel takes one immense and variegated time span, from the time
of the Roman world to the time of Luther, and makes of it one single
great travail of the Christian consciousness within a Christian cosmos;
and this, the richest of all Hegel's dialectical dramas of the mind, finds
an equivalent expression in the richest of all Ibsen's dramas, *The
Wild Duck*.

Though the claim that *The Wild Duck* is dramatizing a specifically
Christian world view may at first be novel to the reader, I think that
only a little reflection upon the play's action, imagery, and character
portrayals will reveal the obvious rightness of this claim. A Son descends
from above to raise up a fallen family in opposition to his Father; he
discovers this family to be in the power of a deceiver, an old enemy
of the Son who fought with him up in the heights (Høydal) and now
resumes the battle below over the fate of this fallen humanity. This
deceiver lives below, indulging in "orgies." The crisis of the play's
action is an act of self-sacrifice, after which the Son and his opponent
continue their quarrel as to the possible redeemability of humankind.

In a very attractive interpretation of the play, Robert Raphael draws
attention to certain Christian metaphors, metaphors that correspond,
by the way, to Hegel's account of the dualistic consciousness. He
comments:

> Hedvig and her grandfather approach their world [the attic] with a
> devotion and ritual akin to religious reverence, for the attic with the duck
> and other treasures may be considered a metaphor for the Christian paradise:
> it performs in their lives exactly the same function as does a traditional
> church for many people. Existing on the top floor of the Ekdal microcosm,
> the attic is the *summum bonum* in their lives; it provides them, just like
> heaven, with a world of pure value, a realm of nearly perfect orientation.
> The Ekdals keep returning to this private religion for sustenance just as
> people do with any traditional illusion that is sacred to them.[37]

And Raphael goes on to note how old Werle resembles a god who has
provided everything in the Ekdal world. This sensitive response to
the structure of Ibsen's play reveals how its universal meanings *can*
be detected through the delicate realism; how Ibsen's choice of images
and experiences, his exquisitely *felt* human world, while sacrificing
none of its subtlety and human poignancy, still creates in the perceptive
viewer an awareness of the great shaping images of his art.

Ibsen gently aids our comprehension of the spiritual condition he
is dramatizing by drawing upon our memory of the *visual* arts of this

phase of spirit, a visual quotation that parallels the verbal quotations and the recollected actions in the play (so that we must see his art as very richly and complexly mnemonic). He insisted that lighting effects were of particular importance in the production of this play and it was precisely the use of light, the play of light against darkness—chiaroscuro—precisely to achieve the effect of a third dimension (as Ibsen's staging with its inner room revealing a whole new world), that was of such symbolic importance in later Christian art: especially in the art of the great Rembrandt,[38] an artist whose mellow realism which converts great classical and biblical subjects into images of the familiar world of Rembrandt's time, seems very similar to the realism of *The Wild Duck*. The humbleness of the Ekdal home, the loft of animals in the background, the light streaming down from above (through the skylight, especially in the mysterious moonlight disclosure of the loft to Gregers in Act II) irresistibly call to mind such Christian iconography as the humble family in the foreground of the stable, the animals behind (like an unconscious acknowledgment of the lost natural world) and the light streaming down through the traditional hole-in-the-roof. We might pick up further visual quotations in the fact that Relling lives *below* the Ekdals, like the conventional devil, that the group about the dead body of Hedvig in some way reminds us of the group about the dead Christ, that Gina and Hjalmar carry Hedvig's body offstage like a deposition from the Cross. I do believe Ibsen is cunningly and delicately orchestrating our responses in this way and this, together with the play's very definite and vivid recollections from the dualistic art of Cervantes and Shakespeare (and possibly Molière), makes the play an extraordinarily rich *Gesamtkunstwerk*, though a good deal less solemn in its *"galskap"* than that of Richard Wagner.

Ibsen's first biographer and friend, Henrik Jaeger, indicated the similarity of Gregers Werle and Don Quixote, that disastrous idealist and visionary: but even more rich is the rather irreverent parody of Shakespeare. The play opens, for instance, with two servants in the foreground commenting on the feasting at old Werle's "court" where Werle is proposing a long toast, before his audience, to his mistress, Mrs. Sørby, when suddenly they are startled by the apparition of the old, ex-military Ekdal, and as this strange figure shuffles offstage we hear from the servants of his fall from grace. The whole little scene seems like a quotation from the opening of *Hamlet* and, like the ghost in *Hamlet*, old Ekdal even appears a second time, this time to his son, the similarly named Hjalmar. This second appearance, startling Werle's feast, also carries overtones of Banquo's ghost. The Hamlet themes are surely continued in the fact that young Gregers, the other Hamlet figure in the play, has just returned from a long absence, like Hamlet from Wittenberg, to be present at a feast where Werle is about to embark upon a questionable marriage. And after he sees old Ekdal in Werle's drawing room, Gregers discovers there is something rotten in the Werle world. It seems that the two aspects of Hamlet's character are divided between Hjalmar, who shares the prince's rhetorical ineffectuality, and Gregers, who shares the prince's self-disgust.[39] Other Shakespearean details seem to be Hjalmar's Lear-like rushing out into the storm (wickedly deflated by the insuperable problems of packing and of taking the domestic animals with him, and his rhetorical and Lear-like declamation against God over the dead body of his daughter, while a chorus of onlookers comments on the tragedy. The idea that Ibsen is parodying Shakespeare possibly will offend some readers more than the idea that he is parodying Christianity. There is, however, the consolation that this play in which Shakespeare's spirit is so irreverently present is acknowledged to be one of the deepest and richest that Ibsen has created.[40]

Apart from Hamlet, another gloomy Dane, Søren Kierkegaard, has been detected in the character of Gregers Werle. Kierkegaard was in revolt against his father, who, like Gregers, represented a quixotic and somewhat inhumanly uncompromising attack upon the world of established "Christendom" in the name of a more fundamental Christianity; living just long enough to exhaust his finances, as Gregers foretells of himself and, with better reason, disliking his own sombre name, he is himself a clear example of that Unhappy Consciousness of Christianity so penetratingly analyzed by Hegel. It is now a familiar part of the criticism of *The Wild Duck* to see in its two major characters, Gregers Werle and Hjalmar Ekdal, smaller-scaled versions of Brand and Peer Gynt and, certainly, the all-or-nothing requirement Gregers demands of the fallen Ekdals is similar to the demand of the Kierkegaardian Brand.[41]

We have suggested that the dialectic of *Rosmersholm* was the logical development of the dialectical situation of *The Wild Duck*, and this continuity of theme can also be detected in the historical recollections undertaken by the two plays. *The Wild Duck* presents us with a profoundly divided world into which an idealistic force erupts creating a fatal crisis of suffering and sacrifice, corresponding closely to Hegel's account of the Christian eruption into the profoundly divided Roman consciousness, and the later Lutheran challenge to a Roman Europe. *Rosmersholm*, on the other hand, tells of a profoundly divided aristocratic world into which a northern "pagan" force erupts, its action also creating death and sacrifice. It is an action that quite closely corresponds to Hegel's two examples of the explosive encounter between the Germanic northern and Romanic southern traditions of the European consciousness: the early pagan and northern conquest of the divided Roman world which, however, led to the spiritual conquest (the Christianization) of northern paganism; and, in the realm of the intellect, the later attack upon Roman Christianity by the northern Enlightenment.[42]

The two plays present strikingly similar actions, but with two strongly contrasting spiritual powers (Gregers Werle and Rebekka West) as the revolutionary instigators of the action. There is an appropriateness in the fact that the Christian Knight of Faith, Gregers Werle, sees his mission as rescuing the fallen, humble, insulted, and injured, whereas that pagan missionary, Rebekka West, engages against the aristocratic order of the world. Both actions are conceived to raise and ennoble humanity, but in diametrically opposite terms. For Gregers Werle this ennoblement requires humility, confession, forgiveness, a sacrifice and faith that will work a "transfiguration" of reality, and these Christian details are continued in the play's imagery. Hjalmar's bitterest moment is, to Gregers, also his most "sublime," for after Hjalmar and Gina have "laid bare their souls" to live together "in truth" Gregers expects to be greeted by "the light of radiant understanding" shining from their faces. Instead, Hjalmar admits only to having drunk "a bitter draught" like Christ in Gethsemane. Ibsen quite outrageously depicts the little realistic action as an almost farcical parody of its great New Testament archetype. *The Wild Duck*, I think, has much of the quality of Christian myth itself: a *homeliness* of detail, together with the most extravagant spiritual claims ever made by a religion, a disparity and incongruity between means and meaning which spirit will be impelled to overcome, in Hegel's account, by a dialectical process that will culminate in the French Revolution.

The ideal of the Enlightenment action of *Rosmersholm*, on the other hand, is that of raising men up "in friendly rivalry" to the condition of a new "aristocracy" of spirit. Here the ideal is pagan with its emphasis upon human nobility and fulfillment. The contrast between these two concepts of spiritual revolution, the Christian and the pagan, is found again and again in the literature of Europe from the Enlightenment onwards. Goethe and Schiller, for example, quite openly gave their allegiance to the Hellenic ideal of human education and fulfillment; and Ibsen sets the two concepts in opposition in *Emperor and Galilean*.[43]

Once again, I understand the possible objection to this way of interpreting the play and if we merely were to turn Ibsen's plays into a form of philosophical allegory, where all the characters "stand for" certain principles and forces as in a medieval morality play, then the objection would be valid. But this is not what we are claiming; we propose the much more complex idea that Ibsen's plays manage to contain or exemplify such universal principles and forces yet within a human action the rhythms of which are poignantly intimate and searching. Greek and Elizabethan drama managed to subtilize universal abstractions, yet it is these abstractions that, finally, make the plays infinitely more true of the human condition than the intimate "slice of life" realism of recent times. The figure of Falstaff is increased and not diminished in dramatic value by his derivation from the Morality play Vice of Gluttony, and the human world of *King Lear* is all the more affecting for being a metaphor for the same universal realities naively set out in *Gorboduc*. We have to move away from William Archer's very eccentric idea of drama as a surrogate for everyday life and back to the great tradition of European drama which always has presented universal realities. Nothing puzzles young students of the drama more than reading a traditional account of an Ibsen play as a modest little exercise in bourgeois psychoanalysis and then encountering the claim that Ibsen is a dramatist who can be ranked with Sophocles and Shakespeare. Such an account betrays as drastic a misunderstanding of what great drama is all about as of what Ibsen's dramas are all about.

The plays are events in a *theater*, on a stage, and not within real-life psyches; and theater, more than any of the literary arts, has to convey its image of reality by means of universal metaphors economically depicted in dialectical conflict. Ibsen's Cycle, for the first time since Shakespeare's, sets out to be a consistent total theater, a scene for a mighty Argument rivaling the most ambitious of the nineteenth century's many greatly ambitious art works. *Rosmersholm*, while a deeply felt and explored human drama in its own terms, also is one stage of this Argument and we have to demonstrate how this Argument is as full of dramatic interest and esthetic possibilities as the human drama. This I attempt to do in the second part of this book where the reader will find an interpretation of the dialectic of *Rosmersholm*.

In Hegel's account, after the fight to the death between the forces of superstitious authoritarianism and the forces of enlightened freedom in which the whole enlightened enterprise collapses in the recognition that it is one with the forces it at first set out to oppose, Spirit embarks upon the most extreme of its dualistic dramas, lured towards the concept of an Absolute freedom, as boundless as the sea and recognizing no limits but Death. Such freedom, being unlimited, "can thus produce neither a positive achievement nor a deed; there is left for it only negative action; it is merely the rage and fury of destruction."[44] It attempts to destroy "the organization of the actual world" and "the sole and only work and deed accomplished by absolute freedom is therefore death—a death that achieves nothing, embraces nothing within its grasp."[45] In an analysis too complex to summarize here, Hegel shows how Spirit retreats from the "terror" of this absolute freedom into a mode of morality (of human responsibility) expressed philosophically in Kant's Categorical Imperative.[46]

The problem of maintaining his dramatic metaphor of the domestic setting of one or two psyches to be explored in depth (like Ingmar Bergen's method, later) yet, at the same time, of finding a place for the perspectives of "absolute freedom" and its subsequent "terror" forces Ibsen, in *The Lady from the Sea*, to create the most drastically dualistic of all his actions, though this is perfectly appropriate for this climax in Hegel's account of the dialectic of the dualistic consciousness. For the world of *The Lady from the Sea* is split into hostile halves that have no possibility of joining together: the absolutely nihilistic world of the Stranger, as boundless as the sea, and the confined and responsible world of the Wangel home, as bounded as the carp pond.

Ellida, haunted by the memory of her nihilistic lover who seems to resemble the formless, restless power of the sea itself, had pledged herself to him at a time when he had killed his captain, an action strongly suggestive of the Revolutionary regicide. Now, much later, he reappears, demanding she honor her rash pledge, rather as if the modern (nineteenth-century) spirit were asked to live up to *its* Revolutionary commitment in the past. In the play we find a contrast between a life elaborately and variegatedly *compromising* with unsatisfactory reality (in this as in other details somewhat resembling the condition of *The Wild Duck*) with the result that no one lives at a very high intensity of happiness or significance and, on the other side, a life (that of the Stranger) which accepts no compromise whatsoever, refuses to change with changing events so that even Ellida's firm breaking with the Stranger in her letter and her later marriage to Wangel seem to be entirely unimportant considerations with him. It would be easy to see the play as agreeing with Ballestad's advice that man must learn to "acclimatize" himself to a modest reality and not strain unhappily for an impractical and alarming liberation for which he is not equipped; but the "Prospect" scene of Act II with its view over distant mountain peaks and fjords suggests that the retreat that the ending of the play makes into a common-sensical and restricted reality is not a decision the Spirit can long be happy with. Is it for this reason that the most restless inhabitant of this world,

Hilde Wangel, is allowed to escape it and to open up the actions of release into spiritual liberation and death of the last group? Certainly, Hegel's treatment of consciousness's Kantian decision is tinged with a fairly heavy irony and we cannot help reflecting that, with Ellida's decision to renounce the alarming freedom offered by her lover and to accept the realm of responsibilities offered by Wangel, we are moving towards the intolerable confinement of consciousness of *Hedda Gabler.* In Hegel's words:

> These individuals, who felt the fear of death, their absolute lord and master, submit to negation and distinction once more, arrange themselves under "spheres," and return to a restricted and apportioned task, but thereby to substantial reality.[47]

J. Loewenberg observes that though the post-revolutionary world never can be "conducive to individual enjoyment of absolute freedom ... such freedom, though not attainable in the world, is inexpungible from the sphere of the individual's moral consciousness."[48]

The appropriately fluid, undersea movement of the play with its ebb-and-flow yearning towards and retreat from possibilities of larger realities, and its strange restlessness, is well represented by Act II, in which groups of rootless people, couples, tourists, and such indeterminate characters as Ballestad, jack of all arts and trades, and Lyngstrand, a would-be sculptor already dying, all move across the stage like shoals of fish, visually establishing their restless movement against a scenic background of the fjord and the enduring mountain peaks. The depths of the sea and the mountain summits are, as Rolf Fjelde has noted, the extreme limits of biological life on earth, the sea perhaps representing regression to the pre-human, the mountain summits advance to the superhuman.[49] In the contrast between the extreme depth from which the Stranger has emerged, and the extreme heights of the distant peaks seen from the middle-heights of the Prospect, we see the dualism of this group of plays given its extreme geographical definition. Similarly, the central drama of this play is a psychological dualism bordering on schizophrenia in the heroine. (As a native of the "headland" of Skioldviken, Ellida also derives from an environment of continual tug-of-war between sea and land.) Almost midway in the Cycle (and precisely midway if we see its spiritual "awakening" beginning with *A Doll's House*) the scenic details of *The Lady from the Sea* stretch back to the origins of biological life itself, the sea, and forward to the utmost limits of human aspiration, symbolized by the mountain peaks. Between these two extremes, the play seems to indicate, humanity must establish its complete and adequate identity spatially and temporally, foregoing the lure of a perhaps pre-human absolute freedom whose culmination only can be the negation of life, yet, at the same time, I think, looking upward beyond the carp-pond acclimatization which would resemble the troll-like condition depicted in *Peer Gynt*.

The acute dualism of this play emerges also in the somewhat incongruous juxtaposition of the Romantic and the bourgeois imaginations, a dualism that was, of course, "there" in the period the consciousness of which Hegel is analyzing. It was a period that could contain both Lord Byron and Jane Austen, the gradual *embourgeoisement* of European society forcing upon the non-conforming individual and artist the necessity for the most extravagant forms of rebellion or rejection. The Romantic agony and aspiration appeared before a public whose reality was the reality of Dr. Wangel and not that of the Stranger; yet it was the sensitive souls within the world of Dr. Wangel who were fascinated by Byron, drawn to Werther, and, later, were to be thrilled by Wagner's *The Flying Dutchman*.[50] The disjunction in reality between the world of the Stranger and that of "Dr. Wangel and the pert daughters"[51] imposes a considerable strain upon the structural consistency of the play, but this is a great part of its interest, for the viewer senses the extreme dualism inherent in this reality and responds to its dramatic dialectic. The strain between the Romantic spirit and its bourgeois imprisonment only can be ended by eliminating the possibility of Romantic aspiration altogether or, conversely, courageously transcending the world of bourgeois limitation and living by visionary reality. In *Hedda Gabler* we find the first alternative; the second is attempted in the last four plays.

If the spiritual dualism of *The Lady from the Sea* calls to mind Romantic drama and literature, that of *Hedda Gabler* calls to mind the theater of the Scribean well-made play. It is, in fact, the apotheosis of the well-made play. Its "fatal" drink, misplaced manuscript, *femme fatale*, its *demi-monde* (in Mlle. Diana and her circle), together with the sensational pistols, the *ménage-à-trois* desired by Brack (who is himself a combination of *roué* and *confidante*), the brittle suburban tone of the dialogue, the shapely mechanism of the ingenious plot with its sensational curtains culminating in Hedda's suicide: all these are handled with more than the skill of Scribe & Co., and suggest that Ibsen had the French theater directly in mind as he conceived *Hedda Gabler*.[52] Hedda herself strongly calls to mind Emma Bovary although Ibsen, unlike Flaubert, has given his heroine a disturbing intelligence and fastidiousness. This "French" aspect of the play would be suitable to the phase of consciousness it is depicting, that of the post-Napoleonic bourgeois culture of Europe dominated by the *memory* of the great

general and emperor, a period that Hegel scathingly termed that of
"valets of the moral sphere" not only incapable of greatness but
incapable, also, of recognizing it. In this phase, which followed the
collapse of Romanticism and of revolution, the old aristocracy has
been displaced by the new bourgeoisie and society is divided only
between this new bourgeoisie and a developing bohemianism. In the
German world, we find the contrast exemplified in the militant Hellenism
of Hölderlin and, later, of Nietzsche (*The Birth of Tragedy* and other
writings which oppose the growing mediocrity of modern society).
The god of the well-made-play is Mercury, god of merchants, but the
gods of Ibsen's play are the Nietzschean pair, Apollo and Dionysos.

  Hedda Gabler is the last play before the great final group which
will present a transfigured, new reality; so that the subject matter is
the phase of consciousness that stretches from the post-Napoleonic
world of Hegel's analysis up to Ibsen's own day. It is probably for this
reason that the play always has struck commentators as the most
"modern" in the Cycle, for it appears to lack those historical and
archetypal dimensions that lie behind the modern actions of the preceding plays. It is for this reason that its subject matter, also, has
struck commentators as being in some way slighter, more nearly a mere
study in neurosis (and suburban neurosis at that!) than the other
plays. Thus, it is necessary to indicate the way in which the play
actually very cunningly conceals great depths beneath its satirically
glittering surface. For the argument of *Hedda Gabler* is nothing less
than that of *Emperor and Galilean* and of Neitzsche's *The Birth of
Tragedy*. One of the meanings of the play emerges from the fact that
this immense subject matter is forced into an intolerable confinement
as Ibsen makes the well-made-play structure contain what it had been
designed, precisely, to exclude: those perspectives of the human spirit,
its history and destiny, for which the materialistic and sophisticated
subjects of the nineteenth-century Bourbon rulers had no more relish
than the patrons of Broadway today. The well-made-play, with its
cynical philosophy that even the greatest issues were decided by the
most trivial events and that, therefore, ethical or political or metaphysical concerns were irrelevancies, pathetic human attempts to dig-
nify a mechanistic Chance and Accident, was the useful refuge of the
modern bourgeois anxious only to set about the business of making
money and to avoid the kind of consciousness that once inspired a
revolution. The well-made-play cunningly transferred the audience's
interest from ideas to objects, from an argument to a mechanical plot.
Intense interest was focused upon a concealed letter, a locked cabinet,
a fatal drink, a glass of water. The mechanical plot depended upon a

technically complex situation subject to the urgent pressure of artificial theatric time, the crisis of the play being, not a crisis of perception (as in even the most melodramatic of Enlightenment plots), but the crisis of *suspense*: of the wished-for or feared event teasingly delayed or obstructed, then finally achieved or avoided—the suspense, in fact, of the stock market, an analogy acknowledged by Dumas *fils* who sarcastically hailed Scribe for the great dramatic discovery that perfect felicity was not merely winning the beloved but a handsome fortune at the same time.[53]

This reduced dramatic ritual and its limited vision are part of the subject of *Hedda Gabler* which wonderfully takes up this little dramatic structure and then reveals its unexpected capacity for expressing the immense Ibsen themes. Compared with the other plays in this group (and with the plays that are to follow), we are struck by the extreme paucity of Nature imagery, either in direct presentation (as in *The Lady from the Sea*) or by verbal reference (as in *The Wild Duck*). In place of this usually present rich source of metaphor, we have, merely, the honeymoon (outrageous euphemism!) of Tesman and Hedda in the Austrian mountains reduced onstage to a short, dry, and risqué conversation over a photograph album. The cut bouquets of the first act, and the yellowing leaves of the dying year are the only other Nature details except for one moment when Løvberg, tactfully lying to Thea, describes his manuscript (their "child") torn into a thousand pieces and drifting out into the fjord as another "child," Little Eyolf, will in a later play. This extreme confinement of the imagery of the dialogue is continued in the extremely confined scene of the play (which is throughout the same drawing room) and the nature of the characters within that scene. Never before has Ibsen assembled so unpromising a group and allowed them to say so little: Aunt Julie, Berte, Tesman, Thea, Brack—there seems to be nothing here that could carry the themes of a lofty and urgent spiritual dialectic, but in this play Ibsen is at his most cunning. We noted that the phase of consciousness is that of the modern bourgeois world living on the memory of Napoleonic greatness, as in Stendhal's *The Charterhouse of Parma*, but itself retreating into the "spheres" of petty duties; and to convey, visually, something of this idea, Ibsen has the domestic and petty action of the play overlooked throughout by the impressive portrait of the uniformed General Gabler whose presence is an un-assimilated anachronism like his daughter's.

Ibsen's notes to the play continually stress this contrast between an omnipresent pettiness and the spirit yearning for higher and freer regions. One note goes:

The manuscript which [Eilert Løvborg] leaves behind is concerned to show that the task of humanity is: Upwards towards the bringer of light. Life on the present social basis is not worth living. Then imagine yourself away from it. Through drink, etc. Tesman is correctness, Hedda is the blasé. [Thea] the nervous-hysterical present-day type. Brack the representative of the personal bourgeois attitude.[54]

The note poignantly depicts the highest level of consciousness in the play—that of Løvborg and of Hedda—as trapped in a world which, for the first time in the Cycle, is totally denied a sight of the divine, and the reference to "the bringer of light" looks forward to the next play, *Bygmester Solness* (*The Master Builder*) with its very emphatic sun-and-light imagery, and the movement "upwards" that it inaugurates.

Any approach to *Hedda Gabler* must first come to terms with its extraordinary design: the symmetrically perfect arrangement of its four acts, its exact balance of characters, and its beautifully circular action. If Apollo and Dionysos, gods of the drama, haunt the play, they are discoverable if we first detect the esthetic compulsion creating the play's form. Act I exactly balances Act IV while the two inner acts, II and III, form an action and unit themselves, so that the "shape" of the play could be set out:

Act I	Act IV
(Hedda's frustrated	(Hedda's retreat
aggression)	to die)
Act II	Act III
(The Løvborg	(The Løvborg
"army" launched)	"army" defeated)

The halfway point of the action actually is reached *between* Acts II and III in surely one of the most consequential offstage actions in all theater. It is at this halfway point that the "life" themes of the first half of the play now give way to Hedda's "death" themes, and this moment is delicately signaled in the opening of Act III when a letter arrives announcing Aunt Rina's dying. The basic choreography of the play is circular, following Hedda's emergence from her inner room (associated with her private world of values), her first attacks upon her enemies in the form of minor aggressions, the major campaign when she launches the bohemian Løvborg against the philistines, his defeat, and Hedda's beautiful death like a pagan warrior preferring death to dishonor.

In Act I Hedda's aggressions are frustrated minor skirmishes: her barely covert malice towards Tesman, her frontal assault upon poor

Aunt Julie's hat,[55] her easy intimidation of Thea. But in spite of these aggressions we are aware of the logic of circumstances defeating Hedda. The bouquets from the world of the aunts have invaded the room, the financial problems prevent her attaining a "style" above the *petit-bourgeois,* and the small, stifling, benevolently mediocre world of the aunts, Berte, and Tesman, have taken possession of her as a plebian mob in Rome might have acquired a defeated empress. It is only when Thea arrives with her startling disclosures about Løvberg that Hedda finds herself at last equipped with an army by means of which to mount a major attack. In Act II she launches this army: it will carry the Hellenic values of beauty and joy-of-life against the Christian world of decent society. In Act III, with her army in grotesque retreat, Hedda has to face a squalid and ignominious defeat; but, in Act IV, she converts this defeat into a moment of subversive, militant *beauty,* retreating loftily to her inner room to die.

There are, therefore, two major movements in the play: one, connected with the world of Tesman and the aunts; the other, with Hedda, Diana, and Løvborg, and underneath the plausible everyday surface this social and psychological dualism takes the form of a completely ruthless *battle.* Ibsen drew attention to this dualism in describing the play to an actress who was to impersonate Hedda:

> Jörgen Tesman, his old aunts, and the faithful servant Berte together form a picture of complete unity. They think alike, they share the same memories and have the same outlook on life. To Hedda they appear like a strange and hostile power, aimed at her very being.[56]

In Act I, Tesman and the aunts are in the ascendant and *their motifs* of flowers, light, new birth (and the "new book" of the Thea-reformed Løvberg) successfully engage with Hedda's more deathly imagery: the curtains she draws against the light; her disdain of her own pregnancy; her indifference to the new book; the lethal pistols. In the last act it is Hedda's death imagery that is in the ascendant, despite her defeat. The bouquets and the light of the first act have become the mourning *insignia* and the fully curtained windows of the last. The birth imagery of a new child, new book, gives way to a multiple mourning (Aunt Rina, Løvborg, Løvborg's book, Hedda, and her unborn child), which makes of the last act a miniscule *Götterdämmerung* which Hedda forces upon an action that began so hopefully with flowers and anticipations of new life and work.

The dialectical balance of the conflicting forces in the play can be seen in the play's structure. In our diagram on page 128 we notice that the two central acts were given over to Løvborg's action and these two acts which are the only ones in which Løvborg physically is present are the only acts in which Aunt Julie physically is absent, suggesting that the forces represented by Løvborg *displace* those represented by Aunt Julie, and *vice versa.* A subtle indication of the moment when the aunts are about to return, thematically, is the delicate detail of Aunt Julie's letter slipped through the letter box as Hedda is waiting for news of Løvborg. As this still is a "Løvborg Act" Aunt Julie will not physically appear but there is, as it were, "a movement from that direction." In a play whose rather coarse cynicism on the surface can obscure the depth and subtlety of Ibsen's vision, we should detect the great frequency of such delicate plotting and imagery. The book-of-the-past, the book-of-the-future, the mythic overtones of the "dis-memberment," burning and loss of the "child" and its parodic pedantic resurrection, the unexpected similarities between the "correct" Hedda and the bohemian Mlle. Diana, and so on, all alert as to a complexity and subtlety of artistic intention on Ibsen's part that obviously goes far beyond entertaining us with a voyeuristic study of a neurotic woman. *Hedda Gabler* is neither a moralistic nor philosophical tract, nor is it a psychological casebook; it is a beautiful dramatic design, an image, in theatrical terms, of a total condition of spirit seen as an artistic prob-lem to be solved by the dramatist and meditated upon by his audience.

Already our account of the play suggests that it resembles, more than anything else, a battle—a campaign that is launched and which suffers defeat. This idea of a battle gains in plausibility when we reflect that Hedda is the daughter of a general, that she inherits, and uses, his pistols, and that the general himself, in portrait, overlooks the whole action as if from the vantage point of the general's tent. The battle seems symbolically launched at the opening of Act II when Hedda fires her pistols at the sky (a fine image of the unbearably *blank* infinity surrounding this demythologized world) and news of the battle and of its loss arrives in a series of reports somewhat resembling the messenger speeches of Greek drama as well as the *aide's* report to a general.

A battle requires two armies, each representing a distinct, even if unconscious, cause, and the reader by now will not be too astonished at the suggestion that these two armies can be designated, respectively, pagan and Christian as these forces of the psyche had developed into the dualistic consciousness of Ibsen's own time. The Christian group, with Tesman, the aunts, and Thea, shades off into the ambiguous Judge Brack; the pagan group of the general, Hedda, and Løvborg shades off into the disreputable Diana.[57] Thus the pagan-Christian conflict of *Emperor and Galilean*, present in the Cycle all along, now ranges itself into clear dialectical confrontation within the psychological-social terms of the late nineteenth century and it is for this reason that *Hedda Gabler*, while lacking the richness of the historical perspectives of the earlier plays, is still able to re-enact the drama of *Emperor and Galilean* even through the medium of the Scribean theater.

The pagan army in the play is a distinct group. Hedda rules the "day" world of social convention while her alter ego, Diana, rules the "night" world of bohemian orgy. It is easy to show that Diana *is* Hedda's alter ego; Hedda dreams of the orgies in which Diana takes part yet rules the world from which Diana is excluded, like the sun-moon division of Apollo/Artemis. Thea's description of the strange woman in Løvborg's past, and Hedda's suggestion that it is Diana, link the two together. Løvborg accuses Diana of committing the crime (killing the "child") that Hedda commits. He is shot in Diana's apartment with Hedda's pistol and Judge Brack threatens Hedda with the possibility of her appearing with Diana in court, as if in public acknowledgment of their alliance. The mutual exclusiveness of the worlds of the two women indicates a need for their integration, for if Diana's soirées lack the elegance and refinement of Hedda's social world, Hedda's refinement, without passionate experience, is spiritually decadent—for dcadence comes from the insufficiency, not the excess, of passion. Løvborg, caught between his reformed life up in the hills with Thea, and his pagan life in town with Hedda/Diana, is in very much the situation of Wagner's Tannhäuser, torn between his Christian "saint" Elizabeth and the temptations of Venusberg. In this very cunning play I think we are meant to be on the alert for such ironic Joycean archetypes.

The Christian army is as distinct, comprising the aunts, the maid Certe, Tesman, and Thea. Judge Brack, whose night parties for bachelors parallel Diana's parties with her group of women (as Artemis is surrounded by her women) is, I think, the Mephistophelean or "satanic" aspect of Christianity, here very playfully suggested. Hedda's first greeting to him, "It is a treat to see you by daylight, Judge Brack," implies he is a figure of the night. Aunt Julie, who gives her whole life up to charity, requires a sick world to minister to in contrast to Hedda who cannot bear ugliness and sickness; and the aunt's joy over Løvborg's reported "fall" in Act I tells us that this sweet old lady can be indiscriminatingly ruthless where her beloved nephew's interests are at stake. Thea Elvsted, too, though a little fool, is, with her halo of golden hair, something of a little saint exhibiting that spiritual power-without-intelligence that so exasperated Julian in the Christians.[58]

For this last play of the second group, therefore, which brings us to the culture and theater of Ibsen's own day, the dramatist has taken his own *Emperor and Galilean* as the philosophic and dramatic statement of the *Zeitgeist*, and has given it the theater of the day which Ibsen's own art is transfiguring with his great thematic archetypes, so that *Hedda Gabler* presents us with one of the largest of his conflicts within the most reduced of his theatric methods. A recollection of the method of the previous play, *The Lady from the Sea*, with its Romantic overtones and its extensive scenography, will bring home the extreme *confinement* of *Hedda Gabler*. This confinement of the spirit is symbolized by Hedda's final retreat from the drawing room whose curtains are drawn against the outside world, into her inner room whose curtains are drawn against the drawing room, giving the impression of layer after layer between this final retreat of the spirit and the outer world; but this play is the prelude to the last group which, *beginning* in this extreme confinement, is given over to actions of the spirit breaking free and regaining the natural world.

The phases of consciousness encompassed by this second group, from *The Wild Duck* to *Hedda Gabler,* are the most varied in the Cycle, accounting, perhaps, for the greater variety of dramatic styles of these four plays. The relation of the plays to the Hegelian account of the evolution of consciousness is all the time a highly imaginative and independent one: an astonishing re-creation and actualization of Hegel's obscure and highly abstract text into a vividly inhabited, solidly conceived dramatic world. From *The Pillars of Society* to *Hedda Gabler* the correspondences between the plays and the Hegelian argument have been clearly chronological; for the rest of the *Phenomenology* Hegel abandons this strictly chronological process, or, rather, the *historical* underpinning to the argument no longer is strictly chronological. Entering upon an account of the highest possible level of consciousness Hegel describes the apotheosis of the human mind through its myths, religions, cults, arts, and philosophies. The cosmos suddenly expands and, with its expansion, the human consciousness expands, too, embracing an order of reality more profound and more sublime. The most outlandish as well as the most familiar myths and legends, cults and beliefs, now invade Hegel's texts, *not* to illustrate social/political conflicts in the Objective world, as in the first group, nor to illustrate conflicts within the Subjective world, as in the second group, but as direct spiritual realities in their own right, beginning with the Persian religion of the sun to the rational Christianity of Hegel's own philosophy. And this alarming but exhilarating expansion of the imaginative universe and of the human consciousness that seeks to grasp it constitutes the liberation or "awakening" of the final series in Ibsen's Cycle, beginning with *The Master Builder*. The empty sky at which the blasé Hedda had fired her pistols now becomes numinous, filled with spiritual powers.

THE LAST GROUP

If we consider our overall impression of the last group *as a whole*— the scenography it encompasses, the wealth of recollected mythopoeic detail—I think we will agree that a tremendous expansion in time and space occurs. Time now is crammed with direct and consciously recollected *memory*; the act of recollection, in fact, becomes the major action of these plays, displacing the elaborate "plots" of the earlier plays, and this recollection of the Past, whose perspectives open up so clearly and so vastly, is made utterly to transform the reality of the Present. *Spatially*, too, these last four plays gradually recover the huge natural landscapes of *Brand* and *Peer Gynt* and of the "Prospect" scene of *The Lady from the Sea*, and these spatial perspectives have their own Natural themes of day and night, seasons of the year.

This great expansion of temporal and spatial metaphors matches an expansion in dramatic character. The characters of the last plays take on the dimensions of semi-mythic figures locked in archetypal conflicts, and the elaborate realistic plausibilities of the earlier plays now almost shamelessly are discarded as Ibsen swiftly and economically designs striking characters and actions to carry his increased burden of myth-opoeic meaning. It is precisely because these plays have to say and to recollect so much that Ibsen cannot be employed upon minutely ingenious plotting as he was in the infinitely cunning structure of *Hedda Gabler*. This does not imply any qualitative judgment between the last plays and those that precede them. Between intentions so unlike, such judgment would be meaningless.

Before prospects so imaginatively alarming, the reader might well implore caution from the interpreter; but caution is a virtue not notice-ably absent from Ibsen criticism and the interpreter has an obligation, also, to respond to the immensity of Ibsen's dramatic vision. In the pages that follow I will not be concerned with the solidly and finely rendered human world of the last plays, already very well dealt with in a number of excellent studies, but, rather, with the mythopoeic and metaphoric areas of the plays. This, I agree, will not be an adequate *full* interpretation of the plays (that would expand far beyond the limits possible in an account of the Cycle as a whole) but I hope it will provide an exciting and useful starting point for a later re-examination of their full range of intention.

No more abrupt and startling a transition could be imagined than that between the world of petty proprieties, cynical pragmatism, and irresponsible bohemianism of *Hedda Gabler* and the exhilarating and alarming invasion of the Solness household by the "mountain-climbing" Hilde. Only Lona Hessel's arrival by sea that opens the Cycle can match it in buoyant energy; but Hilde's arrival carries ethereal connotations (of mysterious origins, intentions, and destination) totally remote from the pragmatic and eminently "ethical" Lona Hessel. If *Hedda Gabler* had given off a stale odor of Parisian worldly cynicism, "like a corsage the day after the ball" in Hedda's phrase, *The Master Builder* obviously blows with a fresh breeze of spirit descending with Hilde from the mountains.

We will find, in these plays, no merely objective human world of ethical values and contradictions to comprehend, nor merely a brooding inward world of the subjective spirit that cannot be reconciled with the outward structure of society; instead, the characters of the last plays live at an altogether higher level of consciousness and reflection, are animated by and lured toward possibilities quite outside the categories of the earlier plays. They have undergone the phases of the earlier plays and thus contain within themselves these phases as memories, often as still rankling errors, wrongs, or losses; but in the actions to which the last plays impel these characters, Solness, Allmers, Borkman, and Rubek, they are confronted with ultimate questions as to the meaning and purpose of their lives. They are brought, abruptly, to call their entire lives into question and to measure up to the highest or most penetrating demands. Such a level of experience is one in which the work of consciousness has been completed before the plays begin so that the realms of subjective intentions and objective results now lie fully exposed to view and ready for the most searching judgment. Fully exposed is both the nature of the psychic realm with its tensions, conflicts, guilt, and fears, and the nature of the objective world which consciousness both has created and has been created by: that complex of interacting and mutually affecting realms, subjective and objective, which it was Ibsen's particular genius to comprehend and present almost from the beginning of his career.

Consciousness completed as a network of inward causes and outward events—and *vice versa*—can know itself (become an object for itself) and so rise to the level of art, religion, and philosophy as it does in the last section of the *Phenomenology*.[59] Modern man, at his *highest* level of reflection, transcends the terms of the present and considers his entire revealed history, much as the epic poets, Homer, Virgil, and Milton, invoke their Muses to lift them out of the context of the Present so that they might "see" the "great Argument" of which they will be the vocal instrument. This third, overarching, phase of Spirit's development is as distinct a break with the previous text as Ibsen's last four plays are with the plays that precede them in the Cycle. Precisely such a momentous transition into another (more visionary) mode of consciousness occurs at this point in both sequences, just as, earlier, there had been a decided transition from the Objective to the Subjective realms of consciousness. The realm of arts, religions, and philosophies, though it still demands painful dialectical development, the outgrowing of inadequate truths, represents the somewhat exhilarating point at which the individual can transcend his own historically determined condition and enter into that "community of consciousness" that Hegel saw as the goal of all human striving and whose universal expressions as myths, religions, arts, and thought are the common heritage of all mankind.

Not only is there a difference of subject matter in Hegel's account of this level of the human consciousness; there is also a major difference in method which, I believe, is also reflected in Ibsen's dramatic method in the last four plays. In an ingenious image Hegel describes the advance of Spirit in the previous sections of the *Phenomenology* as resembling a line marked by "knots" marking the stages (along the line) of the dialectical progress.[60] But *now* at this higher level of consciousness, these knots or universal moments are the points at which the line is broken up and made "into a single bundle" symmetrically combined "so that the separate distinctions in which each separately took shape within its own sphere, meet together." What this means is that the whole rich substance of human consciousness (Spirit), both Objective and Subjective, which had unfolded as a logical/historical series of spiritual crises and conflicts, now is totally to be grasped all at once by consciousness which carries them all together along this final and highest mode of advancing. This naturally creates a method of dialectical recollection of extreme complexity, in which all the previous dramas continually are reappearing in unexpected places in the later dialectic: a difference from the earlier mode of proceeding as complex counterpoint is different from monody.

For the consciousness now is liberated from confinement merely within one historical form (*gestalt*); at this higher level all previous phases must return to be ultimately understood just as the thinker or artist of consummate culture now can traverse and comprehend all earlier cultural forms. Therefore, in what at first seems to be an astonishing retrogression to its infancy, Consciousness in Hegel's account returns to its very first myths, rituals, and cults, the very origins of its dialectical life; but this regression to immediate archetypal recollection is, paradoxically, an advance to the highest level of consciousness in which these mythopoeic and spiritual expressions are now fully comprehended in all their universal significance. From this point on, in a form of spiritual mountain climbing, consciousness moves upwards in an ether of universal realities to a peak of promise whose summit is Absolute Knowledge. This goal will strike our modern and more sadly pragmatic age as hardly a sober one but we can be moved and inspired by the poignant attempt finally to justify existence (by comprehending it) to the human consciousness. The only alternative, of similarly respectable dimensions, would be to damn all conscious existence for its final and horrible meaninglessness, and in these two alternatives we can see on the one side the artistic affirmations of Ibsen and Joyce and, on the other, the total denials of the art of Samuel Beckett, or of Kafka.

Obviously, such a mode of consciousness will encompass all levels of existence from the most primitive and undeveloped to the most etheric, and such an expansion of subject matter, from the most physical to the most etheric, is, I believe, the experience of the reader or viewer of these last plays. They are plays that move from the most shocking or heart-rending inward and personal experience (complex interpersonal betrayals, erotic enmities, and jealousies, parental-filial conflicts and so on) outward and upward to those etheric affirmations with which the plays end: "harps in the air"; "towards the peaks. Towards the stars. And towards the great silence"; and towards "the peak of Promise."

Giving an account of Hegel's bewilderingly rich text is far more difficult at this stage than previously, for the expression of metaphysical universals ecstatically apprehended and experienced obviously defies sober analysis and explanation and many Hegel commentators, philosophically far better skilled than the present writer, throw up their hands in despair in trying to understand this section. Here, at least, Hegel's procedure reminds us of that "bacchanalian revel in which no member is not drunken" which Hegel oddly described his dialectical development of consciousness to be. Practicing a form of mythopoeic, religious, and philosophic counterpoint, Hegel, like a medium at a sublime séance, actually mimes (re-enacts) the visionary experience of the major spiritual traditions of the Western consciousness: an astonishingly bold philosophico-dramatic performance which, however, must leave most of even the devoted coterie of readers greatly in the dark. But this, at least, will remind many readers (almost as small and devoted a coterie!) of the similar situation in Ibsen's last plays, of our feeling certain that there is a method and rationality behind the seeming madness of rich detail and suggestion, and even evidence of a distinct progression within the whole group of four plays; but, nevertheless, though we may be moved by this art of archetypal recollection more than we consciously are aware, we cannot easily enter into the worlds of these plays. Are they, for this reason, failures? No, for Ibsen has every right to pursue his own visionary meanings and to create artistic unities expressing his highest insights and to expect us to liberate ourselves from our spiritual sleep and to comprehend his art. It is not by debasing the visionary meanings to our world that his art best will serve us, but by holding out before us the possibility of our difficult but free development to its level of vision. And Ibsen, with as visionary an imagination as William Blake, has, in fact (as Blake did not) given us a basis of familiar everyday realism from which to begin our journey upwards.

Ibsen himself, in his old age, was preparing to enter "the great silence" and it is more than likely that his imagination found more truth and reality in the old religious myths and conceptions than in the busy immediate events surrounding him in his world. Even the most bizarre of the old spiritual fables or practices were concerned with ultimate issues: with the meaning of life and the extension of the human spirit shaping a spiritual cosmos from only the most universal perceptions. At such a point in his life, his dramatic action of returning to and reliving the old universal concepts of the human mind must have seemed more relevant than ever.

The last plays are almost immobilized by the sheer weight of mythic recollection they must carry, for they are depicting states of consciousness rather than crises of action. In my analysis of *The Master Builder* later in the book I offer an account of the great complexity of the spiritual substance of one play and of the manner in which Ibsen's method and subject matter expand (like the expansion of light at the sunrise) in order to embrace the new perspectives of this phase of consciousness.

At the close of the second group, consciousness had *contracted* into a scene of the greatest possible confinement: the Tesman drawing room, curtained off from the outside world with Hedda retreating from this into an even further confinement. Hedda, lacking the courage and free will to break free of this confinement, possessed at least the courage not to accept life on such terms, and her "beautiful" death (shooting herself in the temple) at least set up a provocative challenge to the mediocrity into which the spirit had been trapped. Her chosen death within the mediocre "best of all possible worlds" is not unlike those strange events about which one reads in the newspapers occurring in modern suburbia: a strange murder or suicide that at least briefly disturbs the usually placid round of supermarket shopping with the faintly uneasy suspicion that perhaps some vital center *is* missing from our lives and that maybe our acceptance of life at such a level is more horrendous than the scandalous event we are reading about.

The Master Builder begins in a scene and condition of intolerable confinement more oppressive, even, than that of *Hedda Gabler*, but from the windowless work room and its complexly baffled and frustrated spiritual life, the play gradually enlarges, act by act, to the vistas of sky and sunset of the last act. This movement from confinement to greater spatial freedom is the movement of the whole group which gradually recovers the landscapes of *Brand* and *Peer Gynt*: a spatial recovery paralleling the recovery of the great temporal perspectives of *Emperor and Galilean*. In other words, the human consciousness in these plays extends its visionary dimensions in time and space as far as is poetically conceivable: the apotheosized spirit searches for a cosmos adequate to its demands. Obviously, this interpretation contradicts the usual ones which see these last plays as private, interior, and secretive, but the evidence of the scene directions alone is clearly on our side.

The spiritual reintegration of man within his cosmos,[61] then, is both temporal and spatial: a reintegration of man with his total history (the history of the world) and with the laws, forces, and Spirit of the external universe. This *simultaneous* extension in time and space, of the human spirit moving through its own total history and through the rhythm of the cosmos, makes up the difficult texture of Ibsen's last plays. They explore a definite physical landscape with its seasons of the year and times of day and night and this exploration is at the same time a gradual *ascent*, the stages of this ascent following the gradual progress of consciousness through its mastery of its total past and its arrival at the level of total spiritual maturity and self-knowledge. This ascent is finally to a height at which human life cannot be sustained, as with the Ice Church in *Brand*, and in this last group one character will be swept out to the depths of the sea while Solness, Borkman, Rubek, and Irene all die as they ascend, reaching for the heights.

These last four plays, then, move gradually upwards and through a space-time of four seasons, through a Night to a Dawn. The sequence of last-act endings is Evening; Late Evening; Night; Dawn *before* the sunrise—a sequence that is not likely to be accidental. The following diagram might enable us to see the progression both in vertical Space and, temporally, through Space-time:

Mountain Peak

*When We Dead
Awaken*

Wooded Hill

*John Gabriel
Borkman*

Garden Hillock

Little Eyolf

Tower

*The Master
Builder*

(Autumn)   (Early Summer)   (Winter)   (Summer)

Last Act   DAWN BEFORE
Endings: EVENING   LATE EVENING   NIGHT   THE SUNRISE

Because the huge extensions of consciousness through Space and historical time are rendered in terms of the life histories of particular dramatic characters whose vivid actuality commands our engrossed attention, they generally are overlooked. These individual life histories, however, if we carefully follow Ibsen's Ariadne's thread of symbolism through the maze of particular details, will lead us to the *universal* human realities they embody and from which they originate. For particular individual consciousnesses are only aspects of Consciousness. Myth and literature have presented the essence of universals of human existence in terms of Autumn, Spring, Winter, and Summer archetypes and these are patterns to which human consciousness continually will return consciously and unconsciously, investing local human experience with archetypal significance.

The entry into the *Phenomenology* of this archetypal or religious level of consciousness is a "height" of Consciousness not unlike the mountain summit from which Rubek promised to show both Maia and Irene "all the power and the glory of the world," i.e., the entire realm of human secular (power) and spiritual (glory) achievement.[62] For it is from this religious level, Hegel claims, that the entirety of reality— all that preceded it in the long dialectical journey of consciousness—now can be seen and comprehended in its wholeness.

The parallels between Hegel's strange text and Ibsen's last four plays begin with the opening sequence of this journey of the religious consciousness:

"God as Light"	*The Master Builder*
"Plants and animals as objects of religious consciousness" (pantheism)	*Little Eyolf*
"The artificer" (minerals)	*John Gabriel Borkman*
"The artificer" (statue)	*When We Dead Awaken*

This, however, is only a very short step along the dialectical path that the religious consciousness takes and, after providing the brief sketches of these origins of Western Religion above, Hegel proceeds to amplify his account of the religious consciousness by drawing upon an enormous range of mythic and religious sources. These additional details continually bring to mind details in Ibsen's four plays, but it no longer is possible to assign any one play to any phase in Hegel's argument. Thus, the sun and light details of the God as Light section reappear again and again in later passages in Hegel's text and seem to have direct bearing upon the imagery of *The Master Builder*, as I hope to demonstrate in my study of that play at the end of this book. This is true, too, of the other religious modes set out above so that, in fact, the entire section of the religious consciousness is relevant to each play. One *might* describe Hegel's procedure in this grand finale to his dialectic (a procedure which has baffled more than just the present writer) that the four religious modes, Light, Pantheism, Mineral Forms, and Art (the Statue) are the four basic themes which are contrapuntally developed throughout the succeeding passages so that continually we find them reappearing, then disappearing, to reappear again. The whole movement climaxes in the arrival of the "Revealed Religion" (Christianity) from whence Consciousness intrepidly proceeds to Philosophy (and Hegel's philosophy, at that!). If all this was not complicated enough, it is also obvious that Ibsen is using this analysis of the religious consciousness in a very independent way, bringing in whole traditions of myth ignored by Hegel. We *can* say that Ibsen follows Hegel in seeing the religious consciousness as the highest stage of Spirit's long odyssey, that he *does* accept Hegel's initial outline of the origins of the Western religious consciousness, that he *does* use details from the later development of Hegel's argument; but after establishing this, we have to see Ibsen independent of and perhaps in disagreement with Hegel's conclusions—as we would expect from the author of *Emperor and Galilean*.

The first phase in Hegel's analysis is the Iranian religion of the sun and of light, and the first play of the last group in Ibsen's Cycle is *Bygmester SOLness* whose hero, SOLness, is named after the Sun; he once climbed a tower at Lysanger ("lys" is light) and once again will climb a tower in the evening of the autumnal equinox, falling against a sun-streaked sky. The text of the play is filled with visual and verbal sun, light, dawning-day and sunset images. The immediately succeeding phase in Hegel's text is that of pantheism, in which plants and animals in the cosmos are invested with spiritual power and the play immediately succeeding *The Master Builder* is *Little Eyolf*, the details of which are filled with plant and animal imagery: Rita's gold and green forests, the water lilies from the fjord where Eyolf drowned, the plants and trees of every scene, the Rat Wife, her dog and the rats, and the strangely responsive cosmos of this play. John Gabriel Borkman is a miner's son who dreams of freeing the imprisoned mineral spirits of the earth and who dies uttering a vivid prose-hymn to these spirits that he worships and loves. Religion in abstract mineral form is the next phase of Hegel's argument. Finally, as *this* phase merges into that of the Statue leading to "Religion in the Form of Art," so Ibsen's next and final play is *When We Dead Awaken,* whose hero is a sculptor whose major work, the statue of Irene named "Resurrection Day," is the central metaphor in the play.

The process of this development of the religious consciousness from the impalpable Religion of Light through that of plants and animals, then of man working upon minerals, and, finally, giving to a statue an image of divinity as a human figure, is not as arbitrary as it at first seems; obviously, Hegel here is describing the gradual *concretization and anthropomorphization* of the religious consciousness—from nebulous light, to living things, to abstract art works and, finally to the human form. Nevertheless, Hegel's procedure in this last phase of the *Phenomenology* is probably the most questionable of the entire development and it would entail no great contradiction on Ibsen's part to have made use of Hegel's argument up till now with a good measure of fidelity to its argument (which, after all, *did* have direct, if not always acknowledged, historical backing) but to have felt free to depart from Hegel's strict argument when it offers judgments less grounded in actual history.

In this last section of his *Phenomenology* Hegel is at his most vulnerable and many commentators who have followed him to this point have seriously questioned the manner of his proceeding beyond that point. Much of this is not Hegel's fault; he is permitting himself judgments upon a very wide range of religious and spiritual phenomena of which little was known until after his death when scholarship, particularly in Germany, began investigating far more deeply the nature of the Oriental and pagan religions. And one major spiritual tradition, which Hegel so oddly neglected to treat, was to emerge powerfully as a cultural force in later years: that of the Germanic/ Scandinavian tradition of myths and cults for which Hegel felt little sympathy.

Ibsen's procedure in the last plays, nevertheless, closely resembles Hegel's in the main thing: the action of a huge recollection of the entire spiritual inheritance of Western man as expressed through a form of consciousness responsive to a high degree to the religious, mystical, sublime, and profound areas of the human consciousness, utterly transfiguring the nature of reality hitherto depicted. What differences there are between the two texts most likely derive from a final difference of judgment on the course of human history (a difference we would expect when recollecting the non-Hegelian conclusion of the Hegelian *Emperor and Galilean*) but to speculate on this strikes the present writer as (at present) unprofitable, for our main interest is in Ibsen as an artist. We are interested in the nature of Ibsen's subject matter only insofar as it enables us to see the shaping of this subject matter in terms of dramatic art.

However, a confrontation with the *total* intention of a late Ibsen play cannot be evaded and I have attempted to fathom such a total intention in the lengthy analysis of *The Master Builder*. For the remaining three plays in this group I can do no more at present than indicate the broad nature of their spiritual dialectic in order to give an idea of the "atmosphere" of this last group. This account in no way claims to be dealing with the entire intention of the plays and it deliberately leaves out of account the complex human stories in order to focus attention upon the salient metaphors and images.

Little Eyolf, we suggested, creates a "pantheistic" world that emerged out of the Sun and Light imagery of the preceding play. (We are talking, here, about *predominant* themes and images; for obviously one can point to plants in *The Master Builder*, especially in the last act, and to the presence of sun and light in *Little Eyolf*. Just as in Shakespeare, each play has a predominant imagery as well as, of course, details it shares in common with other plays.) The pantheistic phase is the "religion of Perception" and takes the form of an at first gentle, innocent flower and plant religion of "the selfless idea of the self" and of "the quiescence and impotence of contemplative individuality."[63] This gentle and contemplative consciousness, however, is forced to give way to "the seriousness of struggling warring life, to the guilt of animal religions" and of "the destructive activity of separate self-existence,"[64] the recognition, by consciousness, of a cosmos of conflict and fighting and of murderous forces, both outside and within the human spirit. Similarly, I think, the "innocent" world of Allmers's and Asta's childhood past, their non-sexual (non-animalic) relationship, the plant and flower aspect of Rita's world with its gold and green forests and, also, the contemplative and withdrawn life of Alfred Allmers (his preoccupation with his book) all are violently disrupted by the intrusion of struggling, warring, and conflicting egos, of sexual jealousy and the loss of innocence in the relationship of Allmers and Asta. This whole new development to a more violent mode of consciousness finds its central symbol in the startling intrusion of a folk figure associated with animals and with the death of animals: the Rat Wife who herself hints that she has murdered her lover. Guilt, too, has intruded into this world: guilt for the crippling of Eyolf during an hour of sexual pleasure, and Eyolf will be drowned while his parents are egotistically quarreling again over guilt and passion. Eyolf himself, the gentle crippled boy in a *military* uniform, seems to be an emblem of the contradiction of this form of consciousness, and his fate of being drowned and swept out to sea by the "undertow" suggests that, unable to advance within the developing harsh realities of the warring animalic world, he returns to the origins of the spirit.

Hegel goes on to observe of this phase of religious consciousness (the pantheistic): "the animation of this spiritual kingdom has death in the heart of it," and that the spiritual development now "becomes a hostile process, in which the hatred stirred up by independent self-existence rages and consumes." Death is in the *heart* of the world of *Little Eyolf* as in no other play. Allmers says that he encountered Death as a traveling companion on his mountain tour; the Rat Wife is a conscious agent of animal and human death and Death intrudes into this play, early on, as a fact of consciousness to which the individuals must reconcile themselves. In a somewhat portentous phrase Allmers describes this pantheistic process of continually dying and renascent life as "the law of change"—the pantheistic philosophy of Libanius in *Emperor and Galilean* where, he tells Julian, "godhead" is "The uncreated in the changing," "Reunion with the primal source," and "Reunion as of the raindrop with the ocean, as of the rotting leaf with the earth that nourished it." And Libanius then departs, by boat, across the ocean. The sea death of little Eyolf is just such a reunion with the primal source and so is the other, stranger "death" of the fictional, idealized Eyolf which, we hear, Asta impersonated for Allmers in childhood, even dressing in boy's clothes for the part. The seeming sister, impersonating the role of brother, only to disclose that she is not a sister after all is the very essence of fluidity and change so that this disclosure is itself a form of death. (Allmers had claimed that the relation of brother and sister was the one thing that did not suffer from the law of change.)

In a play whose religious consciousness is that of *Perception*, it is noteworthy that there is a great emphasis upon *eyes*: animal, human, supernatural, and cosmic. The trinity of Allmers-Asta-Eyolf, from which Rita feels shut out, are all described in terms of their eyes (unlike Rita and Borgheim). Allmers is "mild eyed"; Asta has "deep serious eyes"; Eyolf, "attractive, intelligent eyes." This "eye detail" (noted by J. C. Kerans) undergoes further important variations. The Rat Wife has "deep, piercing eyes" and the "expression" of her dog, Mopseman, produces a fascinated, staring response from Eyolf. There is reference to the "evil eye," to the staring eyes of Eyolf and the bottom of the fjord; the lights like eyes of the steamer bearing away Borgheim and Asta, the likening of the stars to eyes at the end of the play and, finally, there probably is an eye reference in the very title of the play for there is a close assonance between the Norwegian for "eye' (*øye*) and Eyolf.

The Rat Wife herself, a dramatic presence as startling as that of the Stranger in Ibsen's other sea play, *The Lady from the Sea,* seems a brilliant dramatic equivalent of one of the most notable forms the pantheistic spirit, in Hegel's text, takes on:

> The actual self-consciousness at work in this dispersed and disintegrated spirit, takes the form of a multitude of individualized folk spirits who fight and hate each other to the death, and consciously accept certain specific forms of animals as their essential being and nature; for they are nothing else than spirits of animals, or animal lives separate and cut off from one another, and with no universality consciously present in them.[65]

The Rat Wife, who claims to have killed her lover, whose intrusion into the Allmers home impels it to fierce conflict; who identifies with the rats and identifies Eyolf with them); and who is a personification of the animal violence and death in the heart of the world of the play is, as much as is possible within the terms of modern realism, the embodiment of Hegel's folk figure. In the early drafts of the play the Rat Wife's name, "Varg"—a Germanic form of "wolf"—better suggests this taking on of the form of a ferocious animal: in northern folklore the Devil came to call for souls in the form of a wolf, often accompanied by a black dog like the Rat Wife's black dog.[66]

The reader should not be dismayed that the play's beautiful imagery of plants, forests, mountains, sea, water lilies, stars, animal forms, and so on, and the whole pantheistic atmosphere of this strange and lovely play, is rooted in serious rational and philosophical intentions, for the rational intention does not destroy but amplifies the imagery, controls it with a higher purpose than mere evocativeness. The Rat Wife, that emblem of animal violence and death in the heart of the Allmers world, is an effectively startling presence in a naturalistic play as well as a richly symbolic figure. Her "deep piercing eyes," "old-fashioned flowered dress" covered by "a black hood and cloak," and the red umbrella she carries create, for the viewer, an immediate suggestion of a figure from a folktale, yet at the same time she is not an impossible inhabitant of Ibsen's Norway. Her piercing eyes, black hood and cloak, and her action of "luring" animals and humans into the sea, suggest Death; but the flowered dress, and her odd sympathy with the animals, suggests, also, Life: the duality inherent in pantheism.

Christian mythological details also seem to be worked into the play. In the plant and flower "Eden" of Rita's estate, little Eyolf fell and was crippled during one "entrancingly beautiful hour" of sexual pleasure, as if, from *this* mythological tradition, humanity must permanently be crippled; this later leads to the terrible quarrel of the guilty pair in the Garden (Act II); the strange detail of the incarnation of the ideal Eyolf by Asta (as if prophesying for the messianic event which, however, was incapable of actual incarnation?); the crucifixion detail of Eyolf's death and the cross-like crutch that continues to float in the imagination; the resurrection motive in the Easter-like (the play is set in *early* summer) water lilies "that stretch up from deep down at the bottom" of the fjord where Eyolf was drowned; and the final resolve of the "earthbound" Allmers and Rita to gaze up at the sky for the "big" (ideal) and little Eyolf—"up to the peaks and the stars." Rita's words "the peace of the sabbath will rest upon us from time to time," remind us of the pentecostal descent of the spirit. (The "sabbath" [Shabuoth] and the pentecost occur at the same time.) The Easter suggestions of the play help to link Eyolf's death to the Christian sacrifice and it is probably for this reason that the play in many respects calls to mind *The Wild Duck*. It may be, as interpreters have suggested, that the ending of the play is ironic (Ibsen himself expressed strong doubts as to whether Alfred and Rita would be able to keep to their resolution of serving fallen humanity), and this, I think, expresses Ibsen's very non-Hegelian reservations as to the claims of Christianity, but this should not be overemphasized. Alfred and Rita renounce "life" in terms of the flesh and its pleasures, so that the future does not seem to lie with them so much as with Borgheim the "road builder" (an obvious emblem of one who strikes out new paths for humanity to follow, and *also* an anticipation of the "minerals" of the next play) and with Asta who brings with her the death of the ideal Eyolf in her black bag, as the Rat Wife brought the death of the actual Eyolf in *her* black bag.[67]

While the sacrificial action of *Little Eyolf* and its consequences as guilt and atonement seem predominantly Christian, we also can detect other spiritual forces within the story. Pantheistic and Greek details seem to inhere in the sensuous Rita, the Athene-like Asta, the "military" aspect of Eyolf's uniform, the Demeter quality of the Rat Wife and her flowered dress and the whole strangely numinous cosmos of this play. All the traditional four elements of the cosmos seem actively to be involved in the human drama (a perfect illustration of Hegel's insistence that at the highest level of mind consciousness is extended *into* the cosmos). The earth with its gold and green forests, its plants and trees of every scene, to which Allmers and Rita are "bound"; the water, with its undertow that takes the child, and which yet sends up the lilies that shoot up from the depths; the air, that carries the cries of the children up to the house, and especially the terrible cry, "the crutch is floating" (*krykken flyter*); and, beyond the peaks of the earth, the fires of the stars that look down like eyes upon Allmers and Rita. The play ends, in fact, invoking the "spirits" of this cosmos, as if the human elements of both little and big Eyolf have melted into it. Little of this superbly rich detail is to be found in the Hegelian source; the source only alerts us to the full extent of Ibsen's artistic triumph.

The transition from the gentle plant and flower world of *Little Eyolf*, torn apart by passionate confiict, a drama of spring and its passions, to the winter world of *John Gabriel Borkman*, where the vital passions are all of the past and the human and natural worlds are imprisoned by the cold, is a masterful stroke of contrast on Ibsen's part and alerts us to the imaginative audacity of his poetry. *John Gabriel Borkman* is Ibsen's most northern play as its constant emphasis on winter, snow, and cold suggest, and if there *is* such a thing as a world soul this is the drama of its polar regions. The main area of conflict in the play, Mrs. Borkman's drawing room, reveals, through its windows and glass door, an outer world of driving snow, and throughout the finely "cold" first act we stare beyond the human drama being acted out in this flimsy human structure to the inhospitable and deathly universe surrounding it. Filled with echoes of Germanic folklore, especially, I think, the Nibelung myth of the theft of gold and the betrayal of love, this is a metallic play. It is the metallic sound of sleigh bells that opens the play, bringing a brief spasm of life to the Borkman home and this same sound of bells signals the escape of Erhart and his companions south converting the metallic death forces of Borkman into the life force of Mrs. Wilton.

This is perhaps the strangest of Ibsen's realistic plays as it is also one of his most "classical" in structure. It is a world (that of the Borkmans) in which the life impulses have been so long repressed that the characters actually have created "norms" out of the condition of insanity so that, for instance, Gunnhild Borkman is "astonished" at Ella's suggestion that in the eight long years since Borkman's release from prison and confinement in the house the husband and wife should have even *once* laid eyes on each other, and Gunnhild is equally helpless in comprehending that her son, rather than follow her manic scheme of rehabilitating the name of Borkman, should be capable of such simple impulses as love for Fanny Wilton.

The drama of the miner's son who dreamed of releasing the spirits of the earth's imprisoned minerals corresponds unmistakably, if not exactly, to the phase of consciousness, succeeding that of pantheism, in which the human spirit worships mineral forms that have not, as yet, received *human* attributes. In its original expression of this phase, consciousness sacrificed human life and labor to monstrous monuments of *pride*: pyramids, obelisks, etc. Such abstractions in mineral form "only receive spirit into them as an alien, departed spirit, one that has forsaken its living suffusion and permeation with reality [pantheism?] and, being itself dead, enters into these lifeless crystals; or they take up an external relation to spirit as something which is itself there externally and not as spirit."

Ella Rentheim, whose capacity for love was sacrificed to Borkman's pride, insists that his metal kingdom is deathly, that it sends "a freezing breath" into the human world. At the end of the play an ice-cold metal hand clutches Borkman's heart and the miner's son dies uttering a hymn to the metallic spirits he worshiped, for their *proud* attributes:

> I seem to touch them, the prisoned millions; I can see the veins of metal stretch out their winding, branching, luring arms to me. I saw them before my eyes like living shapes, that night when I stood in the strong room with the candle in my hand.[68] You begged to be liberated, and I tried to free you. But my strength failed me; and the treasures sank back into the deep again. (*With outstretched hands*) But I will whisper it to you in the stillness of the night; I love you, as you lie there spellbound[69] in the deeps and the darkness! I love you, unborn treasures, yearning for the light! I love you with all your shining trail of power and glory! I love you, love you, love you.[70]

The displacement of spiritual values, "power and glory" (*makt og ære*), onto metallic forms is, as G. Wilson Knight has observed of this play, the very expression of the deepest spirit of modern industrial capitalism, for Borkman dreamed of utterly transforming the world by this metallic power so that fleets of ships would carry its treasures round the world. The shining treasures in the darkness are also powerful details of northern mythology[71] and, in Wagner's treatment of the

Nibelung myth, are even the cause of the downfall of the Germanic gods (that is, of the northern world view itself). Like Wagner's Wotan, Borkman has forfeited love for metallic wealth and power which, again like Wotan, he attempted to gain by fraud. Wotan (Odin) often took the guise, in northern myth and legend, of the huntsman or Wild Hunter, and Grimm gives many instances of this hunter identity. In these legends there is a frequent and notable imagery of the forest, the chase, of Wotan appearing in hunter's guise to men of the north after his disgrace and long ostracism by the Church. Of all the identities later assumed by Wotan/Odin, this of the hunter is the most vivid that Grimm records and is the one that would remain in the mind of the poet resurrecting this myth. The figure is given complete resurrection, I think, in the figure of Ulfheim in *When We Dead Awaken*, but there seems a strong anticipation of it in Act II of *John Gabriel Borkman* for in this act, which is placed in Borkman's own exiled realm of the upper gallery, we hear this "sick wolf" and watch his movements against the background of old woven tapestries "representing hunting scenes, shepherds and shepherdesses, all in dim faded colors." It is hard to see what other reason Ibsen could have had in mind, with this odd specification, than that of drawing upon this hunter identity and its "faded" currency in the modern world, and it is precisely this union of the northern legendary details with the metallic and modern details that is, mythopoeically, so compelling. The imprisoned spirits of the metals that lure Borkman to his crime are similar, not only to the Nibelung gold, but also to the powers of the northern underworld, the elves and dwarfs, created by the gods as skilled metal workers and craftsmen whom both Wotan and his rival, Albericht, seek to control in the *Ring* cycle.

The many other mythic details which I believe to be present in the play require a separate study. The reader will remember the reference to the medieval dance of death, and Mrs. Wilton's odd little exchange with Erhart where she lightheartedly casts a spell on him: a mere pleasantry, perhaps, but it results in Erhart reacting in exactly the way Mrs. Wilton predicts he, under her spell, will react. The two rival women, Gunnhild and Ella, resemble Ibsen's perennial female duality of Furia-Aurelia, Hjørdis-Dagny, Hedda-Thea, Rita-Asta: a duality that itself derives from northern saga. In Ibsen's reworking of this source for his realistic dramas, the two women obviously stand for alternative forces influencing the hero: pagan versus Christian in *Hedda Gabler* and in *The Vikings at Helgeland,* and one senses some such archetypal identity behind Gunnhild and Ella, giving their quarrel its fierce, overlife-size, universal quality. Their old quarrel, resumed immediately they meet, seems the last steps of a dance of death they have been performing for centuries, understanding its complex and bitter choreography by heart. Erhart's escape from this deathly dialectic will seem all the more sympathetic and convincing, for all its tentative nature, if a production of the play can suggest the spiritual sterility of this ancient quarrel where the moves, though passionate, have a mechanical or even somnambulist (nightmarish) quality. The contrast, then, between the life-craving Erhart who, so far, has been denied knowledge of what is implied in "life" and is discovering it, in Fanny Wilton, for the first time, and the discredited dialectics of a way of life that has lost its justification for survival, will be poignantly relevant to the present as well as faithful to the main thrust of the play. The play needs interpretation along the lines of a spiritual crisis if its puzzles are to be solved, though I would agree that the main thing is not the solving of puzzles but the adequate appreciation of Ibsen's superbly multi-layered, multi-textured dramatic metaphors. Even if we are not completely sure of the full meanings behind the details we can, as with Shakespeare's late plays, appreciate the fine complexity and density of this art.

This is nowhere more true than of the "Epilogue" to the whole Cycle, *When We Dead Awaken*, which, to adherents of common-sense realism is an unstageable perversity but, to the imaginative Ibsenite, like James Joyce, is, from its first speech on "hearing the silence," a source of the same kind of pleasure as one derives from the first, weird, atonal sound of a late Beethoven quartet: for we know we are in for a feast of "decadent," ugly, tortuous, and compellingly fascinating music. Its polyphony of *leitmotiv*, like that of *Götterdämmerung*, recollects the richest wealth of spiritual content for, in this last summing up before the silence, Ibsen is setting out most fully and explicitly the spiritual dialectic of the whole Cycle. Greek, northern, and Judeo-Christian themes and identities interfuse and separate in a series or network of bewildering parallels, antinomies, difficult chronologies and sequences, within an almost perfunctory plot. In fact, "plot" in this play is almost entirely internal: the action of casting up accounts, passing judgment on the self, moving toward liberation from the past. The play binds the whole Cycle together, in circular form, like *Finnegans Wake*, with the references to the "animal world" from which the whole Cycle emerged.

Consciousness, in the corresponding section of Hegel's text, moves from the abstractions of the previous phase to, first, a symbolic art of plants and animals in stone, then to shape half-animal, half-human forms, "ambiguous beings, a riddle to themselves, the simple inner with the multiform outer, the darkness of thought mated with the clearness of expression—these break out in a language that is darkly deep and difficult to understand."[72] This phase of consciousness, typical of symbolic art, precedes the triumphant humanism of Greek art, which, for Hegel, is *the* supreme development of art, a religion of the esthetic consciousness. Similarly, Rubek relates how he had created half-animal, half-human portrait busts, sculptural monstrosities whose meanings no one had fathomed, but that his *masterpiece*, the statue "Resurrection Day," depicts the perfect *human* body, the naked Irene who is awakening after emerging from the earth crust that is bursting with figures with dimly suggested animal faces.

The half-animal, half-human portraits, and the masterpiece have been gazed at and admired by the great public, making Rubek world famous, but this public, Rubek "growls," "knows nothing! Understands nothing!"

MAIA: Well, at any rate it can divine something—
RUBEK: Something that isn't there at all, yes. Something that was never in my mind. Ah, yes, that they can all go into ecstasies over! (*Growling to himself*) What is the good of working oneself to death for the mob and the masses—for "all the world."[73]

To see this as Ibsen's own discontent with his public fame is an attractive idea and, moreover, a very short cut into the play's possible meanings; but I believe Ibsen is too good a dramatic poet to muddy and confuse his objective artistic structure with such blatant confessional devices and so make it impossible for the theater audience to grant to Rubek total consistency as a dramatic character. It is better, I think, to see Rubek as the archetypal Artist and his feeling of discontent as that which is inevitable to this *role*. It is just the discontent which Hegel sees as inevitable to the artist of this phase of consciousness, the *sculptor* whose art lacks language. Hegel describes the sculptor as conscious of "an admiring multitude" honoring what it considers to be the spirit of the artist's works, but how the sculptor "knows how much more his act is than what they [the multitude] understand and say." And so the religious artist gives way to the Oracle, which can speak its meanings.

The half-animal, half-human portrait busts were, Rubek tells Maia, the "dear old domestic animals which men have distorted [*forkvalet*] in their own image and which have distorted men in return." This seems to suggest that the forms created by human consciousness—gods, myths, religions, systems—are created out of the (animal) passions and "distorted" into the images of men, but, once created, these images or forms take on independent life and distort the human consciousness in turn—as man *is* shaped by the historical world that man has shaped. The word *forkvalet* is difficult to translate. Archer uses "bedevilled" which is distracting. *Forkvalet* means to cripple, warp, or even make a mess of, bungle, as an artist might spoil his material. Not just the sculptor, then, but man himself is an artist (though a bungling one) whose material is his animal passions, shaped by his consciousness, creating the forms of his conscious life and, through his evolving spiritual history, being molded and warped by these forms: an idea that at least accords with what we know of Ibsen's thinking, however freely this might be adapting Hegel (it seems, in fact, a directly ironic rebuttal of Hegel's claim for the finally achieved realm of human reason).

Ulfheim is to compare his own activity—bear hunting and slaying—with Rubek's sculpture. The hunter represents the basic human struggle against the directly animalic world from the victory over which the *human* community will commence; and the human community itself will create forms of consciousness out of its animalic passions. The artist, from his primitive origins (as the cave-painters of the Magdalenian period) to the present-day reflective consciousness of Henrik Ibsen (that is, the universal, archetypal artist in whom all prior phases are present), is engaged in evolving a fully human world of controlled artistic forms (perhaps thus correcting the bungling work of mankind) by more successfully sublimating his animal passions, as Rubek sublimated his sexual passion for Irene. But this sublimation creates art at the expense of life; the artist creates an alternative and ideal world at the expense of losing the real world.

Like the sculptor, the hunter wrestles with difficult and intractable material; but Ulfheim's activity does not distort or warp the animal forms he engages with: he struggles with and kills them, but the animal realm remains unchanged. Like an animal predator, therefore, Ulfheim neither changes his world nor is profoundly changed by it. He lives at an animalic, pre-human (that is, pre-*historical*) level which refuses to embark upon the tortuous but human dialectic of consciousness to which the Artist is committed (hence the evolution of artistic forms) and which is outlined in Hegelian philosophy. As non-historical man, Ulfheim is free from the complex sickness of the modern consciousness, represented by Rubek's tortured conscience. Ulfheim and Rubek face each other, therefore, as the "brutal" and the "intellectual" hero. Ulfheim is not a fascistic character, for his "brutality" is the result of innocence of history, whereas fascism is a decadent longing for the abrogation of history, a *nostalgia* for a toughness that will drastically simplify *modern* complexities.

Ulfheim despises the sanatorium where *sick* humanity (mostly female) is gathered, and his particular target is the Inspector of the Baths, a Kafkaesque figure of benignant but authoritarian regulation, like the bureaucratic officials of an efficiently run but spiritually nonvital society. One might see in Ulfheim an anticipation of the primitive hero of much modern fiction: Knut Hamsun's Lieutenant Glahn; D. H. Lawrence's passional heroes who challenge the accumulated sickness of modern consciousness; the Hemingway heroes seeking a rapport with the lost natural world; or O'Neill's "hairy ape" or Emperor Jones. Indeed, the adulterous seduction of Maia by the landowner, Ulfheim, anticipates the similar knight-errantry-in-reverse of gamekeeper Mellors's rescue of love-starved Lady Chatterley! Ulfheim is able to be integrated with the natural forces of the earth simply because he has not embarked upon that complex humanization of his consciousness which now stands as a barrier between modern man and the natural world. If the play is, as the conventional accounts say, dramatizing the regret of the artist for a misspent life of art instead of being at one with "the inscrutable earth-life," this is a regret felt on behalf of the artist as a universal figure, not as a flimsy disguise for the situation of one particular artist— Henrik Ibsen!

In an ironic reversal of the Pygmalion myth in which, now, the living model has "died into" the sculptor's statue, Rubek and Irene are linked together through their relation to the statue "Resurrection Day": the relationship of artist, model, and achieved art work which synthesizes the artist's idea (the universal) and the model's partial embodiment of that idea which the art work will fully objectify. We see here that contrast between the universal realm which needs particular embodiment, and the particular realm, which needs universalizing significance, which we already have suggested as the basis of Ibsen's realism. The account of the masterpiece is somewhat complicated; it has a history of its own, independent of, but parallel to, the history of Rubek and Irene. It has gone through the stages of living model (Irene), artist's idea (Rubek), clay model (their "child"), and, finally, marble masterpiece, placed in a museum after the accretion of many new figures. This evolution of the progress of "Resurrection Day" can be set out as follows:

PARENT STAGE

(a) Absolute Idea ...... (b) Artist's Idea .... (c) Living Model

CHILD STAGE

(d) Clay model .... (e) Marble model .... (f) Museum piece

In the "parent stage" of the masterpiece the sculptor perceives in the living model (particular humanity) a universal meaning within the particular example, an "Idea" which the artist perceives in or projects upon the particular: and this Idea, in turn, derives from the artist's awareness of the ultimate source of universal ideas, the Absolute Idea or Absolute Reality, itself: the realm of universals, which "need" to be embodied in the realm of particulars. This is a non-Romantic idea of poetic insipration, to be sure; it does not indulge in the usual cant about the unfathomable mysteries of creativity but insists on the ultimate rationality of art: thus Rubek is far from being the conventional stage-artist of inspired irrationalities (like Shaw's Eugene Marchbanks) or of Svengali-like mysterious powers. He is eminently a Hegelian artist for whom the sublimities, abysses, and mysteries of life are all discoverable within a recognizable reality, within the experience of our consciousnesses within the known categories of time and space. Rubek, the artist, seems the mediating term (Spirit) between the Idea (striving to be embodied) and Nature (Irene) yearning to be lifted "up" to universal significance—hence Rubek's promise to take Irene to a height where she would see "all the power and all the glory of the world," the same height Solness promises he will build for Hilde Wangel. The artist is the mediating term between the realm of universals (essential life) and the realm of spiritually unawakened life, and from his synthesizing function emerges the art work ("Resurrection Day"). It is the artist's desire to give to the sensible (and sensory) world the life of the spirit: to make the world of the senses incandescent with the life of the spirit, in music, painting, sculpture, architecture, or poetry. But this allegiance to the Idea, to the life of the Spirit, runs the risk of betraying natural, instinctual life itself, and this seems to be the crime of which the sculptor, Rubek, is guilty. In the "child stage" of the masterpiece, from clay model (the form in which Irene knew it as her child) to the complex marble masterpiece with added figures, and finally to the museum piece stared at by the uncomprehending multitudes, we seem to be presented with a further and further betrayal of the natural and instinctual for the complex and manipulated. Yet the play is not a simple-minded indictment of art and of the intellect on behalf of primitivism: as always, with Ibsen, it is the dramatization of a complex condition of consciousness the main value of which is the grave high level of the argument.

The statue, after the separation of Rubek and Irene, has been debased from the high point of Rubek and Irene's meetings in his studio where he worked on the statue with "saint-like passion and such ardent joy" and in which they "met together every morning, as for an act of worship," to the ludicrous low point where the statue is a tourist bait in a a museum. Rubek describes his work on the statue as if it were sacramental, as if it *were* an act of worship in which the individual spirit is joined with the universal spirit. Irene's history of gradual debasement parallels that of the statue: a movement away from the intense reality of the creative moment in which the artist and the model joined in a sacramental act, to her later life history of disastrous marriages, performances at striptease shows, and so on. The statue had declined from the intense vision of the creative moment to the low intensity of the admired masterpiece, and Irene's life has been a decline from the intense moment of her rapturous *conception* of Rubek's vision, to the death-in-life of her incarceration from which she is only now beginning to awake. Irene now is a walking corpse, her arms crossed over her breast, her white figure closely followed by the black-clad Deaconess (an emblem, it seems, of the dead spirit followed by the Church).

In the guilt-ridden account that the play offers, it seems that the natural and instinctual, *and* the spiritual and visionary, qualities die in the art work which then remains as an ironic *monument* to the death of both, forgiving the death, and attempting to reconcile the human consciousness to this dual death. The art work that is to celebrate the tremendous liberation of Resurrection Day becomes the tomb marking its demise.[74] The statue was that of a young naked woman "awakening to light and glory," yet Irene, the living model of this statue, is to suffer a "self-murder" and a "slavery." Now, awakening from the somnambulism of the many years that followed the completion of "Resurrection Day," she bitterly accuses Rubek of being a "poet":

RUBEK (*annoyed*). Why do you keep calling me a poet?
IRENE (*with malign eyes*). Because there is something apologetic in the word, my friend. Something that suggests a forgiveness of sins—and spreads a cloak over all frailty.[75]

The poet or sculptor can forgive and acquit the unfreedom that his masterpiece *esthetically* indicted. The masterpiece reproached the world with the vision of an ideal spiritual freedom (Resurrection Day) but the very nature of the artist's commitment required that both artist and model be *actually* unfree: realized as "ideas" but not as free living beings. The whole Cycle, we saw, is a massive and complex subversion of repressive reality, a whole procession of individuals, on the stage, liberating themselves from contexts of unfreedom and untruth: a superb artistic achievement that would be impossible without an unfree world as its subject. The entire artistic endeavor, therefore, might well guiltily acknowledge its necessary "stake" in the unfree world and the esthetic achievement; the more consummately it renders its subject, even the more penetratingly it analyzes—and indicts—itself, the more it creates an artistic realm that compensates for the unattained *actual* freedom. The better the artist the more we feel the world well lost for his art! Rubek expresses this dilemma of the artist when he tells Irene that his situation as an artist is as painful as her situation as the model of an "episode":

> RUBEK. . . . let me tell you, too, how I have placed myself in the group. In front, beside a fountain—as it were here, sits a man weighed down with guilt, who cannot quite free himself from the earth-crust. I call him "Remorse for a Forfeited Life." He sits there and dips his fingers in the purling stream—to wash them clean—and he's gnawed and tortured by the thought that never, never will he succeed. Never in all eternity will he attain to freedom and the new life. He will remain for ever prisoned in his hell.
> IRENE (*hardly and coldly*). Poet![76]

In the very convoluted dialectics of Ibsen's late manner, even the artist's remorse over making life a "subject" itself becomes the artist's subject: "Remorse for a Forfeited Life"! Rubek and Irene seem trapped in a labyrinth of consciousness where every direction taken is a return upon itself. Irene, too, has forfeited "freedom and the new life." Recalling her first encounter with Rubek, she exclaims:

> But I was a human being—then! And I, too, had a life to live and a human destiny to fulfill. And all that, look you, I let slip—gave it all up in order to make myself your bondswoman. Oh, it was self-murder—a deadly sin against myself. (*Half whispering*) And that sin I can never expiate.[77]

It might be worthwhile attempting, despite the obvious risks, a paraphrase of the difficult argument as it applies to the question of art, the artistic consciousness, and the artistic subject, though we should not see this argument as comprising the whole of the play. Man, as artist or shaping consciousness, has conceived forms that mediate between universal reality and newly awakening life (Irene?). These universal forms, at first new and vital conceptions (as with the earliest myths at the dawn of human consciousness), have further been modified as poetic conceptions (and, perhaps, religious and philosophic conceptions) that more and more imprison, while offering to "uplift," potentially free consciousness. The very art that wishes to serve the cause of freedom must use forms and conceptions that are the expressions of unfreedom so that behind these forms the unliberated spirit still reproaches the artist whose subject is unfreedom. Even if the artist takes the reproach into his art it becomes but another layer of his art! The history of the human spirit, after all, *is* of its being trapped, in culture after culture, in one particular shape (*gestalt*) of thought and belief fashioned by human consciousness and, in turn, fashioning it, creating that nightmare of history from which Stephen Daedalus wished to awake. With anything less than the whole of consciousness (which both Ibsen and Joyce attempted to bring into their art) one is still trapped within one or more of its forms; but the comprehension of the whole is the self-analytical labor of a lifetime, that unceasing judgment day upon the soul which Ibsen saw as the poet's task. The only escape from this dilemma of the fully *human* consciousness seems to be that of Ulfheim, of refusing the dialectic of the human consciousness altogether (in *his* house there are no works of art) and remaining at the animalic level. But even of Ulfheim this is not strictly true, for by the very fact that he can converse in human language, he has at least embarked upon the dialectical journey, though he may be at the beginning of this journey as Rubek is at the end. For the guilt and suffering of Rubek and Irene is not an *indictment* of what they represent, but an analysis of a seemingly inescapable condition.

When We Dead Awaken draws a sharp contrast between an enclosed, interior, isolated dialectic of spirit structured upon sacrifice, guilt, and suffering, finally attempting an ascent to an ultimate affirmation and an objective world of nature, of the cosmos surrounding this interior drama and supplying, even, an objective correlative for its spiritual gestures in terms of a metaphoric landscape of season, time of day, vertical geography, and the final "gesture" of the avalanche. The two rhythms are separate but complementary, as in *Brand*, and while Rubek's and Irene's bid for ultimate aspiration seems to be rejected by the cosmos, Ulfheim and Maia can be said at least tentatively to reintegrate themselves with the natural and cosmic rhythm: as if, perhaps, the "emperor" and "Galilean" halves of man's spiritual nature still resisted integration and here decisively separated.

That the realm of art (or religion or philosophy) is a realm of dead forms, mere ghosts of the living spirit (ironically recognized only at the end of the whole dialectic), is suggested in Maia's odd description of the realm to which, like Bluebeard, Rubek lured her:

He lured her to a cold, clammy cage, where as it seemed to her, there was neither sunlight nor fresh air, but only gilding and great petrified ghosts of people all round the walls.[78]

This recalls Hegel's description, at the end of the *Phenomenology*, of the finally comprehended consciousness or Reason, where all the phases of Spirit, unfolded in space and time, resemble "a slow procession and succession of spiritual shapes [*Geistern*], a gallery of pictures...."[79] It might seem a mordant irony that Ibsen seems to convert Hegel's triumphantly achieved realm of Reason into a Bluebeard's Castle into which life is lured and trapped, but this pessimistic vision really is not so alien to Hegel's text. And certainly, the whole "winding stairway of despair" upon which consciousness, in Hegel's account, must embark, is one before which the innocently awakened consciousness might well recoil.

We already have suggested that *When We Dead Awaken* represents an extremely complex concept, a tragedy of consciousness, embodied and animated as human drama and where, I think, the tension between the dramatic art and the concept that art is realizing is more acute than in any other play in the Cycle. We find ourselves confronted by a strange contrast between a *texture* of extraordinarily complex and allusive detail on the one hand, and, on the other, a dramatic *structure* of extreme simplicity. A couple comes to a place of convalescence, each finds another partner, and the couples separate. The movement is a straightforward act-by-act ascent and a straightforward temporal movement from morning, to late afternoon, to dawn before the sunrise. Act I is on the lowest (sea) level of the play's action and the setting is a baths populated by sickly inhabitants. In this act Rubek is at his most repellant and ugly, like Solness in the first act of *The Master Builder*. The scene is open-air, but presents the façade of an hotel; already we have moved from Ibsen's constant scenic metaphor in the Cycle—the home and the domestic setting in which the actions are enclosed and by which they are defined as by defining environments. The facade, in *When We Dead Awaken*, is that of an hotel, a *public* not domestic building, and it is juxtaposed against huge natural perspectives—that natural world that will totally take over the scenic realm of the play.

To grasp the radical departure in scenic metaphor, we need only recollect such a setting as that of *The Wild Duck*, where the entire consciousness of the play was enclosed within the small domestic setting and where the world of Nature was submerged and invisible, emerging only secretively through the realistic dialogue, or covertly re-created in the fantasy attic. In *When We Dead Awaken* the once submerged and covert world of Nature now has taken over, entirely, the foreground of the drama and it is the sickly interior world that is relegated to the background. Though we hear constantly of sickness and guilt in this first act we survey sweeping prospects of fjord and sea and distant islands.[80]

Act II takes place at a higher altitude, a "mountain health resort" with a background of treeless mountains, snow peaks, and an uninhabitable natural scene. The impression, appropriate to the themes of this act, is of reviving health, recovery, and a new vigorous life, and throughout this act *children*, in town and peasant clothes (one of the play's many dualisms), play, laugh, sing, and dance, surveyed by the artist, Rubek, who catches, every now and again in their spontaneous actions, moments of "harmony": "And it amuses me to sit and watch for these isolated moments—when they come." (This suggests, to me, the artist's

detection of universal moments behind the accidents of everyday particulars: the idea of Ibsen's "realism" that this book has propounded.) Act
III takes place on "a wild riven mountainside" with "sheer precipices,"
"peaks," and drifting mists—a scene not only pre-human but actively
hostile to human life.

Structural and textural details of the play take the form of an extremely
sharply drawn series of dualisms: the division between body and soul,
flesh and spirit, life and art, Dionysos and Apollo, paganism and Christianity, health and sickness, freedom and imprisonment, death and life,
and so on. Ulfheim, the animalic male, is the counterpart of the intellectual Rubek. Maia and Irene, so opposite, have curiously parallel life
histories, for each was promised the mountain-summit vision by Rubek,
each was imprisoned in a tomb-like cage, each was raised up from
nothing, and each will be awakened. Ulfheim recalls being deserted by
a young woman, as Rubek will be deserted by Maia. Ulfheim's enemy,
the Inspector of the Baths, attends the physical ills of his patients, as
the Deaconess (whom Ulfheim also abhors) attends the spiritual ills
of Irene. Even the long train journey through the night, recollected by
Rubek and Maia, was punctuated, at all the station stops, by the shadowy
appearance of *two* men (one with a lantern). This dualism is a persistent
motif throughout the play.

The three major spiritual traditions we have insisted make up the substance of the Cycle, the Hellenic, the Judeo-Christian, and the Germanic, are more openly presented in the Epilogue. The bear hunter,
Ulfheim, for instance, is variously identified as Faun, Devil, and Huntsman; that is, in each spiritual tradition, he is Dionysian man, the animalic,
in contrast to his spiritual alter ego, the Apollonian artist-man, Rubek,
and this identification of Ulfheim with the world, flesh, and devil can
account for his particular abhorrence of the black-clad Deaconess. Maia,
fascinated with Ulfheim, imagines him with horns and goat legs, and it
is she who calls him a "faun." Ulfheim likens himself to the devil, and
jeers at the Inspector for fleeing from him as from the devil.[81] This
Graeco-Roman faun and Christian devil identity is supplemented by the
northern huntsman identity with which, we have seen, Odin was identified as another type of the devil. Ulfheim, whose name means "wolf-
home," is accompanied by hounds and very obviously is associated with
the natural world.

Like Ulfheim, Maia patently represents life-and-nature values. Her
name, apart from suggesting May or Springtime—renewing life—is that
of the goddess Maia (mother of Hermes) who was closely related to
Fauna (or Bona Dea) in the orgiastic Lupercalian festivals which "symbolized the earth's spring fertility and was honoured in May."[82] The

orgiastic and animalic details of the rites of Faunus and Fauna-Maia were the ancient world's escape from the intellectual and spiritual dialectic of evolving consciousness: a regression and breakdown of order preceding the return and renewal of order, one of many such pagan rites which, Mircea Eliade has shown in *Cosmos and History,* was the "primitive's" way of preventing the nightmare of history from occurring.[83]

Rubek's artist-identity, like Ulfheim's animalic identity, synthesizes the three spiritual traditions. The sculptor and the "Statue" phase of consciousness exemplifies, for Hegel, the Hellenic religion of art, yet Rubek's masterpiece adopts the Christian title "Resurrection Day." The opposite of Ulfheim, Rubek renounced the claims of the flesh for the discipline of art, turning from "whatever is begotten, born and dies," to "the monuments of unageing intellect" of Yeats's *Sailing to Byzantium.* With Irene, Rubek recollects the Germanic Lohengrin myth (in a play which, we will see, recalls details of *Parsifal*), and in one odd passage he confesses that when he abandoned Irene, he wanted to return to the forest (associated, since Tacitus, with the northern peoples).

Irene, Maia's opposite, sacrificed her physical life for the spirit, though her identity is complicated, existing both as the ruined woman and the successful statue. She first appears onstage after we have heard of her strange appearance, at night, as the white-clad lady, as a walking corpse, her arms crossed over her breast (as for burial?). Her name, Irene, and her statue identity as the naked young woman, are Hellenic but, as the heroine of "Resurrection Day" and as followed by the Deaconess, she also is Christian. From the identity of the virginal young woman of "Resurrection Day" she has degenerated into a series of disastrous marriages and alliances, murderous relationships with men of many nations though, of course, on the strictly realistic level of this information, we must consider her narrative as, to a great extent, fantasy. After appearing in striptease shows, she became insane and was put into the care of the Deaconess. Paralleling the statue's removal to the dead museum and Maia's entrapment in the "cold clammy cage," Irene was "lowered into a grave vault" whose walls were padded "so that no one on earth above could hear the grave shrieks," but, she announces to Rubek on their first reunion, she is "beginning to rise from the dead." Of course, on the level of strict realism, this is merely Irene's extravagant way of saying she was shut up in a mental asylum and now is beginning to recover her sanity, but the imagery insists upon a larger meaning with such mythic overtones as Proserpina dragged, shrieking, into the ground, but who returns to earth in the spring.

It is true that such mythopoeic interpretation lands us in a number

of great difficulties, but I believe they are difficulties inherent in the
play and that they light up more rewarding possibilities than the practice
of discounting the imagery of this dialogue as just so much unfathomable—or irrelevant—extravagance. The northern and Germanic identity
of Irene also is prominent. In Jacob Grimm's *Teutonic Mythology*, one
of the most poignant and beautiful figures, quite as striking as the huntsman and his hounds, is that of the white-clad lady, a ghost from the
banished northern folklore who appears, bewailing her sorrows and
"craving deliverance, as Condwiramurs did of Parzival," and Grimm
comments, after citing a number of such legends of the white-clad lady:

> Now the prevailing thought in all this of *being banned* and longing for
> release I take to be just this, that the pagan deities are represented as still
> beautiful, rich, powerful, and benevolent, but as outcast and unblessed, and
> only in the hardest terms can they be released from the doom pronounced
> upon them. The folk-tale still betrays a fellow feeling for the white woman's
> grief at the attempted deliverance always interrupted and put off to some
> indefinitely distant date.[84]

The similarity of situation in a play recollecting the Lohengrin and
Parzival legends is striking. Irene is closely akin to Kundry in Wagner's
Parsifal and to Grimm's account of Condwiramurs. Like Kundry she is
both victim and betrayer, and like Kundry and Condwiramurs she craves
deliverance from her situation. Thomas Mann noted the similarity between *Parsifal* and *When We Dead Awaken*. Both open at a healing
place and both end with an ascent, though Ibsen's play lacks Wagner's
luxurious Christian consolations. These mythic patterns woven into the
play do not disqualify the play as a modern action; on the contrary,
because of them the play speaks more immediately to our own age than
if Ibsen had fashioned a tale entirely of his own age. The mythic substance of the play reminds us that we exist in a continuum of time, not
a series of discrete "ages," and that the vivid identities created by "past"
stages of our communal consciousness better express the enduring substance of that consciousness.

When We Dead Awaken ends "at dawn, before the sunrise," and the
last four plays, we saw, have brought us through a long, dark night of
the world soul, haunted by a multitude of ghosts, to the expectation,
only, of that Sunrise in which the ghosts of the Past, presumably, would
be dispelled. Thus the Cycle, as a whole, remains in the old order that
must pass away, as Ibsen declared in the speech at the Stockholm banquet. With something of a Mosaic pattern, Ibsen had descended from the
poetic and visionary heights of *Brand*, *Peer Gynt*, and *Emperor and
Galilean*, down into the land of the imprisoned spirit and, gradually
freeing the spirits from their imprisonment, had led the human mind

to regain the Pisgah heights of consciousness from which to envision the Promised Land: a parallel that Ibsen himself, so thoroughly steeped in the Bible, might not have rejected. Odd though this lifelong artistic endeavor must seem to the modern reader, it represents the kind of overweening sense of artistic vocation typical of the nineteenth century. It is, for example, obviously the action of Ibsen's Brand, and we cannot possibly fathom Ibsen's full intention if we close our eyes to this visionary and prophetic aspect of his art.

Appropriately, *When We Dead Awaken*, for all its action of ascent, is an ambiguous conclusion to the Cycle. It finally exteriorizes the long interior dialectic and indicates perspectives of a natural world which may or may not be a more adequate context for the liberated spirit. At the same time, the foreground dialogue of Rubek and Irene is the most secretive, interior, and convoluted that Ibsen has created, and the attempts of the protagonists to break free of it end only in death. This very Janus-faced play turns its gaze both inward and outward: back to the remotest past and forward to an uncharted future; into the depths of the imprisoned consciousness and outward and upward to the heights of the liberated spirit. It is filled with echoes of past myths, legends, literatures and arts, yet filled, also, with pregnant anticipations of major developments in twentieth-century writing.

Its opening image of humanity convalescing at a health resort, supervised by a bland controlling Inspector of the Baths, anticipates Thomas Mann's *The Magic Mountain*, T. S. Eliot's *The Waste Land*, or the spiritual malaise of Kafka's *The Trial* and *The Castle*, while the archetypal recollection at the same time keeps in the reader's mind layer after layer of past literature. The dualistic emphasis we noted is repeated in the dualisms of Samuel Beckett's dramatic structures while the dialectical method, so central to Ibsen's art, links him with the modern dialectical dramatists Shaw, Brecht, and Peter Weiss. The play depicts the human consciousness struggling within the labyrinth of its own making, yearning upwards to Galilean heights yet, at the same time, in Rubek and Irene's duologues, yearning also for "the love that belongs to the life of earth—the beautiful miraculous earth-life—the inscrutable earth-life,"[85] that regret for the non-fulfillment of *human* and earthly promise which the dying Julian expresses in *Emperor and Galilean*:

Beautiful garlanded youths . . . dancing girls . . . but so far away. Beautiful earth . . . beautiful life on earth . . .

so that, it seems, the dualism of *Emperor and Galilean* has not been overcome, a meaning we can see in the drastic disjunction of the separated couples at the end of the play, where the "earthly" Ulfheim

and Maia descend to live and the "spiritual" Rubek and Irene ascend
to die. The invocation of the "inscrutable earth-life" evokes the modern
celebration of the instinctual and passional against the intellectual and
spiritual, but in Ibsen the intellectual, with its great and tragic legacy
of consciousness, also is honored.

The demands the play makes upon the resources of the theater make
us feel that Ibsen might be happier with the cinema—a very Bergman-
esque cinema to be sure. No other play by Ibsen, with the exception of
Emperor and Galilean, is so rich in anticipations of the themes and
methods of contemporary literature and drama. Because the archetypal
action so thoroughly breaks through the careful form that Ibsen had
evolved and maintained throughout the Cycle, this "Epilogue" leaves
us uneasy, yet, I think, more profoundly challenged than before. It
emphatically is not tired or "decadent" work: on the contrary, it
presents us with the dramatist working at his most astonishing intensity,
concentration, and economy and with the greatest depth and width of
conceptual implication to which the foregoing account hardly has done
justice.

The dramatic method of the Cycle, and especially of the last four
plays, makes formidable demands upon the audience's capacity for complex meditation combined with a highly sophisticated and distinguished
theatrical sense on the lookout for the deep and delicate thing, not the
cheap great "effect." The human consciousness, summoning itself and its
entire content for a total recollection or judgment day, seems an intractable subject for drama, but Ibsen does astonishing things to overcome the seemingly undramatic nature of his subject matter.[86] The
last four plays carry an awesome burden of archetypal recollection, but
Ibsen contrives, to counter this, startlingly vigorous and memorable
actions. Solness's evening ascent and fall, little Eyolf's drowning, Borkman's abrupt emergence from his long incarceration, and the suicidal
mountaineering of Rubek and Irene integrate the complex intellectual
dialectic with a world of emphatically *physical* reality. Whatever their
total success, these last plays, employing so complex a contrapuntal
mythopoeic method, attempt in the theater an esthetic complexity,
subtlety, and adequacy as ambitious as that which Joyce was to claim
for the novel. The whole Cycle strains realistic form in the theater to
its limits, beyond which dramatic realism hardly can go so that it is
obvious that any major achievement in the theater, in good Hegelian
and dialectical terms, cannot return to the form that Ibsen has exhausted. Ibsen himself recognized this when, intrepidly contemplating
a new work to follow this "Epilogue" to the Cycle, he said it probably
would be "in another context; perhaps, too, in another form."

PART II

CHAPTER 4

Archetypal Repetition in Ghosts

It is strange how history repeats itself in different forms like variations on a musical theme.

Ibsen in a letter to John Grieg, 1866.

We are first of all, of course, struck by the title *Gengangere* (Ghosts), those who return to walk again, which immediately suggests the fearful, primitive, and occult. The feared return of the dead to plague the living is one of the most primitive and basic of all human fears, considered by many anthropologists to be the origin of religious practice and myth. Such a fear begot elaborate burial and memorial practices, even including the actual binding of the dead body before burial to prevent its returning from the grave.[1] It may seem a long way from this pre-historical nightmare to the sophisticated structure of Ibsen's family drama, but it is just this nightmare that is reexperienced by the modern consciousness in the famous climax to Act I when Helene Alving cries out:

Ghosts. Those two in the greenhouse have come back!

In fact, close analysis will show that the play's major action consists of a desperate but futile attempt (and by means of a memorial to the dead) to keep the dead buried in their graves. Though consciousness has advanced beyond physically tying the dead body in its grave to prevent its return, Helene Alving has attempted the same action by sophisticated modern means: by legal deeds, by an alien moralism which only faintly disguises the animus felt by the living wife towards the dead husband. Beyond the immediate dead, too, hover the hosts of the spririt's past always ready to overwhelm and repossess the little foreground world of human reason.

We have noted how Hegel's analysis of the conflict between the law of man and the law of woman (on which Ibsen structured his *A Doll's*

House) dialectically evolves into the conflict between the Living and the Dead[2] and how a note to *Ghosts* (the play that immediately succeeds *A Doll's House*) shows that Ibsen, too, was musing upon the relation of the living to the dead:

> Among us monuments are erected to the *dead*, since we have a duty towards them; we allow lepers to marry; but their offspring—? the unborn—?[3]

As in Hegel's text, and the Greek tragedies upon which that text draws, there is in *Ghosts* a striking contrast between the modern world with its rational, civic sensibility, and the substratum of primitive pieties upon which that sophisticated structure is based. For Hegel, the Greek *polis* best exemplified the Ethical (*sittliche*) Consciousness, and the dialectical heart of this consciousness had been explored profoundly by the Greek dramatists. Their plays do not belong to the past, for the ethical consciousness is a part of the ever-present structure of the total Consciousness. Though, therefore, the form and terms of performance of this drama belong to the past, their *arguments* will be valid wherever humanity has attained the level of the state.

The Greek quality of *Ghosts* has been recognized by a number of commentators. Almost as soon as the play appeared a countryman of Ibsen's, the classical scholar P. O. Schjøtt, saw in the play a modern version of the hereditary curse of Greek drama. G. Wilson Knight observes that the heritage of guilt in *Ghosts* "is like the curse on the house of Atreus in the *Oresteia* . . ."[4] Other critics have pointed out the Greek structure of the play: how its method of recollecting the past within the *agon* of the present resembles the method of *Oedipus Tyrannos*, how its almost obsessive mathematical procedure (reducing the characters onstage one by one) has a stark Sophoclean rationality. The subtitle of the play, too, *A Family Drama* (*Et Familiedrama*), recollects the subject matter of Greek tragedy. When, therefore, we recognize that the dialectic of the play is based on Hegel's account of the ethical society whose conflicts are illustrated by Greek tragedy, we are not violating but substantiating the most perceptive of accepted commentary upon the play. It should, therefore, be possible to suggest, without incurring too much protest, that Ibsen, concerned to resurrect the spirit of Greek drama, has drawn upon the greatest achievements of the three major tragedians of Athens: the *Oresteia*, the *Oedipus Tyrannos*, and *The Bacchae*.

As the dialectical center of the first group of four plays, *Ghosts* draws together with extraordinary concentration the themes of individual-family-society which make up the ethical consciousness. *Ghosts* stands in relation to the other plays in the Cycle in the same way that Greek classical drama stands in relation to the drama of the West. It is a hard, spare, objective masterpiece, indubitably as great as the more subjective and romantic plays of the second group or the richly mythopoeic last group. The formal perfection, ethical power, and clarity of the play are as fine as anything Ibsen has written and the impact of its arrival in the Cycle, causing both extravagant dismay and awed admiration among Ibsen's contemporaries, testifies to the strength and power of the Hellenic spirit when brought to bear upon the stuff of the Present. The concentration and economy of *Ghosts* are disciplines which, in their severe and distinguished difficulty (reminiscent of Sophocles) are as admirable to the serious student of drama as the imaginatively more expansive method of *The Wild Duck*.

Though, in structure and theme *Ghosts* is, as critics have observed, Greek, its total spiritual subject matter is, of course, that of Ibsen's own day, so that there is no contradiction in the fact that within this Greek structure we can find spiritual archetypes obviously deriving from other mythological traditions, such as the Germanic and the Judeo-Christian. These other forces, however, are assembled for a distinctly Greek dialectic so that even the Christian priest, Manders, is a social rather than a spiritual leader, his function expressing itself in terms of social convention and social *duties* (*duty* is a key term for Hegel in this phase of his argument). It is not the messianic idealism of a Gregers Werle, or the later Christian tradition of Johannes Rosmer, a sensitive and civilizing though constraining force in society. Manders is, rather, the reflection of orthodox social *mores* (his conventional pietism would be as happy with one religious tradition as with another) so that Ibsen is not setting him up as an easy anti-Christian target but is using him to portray the somewhat pathetic inadequacy of a level of consciousness that attempts to function entirely in terms of conventional pieties. Thus there is, in Ibsen's portrait of Manders, no bias to be outgrown (somewhat late in life!) in the later plays; I think Ibsen can be taken as speaking the truth when he observed, "in the whole book there is not a single opinion, not a single remark to be found that is there on the dramatist's account. . . . The method, the technique underlying the form of the book, was in itself quite enough to prevent the author making himself apparent in the dialogue."[5]

The world of *Ghosts* is a historically determined one, in which the condition of the Present can be understood only by a process of imaginative historical recollection and analysis. Identities on the stage, for all their vivid particularity and immediacy, also are universal and archetypal: the priest, Manders; his "satanic" complement, Engstrand; the intellectually inquiring Helene; the artist, Osvald. These characters exist firmly as modern figures in a modern situation, but only the most superficial judgment would claim that the modern consciousness is truncated from the history that has shaped it or that the poet who was to give us an adequate portrait of the present would not have to explore the whole evolution of human consciousness. Religion, art, and intellectual inquiry, which are as important to the play's meanings as the life histories and destinies of fictional individuals, did not drop full-blown from heaven onto the modern scene, but became what they are through the process of history: a point acknowledged by Ibsen in a note to the play:

The key-note is to be: The prolific growth of our intellectual life, in literature, art, etc.—and in contrast to this; the whole of mankind gone astray.[6]

Very obviously, here, Ibsen is considering a culture crisis within a moment in history, and if it is protested that this does not apply to the *individual* within that culture crisis, that here, at least, we can dispense with that historical awareness that Ibsen insisted was indispensable to a modern author, another note to *Ghosts* shows that the individual human being is also a product of culture:

The complete human being is no longer a product of nature, he is an artificial product like corn, and fruit-trees, and the Creole race and thorough-bred horses and dogs, the vine, etc.—
The fault lies in that all mankind has failed. If a man claims to live and develop in a human way it is megalomania. All mankind, and especially the Christian part of it, suffers from megalomania.[7]

Admittedly these utterances, like the many gnomic apothegms scattered among Ibsen's notes, are more tantalizing than clear; but the reference to the "complete human being" surely should bring to mind the theme of *Emperor and Galilean* and its ideal of humanity which would be a synthesis of pagan and Christian powers. That world-historical drama recorded the failure of the synthesis, a failure that was to continue up to the present, so that the claim of being a complete human being today *would* be megalomania; and the Christians, proclaiming that their spiritual condition has successfully superseded the pagan and pre-Christian, that, in fact, Christian man is superior to pre-Christian man, more whole than Homer, Aeschylus, Sophocles, Socrates, Plato, Alexander, or Caesar, are guilty of that fault condemned by the Greeks: *hubris* or megalomania. One would expect, therefore, that something like this *hubris*, this comfortable moral sense of having overcome a spiritually or ethically inferior way of life (i.e., the pagan), would constitute the tragic error (*hamartia*) of *Ghosts*, to be punished by means of its total action.

Not only do the ethical formulations of the modern consciousness and modern society express our Hellenic heritage: the very art form, drama, which, for Hegel, best sets these out, and which Ibsen himself is employing, is Hellenic. The acknowledgment of our Hellenic identity, therefore, is inescapable to anyone capable of thinking, and most especially to an audience assembled in a theater.[8] But not only are we to acknowledge our Hellenic identity: we are to be asked to rise to its highest level of ethical courage and esthetic achievement. Resurrecting the Hellenic spirit means reactivating it within our consciousnesses as an ethical, esthetic, and philosophical faculty, and not merely bringing back Greek myths and themes from classic drama. While we are held by *Ghosts*, we assume a Hellenic universe, subject to a particularly demanding scheme of guilt and responsibility.

Not only, therefore, is it necessary to recollect our Hellenic heritage in order to understand the structure of reality of the Present: it is necessary to recollect it in order to be capable of living up to that reality. Truth and freedom require that the modern consciousness challenge and judge the entire structure of reality, both objective and subjective, and, here, the use of the Past is ambiguous, for it demonstrates to what extent the structure of reality is a structure of dead conventions, accepted and unexamined premises, a system of spiritual repression (conscious and unconscious); and at the same time it brings to bear upon the repressive Present values and standards from the Past, tabooed by the Present, whose resurrection would lead to greater truth and freedom.

Before we examine the Hegelian argument upon which the dialectic of *Ghosts* is structured, let us consider the earlier suggestion that, like Hegel's text, Ibsen's play resurrects themes and situations from the major Greek tragedians, for here the parallels are more directly striking.

1. In the *Oresteia*, the military father, Agamemnon, is slain by his wife, Clytemnestra (twin sister of Helen), who then sends her son out to strangers. To set right her troubled and frightened conscience, the wife attempts to placate the wronged and buried father (many years later when her son has grown into a young man) by a fraudulent memorial ritual at his grave. The son returns from abroad at this moment and leagues with his sister to avenge his father. (These details are repeated in Sophocles' and Euripides' treatment of this myth.)

In *Ghosts*, the dead military father, Alving, has been wronged by his wife Helene who has sent her son out to strangers. Helene tries to lay the ghost of her husband once and for all with a fraudulent ritual: as she is making arrangements for this her son, Osvald, returns from abroad and soon will league with his sister, Regine, against the whole world of pious untruth created by Helene against the values represented by her husband. In *The Libation Bearers*, as in *Ghosts*, after the father has been avenged, there is a powerful invocation of the sun.

2. In *Oedipus Tyrannos* the present action of investigation of a present distress (the plague at Thebes) uncovers more and more of the polluted past. In the Oedipus myth the son was sent from the house to avert the catastrophe that the action fulfills. Mrs. Alving's tragic journey into enlightenment parallels closely that of Oedipus. There are minor similarities, perhaps, in Oedipus's duel with Tiresias and Helene's with *her* priest, Manders, and in the *incest motif* of both plays, though these parallels are very slight. The major parallel is the theme of the tragic family history, the polluted house, and the action of passionate and tragic retrospection.

3. Between *Ghosts* and *The Bacchae* the parallels are mostly thematic, but still powerfullly striking. In Euripides' play the god of wine and joy-of-life, Dionysos, revenges himself upon the family that attempts to deny his divinity. The play ends with the mother, Agave, confronted by the mutilated body of her son, killed by herself—a terrible testimony to the power of the god she has offended. In *Ghosts*, Helene Alving, representing the pietistic and life-denying tradition of puritan Christianity, had set herself against the force of "joy-of-life" (*livsgleden*, an untranslatable word which means something much more profound, such as the life impulse itself) and had erected, over her victory over this power, a triumphant lie which will be terribly destroyed (as in Euripides' play, there is the destruction of a building). *Ghosts* ends with the mother confronting the wreckage of the son whom her crime helped to destroy.

These parallels can no more be coincidental than the parallels between other plays in the Cycle and their completely appropriate sources in Hegel and world literature and history. In Hegel's account of the ethical society, we move through an ever-widening circle of conflicts, the circumference of meaning continuously being pushed through individual, familial, societal, ethical, cultural, and religous dimensions of reality until the whole structure of reality is encompassed. The central conflict (symbolized by the conflict between Antigone and Creon, or Oedipus and his fate) detonates the devastation of the whole substance of this particular world view (the ethical consciousness); and this is true, too, of the action of *Ghosts* which involves:

(a) The struggle of the individual consciousness against the structure of conventional society. (Helene and Osvald.)

(b) The conflicts within the family of husband-wife, parent-child, brother-sister relationships.

(c) A social and cultural world whose divisions are illustrated in the discrepancies between Captain Alving's Orphanage and Chamberlain

Alving's brothel; Osvald's "Parisian" values versus Manders's pietism; the collision between enlightened knowledge and conventional orthodoxy.

(d) The religious discrepancy between Manders's careful, spiritual orthodoxy and the lonely spiritual quest of Helene Alving, brought to test the validity of her entire conventional instruction.

The detonation at the nucleus of the drama sets off a reaction not completed until the whole substance of this world view is destroyed: a destruction, in the Hegelian paradox, essential to the continuing life of Spirit.

As the *Phenomenology* advances, so it attains greater spirituality of content, for it is all the time taking up earlier, exhausted modes of consciousness into the succeeding ones. At a relatively early stage in the dialectic of Spirit, such as the section upon which *Ghosts* is structured, the mode of life, for all its ethical clarity and courage, is still at a great remove from the spiritually more adequate, even numinous world of the last part of Hegel's work and of the last four plays in Ibsen's Cycle. In *Ghosts*, I think, we sense this distance between the naturalistic action with its predominantly ethical emphasis, and the total spiritual content it struggles to reveal—a distance that is bridged by a somewhat violent symbolism, such as the burning orphanage, the hereditary disease, the rain, and the rising sun. The play, in fact, demonstrates the inadequacy of the ethical consciousness as a fully *human* consciousness: the bifurcation of reality between the individual consciousness and the startling operation of Objective ethical powers (gods in Greek drama; objective scientific and natural forces in *Ghosts*) is one so intolerable that it must be overcome. As in Greek drama, the ethical structure of *Ghosts* completely lacks *moral* correlation. As in the Oedipus story, it is by acting by what they feel to be the *best* motives that Manders and Helene Alving create such appalling consequences. The insight that the universe refuses to conform to our moral concepts; that with the best intentions, in our ignorance, or in our pride, we set off consequences that will destroy us and those we love, is, perhaps, a truth that Greek tragedy still can teach us but, in Hegel's account, it is an insight which is insufficient for human consciousness, which will strive, even at the price of the greatest suffering, to discover a more adequate human reality.

Within the limits of the world view of *Ghosts*, which excludes the brooding subjectivity of the second group, and the visionary and transcendental consciousness of the last group, Helene Alving explores all the possible permutations of realistic speech and action, from humor and joy at the beginning of the play, to serious inquiry, concern, anxiety, and finally anguish and terror. With all these permutations exhausted she is finally left standing immobile and speechless while the sun, that Hegelian emblem of a new dawn of Spirit, floods the devastated Alving home.

In Hegel's account, *Consciousness,* in the ethical society, cannot but discover itself confronting alternative and contradictory laws, so that, as Loewenberg summarizes, "no act can escape turning into guilt... the individual must offend one power when he acts in obedience to the other."[9] Hence the paradox that "every law-abiding person inevitably becomes at the same time a lawbreaker," for the ethical realm is made up of laws and duties mutually exclusive yet equally imperative. In this world guilt belongs to the action rather than to the actor who is fated to perform it. In *Ghosts,* for example, Alving's "law"—*livsgleden*—inevitably offends the laws of those pieties for which Helene stands; and, in turn, her action, on behalf of her offended values, becomes a crime against the law by which Alving lived. "Acknowlegement of guilt, whether by an Antigone or an Oedipus, is acknowledgement that the law violated is no less real or no less necessary than the law from obedience to which guilt ensues."[10] The ethical dilemma posed by such a world can be evaded only by an innocence "that belongs solely to inaction:... to the mere being of a stone, a state which is not even true of a child."[11] This, I think, helps us to understand the nature of the realism of *Ghosts,* which is that of an Objective rather than a Subjective valuation. In the later *Rosmersholm,* for example, guilt is very definitely bound up with subjective character: with the precise nature of motives and subjective intentions, so that the dramatic rhythm of this play is far more one of self-examination. In *Ghosts,* however, the recognition by Mrs. Alving of the nature of her guilt is at the same time the recognition, not of her guilty unconscious motives, as with Rosmer and Rebekka, but of a flaw in the structure of reality which had brought her up in obedience to a one-sided law:

> MRS. ALVING: They'd drilled me so much in duty and things of that kind that I went on here all too long putting my faith in them. Everything resolved into duties—*my* duties and *his* duties, and—I'm afraid I made this home unbearable for your poor father.[12]

Mrs. Alving's insight, which results in self-condemnation, is, actually, a condemnation not of her personal character as an independent force operating upon the world (as with Rebekka) but of a law or tradition, independent of herself, to which her own life has been in allegiance. It is not Mrs. Alving who stands condemned by the action of the play, therefore, and interpretations that reduce it to this psychological dimension are going against the deliberate "objective" nature of its dialectic; instead it is an inadequacy destructive of a whole cultural tradition in the West that is condemned.

Once the implications of the ethical consciousness are pushed honestly and courageously to their conclusions, this consciousness is forced to evolve beyond a society "subject to customary powers sanctioning conflicting imperatives. In the new order growing out of the old, the concept of right supplants the concept of custom."[13] This later development, however, necessitating the breakdown of the ethical community, takes us beyond *Ghosts* to *An Enemy of the People*.

In the relationship of the living to the dead, Hegel demonstrates, we have the clearest example of the ethical consciousness within the realm of the family, and the potential conflict between the realms of the family and of the state. The individual who is dead has been "wronged" by "nature" through the process of bodily corruption, and in order to remove this wrong those who share his blood perform a work of their own doing, for the dead belong wholly to the family and not to the state. This work is both burial and memorial, *and* vengeance.[14] In *The Libation Bearers* both actions are presented when we see Clytemnestra attempt to appease the shade of the husband she has wronged by a ceremony at his grave at the same moment that Agamemnon's son returns home to avenge him, and *Ghosts* shows us Helene preparing the memorial ceremony that will finally dispose of Alving at the same moment that Alving's son returns carrying the disease that is the terrible vengeance of Alving's repressed *livsglede* or sexuality against his wife. To be sure, Osvald's avenging of his father (in which, like Orestes, he will also be a victim) is more unconscious and unintentional than that of his Greek prototype, but it will, similarly, destroy his mother and bring upon himself the furies of his *aandelige nedbrudd* or spiritual collapse. This somewhat intellectualized manner of discovering the past in the present is, as Nietzsche insisted in *The Birth of Tragedy*, the only way that modern man can (as he must) return to the "once-living reality of myth." In the same intellectualized way, James Joyce rediscovered the mythic and historical past in *Ulysses*. Just as, for example, Leopold Bloom re-creates Odysseus's act of slaying the suitors of Penelope by reasserting himself in Molly Bloom's consciousness, so Osvald "slays" his mother when he forces upon her the recognition of the guilt of her whole ethical substance, the whole world of values she has built up over a lifetime.

The ritual of burial and memorial is to ensure that "the ethical realm remains ... permanently a world without blot or stain."[15] But, as we have seen, such is the nature of the ethical consciousness, that such an action (as in the *Antigone*) can itself be destructive of the ethical realm. At such a phase of the ethical consciousness we witness "a transition of opposites into one another by which each proves to be the annihilation rather than the confirmation of its self and its opposite."[16] So Orestes, to represent the rights of his father, must not only violate those of his mother, but, at the same time, bring upon himself and the whole ethical realm complete destruction. In *Ghosts* the transition of action is precisely from the opening note of harmoniously complementary opposites to terrible mutual destruction: from the seeming situation of the dead father honored by the living wife and by society; the son returned to the family, the individual (Mrs. Alving) settling her accounts with her conscience and with society, to where these elements will reveal themselves to be explosively at odds and unable to withstand the pressure of truth and freedom exerted upon them. In no other play by Ibsen is the dialectical pressure and tension so great beneath the placid-seeming surface and this no doubt accounts for the Greek swiftness and remorselessness of its retributive logic. Hegel describes this reversal from harmony to deep conflict in the following terms:

It becomes the process of negation or destruction, the eternal necessity of awful destiny, which engulfs in the abyss of its bare identity divine and human law alike, as well as both the self-conscious factors [the conflicting protagonists] in which these powers subsist; and, to our view, passes over into the absolute self-existence of mere single self-consciousness[17] [i.e., the objective ethical drama becomes located in the action and suffering of one individual consciousness].

A key term in this movement described by Hegel—Duty—is also, readers will recall, a key term in *Ghosts*. We find, writes Hegel, not the comic collision between duty and duty within the consciousness, but instead the condition whereby consciousness gives itself over entirely to *one* law, *one* duty, which, for it, is the essential reality.[18] The feminine, divine law sees in human law "mere arbitrary fortuitous human violence" while human law sees in its opponent "the obstinacy and disobedience of subjective self-sufficiency,"[19] phrases which, while drawing upon the Creon-Antigone conflict, and thus applicable to *A Doll's House*, call to mind, also, Manders's exasperation with the obstinacy and willfulness of Helene Alving. In the dialectic of *Ghosts* Mrs. Alving, in the past, violated her duty to herself and gave herself over to her community and its mores and at the time when the play opens, is attempting a reversal where, at least vicariously through her son, she will honor duty to self at the cost of offending even the deepest conventional pieties (e.g., those taboos on incest she is *intellectually* willing to discard). At a deeper level is the conflict of *The Bacchae*, a conflict between the life that denies or that which accepts, Dionysos; between conventional duties and that joy-of-life which, as Euripides demonstrated, was also an important duty.

The ethical consciousness must expiate its guilt towards the violated law that demands revenge:

> The ethical consciousness cannot disclaim the crime and its guilt. The deed consists in setting in motion what was unmoved, and in bringing out what in the first place lay shut up as a mere possibility, and thereby *linking on the unconscious to the conscious*, the nonexistent to the existent. In this truth, therefore, *the deed comes to light*; it is something in which a conscious element is bound up with what is unconscious, what is peculiarly one's own with what is alien and external:—*it is an essential reality divided in sunder, whose other aspect consciousness experiences and also finds to be its own aspect, but as a power violated by its doing and raised to hostility against it.*[20]

Despite the difficulty of this passage, its relevance to the action of *Ghosts* is clear. In the dialectic of Ibsen's play, Helene Alving and the audience are brought gradually to recognize and acknowlege the validity of the law (*livsgleden*) violated, and to recognize that this violated law, as part of the structure of reality, is an essential aspect of the consciousness that violated it. Thus the power that is merely in the background and unconscious in the beginning of the play, moves into the foreground and the light of consciousness at the end. And when Hegel goes on to quote from Antigone, "Because of our suffering we acknowledge we have erred,"[21] we seem to be at the heart of Ibsen's play. Such a recognition, however, leads to the destruction of the offending consciousness which has lived by another universal law, for

> the ethical individuality is directly and inherently one with this its universal, exists in it alone, and is incapable of surviving the destruction which this ethical power suffers at the hands of its opposite.[22]

In the figure of Osvald Alving, who is the ground upon which the battle of his parents is fought, the ethical consciousness, in which both duty and joy-of-life collided, is destroyed. Agamemnon-Alving, Orestes-Osvald, Clytemnestra-Helene—these parallels indicate the nature of Ibsen's use of the past and the marvelously demure manner in which it is worked into the realistic fabric of the play.

Because this is Ibsen's central drama of the Ethical phase, its dialectic is neater and more stark than that of the plays that follow. In *Ghosts* Ibsen is organizing the material of the Cycle into an ethically concentrated, Hellenic form: but *Ghosts* is but a part of the total pattern of the Cycle. We should come back to it, reflecting upon this stage of Consciousness's evolution, after having experienced the full evolution. It is one of Ibsen's most perfect plays, and one of his most effective, and it completely justifies his whole method that such a Greek structure had such an impact upon the life of Ibsen's own age. For it is only by creating dramas sufficient unto themselves that the decision to find a human and theatrical world equivalent to Hegel's psychoanalysis of the *Weltgeist* could be justified. In *Ghosts*, from the very highest motives, Helene Alving heroically had offended the Hellenic values of joy-of-life, and so she will be at the same time both punished and transfigured by the supreme Hellenic art form: Tragedy.

The somewhat dreadful nature of Ibsen's humor can be gauged from *Ghosts'* subtitle, *A Family Drama.* It brings to mind the familiar nine-teenth-century phrase "family novel" or "family play," an assurance, to a squeamish public, that the "wholesome" contents are fit to be en-joyed by the entire family. The subject of *Ghosts* is the family, and its central metaphor, syphilis, destroys the generative source of all families, a superbly *tasteless* irony calculated to offend in the same way as the even more tasteless joke embedded in the situation of *Oedipus the King.* From Latin, Ibsen might well have been aware of the pun on *spiritus*, familiar to the Elizabethans, for example, equating it with semen ("the expence of spirit in a waste of shame . . .") which would make the meta-phor of syphilis stand duty for the polluted spirit in a double sense: a finely appropriate synthesis of physical and metaphorical meaning. For if, as the powerful note to *Ghosts* implies, "all mankind is on the wrong track," this is not to be attributed to local moral and medical causes but to a major crisis in the history of the human spirit. This, admittedly, is a big subject, but I am convinced that Ibsen was interested only in big subjects—of the magnitude, in fact, that kept him occupied so long on the world-historical drama *Emperor and Galilean.* If the whole of mankind is on the wrong track—and the right track, one imagines, would lead to the "third empire of spirit"—then the error of misdirection began far back in history, near the spiritual origins of modern man. Thus it will repay considering the subject of physical and psychical origins in terms of polluted streams, and of the interconnection of these two realms. Infected or diseased spiritual streams will set up the cultural conditions of repressed Eros in rebellion, and syphilis will extend from being a mere medical symptom into a genuine tragic Nemesis. It is genuinely tragic, not only for its appropriateness (poetic justice in the very prose of prose), but also for its universal scale of reference, which is nothing less than the history of Europe. Thus the horrible suffering of Osvald and his mother, which has struck so many commentators as rooted in a pessimism, or in a merely local criticism of a particular morality, and in either case thus denied tragic dignity, completes a *universally* tragic pattern. For, as we have noted, in the world of the ethical consciousness, it is the action, rather than the doer, that is guilty, for the guilt attaches to the universal law to which the victim is inescapably committed; so that the tragic insight does not remain at the level of pessimism or a particular didacticism, but completes itself in an awareness of universal forces and purposes behind the localized action. The insight that emerges from *Ghosts* is that life lived entirely within the limits of the ethical consciousness (and much contemporary and honorable social conflict is thus confined) is tragically inadequate—an insight, however, that is possible only if one has, at least imaginatively, accepted the terms and logic of the ethical consciousness. The perception of the inadequacy of any stage of the Cycle is the privilege only of those who can rise up to and surrender themselves to each of its "Moments." It is, of course, possible to evade the entire dialectic, but only at the price of spiritual insignificance, of not being "awakened" into spiritual life. Such is the level of the guards, mere common-sensical functionaries of Antigone's tragedy; or of Engstrand and Manders, warily avoiding inconvenient insight, in *Ghosts*. Tragedy is the privilege of the spiritual aristocrat and if we pronounce these vehicles of the ethical consciousness "inadequate" we have to confess that even *inadequacy* at this level of spiritual life is far above our level. For these are the inadequacies of heroes, and only heroes are worth bringing to the judgment day upon the human spirit.

If the play's action sets out an image of the tragic misdirection, or dissipation, of the major spiritual streams—Hellenic, Judeo-Christian, and Germanic—that make up the life of the modern consciousness, the image of the dawning sun at the close of the play suggests the possibility of renewal of forces and energies that cannot be confined by local human error. Not only is this image of the dawning sun a constant metaphor in Hegel for spiritual renewal; it appears, powerfully, in the closing words of the Old Testament:

For behold the day cometh, that shall burn as an oven; and all the proud, yea, and all that do wickedly, shall be stubble; and the day that cometh shall burn them up, saith the Lord of hosts, that it shall leave them neither root nor branch. But unto you that fear my name shall the Sun of righteousness arise with healing in his wings; and ye shall go forth, and grow up as calves of the stall. . . . Behold I will send you Elijah the prophet, before the coming of the great and dreadful day of the Lord: and he shall turn the heart of the fathers to the children, and the heart of the children to their fathers, lest I come and smite the earth with a curse.[23]

It is very likely only a coincidence that the words in the Bible that immediately precede the great spiritual renewal claimed in the New Testament contains the images of Sun and Fire and the reconciliation of fathers and children, all of which are important in the action and imagery of *Ghosts*, though Ibsen's thorough knowledge of the Bible should make us consider the possibility of a conscious parallel. But hardly coincidental can be the appearance of the sun imagery at the close of Aeschylus's *The Libation Bearers*, when the military father, Agamemnon, has been avenged, like the finally exonerated Alving. That Greek Osvald, Orestes, turns to the audience and chorus in the Greek theater and proclaims:

> Behold again, O audience of these evil things, the engine against my wretched father they devised, the hands' entanglement, the hobbles for his feet. Spread it out. Stand round me in a circle and display this net that caught a man. So shall, not my father, but that great father who sees all, the Sun, look on my mother's sacrilegious handiwork.[24]

The parallels, here, between the dramatic moments of both plays (the exoneration of the fathers, the Furies that afflict Orestes and the mental affliction of Osvald, the destruction of the mother and the invocation of the sun) are surely too numerous and too striking to be coincidental, even though the terms of the old Greek drama of Fate have been thoroughly translated into those of a consistent modern fatalism.[25]

The main action of *Ghosts*—what, in fact, constitutes Helen Alving's fate—is the comprehension and exoneration of the life values, or laws, of Captain Alving; at first they are seen merely as a material inheritance tarnished by corruption and deception, a ghost to be laid forever to rest, but finally comprehended as a violated right whose suppression has resulted in a terrible Nemesis. The dialectical crisis of the play, interrupted by the outbreak of the orphanage fire, is the moment when Helene, stirred by her son's remark about *livsgleden* (life affirmation), suddenly "sees it all"—the whole pattern in which she recognizes herself, for the first time, as a destructive agent. The central figure in this pattern is that of the young, life-craving lieutenant before he was broken by the net of duties which his wife enlisted from that pietistic community of which Manders (her intellectual Aegisthus) was the representative and spokesman. This image is the last and most powerful ghost to haunt the play, achieving that unity of recognition scene and reversal which Aristotle praised as the most perfect of tragic effects, for when Helene Alving is brought to recognize the nature of her husband and the nature of her crime against him, not only does her life work "burn up," but the entire direction of her quest—to be free of the influence of the hated husband—is reversed into its opposite: to rescue and rehabilitate all that he stood for.

Captain Alving, though dead, is Helene's invisible antagonist, striking back, like Agamemnon, through his children. He thus is of far more consequence as a dialectical presence than Manders or Engstrand who, we noted, never risk the level of essential dialectical confrontation. Like a

Socratic dialogue, the play's argument proceeds from error and misconception to final comprehension, and Helene's journey into light through recognition of error and guilt is a miniature model of the modern spirit's difficult recognition of the misdirection of its own spiritual history: the recognition prompting the note to *Ghosts* that "all mankind is on the wrong track" and which also is the clear message of *Emperor and Galilean.*

Ghosts is able to contain, within an action that is recognizably of Ibsen's own times, both the historical perspectives that have gone into the making of the modern consciousness, and one of the major (or archetypal) forms of that consciousness—the Hellenic. Thus the condition of consciousness esthetically enacted by the play and, hopefully, activated in the audience, is a complete form, being archetypal, historical, and contemporary. This continuous interaction of more than one plane of reality throughout the total action must be kept in mind in our analysis of action and character, if our response is to be adequate to Ibsen's challenge.

Our analysis of character, for instance, must get beyond preoccupation with individual motives and character assessment, to a concern with the ethical, intellectual, and esthetic implications of the interaction of the total character grouping—the total consciousness—depicted by the play. That is to say, we should look at *Ghosts* as if it were, in the Miltonic phrase, a "great argument," the characters of which carry as much thematic as psychological qualities, and draw our attention outward, to the expanding circumferences of meaning and implication, as well as inward, to the motives, velleities, and nuances of the individual psyche. It might help, in fact, to look at the character grouping of the play, for a moment, as if it were a visual design:

Old Testament	*Pre-Christian*	*Post-Christian*
Fallen Man	*Pagan Man*	*Pauline Man*
Jakob Engstrand	Lt. Alving	Pastor Manders

| | Johanna | Helene | |

| | Regine | Osvald | |
| | (Body) | (Mind) | |

| | | Orphanage | |
| | | (Destroyed by Fire) | |

Alving Sailors' Home		Collapse of Artistic Work
(Destruction of physical		(Destruction of spiritual
Eros)		Eros)

This diagram will startle those for whom *Ghosts* is very obviously an examination of an erroneous life style within a local social situation; but it will not surprise the reader of *Emperor and Galilean*. Ibsen called *Brand* a "syllogism" and this syllogistic structure behind the Cycle and each individual play within it is merely another element of the total consciousness that each play represents. The three male figures, Engstrand, Alving, and Manders, all are involved in the past of Helene Alving, and are the subjects of choices and decisions she has made and now, in the action of the play, must reexamine and revalue. On the purely psychological and moral level they represent her old revulsion from Alving's life style, her attachment to Manders's pietism, and her bad conscience over the consequences of her husband's way of life—all of these valuations emerging from her own particular upbringing and world view. This is a very important area of the play's existence and of its full meaning, but it also serves to embody, or actualize, a wider realm of consequences and causes, and to see the characters also in terms of this wider range of meanings is not to violate the nature of the play but to be faithful to its *full* rhythm and resonance. I would even say that, as a *limitedly* realistic play, in which the poet makes a fairly narrow range of consciousness (e.g., psychological and social) carry the full richness of his meaning, *Ghosts* is as unsatisfactory as *Antigone* or *Oedipus the King*; and it is only with our awareness of the greater dimensions of its intention that the subtle and complex artistry begins to work, and that the language and the dramatic method, which otherwise would seem "stagey" and nonrealistic, is shown to be dialectically far more complex than strict realism, for it expresses a continuous interplay of universal and particular reference in which *both*, universal *and* particular, must be simultaneously present.

The significantly named *Jakob* Engstrand should impress us, not merely as a particular fallen and graceless individual, but as vividly representative of fallen man in whom the pagan categories of eros and *livsglede* have degenerated into "sin" and the brothel. Young Lieutenant Alving, with his baffled "joy-of-life," is suggestive of an alternative, guilt-free, energetic and *creative* eros whose values have been unhappily *divided* in his children. The virginal, life-denying Pastor Manders, while being a plausible individual "character," transmits into the play's dialectic the spiritual tradition of Pauline Christianity which has helped to shape the structure of modern culture and of the modern consciousness: the culture and consciousness of the audience before which the play, *Ghosts*, is presented as a mirror held up to Nature. In Ibsen's theater, the "characters" are significant enough to find a place in the Cycle when, in fact, they are strong enough to carry archetypal identities.

From this perspective, the Alving family history becomes the "diagram" of a wider spiritual history; not, of course, a dogmatic assertion on the course of Western history, but a model that can help us better meditate upon and understand its salient aspects. In *Emperor and Galilean*, a play that Ibsen insisted (rightly, I think) was relevant to the present, there is demonstrated an unresolved and disastrous conflict between the pagan qualities of life affirmation, exemplified in Hellenic culture, and the uneasy victory over this life affirmation by Christian spirituality. In that world-historical conflict, the division is nakedly apparent, the armies of both paganism and Christianity carrying their banners into open battle. In the Cycle, the same battle is being fought out, but now covertly and unconsciously, through the forces of a reality whose surface details do not immediately declare their spiritual origins.

The offspring of Alving each have an actual and a pseudo-father and a different mother. Regine's putative father is Engstrand but actually Alving. Osvald is the legitimate son of Alving, but his mother's emotional allegiance to "pastor" Manders (to the point where she claims Osvald actually resembles Manders) gives him, too, a second father. (In fact, the pillar of society that Helene brought up Osvald to consider his father to be is Alving remade in the image of Manders.) Alving's two partners, the unwilling but legitimate Helene, and the willing but illegitimate Johanna, are each "infected" by their own previous alliances, Johanna with Engstrand, Helene with Manders. (The fact that it is Helene's offspring that carries the hereditary syphilis is as much a thematic joke on Ibsen's part as a medical curiosity.) The appropriate shortcomings of the two offspring, Regine healthy in body but disastrously lacking in mind, Osvald intellectually creative but crippled physically,[26] are thematically linked to the shortcomings of Alving's two partners, Johanna and Helene. The two children divide between each other aspects (physical and mental) that can function creatively only in union and mutual interaction, and though these two functions or aspects are capable of being reduced to individual inadequacies, they quite obviously bring to mind the whole area of life subsumed under the categories of Flesh and Spirit. Regine's destination, Chamberlain Alving's sailors' home, should carry all the resonance of the most moralistic Victorian use of such emblems, as much as the collapse of Osvald's function as an artist should imply all that the nineteenth-century use of the figure of the Poet or the Artist in decline implies and our modern embarrassment with such archetypal identities (though Ibsen subtilizes them more than his contemporaries) is not necessarily to our credit.

A central metaphor of the play is that of the Orphanage. We notice that all the living characters are involved in it. It is Helene's memorial

which (contrary to a true memorial) attempts to *eliminate* the memory
of her husband. Manders will assist in this process of elimination or
obliteration, by his conventionally pious memorial service. Engstrand
is employed to work in the orphanage and this, too, seems to be Regine's
destined task (in Helene's mind). Osvald has returned home to be present at the memorial ceremony. An orphanage is a place for homeless
children just as a sailors' home (which also will bear Alving's name) is
a place for homeless adults, and in both instances the sexual connotations of illegitimacy and sexual license are obvious. (It is likely that
the sailors will create the need for the orphanage, so that the Alving
name on both institutions recognizes the connection.) Ibsen—whose
hero Julian admired Hellenic culture, which contained such convenient
and holy institutions as the Corinthian Aphrodite—is not likely to be
morally outraged by this: it is the peculiar *dreariness* of these institutions
in the modern world that more likely offended him, a dreariness deriving
from a lack of faith in either the Hellenic or the Christian world views.
The lack of parentage, in the larger design of the play, could represent
the truncation of the modern world from these two spiritual sources, so
that the buildings of this orphanage, schoolhouse (Hellenic), and chapel
(Christian) are, indeed, memorials to a dead past. In *Emperor and
Galilean* Ibsen explicitly affirms this. The Church (Act I) and the
University (Act II) are both shown to be spiritually bankrupt, and it is
only a further degree of reification to translate Church and University
(standing for Faith and Learning) into local chapel and schoolhouse.
The diagram of the play set out on p. xxx is not the whole play but it
can alert us to the universal and abstract argument which the details of
scene, character, action, and dialogue render in terms of tangible reality
and tangible art.

The scene of *Ghosts* is a coastal town in Western Norway, set apart
from the large world (as in *The Pillars of Society*) and from large
spiritual conflicts. We learn, from details that emerge in the dialogue,
that this local community is suspicious and watchful, moralistic and un-
forgiving to those who are morally vulnerable. This community has to
be placated, its opinions, however narrow, having to be taken into careful consideration, and Manders, the committee pastor with neither time
nor talent for larger spiritual realities, goes in fear of it. The tyranny
this community subtly exerts over spiritual freedom, in fact, though less
dramatic, is as effectively inhibiting as the world of intrigue, power, and
hypocrisy analyzed in Act I of *Emperor and Galilean*, where Julian,
inwardly tormented, goes in terror of the agents and spies of the Christian emperor. The society of these first four plays, in fact, is essentially
the same: forcing the energetic Bernick into multiple hypocrisies; cre-

ating the threatening economic and ethical dangers inhibiting Nora's
(and Torvald's) freedom, and, finally, when directly challenged in *An
Enemy of the People*, violently turning upon the doctor who, like
Socrates, seeks to cure its ills.

At the entrance to this world, in "Little Harbour Street," Engstrand
intends to set up his "sailors' home" in order to lure in the "wandering
sea-farers of the world's oceans." This portentous phrase, used by Engstrand, seems to be echoed in Manders's account, to Helene, of the "intellectual currents" (*aandelige strømninger*) "in the larger world—
where you've let your son wander so long."[27] These two images—the
sailors wandering on the seas, to be lured into the "home," and the son
wandering among the intellectual currents of the wide world, to return
to the life lie of his society—suggest, again, both flesh and spirit "on the
wrong track."

Set apart from this community, and reached by boat, is Rosenvold,
now a center of some enlightenment with its books, periodicals, and
the belatedly freethinking (i.e., Hellenic) Helene. "Rosenvold" suggests
an aristocratic vantage point, somewhat like "Rosmersholm," and if
Ibsen chooses his names with the same care as other details in his play,
there may be connotations, here, of the pagan categories of love (*Rosen*—
rose) and force (*vold*) more decisively concentrated in the philandering
Lieutenant Alving. Part of the Rosenvold estate is Solvik, which Helene
will relinquish, reckoning it to represent the "value" of Alving as a
marriage partner. It is to be noted that this particularly sordid interpretation of the relationship is Helene's, not Alving's, and alerts us to view
skeptically her whole account of that marriage. Upon Solvik is erected
the schoolhouse and chapel of the Orphanage: both vehicles of an
orthodoxy that Helene has, in fact, outgrown, thus compounding her
hypocrisy in erecting the memorial. *Sol*vik brings to mind that constant
sun metaphor in Ibsen's work (Sol, of course, is sun) and Helene's re-
linquishment of Solvik is at least in keeping with her whole sacrifice of
livsglede (life affirmation), the Dionysiac energy indispensable to the
health of the human spirit; and Osvald's collapse, with the words, "Give
me the sun, mother," brings home the full disastrousness of this sacrifice.
"Solvik," as embodied in the legal documents in Pastor Manders's traveling bag, seems a conveniently pragmatic reduction of the ghosts that
Helene seeks to exorcise, and her pathetic attempt to dispose of the
past by these eminently pragmatic means is terribly reproached in the
same way as Julian's attempt to dispose of the Christian past by per-
suasive pamphlets: for the Christian buildings she erects upon Solvik
are destroyed just as Julian's temple in Jerusalem is destroyed in *Em-*

peror and Galilean, and the dreadfully ascendant sun reveals the equally as invincible power that Helene has offended.

The geography—or topography—of the world of *Ghosts*, therefore, is a metaphoric landscape where even the most prosaic-seeming details (schoolhouse, chapel, sailors' home, orphanage, and family home) carry universal as well as particular connotations, and when Ibsen invades this landscape with a history and with human consciousness, larger perspectives open up. We must, I believe, be alerted to visual echoes and quotations in Ibsen's work as well as verbal ones, and some such visual suggestion is evoked, surely, when the limping Jakob Engstrand attempts to enter a garden room and is intercepted by a young girl, Regine, who brandishes a weapon-like garden syringe and tries to prevent his entering. The satanic figure, entering a garden and being intercepted by an at least visually angelic figure, is continued in the dialogue with its debate on "the Lord's rain" and "the Devil's rain." In Norwegian, there is probably intended a pun on the word *regne* which means both "rain" and "reckon" for this day of rain is also a day of awful reckoning.[28] Regine calls attention to Manders's foot as Peer calls attention to the priest-devil's hoof in *Peer Gynt* and warns Engstrand not to clump about and awaken the "young master" (*den unge herren*) sleeping above. The words "Lord" and "young master" (*Vaarherre* and *den unge herren*) follow closely in the dialogue and Ibsen might, here, intend an at least thematic correspondence, a point we will take up a little later. The Engstrand-Regine dialogue forcefully confirms Engstrand's "satanic" character: he speaks continually of temptations, orgies, weak and fallen humanity, and his oaths are usually associated with the devil (*fanden*) or with blasphemous allusions to the Bible, such as *jøss* (for Jesus), *kors* (cross), *døde og pine* (death and torment). He complains that he always is being blamed for everything and Regine's response to this (somewhat legitimate) satanic complaint is, "Ugh, and then that leg!" In the dialectical pattern of the play, Engstrand's satanism with its "brothel" world and un-Greek ugliness derives from the hostility to the world of the flesh of Pauline Christianity.

An important element in Ibsen's symmetrical design is the character of Johanna, who is in ghostly union with Alving (like the sinister dead pair in Henry James's *The Turn of the Screw*), a union reincarnated in Regine who, with Osvald, reenacts a scene once played by the dead pair. Regine is a vehicle of this Johanna-identity as Osvald is of Alving's. Regine, for example, refuses to join Engstrand's sailors' home with the same words that Johanna once used, in the same house, to refuse Engstrand:

REGINE. Me! Who's been brought up here by a lady like Kammerherrinne Alving. Who's been treated like one of the family, almost . . . ?

Engstrand, soon after this, recalls the words of Johanna's refusal:

ENGSTRAND. Always so stuck up she was. (*Mimics*) Let me go, Engstrand. Let me be. I was three years in service at Rosenvold with Kammerherre Alving, I was.[29]

Both women, we notice, are impressed by the "Kammerherre" title, one
which actually embarrasses Helene Alving. In the course of the Engstrand-Regine dialogue we hear something of Engstrand's past. He was
"thrown downstairs" and lamed, which, in conjunction with his satanic
identity, recollects also the myth of Hephaistos, "thrown by angry Jove."
Hephaistos, whose own notoriously unfaithful wife was seduced by the
military Ares, was, like Satan, associated with fire, and Engstrand is
"sometimes very careless with matches." The parallels between Satan-
Hephaistos and Loki, the Scandinavian mischief-making god, were
pointed out by Jacob Grimm in his *Deutsche Mythologie* (1844), a
major work of that "German scholarship" that Ibsen praised so highly.
Satan, Hephaistos, and Loki were all associated with fire;[30] all three were
lame;[31] Satan and Hephaistos were thrown from heaven;[32] Satan and
Loki both were punished and made to suffer torment.[33] Engstrand, of
course, is a very solid nineteenth-century Norwegian carpenter of the
West Coast, with precise physical and psychical traits; but this dimension of reality, fascinating though it is, is only a small part of Ibsen's
total artistic intention. Engstrand's actions and speeches,[34] unknown to
himself, involve other dimensions of reality; and this is nothing new,
for comparative mythology did not begin in the nineteenth century.
Milton, for one, saw archetypal identities repeating themselves behind
the particular identities of different mythologies. Engstrand's first name,
Jakob, looks back to the Judaic tradition of myth. Jakob Engstrand resembles the biblical Jacob in deceit, cunning, and an unscrupulous self-
interest that allows him to profit under his employer as Jacob profited
under Laban, and the last book of the Old Testament, Malachi, opens,
as it closes, with images reminding us of details in *Ghosts*: for God
promises "Jacob" success and, more grimly, foretells that Edom "shall
build, but I will throw down," an idea that Ibsen, who knew his Bible
thoroughly, may have remembered in the destruction of the Alving
Memorial compared with Jakob Engstrand's more successful building
plans. In his *Deutsche Mythologie* Grimm notes the Christian practice
of erecting Christian buildings upon pagan holy sites, and Helene's
action of erecting on Solvik a building that represents the opposite of

everything that Alving stood for, may carry its own supernatural Nemesis. Though this idea does not accord with the strictest notions of everyday realism, it has the merit of assuming an imaginative continuity between the author of *Emperor and Galilean* and the author of the Cycle: that, in fact, they are the same man.

The satanic connotations (which, of course, are not solemnly horrendous, but to a great extent due to Ibsen's intellectual playfulness— or *galskap*, as he called it) of Engstrand's identity are only further reinforced by his close association with Pastor Manders, an association that, already established in the past, is further cemented in the progress of the play. We have mentioned that Engstrand and Manders are on the same, somewhat low, level in the play's dialectic, incapable of the tragic insights of Helene and Osvald. At the beginning of the play, Engstrand hurriedly exits through one door before Manders enters by another, but in the course of the play, the two figures come closer together until their handclasp and resolve to travel by "the same boat" together, and they exit from the ethically devastated household as unenlightened as ever. This, at first glance, odd alliance of "devil" and priest is new neither in Ibsen nor in European literature. It is, in fact, one of Ibsen's stock metaphors, employed first in *The Pretenders* where, at the sacrifice of realistic credibility, Ibsen brings back the ghost of Bishop Nicholas[35] dressed as a monk, to speak the words of Satan to Christ when he promises Earl Skule: "I will take you up into a high mountain and show you all the glory of the world," and he informs the earl that there are over fifty popes and hundreds of clerics in the lower regions. It is startling to reflect that this same satanic promise is made by Rubek to both Irene and Maia and it obviously stands for ultimate human aspiration which, like the tower of Babel, *can* be regarded as blasphemous. In *Peer Gynt* the devil actually is dressed as a priest and has a deformed foot, or hoof, which has some resemblance to Engstrand's lameness. In *Ghosts*, for the first time, the satanic and priestly halves of the identity are separated, and they seem to be continued, and further developed and subtilized, in the Relling/Molvik, Rosmer/Brendel pairs. This seemingly audacious joke actually is quite ancient: Goethe's Mephistopheles is dressed as a medieval cleric, and Marlowe's Dr. Faustus is even more explicit:

> Go, and return an old Franciscan Friar;
> That holy shape becomes a devil best.

In *Ghosts* this satanic-priestly identity is not of great importance, except as being symptomatic of the moral atmosphere (so un-Hellenic) against which the Hellenic spirit rises, representing the obstacle, in fact, which a resurrected Hellenism would have to overcome and which, in fact, Helene and Osvald have, finally, overcome. It is for this reason that Engstrand and Manders are mainly subordinate comic figures, shut out of the dialectic in which Alving, Helene, and Osvald are engaged. *The Wild Duck*, which is structured upon the Christian world view, treats at far greater depth the complexities of the Christian consciousness.

The similarity of identity between Engstrand and Manders appears in a number of ways. If, for instance, we analyze the Manders-Regine dialogue that follows immediately upon the Engstrand-Regine dialogue, we discover that it is, point for point, a more innocent version of the same themes. It opens, again, with the subject "rain"—Regine this time artfully reversing her earlier judgment and calling it "blessed" (*velsignet*). Manders, just like Engstrand, attempts to persuade Regine to join the highly dubious "sailors' home," using much the same arguments of family duty. Engstrand piously opines that Regine needs a father's care; Manders, over Regine's strong objections, expostulates, "But a daughter's duty, my good girl..." Like Engstrand, Manders observes that Regine has "grown"—though he is less explicit as to the nature of this development. The pastor's oaths are the pious complement of the carpenter's, swearing by God (*Gud*).

The pastor and Engstrand, in fact, are the positive and the negative of the same picture (to adapt the devil's simile in *Peer Gynt*) and if it is appropriate that Manders should represent the Pauline strain of Christianity—under attack from many quarters in the nineteenth century—then it is noteworthy how Manders in his speeches does, in fact, share many of the qualities of Paul, especially the Paul of the epistles to his Greek converts. There is the same denial of all claims of the flesh, the same horror at the life in Paris as Paul's at the fleshly iniquities of the Hellenes, the same philistine indifference to the whole realm of intellectual life and culture classically formulated and represented by Greek civilization. Anyone taking the larger view of the human species and its history cannot but be somewhat jolted by turning from Plato or Aristotle to St. Paul inveighing against long hair, sex, and even, on one occasion, dogs.[36] Paul had great and somewhat forbidding virtues, echoed, perhaps, in Manders's remark to Helene, "What right have human beings to happiness?" but they seem to belong to an eccentric and somewhat disastrously small area of the spirit in comparison with, say, Aeschylus, whose vision seems unclouded by concern with long hair, sexual levity, and dogs.

Both Manders and Paul emphasize *duty*, particularly the family duties of wife to husband, child to parent, and in this they represent a somewhat mechanical and external application of the more living ethical relationships of the ethical society; the spiritual material that led to the gravely and passionately *tragic* rhythms of the *Antigone* or the *Oresteia* are, in Paul, reduced to dogmatic and pious exhortations. The separation of Paul from Christ, which many thinkers of the nineteenth century attempted, would be necessary to Ibsen's program, too, if we see the third empire as combining the best and most essential of paganism with the best and most essential of the Christian spirit.[37]

Manders, like the Church, needs a sick and sinful world to minister to and to sustain his own identity—a role that Engstrand willingly performs for him, but which a healthy paganism would contemn. Equally, Engstrand needs Manders, for his "sailors' home" will be built with the bricks of religion. We see, and hear of, frequent episodes of Engstrand's asking forgiveness of the minister in order better to manipulate him: confessing his sins, repenting, and usefully taking the blame for all wrongdoing. At the beginning of the play he tells Regine he is "blamed for everything," and in Act III he offers to take the blame for the orphanage fire, thus getting the pastor out of an awkward situation. "I am," he tells Manders, "your guardian angel." (The fact that Engstrand most likely *is* responsible for the fire does not alter Manders's ethically dubious behavior in allowing another to take on his guilt.) The collusion of Manders and Engstrand is a perhaps too broad satirical demonstration by Ibsen of *this* level of the Christian consciousness—similar to the satirical portrait of Hecebolius, Julian's Christian tutor, in *Emperor and Galilean*. It is a level of consciousness which, carefully evading full ethical insight or responsibility, is excluded from the higher and more essential levels of the play's dialectic where the Hellenic figures suffer and are destroyed. These latter have moved into a significant pattern that makes up the essential life of Spirit, for significant death, for Ibsen, is preferable to insignificant life. Like an Orestes or Oedipus, Helene Alving pushes forward, reluctantly but ineluctably, to the very limits of desolation. Beyond these limits he does not take her, as Sophocles at last takes the old and blind Oedipus or the stubborn Philoctetes, but she stands more or less where Ibsen claimed he stood as a writer when commenting on the hysterical reception of *Ghosts*: "like a solitary franc-tireur at the outposts."

A tremendous moment in the play, dramatically powerful yet bristling with complexities, is when Manders turns upon Helene the full weight of his reproachful, righteous moralism. As with Tiresias confronting Oedipus, he charges her with willfulness and headstrong rebelliousness, and then glances at her role in marriage and parenthood. Yet, unlike Tiresias, Manders, in invoking tradition, duty, and a higher power, manifests his total inability to comprehend these glibly indicated realities. The great traditional, Christian moral authority that he enlists in his denunciation is discredited by its damning remoteness from the complexities of life. Like the Church pronouncing on modern moral issues, Manders neither can learn to comprehend his times nor learn to keep silent about them, so that his denunciation, for all its force, is a demonstration of his intellectual helplessness.[38]

Ibsen's treatment of this classic confrontation between religious authority and the rebellious individual even includes comedy; and when Helene rouses herself to demolish Manders's whole world view, the complexities deepen. For Helene's defense of herself, with its exposure of Alving, while effectively destroying Manders's authority by demonstrating the disparity between his moral position and his knowledge of the facts, is itself based upon a misconception of values almost as drastic as that of Manders himself: so that these two are stabbing at each other in the dark. In Helene's account, Alving is the great punishment inflicted upon her by Manders, the great wrong from which she still suffers, whose revelation justifies her whole life and shows her to deserve Manders's approbation, from *his* moral standpoint; but in the course of the play she must learn that she, as plausibly, was the great wrong inflicted upon Alving and that her whole life is an elaborate self-deceit and deceit of others to hide that crime. Thus she is *more* guilty than Manders charges!

If we consider the "argument" of *Ghosts* as it emerges, so far, we will find it to be startlingly Nietzschean. There is the same judgment on the Christian tradition, the same exoneration of joy and health, and Nietzsche's aphorism, "Christianity gave Eros poison to drink: he did not die of it but he degenerated into vice," might stand as the motto of *Ghosts*, with Engstrand's "sailors' home" and Alving's syphilis as the motto's terrible emblems. The concept of Eros, in this play, too, is Hellenic, involving the physical, the intellectual, the communal, the esthetic, the religious, and the philosophical levels of consciousness as in Plato's ladder of Eros in *The Symposium*: a concept of Eros resurrected in modern times by Freud, as he acknowledged.[39]

Helene Alving represents a universal as well as a particular identity. Her name, Helene, alerts us to the Hellenic role she is to play, and reminds us, also, of one other wife who fled her home and husband. Helene was the twin sister of Clytemnestra, and is as near as Ibsen can get, in Norwegian, to naming that lady and "Helen," too, is the very symbol of the Greek spirit in European literature. "Helene" is not dissimilar in sound to "Hellener" and her attributes of an inquisitive mind, her freethinking and her ethical consciousness, all suggest the continuing Hellenic tradition of the *Weltgeist*. Her husband's name, Alving, which she bears, on the other hand derives from northern paganism. Jacob Grimm extensively describes the tradition of northern "alvs" (from which we derive "elf" in English) in his *Deutsche Mythologie*, and it is interesting to note that this alv-world contains both beneficent and mischievous figures, the latter resembling such smith-gods as Hephaistos and Wielant, confused with devils by the Christians. The beneficent "alvs" were radiant and beautiful, though very un-Christian in sexual morality.[40] Jacob Grimm continually draws parallels between the northern and the Hellenic mythological traditions and not so covertly implies that both are inimical to Christianity. The condition of consciousness Ibsen is depicting is one that has historically evolved, in which submerged but unextinguished pagan impulses and concepts have been very uncertainly assimilated into the dominant Christian ethos, and this larger history, I think, has created the structure of spiritual reality that the realistic action is exemplifying and continually illuminating. When, for example, Manders justifies making Helene return to her dissolute husband, he tells her, "I was an instrument in the hands of a higher power," invoking the same Pauline phrase as Basileos the Christian at the end of *Emperor and Galilean*. Basileos, like Manders, refuses to see more reality than he can handle, whereas the more profound Maximus, looking into the past and the future, is baffled and defeated. "Pastor" Rørlund, in *Pillars of Society*, speaks the phrase to that latter-day pagan, Dina Dorf, and the phrase can be traced back to the Hegelian dramatist, Heiberg's *A Soul After Death* (*En Sjæl efter Døden*), where Mephistopheles refers to a great man as "et Redskab i Herrens Hænder" (an instrument in the Lord's hands). Manders's phrase, "Jeg var kun et ringe redskap i en høieres haand," closely echoes that of Mephistopheles—and we already have observed that this satanic association is not so incongruous for Ibsen's ministers. Ibsen, with typical irony, allows Manders to pronounce this tremendous phrase of fulfilling universal purposes as he is describing a spiritual disaster.

What we are implying by all this detection of archetypal realities beneath the surface of everyday dramatic realism is not that Ibsen is "enriching" his realism with mythological undertones, making his art "mysterious" and suggesting that many things have happened before,[41] but the more radical idea that Ibsen is interested in the nineteenth century *only* as it embodies those realities that belong to the total, or universal, history of man. We believe that Ibsen looked at the life of his age and was interested when it rose to the level of significance where it revealed its archetypal content, and that this did not dull, but sharpened his eye for what was going on in the present; thus, there is no contradiction between the intentions I here am ascribing to his art, and the firm grasp on the present that always has been considered one of the great features of that art.

The history of the Alving marriage emerges on two levels in the play. In Act I we hear about it through the shocked voice of Helene and the responses of pious horror from Manders who earlier had accused Helen of "throwing off the cross" of her marriage and had congratulated himself on forcing her once again to take up her marriage as a cross. Helene (like Aline Solness in *The Master Builder*) was brought up to place *duties* (*plikter*) above *livsglede*. This was the side of Helene's character that was attracted to the Manders who can ask, "What right have people to happiness?" and it was this aspect of her character, rather than any inherent viciousness in Alving, that corrupted the marriage, as Helene will discover by the end of the play. The fact that she arrives at this discovery by the fine exercise of her duty-bound nature *at its best*, by putting aside concern for herself in order to understand and console her son, is another irony in the dialectic of the play, which, of course, is doing something more serious than making a one-sided criticism of Christian moralism. Poor Manders's moral principles are now revealing themselves to be fatal to the lives of those nearest to him: none more so than the strange perversion of human sexuality that sees marriage as a "cross" to be borne! Beneath the moral complacency of Manders's accounts of his motives and actions, and Helene's justification of herself, something of the *real* horror of the Alving marriage is beginning to emerge. At this moment in the play, however, though Helene is *intellectually* liberated from the past represented by Manders's pious orthodoxy, the depths of her nature still are not freed from this training, so that she is yet unable to prefer the finer vitality of Alving to the life-fearing pietism of Manders. It is only when she is brought to witness the possible destruction of this vitality or creativity in her son that the enormity of the crime against Alving is vividly present to her.

On a first viewing of the play, one is likely to be trapped into either accepting Helene's account of her marriage or rejecting it as an example of Ibsen's own limited puritanism. The verbal counterpoint is extremely subtle; Helene's revelations of the horrors of her married life ironically reveal, unknown to herself or to Manders, the *real* horror of her actions. She recounts to her pastor Alving's "excesses" which forced her to sit up night after night with him, getting him drunk and listening to his silly stories. These cheerless and unsympathetic travesties of bacchanals led to Alving's decline, to Helene, in her own words, having "a weapon

against him" (*For nu hadde jeg våpen imot ham*) and to her taking
over his property, improving it, and disguising "the true nature" of
her husband from the world.

Helene's whole account, given to justify herself, actually describes
her crime against Alving: a crime that, like the protagonist of a Greek
drama, she was, by her very nature, fated to commit for she represented
a law totally opposed to his. At first Alving's energies were confined to
the pietistic little town which so thoroughly reflected Helene's hostile
attitude towards all he stood for, then they were forced into drunken
impotence leading to his loss of control over his estate. Those "silly
stories," too, while quite appropriate to a drunkard in a realistic drama,
in the larger pattern of the play might well refer to the legends and
myths of paganism, still surviving, despite the Church's disapproval,
in the European imagination, often to be maudlinly recalled. Ibsen
at least directly mentions this in Brand's scornful relation of how his
countrymen, when drunk, recall the heroic legends of "king Bele's days,"
and there is a similar situation in *The Wild Duck* when old Ekdal, drunk,
is given to nostalgia over his military and hunting past.

At one point in her revelation Helene tells Manders, in the same
tone of horror, how her maid once was bringing water for the flowers
when that irrepressible pagan, Alving, pursued her. Beneath the outraged moralism of Helene's voice, and Manders's shocked responses,
is buried a lively episode which, in its human terms, is not so unlike
such pursuits as Pan and Syrinx, Apollo and Daphne. Helene concedes
that Alving was "charming" (*hjertevinnende*) and one begins to detect,
beneath Helene's narration, something of that incorrigible pagan joy
that Ibsen's Julian so admired in Alcibiades.[42]

It is important, for our understanding of the play, to see that Helene's
version of the past is a distortion, for we have, here, a form of dramatic
counterpoint where the account of reality given by Helene is played
off against what we begin to detect as the actual truth of the situation.
At this point in the play, the gulf between Helene and her husband
indicates the irreconcilable opposition of the two life principles they
represent: of life as duty or life as spontaneity, joy, a gulf that can be
bridged only by Helene's abandoning her principle and recognizing the
value of its opposite.

The dialectical antagonisms within the *language* of the play thus
enact one of the play's themes—the tragic one-sidedness and mutual
exclusiveness of the opposing forces in the emperor-Galilean conflict.
As the play progresses, Helene is forced to discover a language more
adequate to the reality of the situation until, finally, her Christian
conscientiousness incorporates Alving's life-craving consciousness, so

that the language of the latter moves from the suppressed background
to the foreground, as Helene actually begins to speak with Alving's voice.[43]

The offspring of this joyless marriage, Osvald, brings into the play
the Parisian (and Alving) values of joyful, spontaneous, guilt-free
living. Paris in the nineteenth century not only was synonymous in
the northern world with "immorality":[44] it was also, since the days of
the *philosophes* and despite the restoration of Church and monarchy
and the consequent reaction recorded by Georg Brandes, the center
of the most determined intellectual onslaught upon Christianity until
Nietzsche. The little exchange between Osvald and Manders on the
life style of the Parisian artists, therefore, reflects an actual hostility
between orthodox moralism and the most adventurous imaginative
thought in the spirit of the age, so that Ibsen's audience would have
been able to supply the wider dimension of references which are mostly
lost to us.

Osvald's doctor, in Paris, cynically repeated the Old Testament saying,
"the sins of the fathers are visited upon the children," but Osvald,
knowing nothing of his father's life but Helene's idealistic lie, takes
the blame upon himself and pronounces upon his carefree life in Paris
the judgment that Helene and Manders already have pronounced
upon his father:

. . . that's when I learned the truth—the incredible truth: that this beautiful,
soul-stirring life with my young artist friends was something I should never
have entered. It was too much for my strength. So—everything's my own
fault.[45]

One sees that it is *life itself* that is being slandered here: its whole
possibility of fullness, joy, achievement, represented supremely, perhaps,
by the Athenian experiment, and decried ever since by the vision of
life that can ask, "What right have human beings to happiness?"
Kierkegaard has demonstrated that the "esthetic" way of life was a
genuine and serious commitment, a discipline almost as challenging
as the "ethical" mode of life which, he set out to prove, was its superior.
But Hegel's analysis of Hellenic culture is far more penetrating and
challenging, for it showed the esthetic and the ethical modes of life
to be part of a total objectification of spirit into the supremely creative
affirmation: the creation of the *polis* or adequate human community.
Manders is unsparingly depicted by Ibsen as being anti-life; not only
is he virginal but he fears the manifestation of life in art or the life
styles out of which art arises. Helene, intellectually, has detached herself
from Manders's opinions and can side with Osvald in the discussion on
the life style of his artist-friends, but this intellectual emancipation

is superficial: in the depths of her spirit she is still with Manders and it will require the full shock of Osvald's disintegration to bring home to her the crime against life that her own values represent. When she attempts to remove Osvald's feelings of guilt, she starts upon a course that will remove the guilt from Alving, too, and she will stand self-condemned—the ironic reversal of the opening of the play which was to celebrate her great self-vindication. Her past idealization of her husband, like the memorial, was a lie, ostensibly to hide *his* guilt from the world, but which actually hid her own, for the attitude of mind that saw Alving's life as guilty was itself based upon a lie. In the end Helene exonerates Alving, not by means of lies and a fraudulent memorial, but by means of the truth: a complexity and subtlety of situation and development typical of Ibsen.

Act I, in which Mrs. Alving presents her husband's past in the most lurid light, ends with the ghost of that husband speaking through his children who, though unconsciously, become his avengers as in the Orestes story. Helene has told Manders that on the next day, at the dedication of the memorial to Alving, "the whole comedy" of the past will have been played out. Immediately there follows the famous noise in the conservatory and Helene's terrified whisper: "Ghosts! Those two in the conservatory. Come back to haunt us," as this Clytemnestra and her Aegisthus go in to the unwittingly avenging Orestes and Electra.

The offstage flirtation, covered up by the embarrassed Osvald, which seems, at first, a quaint nineteenth-century inhibition, one of the limitations under which Ibsen worked, becomes, in his hands, an appropriate metaphor in itself for suppressed sexuality. For Osvald not only reenacts his father's philandering; he reenacts its furtiveness and the shock it occasioned in his mother. One's response to this episode, like one's response to Helene's revelations of her husband's offenses, will depend to a great extent on how far one has grasped the meaning of the play whose theme is the calamitous suppression of Eros by forces that still are thwarting its liberation. If one takes the view of sexuality of Manders and Helene, this episode, and Alving's past, is shocking; however, if one looks back at the play from the vantage point of a Hilde Wangel or Maia and Ulfheim, the situation is shocking in quite another way!

Osvald, as the child of both parents, is the battleground on which their opposing laws fight to the death, and if one side of his nature is Alving's pagan values that will be cleared of guilt, the other, which has honored the false image of his father and condemned himself and his life in Paris, derives from Helene's Christian values—a dualism we find acutely present in Julian of *Emperor and Galilean*. Osvald is invested with something of a messianic destiny by his mother who tells Manders that her son will "speak out" the new ideas and beliefs that she, in her solitude, has been formulating. More than once she addresses Osvald as "blessed boy" (*velsignede gutt*) which reinforces Regine's term for Osvald, young master/lord (*den unge herren*), and these overtones of a Christ-like identity surely are powerfully caught up in the closing moments of the play in which Helene wipes Osvald's face, kneels before him, and, as the sun streams behind his collapsed figure, recollects the traditional *pietà* of mother and crucified son. The recollection of Christ's fate is present in the fact that Osvald atones for the guilt of the past, of which he is innocent, and must suffer a "spiritual breakdown" (*aandelige nedbrudd*). Hugh Kenner has pointed out that the syphilis in *Ghosts* really is a metaphor for Original Sin[46]— which, again, refers the pattern of the little local drama to a universal drama. The disease also calls to mind the pagan images of plague and pollution—the unclean presence that works a doom through a whole family. We notice that, in the first group, this image of pollution develops from *A Doll's House* to *An Enemy of the People*, providing a dark undercurrent to the pagan imagery and themes of these plays.

Osvald is torn in half by the collision of the two ethical forces in the dialectic that are designated Duty and Joy-of-life. He has been brought up by his mother to respect the former principle and to honor its supposed existence in his father, but his own nature, both in his life and in his art, impels him towards the latter: a character condition which, in fact, makes the role somewhat difficult to project, for he is neither a thoroughgoing hedonist like Alving, nor a thoroughgoing moralist like his mother, but, rather, an unresolved possibility, the *potential* creative union of these two value systems. Thus he is concerned to defend the honor of his bohemian friends in Paris, while attracted to a way of viewing life that would make such concern for conventional honor absurd. One metaphor for his ineffectual attempt to return to sources of greater instinctual and creative energy and freedom is the champagne, for drink is a frequent and important metaphor, in Ibsen's writing, for the release of the imagination from a repressive reality. G. Wilson Knight observes:

. . . as we watch Osvald asking for drink and yet more drink, we may regard him as a modern successor to Emperor Julian, soliciting the Dionysian fire to re-awake a dead culture and centuries of Christianity-gone-sour from the nature-born and sun-impregnated elixirs.[47]

The desire for drink is an indication in the character of energies and potentialities that cannot find a creative or a permissible outlet in a repressive structure of reality. Weaker or less imaginative natures, such as Manders's, can accept the repressive order and function smoothly within it. A strong nature, such as Helene's, can adapt the repressive order to her own purposes, without an acute awareness of loss. But, in Ibsen's plays, there is an interesting class of characters, imaginative, creative, or of wider vision, who, unable to accept the repressive order or adapt it to firm but narrow purposes, and incapable of altering it, are driven to a somewhat desperate rediscovery of the repressed content of their psyches through drink—the equivalent of the contemporary use of drugs. Such characters as Rank, Osvald, Relling, Brendel, and Løvborg usually are unable to *objectify* their powers satisfactorily; Osvald's creativity has ended. A successfully energetic and objectified talent such as Thomas Stockmann's (the masculine ideal of this first group as Nora, perhaps, is its feminine ideal) can include drinking and feasting with creative work (his science) and with his active role *vis-à-vis* the social structure.

At the moment when young Lieutenant Alving is about to be resurrected, Osvald asks for glass after glass of champagne so that Regine must twice go to the cellar for the bottles. Osvald, drinking the champagne, tells his mother how his art had always "turned on this joy of life.... Light and sunshine and a holiday spirit... and radiantly happy faces." But, in his mother's home and the society surrounding it, all these impulses would, he claims, degenerate into "something ugly," reminding one of Plato's comment that the corruption of the best produces the worst. Thus, by means of the drink, Osvald has traced the course of his father's fall, and it is at this point that Helene "sees it all." She is about to speak out to her son—and speaking out would express her belated but vivid awareness of the value, joy-of-life, her husband represented; but Ibsen delays this moment, for Helene will not be able to articulate to Osvald and the theater audience her insight into this suddenly understood conflict, until she, as well as that audience, also is brought to comprehend its full calamity. The moment of insight, therefore, is interrupted by a piece of obvious but effective and appropriate symbolism: the orphanage, that fraudulent memorial that violates the truth of both Alving's and Helene's life values, now burns up, and with it the possibility of perpetuating this pious fraud in the future, for the building was uninsured.[48] Everything of the past that is inessential to the dialectic is cleared away as the play moves towards the full disclosure of the truth: a process of gradual removal of falsehood and error in Ibsen's dramatic method that G. Wilson Knight has called "spiritual strip-tease."

In the action of Act III, Manders, Engstrand, and Regine are one by one removed from the scene as we move to this play's ultimate confrontation: Helene, staring at the wreckage of her son and of a life's work founded upon the disastrous denial of the instinctual, spontaneous, creative values caught up in the meaning of *livsglede!* It is an indication of the control Ibsen has over the material of this play that he can develop it upon so many levels, one of these levels being fairly broad comedy. Act III opens with the distressed Manders fleeing into Rosenvold pursued by the limping Engstrand and, in an ironic reversal of their situation in Act II, Engstrand now fastens guilt on Manders and magnanimously absolves him of it, thereby binding the minister closer to him and his scheme for setting up a "sailors' home," Chamberlain Alving's Home,[49] and metaphorically emphasizing the collusion of the "fallen" and the pietistic views of the world. To further the founding of Chamberlain Alving's Home, Manders and Engstrand leave to travel by the same boat together, taking with them this now irrelevant and superseded phase of the play's dialectic. With the departure of Manders and Engstrand, the room is sealed off from the outside world (Osvald asks that the doors be shut), and the remaining figures group for a final reckoning. The whole rhythm of the play now shifts from the "busy" realism of the previous action, with its comic villainies, its shocking disclosures, the burning orphanage, to the grave truth-telling and unadorned anguish of Helene's confrontation with her son. This is a height of consciousness, like that of Greek tragedy at its best, attained by nearly unbearable insight and not to be sustained for long; the rest of the Cycle will not present us with such a starkly terrible confrontation again, for it will be concerned to resurrect other modes of spirit and other responses from us. But, for the moment, the Greek aspect of our consciousness is to be awakened for its resurrection day, as we, the audience, are encouraged to rise up to something like the ethical courage of that mode of spirit.

Helene attempts to take the burden from Osvald's mind by at last truthfully exonerating Alving and so exonerating Osvald's own belief in the life value, joy-of-life, to which he has given seemingly disastrous allegiance. She has been shocked and awakened to a new level of perception, and now acknowledges the right, and even primacy, of the law, *livsgleden,* that she previously had violated. In a sensitive analysis of Ibsen's language, Inga-Stina Ewbank has pointed out how, at this moment, Helene "is seeing Alving's life from *his* point of view, and so [her] speech gives us, through the new dimension of understanding, an interaction of two minds."[50] This interaction, one might say, articulates the lost potential marriage of Helene and Alving, glimpsed now through the wreckage of so many lives. Alving is seen as a "child," full of joyous energy but crushed by the silent conspiracy of a joyless, ugly society bent only on business and bureaucracy, to whom Helene herself had brought only cheerless ideas of "duty and things of that kind." "Everything resolved into duties—*my* duties and *his* duties, and—I'm afraid I made this house unbearable for your poor father."

The full disclosure, like many recognition scenes in Greek drama, involves also the discovery of blood ties: Regine is revealed to be Alving's daughter; but, ironically, instead of this revelation cementing the family together, as in the brother-sister recognition scenes of Orestes and Electra, or Orestes and Iphigenia, it serves, like the discovery of consanguinity in *Oedipus the King*, to destroy the family. Regine now leaves Rosenvold to league with her false father in setting up the home named after her true father, so that the stage is left to Helene and the son of the husband she has learned to love too late. Now the doors are not only closed, but locked, sealing off the confrontation of mother and son from the outside world, and giving the audience the sense of unbearable claustrophobia, the dialectical rhythm having reached its ultimate destination in an inescapable prison of logic as Helene is forced violently to face in her son the disintegration which she, long ago, helped to initiate. This terrible scene, with Osvald driving his mother back into the house as she attempts to escape, calling for help, vividly reenacts the confrontation of Orestes and his mother, as does the whole concept of the mother's fate, waiting for years, finally catching up with her in the figure of her son. The modern melodramatic movement of the play, like its dialectic, reaches back and rediscovers (and reactivates) the archetypal mythic situation.

The last stage, or spasm, of this dialectical rhythm, is hideously ironic, for Osvald now asks his mother to do *consciously* what she *unconsciously* has done to his father—to destroy him. In the final stage of her emancipation from the past Helene is brought, by the reincarnation of her husband in Osvald, to a fate worse than that which Clytemnestra suffered: to repeat her earlier crime when her whole spirit cries out against it. She had helped to destroy her husband and the memory of him, through hatred; now, when she has come to love her husband in her son, she must, out of this same love, repeat the action she has come to loathe. Much of the great intensity and power of this moment in the play—the most powerful moment in the whole of the Cycle—derives from the terrible Sophoclean ironies that it gathers together into one action. All the earlier substance of the play is recollected like the many themes of a contrapuntal recapitulation: but they reappear, now, in a sharp new light, with all the force of *Nemesis*.[51]

The alternative to destruction by his mother, Osvald reveals, is a hideous existence not so dissimilar to the drastic condition described by Hegel, "the mere being of a stone, a state which is not even true of a child," when discussing the consciousness that escapes guilt and responsibility. Osvald is terrified of becoming "a child" again, or of growing old as a helpless, senile invalid. So horrible is this destiny in human terms that it might seem both superfluous and unfeeling to suggest that it has a wider application: yet we feel that the right account of Ibsen's dramatic intentions would reveal not only the great *intensive* movement of his dramaturgy to the particular "heart of darkness" of the suffering individual but also its great *extensive* movement to cosmic implications. The images that Osvald employs to describe his possible extension into the future, a helpless child or a senile old man, repeat the contemptuous images Brand employed to describe his contemporaries' concepts of God: either a child at its mother's breast, as in the South, or an inoffensive, somewhat senile old man, in the Protestant North.[52] In opposition to these spiritually undemanding concepts of God, that leave the substance of everyday reality untransfigured by Spirit, and comfortably free of the demands made on an Oedipus or a Moses, Brand announced that he required a god young and strong as Hercules and in this same speech he claims that churches and dogmas decay, that all things are subject to "the moth and worm":

> Yet there is something that remains,
> The spirit that was never formed,
> Set free the same time it was doomed
> Once, in the pristine Spring of Time:
> And, through man's happy pieties,
> Reached from the flesh to Spirit's source.
> Now it is bartered in mere scraps,
> Thanks to today's idea of God
> But from these stumps of broken souls,
> (Torsos of amputated Mind)
> These separated heads and hands,
> A hero, strong and whole shall rise
> In whom God finds his greatest work,
> His heir, His Adam, young and free.[53]

The stature of the god, in other words, defines the stature of the man, and *vice versa*; for man is only as great as his spiritual conceptions, just as his spiritual conceptions, his gods, are only as great as himself. I do not think it is fanciful to recall these terms when considering the devastation-within-the-drawing-room of *Ghosts*: to suggest that the collapse of the house of Alving is an emblem for a larger devastation, of a whole world form. The passage from *Brand* claims that at some period in the past, although already doomed (*fortapt*)—containing within itself the origins of its later Fall?—the human race found redemption (was set free) by building a bridge from the flesh to Spirit's source. This redemption was achieved through a "joyful human faith" (*freidig mannetro*) similar to the "happy pieties" of Keats's *Ode to Psyche*, and is envisioned as a Greek-like statuary and as the innocent Adam, before the later dismemberment of history. This redemption, therefore, in *this* passage, is not the Christian redemption of the broken body, the agony on the Cross, the profoundly painful victory over the flesh, of the New Testament myth, but a redemption *by means of* the flesh. The world of *Ghosts* is one in which the bridge between Flesh and Spirit is broken and each is disastrously separated from the other, and, as in the world of *Emperor and Galilean*, lost without the other, becoming a travesty of the values of both flesh and spirit. This condition is evidenced in the collusion between the world of Engstrand's sailors' home and the world of Manders's piety: here both Flesh and Spirit are debased and contributing to each other's degeneration, or, with terrible conciseness, in the image of syphilis: the very source of life polluted because the sources of Spirit, too, are polluted. Helene's belated recovery of the image of the young Alving, full of energy and joy-of-life, is not unlike the recollection of "happy human faith" (*freidig mannetro*) and the "Adam, young and free" of Brand's speech: an image of human strength and beauty united with spiritual freedom. And this, we have seen, is the constant German Romantic vision of the Hellenic spirit, from the most ardent Hellenists, like Schiller, whose *Gods of Greece* (*Die Götter Griechenlands*) proclaimed, in a stanza deplored by Hegel,

> Since the gods then were more human,
> Mankind was more godlike.
>
> (Da die Göttes menschlicher waren,
> Waren Menschen göttlicher.)

even to such a sober Swabian as Hegel himself. The *military* identity of Alving (and such a fallen pagan as Lieutenant Ekdal) reminds us that Hegel saw the pagan world as epitomized by two young military heroes, Achilles and Alexander,[54] and went on to claim, like Ibsen's Brand, that Hellenic civilization had momentarily (in spite of humanity's later more sombre destiny) built a bridge from Flesh to Spirit:

At an earlier stage I compared the Greek world with the period of adolescence; not, indeed, in *that* sense, that youth bears within it a serious anticipative destiny, and an ulterior aim—presenting thus an inherently incomplete and immature form, and being then most defective when it would deem itself perfect—but in *that* sense, that youth does not yet present the activity of work, does not exert itself for a definite intelligent aim, but rather exhibits a concrete freshness of the soul's life. It appears in the sensuous, actual world, as Incarnate Spirit and Spiritualized Sense—in a Unity which owed its origin to Spirit. Greece presents to us the cheerful aspect of youthful freshness, of Spiritual vitality.[55]

The dialectical recovery of the value of young Alving at the end of *Ghosts* gains, I believe, if we keep in mind this nineteenth-century vision of a lost human potential represented by the Hellenic world. No one reading Herder's *Reflections on the Philosophy of the History of Mankind*, or Hegel's *Philosophy of History*, could fail to be moved by the extinction of the Greek spirit that these authors recorded, nor to feel (though Hegel is concerned to deny this) that mankind somehow lost sight of an important part of its spirit in subsequent history. Such an image of loss haunted the imagination of many nineteenth-century thinkers musing on the spiritual destiny of man (Nietzsche is one example) and it very obviously haunted Ibsen's imagination, impelling him to spend so long on the subject of *Emperor and Galilean*. The image of the young Adam, in Brand's speech, or of young Alving in *Ghosts*, is reminiscent of Michelangelo's Adam in the Sistine Chapel— of Man before the Fall, but placed in a vast history of the human spirit that concludes with Judgment Day and the images of broken, damned souls.[56]

In the dialectical development of the play, the final perception we are brought to is not just the tragedy of Helene, nor just that of Osvald, but of the dead father, too. His suffering, confinement, and decline emerge as the unexpiated wrong that has brought about this day of reckoning. This second, subterranean movement of the play, in which the rights of the dead man, once thrust into the background, as in the dialogues of the opening of the play, now powerfully emerge into the foreground and into the light, is a positive movement in the dialectic that rescues the play from either the cynical pessimism or the lugubrious moralism often attributed to it. This movement is something much stronger, healthier, saner, and less fashionable than pessimism: the dramaturgy is expressing a complex, thoroughly thought-out *concept*, and this intellectual intention behind the emotionally effective dramaturgy, like counterpoint in music, gives Ibsen's art the toughness and complexity and above all the *sanity* that are essential to the highest art. The action of *Ghosts*, then, is not merely the necessary negative one of the destruction of false appearance, but one, also, of recovery of tabooed reality. A false mode of consciousness is painfully discarded and the possibility of a truer mode of consciousness indicated. The rehabilitation of young Alving is rather similar to a process of pictorial restoration, where centuries of accumulated error or distortion are cleaned away to reveal the brilliant original. There are, we notice, many references in the play to false accounts, false teachings, lies, hyprocrisies, the concealment and distortion of the truth, both consciously and, more deeply, unconsciously. The memorial is the flagrant emblem and example of this, but the false documents of Regine's birth, Mrs. Alving's lying letters to her son, Manders's slander of Parisian bohemia, Engstrand's deceptions of the minister, the euphemisms for his "sailors' home," etc., etc., all create a texture of stifling dishonesty within which Helene Alving is brought, struggling, out of her own massive self-deception. Keeping in mind the wider perspectives of the play, these multiple internal and external deceits suggest a huge falsification of historical reality, an experience Ibsen commented on when trying to find trustworthy accounts of Julian the Apostate. This work of falsification is one in which we all have a share and the movement to truth and freedom, which must be experienced in the intimate reality of our daily life as in the larger rhythm of universal reality, requires that the whole substance of our idea of reality be ruthlessly exposed as false: a task requiring the whole Cycle, for *Ghosts* is only one of its moments.

If the action of *Ghosts* reveals what is spiritually bankrupt in the traditions of Europe, in both its pagan and Christian inheritance, it also clears the way for the recovery of what is essential to the future, by separating the false from the true. Such a process is the sustaining principle of the Cycle which always has as its goal that "Resurrection Day" that is the masterpiece of Ibsen's last artist. Ibsen's demolition work is so ruthlessly thorough because he has building plans to justify the devastation. For this reason, his return to the past is totally different from the more sentimental revivalisms of the Celtic, Classical, Viking, or Medieval twilights so typical among artists and writers of Ibsen's times.

Ghosts, then, ends its dialectical movement on an image of recovery and collapse: Osvald, collapsed in the armchair with the sun streaming behind him; Helene clutching the "twelve white tablets," uncertain whether or not to finish him off, and the rising sun, flooding the stage as this long journey into light ends by dispelling the specters of the past.[57] The arrival of the Sun, connected as it is, in Osvald's description of his own art, with *livsgleden*, surrounds the little human tragedy with the invincible creative power of the universe: of great life-renewing energies beyond human power, which terribly and ironically reproach Helene's lifelong battle against this cosmic Dionysos. The human moral order had shown itself to be *contra natura* and, whether the crime was conscious or unconscious, it must be punished, for it cannot be suffered by Nature. The final, terrible conjunction of these two dimensions, that of the aberrant little human order with that of the suprahuman cosmic order, and the quite ruthless and inevitable destruction of the former for its *hubris,* closely resembles the conclusions of many Greek tragedies in which the gods, without malice or dogma, without the *personal* animus of the Christian God, uphold a natural order which the human protagonists have offended. Thus the "small" dimension of Oedipus's personal history is brought up against the cosmic order his history has offended; and the house of Atreus, convulsed and suffering through its generations, affirms the eternal structure of reality against which it had rashly set itself.

In *Ghosts* the intersection of these two dimensions is imperceptibly created in the gradually increasing light, in which Mrs. Alving's little lamplight is absorbed by the greater light of the sun—an effect more apparent in the theater, of course, where the greater light is itself "stage managed." The light of the little lamp is analogous to Helene's lonely, questing intellect, the individual reason which is absorbed in the universal, "Absolute" Reason which is the driving force of the whole Cycle. Thus the horrible human drama is seen as only a particular moment of the total Concept: a moment which, to be sure, requires courage to be comprehended and endured, but which must be endured if the human spirit is to attain to truth and freedom.

The restored image of Alving is as if the broken spirit torsos, the heads and hands of antique sculpture that Ibsen would have seen in Rome, were restored to the masterpiece Brand envisioned. This masterpiece of Greek-like statuary stands in contrast to the Christian icons of Saintly, Fallen, and Crucified Man (just as it was the renaissance of Greek ideals that transfigured Europe in the fourteenth and fifteenth centuries and revived the emperor-Galilean conflict). The opening of *Emperor and Galilean* powerfully employs this contrast where the "overturned statues" of the pagan gods contrast with the Christian church, crowded with "beggars, cripples and blind men at the doors." The pagans of Julian's Byzantium had disdained the Christians' preference for images of broken and mutilated men, and for a god who was a cadaver on a cross.

This Greek image is integral to a play that itself reawakens, through the patterns and rhythms of modern life, the substance of Greek drama. The self-examination that Ibsen conducts on behalf of the modern spirit has reached through every layer of the poet's imaginative life just as he has submitted the structure of nineteenth-century reality, also, to the closest scrutiny. It is this double rhythm, of inward self-analysis and outward analysis of external realities, that makes the texture of *Ghosts,* for all its Sophoclean economy, so rich in implications.

Because we have been primarily concerned with the "argument" of the play—its intellectual bone structure—it has been difficult to do justice to the distinguished and difficult dramatic method Ibsen created for *Ghosts.* Its steady control of its different levels of action, its refusal to indulge in "fine writing" or redundant "character portrayal" derive from a firm and serious sense of artistic and philosophic purposes that is rare in nineteenth-century literature and will always prevent Ibsen from attaining the fashionable *intellectual* popularity of more lurid imaginative writers of the time, such as Dostoievsky or Strindberg, who make more resounding presences in, say, histories of Existentialism. The difficulty and distinction of Ibsen's art make it far harder to appreciate the imaginative scope it achieves and the profundity of its analysis of reality; and this means that Ibsen generally is appreciated and praised for very modest attainments (trenchant social criticism, psychological insight, unsparing self-criticism, good dramatic technique). Much of this interpretation is even rather patronizing, learnedly disparaging Ibsen's learning, urbanely dismissing his own claims as to the central importance of *Emperor and Galilean* to his later work, or of the influence of German culture upon his art, and so on. This is a great injustice, for Ibsen is a *great* writer, comparable with Sophocles, Shakespeare, and Goethe for the depth and scope of his art, its classic restraint, and its concern with *adequacy* rather than with effect.

For all the complexity of analysis Ibsen is conducting in *Ghosts,* the play moves faultlessly to the fully unfolded horror of Osvald's last dialogue with his mother, and it is here that the distinguished *reticence* of Ibsen's method is most striking. An inferior writer would not have been able to resist the opportunity for fine writing, or for pathos: but Ibsen's eye is not upon the "effects" but upon the adequate revelation of his subject which he allows to emerge with Sophoclean severity. He wishes the audience to face the same heart of darkness that the Athenian audience was tough enough to contemplate, and he interposes nothing between the audience and that confrontation that will prevent them from attaining that Greek toughness. It is for this reason, and not for its lurid subject matter, that the play retains its power today—and also retains its value. Ibsen has a long-meditated vision of reality: of human history and destiny which impels him to view the structure of contemporary reality in a certain way. He wishes us to see this vision, too, and his dramatic art is created, not because he has happened to have found a good subject which can be given effective treatment, but, in his own words, to make us *"see."*

Just what the nature of this seeing is, Ibsen's own description of Greek tragedy may help to define. Writing to Bjørnson while he was in Rome, Ibsen asked:

> Do you remember "The Tragic Muse" that stands in the room outside the Rotunda in the Vatican? No statue that I have yet seen in Italy has taught me so much. I would say that it has revealed the essence of Greek tragedy to me. That indescribably sublime, calm joy in the expression of the face, that laurel-crowned head with something supernaturally exuberant and bacchantic about it, those eyes that look both inward and yet through and far beyond the outward object they are fixed on—that is Greek tragedy.[58]

As in Greek tragedy (e.g., *Oedipus Tyrannos*) the conscious, rational and ethical decisions and actions have resulted in unconscious, irrational, and appalling consequences which, however, lead to the truth, and to spiritual growth as conscious activity could not have done. It is by a terrible "cunning of Reason" that the protagonists finally are led to "see," so that, as in the best Greek tragedy, there is a dark, unconscious action counterpointing the conscious action, the intentional action bringing about the more adequate, unintended result. As in *Oedipus Tyrannos* the "little" rhythm of individual and conscious reason is lured, by the structure of reality, to a better comprehension of the universal Reason in reality. It is this ironic movement towards an unwelcome but necessary heart of darkness, revealing the rationality of reality *in spite of* the individual's own confident rationality, that signals the recovery of the tragic dimension, the tragic vision, in *Ghosts*.

CHAPTER 5

The Dialectic of Rosmersholm

The absolutely imperative task of democracy is to make itself aristocratic.
Ibsen in *Letters and Speeches*, p. 320

Ibsen did not merely preach the idea of intellectual aristocracy: he created it.
Ashley Dukes in *Modern Dramatists*, 1907

The title of the play *Rosmersholm* as we contemplate it in our theater program, subtly prepares us for the aristocratic emphasis the play will develop, as the title *Mansfield Park* does for Jane Austen's novel. It suggests tradition, a way of life built round and taking its tone from the dynastic line of the Rosmers. Such an idea of artistocracy, where the spirit has settled into somewhat rigid forms, where the refinement is not intellectual or esthetic but, rather, habitual, is a discredited one in the modern world but it will be the starting point from which we, as audience, will comprehend a truer idea of aristocracy: "an aristocracy of spirit" as in Ibsen's famous speech delivered to the workingmen of Trondheim in 1885. At a time of fierce political controversies and rivalries, Norway needed, Ibsen declared, an element of nobility in its national life:

Of course I am not thinking of a nobility of birth, nor of that of wealth, nor of that of knowledge, neither of that of ability or talent. I am thinking of a nobility of character, of a nobility of will and spirit.
Nothing else can make us free.
This nobility that I hope will be granted our nation will come from two sources. It will come to us from two groups that have not as yet been irreparably harmed by party pressure. It will come to us from our women and from our workingmen.[1]

Nevertheless, in *Rosmersholm* Ibsen centers his drama not within a working-class milieu but within that of the aristocracy; and the heroine

206

of the play displays her belatedly acquired nobility of spirit only at the cost of her will to live. As always, whatever Ibsen's musings on the shape of things to come, his subject is the structure of the present and its complex heritage.

It seems appropriate that during the conception and creation of *Rosmersholm* Ibsen moved his residence from Rome to Munich. Rome, the scene of the ancient Roman civilization and of Latin influence upon the later culture of Europe, found itself forced to exist, reluctantly, within the new Europe shaped by Bismarck's ruthless but dynamically emerging nation state of Germany. Rome had impressed upon the world its traditional and civic values of law, order, civilization, and, later, an established Church, hierarchic, conventional, and absolute. Yet, in its earlier and its later history, Rome had been challenged by the Germanic peoples, who at first devastated the eternal city itself and, later, in the realm of thought and spirit, overthrew the Roman authority. These huge historical antitheses, between Order and Freedom, Law and Anarchy, the disruption of an established, traditional, but stifling way of life by a somewhat ruthless principle of change, are reflected in the dramatic structure of *Rosmersholm*. Within the microcosm of immediate human experience can be discerned the macrocosm of universal human experience which has gone into making up the structure of the modern consciousness. Ibsen's description of the play, in response to a query by Bjørnson's nephew, then at grammar school, in fact refers to both these dimensions of experience:

> For the different spiritual functions do not develop evenly and abreast of each other in any one human being. The acquisitive instinct hurries from conquest to conquest. The moral consciousness—what we call the conscience—is, on the other hand, very conservative. It has its roots deep in traditions and in the past generally. Hence the conflict within the individual.[2]

Ibsen suggests here that the drama of many characters on the stage is really the drama of *one* consciousness (one *gestalt* or shape of spirit in all its dialectical complexity) and that the characters associated with the "acquisitive instinct" on the one hand and those associated with the "moral consciousness" on the other are all qualities and faculties of a single mind. Nevertheless, Ibsen adds,

> . . . the play is first and foremost a story of human beings and human destiny.[3]

Human beings and human destiny, however, are inextricably bound up with the forces of revolution and reaction of Ibsen's own times and these, in turn, can only be understood through awareness of the total spiritual history of which they are the latest expression.

Ibsen, of course, is not unique in seeing the structure of Europe as one in which the Latin and Mediterranean peoples, embodying civic, restraining, and cultural values, continually need rejuvenating by the violent but vigorous peoples from the north. In Ibsen's own time this was considered to be the purpose of northern (and especially Norwegian) literature itself, not only by the reputedly enfeebled centers of European civilization but by the less self-critical of Norwegian writers themselves. Such a north-south polarity was a commonplace of German romanticism, expressed by such thinkers as Friedrich Schlegel in his *Lectures on Dramatic Art and Literature*[4] and encountered in England during the introduction of Norwegian literature—mainly the early novels of Bjørnson—in the later nineteenth century, before the arrival of Ibsen. As in all the plays in the Cycle, Ibsen, musing on human history and human destiny, locates his large themes within the human psyche itself—within consciousness—so that they emerge as a delicate and subtle interplay of minds. We will see that there is good reason for discovering the presence of German Enlightenment dramaturgy and themes in *Rosmersholm*,[5] and one feature of this is the method, so similar to that of Schiller, Lessing, and Goethe, of developing the widest-ranging dialectic of ideas within the interplay of a few highly articulate characters.

This delicate interplay of minds, where the human passions and perceptions reinforce and clarify the idealistic dialectic, creates a texture of "elective affinities" (*Wahlverwandtschaften*) quite unlike the essentially *non*-communicative conflicts of *The Wild Duck*. In a letter to Sofie Reimers, an actress at the Christiania Theater, who inquired after the character of Rebekka which she was to impersonate, Ibsen advised her to read the play many times, and to note what the *other* characters said of Rebekka. Though this is good advice for the understanding of any part in an Ibsen play, it applies with particular force to *Rosmersholm* where, as J. W. McFarlane has observed (and he could be describing, as well, say, Goethe's *Torquato Tasso*):

> The world that Ibsen constructs . . . is a world of relationships, a lattice of conjoined characters linked each to each, in which dramatically speaking it is less important to evaluate the constituent elements as discrete phenomena than it is to see how they stand to each other; less important to see how they separately change than it is to see how, in the flux of changing circumstance, the relations between them change; less important to "place" them by political belief, or psychological type, than it is to note the sightings they separately take on each other, and continue to take (often with unexpected results) in the light of new events; not forgetting that any change in these latticed relationships will be reflected in changes all round, in the sense that Rosmer's relations with Kroll, or Rebecca's, are also functions of their own private relationship, and that any change *there* will have its consequences *here*.[6]

The situation described above is not unlike the condition of consciousness at the level of Spirit in Hegel's *Phenomenology*, in which all the elements of McFarlane's analysis are present, with the *added* dimension that each of these elements is also conscious of, and coming to new relationship with, *itself*, thus adding an *inward* movement, or structure, to the lattice of external relationships. Such a complex of interrelating psyches, moving both inward and outward at once, brings to mind the later manner of Henry James and, in fact, it is to Henry James that one interpreter of the *Phenomenology* likens Hegel's account of Spirit:

> The social-spiritual sphere we have now entered [that of *Spirit*] is said by Hegel to repeat at a higher level the interplay of forces dealt with by the Scientific Understanding. There we had an underworld of distinct forces, mutually releasing and inhibiting one another: here, on the other hand, we have an upper world of mutually acknowledging, conscious persons, who are conscious of their mutual acknowledgement, and who are thereby raised to the fullest self-consciousness. (One is reminded of the Henry Jamesian world where the characters not only see each other, but also see each other seeing each other.) The analogy between the interplay of forces and that of persons is as interesting and as revelatory of the far-flung affinities exploited by the Dialectic as any other instance in Hegel.[7]

"The analogy between the interplay of forces and that of persons" (which Goethe also developed in his novel *Wahlverwandtschaften* [Elective Affinities], applies with particular force to *Rosmersholm*, particularly when we remind ourselves of the interrelationship of physical and spiritual forces in both Hegel's and Ibsen's ideas of reality. Like the Hegelian Concept, the truth of an Ibsen play is only the totality of its developing relationships; it is not the *result* of this development, emerging as a detachable "moral" or character judgment. In *Rosmersholm*, as in German Enlightenment drama, the idealistic dialectic gives to the psychological dialectic a certain quality of nebulousness, or abstractness, startling when compared with *The Wild Duck* but completely successful and satisfying in its consistency.

The wider subject of the play is the confrontation of civilization with revolutionary change, the conflict between the forces of tradition (the moral consciousness) and the forces of evolution (the acquisitive instinct). This dialectic, as we would expect from Ibsen, is seen with a great deal of depth and complexity and neither side in this conflict of forces, neither civilization nor revolutionary change, emerges as the ideological victor. If Rosmer is the representative of civilization and tradition, he also is associated with oppression and superstition, these two qualities emerging in the schoolmaster, Kroll, and the housekeeper, Mrs. Helseth. Rebekka, similarly, coming from Ibsen's metaphoric "north" of spiritual freedom is, on the one hand, the enlightener, combatting the oppressive ghosts of the past; but she is, too, compromised both by impure motivation and inadequate emancipation, these two qualities emerging more clearly in the figures of Peter Mortensgaard and Ulrik Brendel.

The dialectical balance of this character grouping is clearer than in most of the plays and it is the neatness of this dialectical balance that reveals the somewhat abstract nature of its argument. For this reason, perhaps, it is one of the most perfect of Ibsen's dramatic structures, one in which our pleasure in formal values best is satisfied. Only *Hedda Gabler* equals its beautiful balance of act arrangement, and its scenic, character-trait, and action symmetry. This esthetic control is too emphatic for us to see the play as serving or illustrating any *tendency* or judgment; its meaning is inseparable from its shape or movement, and the play's appearance of debating moral and political issues gives way, on closer investigation, to these issues merely serving as indications of spiritual position, "moments" in the total concept, rather than serious propositions in their own right.[8] The movement of the play leads one quickly beyond the little foreground of debate, which is the springboard of the intellectual action, into the play's larger and graver dialectic.

Herbert Edwards, discussing the possible influence of Ibsen upon Henry James, appropriately draws attention to this most Jamesian of Ibsen's plays, noting how, in *Rosmersholm*, Ibsen shapes the subject of each act and of the whole of the play in order to create a formal structure. He observes that the first half of the play deals with Rosmer, the second with Rebekka; that Act I deals with Rosmer's present, Act II with his past; that Act III treats Rebekka's past, and Act IV her present.[9] The balance of details is richer, even, than this and, gratefully extending Edwards's insight, let us look, first, at the total shape of the play.

Act   I   *Evening.* Rosmer's Present. Rosmer and Rebekka prepare to challenge society. Brendel appears, sharing this challenge. Rosmer and Rebekka seem firmly united.
             Action opens with reference to mill-race beyond the window.

Act   II   *Morning.* Rosmer's Past. Society begins to strike back at Rosmer and Rebekka. (Brendel also set upon by lower elements of society.)
             Rosmer and Rebekka begin to move apart.

Act   III   *Morning.* Rebekka's Past. Society defeats Rosmer and Rebekka. They seem to split apart, totally.

Act   IV   *Evening.* Rebekka's Present. Rosmer and Rebekka give up their challenge. Brendel reappears, also giving up challenge.

Rosmer and Rebekka reunite.

Action closes with reference to millrace beyond window.

The movement of the play, we see, is circular, beginning and ending in evening: beginning in the shadows of a past that, it is confidently believed, is about to be overcome and ending with the shadows of this past completely in control of the present. Whatever else the play is about, one important theme is likely to involve this circularity of movement: of the inability of the protagonists to move *linearly*, forward and outward.

We notice also a distinct interplay of inward and outward, individual and social, subjective and objective, forces, and, linked to this interplay, that between past and present. A firm pattern of correspondences, of interlocking dimensions of reality, apparently shapes the world of *Rosmersholm*, in addition to that "lattice" of character interplay noted by McFarlane. It is one of the admirable things about this play that the history of violent psychological, social, ethical, and political *disorder* that agitates the central consciousness of the play and surrounds it as its social and political circumference is made to obey a dialectical movement as formal and controlled as a minuet, in which nothing intrudes upon the stage except at its esthetically and philosophically appropriate moment.

Any experience of the play will beget an awareness of this formal structure: of the ingeniously simultaneous forward-backward movement of the play, of such ironically balancing actions as Brendel's borrowing of Rosmer's clothes to preach their common cause, in Act I, and his return with them, upon the defeat of this cause, in Act IV, moments which the audience in the theater registers with the same satsifaction as, say, the return of the second subject, in sonata form. By means such as these, Ibsen, without the verbal richness of Shakespeare, Racine, or the German *Aufklärung* dramatists, is able to make the theater yield up profound and sophisticated art for our meditation.

The psychology of the characters, for example, functions, like good dramatic psychology, both realistic and non-realistic, to involve us in the human story, but the admonition of L. C. Knight in *How Many Children Had Lady Macbeth* applies with equal force to *Rosmersholm*, where so many possibilities are offered for our speculation by the intriguing triangle of Beate-Rosmer-Rebekka that we could spend a lifetime on this area of character and conflict alone. One of the reasons Ibsen began his play when he did—*after* the piquant and lurid event—obviously was to prevent his theater audience from fastening its attention upon this area. Sophocles, similarly, does not wish to draw our attention

to the marital life of Oedipus and Jocasta. Both writers are stalking
greater intellectual game, and we must see the psychology of
Rosmersholm, for all its fascination at the realistic human level, as
sharing with the psychology of the greatest drama the purpose of
directing our attention through the particulars of the art to its wide-
ranging universals. For this reason, Freud's famous study of Rebekka,
assuming in the fictional character the same unconscious drives as in an
actual human being, must be viewed as an example of misdirected
insights, for it relates the actions and speeches of the heroine to an inner
psychological structure when these details, demonstrably, contribute
to an objective esthetic and ideological structure. Similarly, speculations upon Rosmer's possible sexual inadequacy do not begin to be
relevant until we first see Rosmer's dramatic and dialectical function,
which is that of *opposition to passion.* Civilization is that which opposes
passion, which seeks to subdue it, and Rosmer therefore must be given
actions that demonstrate this function, such as his relation to the
"southern" passion of Beate and the "northern" passion of Rebekka.

We must look at the politics in the play in exactly the same way as
we look at the psychology; both indicate spiritual forces that have taken
on a particular local habitation but which are, in their universal aspects,
independent of local historical circumstances. They represent the Rosmer-
Rebekka relationship and conflict in the larger world of European order
and revolution. Revolution and politics are those functions of the spirit
that divide men and society, creating conflict and opposition, whereas
civilization and tradition are those which *unite.* The political references
in the play, therefore, are not presented for the audience to take sides
with liberal or conservative but to present onstage an image of spiritual battle, of men in conflict with one another. The argument and
imagery of *Rosmersholm* are remarkably similiar not only to those of
German Enlightenment drama but also to those of certain poems of
W. B. Yeats, such as "The Second Coming" or "Nineteen Hundred and
Nineteen," in which an old, ceremonious, traditional order is threatened
with "the blood-dimmed tide" of anarchy, in which,

> Things fall apart; the centre cannot hold . . .
> The ceremony of innocence is drowned.
> The best lack all conviction, while the worst
> Are full of passionate intensity.

If we look closely at the imagery of *Rosmersholm* we will find constant submerged references to battle, "war to the knife," "Blood,"
"a fight to the death," etc., especially when Kroll is speaking. At one
point, referring to his first experience of battle, he uses the Norwegian

phrase, "I have had blood on my teeth," a startling image of animal savagery in strong contrast with Rosmer's endeavor to lift men higher into a spiritual aristocracy. Kroll's frighteningly close-to-the-surface world of animal savagery and Rosmer's Schillerian vision of a universal spiritual brotherhood and aristocracy are the extremes of the play's dialectic and lie beneath the seemingly quiet surface of Ibsen's naturalistic scene. Ibsen first intended to call the play "White Horses," which would have emphasized the retrogressive, superstitious aspect of *Rosmersholm,* those forces which need to be overcome. The decision to rename the play *Rosmersholm* suggests a wish to emphasize the positive qualities of the old order and its value in having subdued the animal side of man. The imagery of animal savagery in the play points to Ibsen's sense of the precariousness of the spirit's gains as well as of the difficulty of spiritual advance. Kroll, who "bit back sharply" at his opponents, already has relinquished his humanity even as he sets up to defend civilization from change, and Rosmer's civilizing efforts have no effect upon him. Rosmer, on the other hand, attempts to retain the best of the past—its civilizing power—while being responsive to currents of change. As an artist of great delicacy and subtlety, Ibsen was bound to have a high regard for the values of civilization and possibly saw in the attractions of such a civilization, as embodied in the aristocracy, a great temptation for the revolutionary. In *The League of Youth* the pseudo-revolutionary Stensgaard succumbs to the temptation quickly (one is reminded of Henry James's American heroes and heroines confronted with Europe):

STENSGAARD: Yes, here! Here there are fine manners: here there is gracious living. Here the floors seem meant to be trodden only by patent leather shoes. Here the armchairs are deep, and the ladies sit prettily in them. Here the conversation is like a game, lightly and elegantly to be tossed to and fro. No blundering remarks here that reduce the company to awkward silence. Oh, Fjeldbo, here for the first time I know what true distinction is. Yes, we really do have our own aristocracy . . . a little circle . . . an aristocracy of culture. And it's this I want to belong to. Don't you feel yourself how this place refines one? Doesn't wealth seem different here? When I think of Monsen's wealth, I think of it as being great wads of greasy notes and beer-stained securities . . . But here! here it's metallic . . . gleaming silver! And it's the same with the people . . .[10]

Underneath the vulgarity of Stensgaard's appreciation and the opportunism of his revolutionary politics (reminiscent of Mortensgaard) one does sense the real clash of revolutionism and culture which Ibsen treats in greater depth in *Rosmersholm*. The attitude to Rosmersholm and its dynastic history draws upon the European sense of what Lionel Trilling, in a study of Jane Austen's *Mansfield Park*, has called "the

Great Good Place: the house where all's accustomed, ceremonious."
It is also infused with a feeling akin to that in W. B. Yeats's "Prayer for
his Daughter":

> How but in custom and in ceremony
> Are innocence and beauty born?

For Ibsen, for whom the human consciousness is a Peer Gynt's onion
of layer after layer of the past yet evolving, by means of this total
content, to new forms, the problem of combining revolutionary change
together with the restraining nobility and delicacy of civilization must
have been acute. The imagery of savagery in the play suggests that
civilization, equally with truth and freedom, is hard won, and that
circumstances can destroy the fabric of centuries. Ibsen's life, from
1828 to 1906, spanned a period of revolutionary uprisings and savage
repressions almost as terrible as our own, climaxing, almost half-way
through that span, with the fearfully bloody suppression of the Communards in Paris (the European citadel of civilized values) in 1871.
In 1864 and 1871, in the Dano-Prussian and Franco-Prussian wars,
it must have seemed that, if the spirit was advancing, it was advancing
through seas of blood. Ibsen's distress at the unscrupulous political
infighting in Norway while he was on a visit immediately preceding
the writing of *Rosmersholm*, is more likely to have derived from his
reflections upon the course of humanity in general than from the petty
motives of revenge and timidity attributed to him even though, doubtless, he was as capable as any of us of these faults.

The sense that civilization's achievements are precarious and that
man can spiritually regress accounts for the ambiguity of Ibsen's concept
of the past which, as in *Ghosts*, often is vaster and even more vital than
the present. As the reservoir of man's spiritual history and the source of
much of his spiritual strength—his identity—it is the past of civilization
and of valid tradition; at the same time the past is like a vampire sucking
the life-blood of the present. The dead but powerful Beate and the
"white horses" strike back from the world of darkness at the world of
the living, while Kroll's atavistic savagery goes far behind the traditional civilization of Rosmer. It is exactly this horrified sense of humanity's capacity to regress to savagery that Yeats expresses in "Nineteen
Hundred and Nineteen":

> Now days are dragon-ridden, the nightmare
> Rides upon sleep: a drunken soldiery
> Can leave the mother, murdered at her door
> To crawl in her own blood, and go scot-free;

> The night can sweat with terror as before
> We pieced our thoughts into philosophy,
> And planned to bring the world under a rule,
> Who are but weasels, fighting in a hole.

Though his reaction is expressed in less violent terms, Rosmer, who requires "quiet, happy innocence," recoils before the same image of human barbarism when, reading the attack upon him by Kroll and his friends, he exclaims, "these are the doings of unscrupulous men. . . . Everything that is good in man will be destroyed if this kind of thing is allowed to go on."[11] Rosmer and Rebekka had planned to bring the world under a rule, a Schillerian vision of mankind no longer in "bitter strife, only friendly rivalry. All eyes fixed on the same goal. Every mind, every will striving on and on . . . up and up . . . each by the path best suited to its nature. Happiness for all . . . created by all."[12] But they are defeated by the forces roused against this endeavor—forces in the larger world of politics and society that correspond to the atavistic forces also within themselves; they are reflected in the ghost of Beate, in the white horses, and in the prejudices and superstitions that even Rebekka has been unable to discard, like her guilt. Here we note Ibsen's fine use of expanding circumferences of action and implication, where the situation of the individual psyche (the core of the onion) expands through layer after layer to embrace the entire objective and subjective structure of the spiritual world of *Rosmersholm*. *Rosmersholm* illustrates how, to Ibsen's vision, no segment or aspect of life can be truncated from the totality and considered in isolation. As in Hegel, reality is a structure of necessary interconnections, a single organic growth in which each part, itself evolving into its succeeding phase as we observe it, can be understood only when we have understood the evolving whole. By somewhat distorting this fluid structure, freezing it for a moment, we might arrive at some idea of the tissue of interconnected realities that make up the total reality of *Rosmersholm* (or of any play in the Cycle [see diagram on page 216]):

This diagram, which need not be taken too solemnly, helps us to see how what one might call the *psychic energy* of the play pushes outward and inward at the same time: that the exploration to the outermost limits of reality (within the confines of the dramatic form) also forces a movement into the recesses of the spirit, so that the dialectic of the play simultaneously reveals the condition of the world in which Rosmer and Rebekka hope to act creatively, and the condition of their own spiritual substance, which makes such action impossible. A *performance* of the play, under a good director, can better bring out

The Structure of Reality of *Rosmersholm*

(f) Aesthetic dimensions enclosing all the others, affirming poetic creativity at its most difficult and distinguished.

(e) Metaphysical realm: ultimate values and realities outside time and space objectively existing, to be subjectively affirmed.

(d) Nature and History: the larger spatial/temporal perspectives beyond individual and social reality. Light/Darkness. Seasons of the year.

(c) Social/ethical realm: institutions, duties, class and political conflict, cultural past (civilization) and revolution.

(b) Intersubjective realm of human relationships: marriage, family, etc. (interlocking pasts and present).

(a) Individual psyche: its conscious and unconscious conflicts and desires. Sexual passions: biological past. (Rosmer's and Rebekka's egos, in isolation.)

Structure and texture of the play and its ideal (f) performance, in which all the prior phases of reality, scene, character, action, dialogue are elements of an esthetic experience.

The "higher idea" for which Rosmer and Rebekka (e) die (the third empire) and this idea's acceptance by the race.

Historical/mythical analogies to contemporary (d) action, showing how the latter are historically determined, representing recurring conflicts in the life of the race. Imagery of light and darkness and white horses.

Rosmer and Rebekka's conflict with conventional (c) society, its outmoded forms and ideas.

Rosmer and Rebekka in love-union and conflict. (b) Beate — Rosmer — Rebekka — Kroll this multi-layered movement than a critical interpretation which finds it difficult to keep so many balls in the air at the same time.

If the poles of civilization and revolution are the two principles that animate, set in motion, the complex structure of reality of *Rosmersholm,* then the idea of subjective and objective reality that is agitated between these two poles will be capable of progression and regression within their terms. The aspect of consciousness that most quickly can regress to animal savagery is the *passionate,* and beneath the controlled realistic surface of the play's action runs, like the furious millrace, a submerged world of passion. It is upon this basis of passion that the civilized world of Rosmersholm is so tenuously built; indeed, the Rosmersholm tradition, *founded* upon force and passion, is a repressive order that has no right to deny the forces and passions raised against it. Inevitably, the virtues of Rosmersholm are ambiguous, issuing from unjust advantage, and civilizedly opposing passion only at a moment of decline. For all their destructive quality, therefore, the passions have a grievance against the repressive order that has suppressed them. The Rosmersholm tradition, we hear from Mrs. Helseth, has spread gloom all around the district. Its children never cry and its men never laugh. Rosmer's recoil from the passions of the two women who have lived with him has resulted in one's being drowned in the mill-race while the spirit of the other has been "broken." Yet only this capacity to subjugate passion gives Rosmer his role of ennobling men, lifting them above partisan passion, into friendly rivalry; it is the program, in fact, of the Marquis of Posa in Schiller's *Don Carlos.* When, therefore, Rosmer comes to doubt the motives from which he contributed to Beate's death (suspecting that the desire on his part for her death, because of his unconscious passion for Rebekka, had worked deviously in the form of enlightened comradeship), he must come to doubt, also, his whole capacity for incorruptible action within the larger realm of human action, where motives must be innocent and pure if they are to effect spiritual change.

Already, therefore, we have outlined a clear and extensive dialectical structure of the play in which the activity of consciousness pushes outward from individual and psychological impulses and motives, through social, political, ethical, natural, historical, and metaphysical dimensions of reality, giving the play the impression of exploring a complete world view or spiritual *gestalt*: the world view explored by Hegel in his brilliant analysis of the Enlightenment, "Der Kampf der Aufklärung mit dem Aberglauben" ("The Struggle of Enlightenment with Superstition"). In this analysis, as in the play, the forces of "Enlightenment" and the forces of "Superstition," under the pressure of the dialectic, find themselves to be *not* the diametric opposites they supposed, enlightenment being less enlightened and superstition less foolish than at first they seemed.

Ibsen's dramatic structure is, in many ways, better suited to Hegel's analysis than the philosopher's method of linear and discursive narrative; for Ibsen can present actions and reactions occurring simultaneously, whereas Hegel rather awkwardly has first to treat the dialectic from the viewpoint of Enlightenment, then recapitulate the whole action from the viewpoint of belief. The inherently *dramatic* nature of the dialectic is best fulfilled in dramatic *form*: the continuous movement, all at once, of a number of parts that change in relation one with another as the parts of a mobile sculpture undergo continuous change within the change of the whole.

The dialectic of *Rosmersholm* grows out of that of *The Wild Duck*. In the earlier play, superstition and despotic authority had controlled the world and had successfully resisted the attempt of the enlightener, Gregers Werle's clumsy attempt to open up this world to truth and light. Superstition, the human reconciliation with unsatisfactory reality, rather than the transformation of that reality, had created for itself a secure alternative world, a *Jenseits* or Beyond, in Hegel's contemptuous phrase; and Ibsen's brilliant metaphor for this was the fantasy-loft of the Ekdals. In *Rosmersholm* the forces of reaction and superstition are on the defensive and those of Enlightenment have come out in the open to engage in battle. That the forces of Enlightenment show themselves to be of questionable motive and nature is completely in accord with Hegel's analysis. On the side of Enlightenment we have Rebekka, Brendel, Mortensgaard, and, in the past, Dr. West. On the side of Belief we have ex-priest Rosmer, the conservative and despotic Kroll, the superstitious Mrs. Helseth and, in the past, Beate. This neat balance is disturbed only by Rosmer going over to the ranks of Enlightenment and Rebekka going over to the area of Belief—a movement described by Hegel. Rebekka, Brendel, and Mortensgaard are all associated with "light." In an earlier version of the play Rebekka's light identity is more blatantly demonstrated, and is explicitly invoked to banish superstition:

ROSMER. And you mean that complete emancipation is to . . .
MRS. ROSMER [Rebekka]. Is to be quit of one's white horses. We must have light, Eilert.
MRS. HELSETH (*in the doorway right*). Here is the lamp, madam.[13]

In this first plotting of his play's metaphors, the lamplight streaming onto the stage from the right is to dispel the ghosts of the past and there is a suggestion of irony in the fact that this light, coming from the "east" (right) is merely the little artificial light, not the terrible

Sun of *Ghosts*. In the final version of the play Rebekka, more subtly, lights the lamp when the conversation turns to Beate, and exclaims, "Ah, the *Beacon!*" when Mortensgaard's paper is mentioned. Brendel's name carries light/fire connotations (brende = burn) as does his *non de plume*, Hetman (hete = heat), while the other enlightenment figure, Mortensgaard, is proprietor of *The Beacon* (*Blinkfyret*).

"The Struggle of Enlightenment with Superstition" describes that phase of Consciousness which, historically, was most typically exemplified in the period immediately preceding the French Revolution although, of course, like every phase taken up in the *Phenomenology*, the dialectic described is part of the structure of "the ever present Spirit." The attack by the Enlightened Spirit upon the forces of the established and repressive order whose representatives are the despot, the priest, and the multitude, is one that continually must be undertaken in the life of consciousness as it has been undertaken again and again in the past. The intellectual assault upon Superstition or Belief in the age of the *philosophes* represents the extreme limit of division, conflict, within the Roman-Christian world, analyzed in such depth in the preceding chapter of the *Phenomenology* (the source of the dialectic of *The Wild Duck*). The dialectic of the Enlightenment depicts the Christian world under attack from the revived paganism of the *philosophes*. We would expect, therefore, that whereas the pagan qualities of the European spirit are submerged and in the background in *The Wild Duck*, they have emerged into the foreground, militantly, in *Rosmersholm*. This attack upon the Roman-Christian world by a militant paganism has occurred twice in European history: when the north Germanic tribes invaded Rome and were absorbed into its declining Christian culture, and in the eighteenth century's attack upon Roman-Christian orthodoxy. If, as I hope to demonstrate, Ibsen has incorporated both of these dimensions of action within his modern drama, this would be perfectly appropriate to his abiding vision of the "third empire." There are thus two major, complementary, but very different actions in *Rosmersholm*, one being fought out in the present, and the other, more violent, recollected from an earlier period:

(a) The present intellectual conflict between Enlightenment and Reaction, which has parallels in Enlightenment thought and drama.

(b) A past, violent, and passionate conflict of murderous crime which has parallels in the first violent encounters between the northern and civilized worlds.

The fact that the second level of action cannot be detached from the first, loftier, level, suggests that, as in *Emperor and Galilean*, the past cannot be resurrected, as the Enlightenment attempted to resurrect it, without its darker aspects re-emerging also. The enlightened quest of the protagonists is brought up against the guilty and insurmountable past: the drama in the background which is "discovered" by the enlightened quest.

Hegel's analysis of the conflict within consciousness in the time of the Enlightenment is extremely subtle and complex, but clear and potentially dramatic forces do emerge. First, there are those three archetypes of the reactionary spirit described by Hegel: the priest, the despot, and the multitude who are the objects of enlightenment's attack, and who reappear, ironically reduced, to be sure, in *Rosmersholm*, as Rosmer, Kroll, and Mrs. Helseth.[14] The ranks of enlightenment are composed of a wastrel with "witty insight" (Brendel), an amoral utilitarianism (Mortensgaard), and the graver development of enlightened thought which discovers its identity to be the same as the Belief it had set out to oppose (Rebekka).[15]

The intellectual/spiritual conflict depicted by Hegel very strongly resembles that of *Rosmersholm*. Hegel describes a seemingly idealistic but actually quite unscrupulous force of enlightenment entering a world whose consciousness is divided between constraining and conservative attitudes on one side and, on the other, an undeveloped (*begrifflos*) consciousness that, if worked upon, can escape this constraining background.[16] As it becomes more and more engaged in its task of liberation, however, this force of enlightenment "becomes untruth and unreason; and as intention it passes into the negative of pure intention, becomes a lie and sordid impurity of purpose."[17]

The dilemma, described here by Hegel, in which Spirit finds itself, *is* that experienced by Rebekka (and by Rosmer insofar as he allies himself with Rebekka's aims) after the achievement of all she has worked for. The disturbing co-existence in Rebekka of high-minded idealism and complete (if mostly unconscious) unscrupulousness, which gives her such complex dramatic identity, is exactly that of Hegel's analysis. Rebekka, entering Rosmersholm, the very citadel of the old repressive order, to further the new ideas, finds herself self-trapped in a sequence of deceptive and even murderous actions that, in Hegel's words, create the very negative of the pure intention with which she set out. Furthermore, Hegel continues, this enlightening force actually discovers that its identity has become the same as the powers it fought against and sought to overthrow: it "comes to know that content as its own, which was to begin with, opposite of itself."[18] This awareness, however, is not a retreat back to the old order, but a completely new phase of self-consciousness: one, however, that must ultimately perish.

Hegel now recapitulates this dialectical action from the viewpoint of belief—of the old order against which enlightenment fought to such an unforeseen conclusion. Belief, too, will arrive at the same strange conclusion. At first, belief sees the work of the enlightened consciousness as merely "destructive negation, simply lying unreason and malicious intent"[19]—the judgment passed upon the enlightenment by Kroll's friends and by Kroll himself.

(One phase of this dialectical action particularly recalls an important detail of the play. Enlightenment comes to consider Absolute Being as "the great void,"[20] a phrase that is spoken by one of the enlightenment characters, Ulrick Brendel: "det store ingenting"—the great Nothing—as he leaves the world of the play to go out into the night.)

Now, paralleling the progress of the enlightened consciousness, the vanguard of belief, engaged in dialectical dialogue with enlightenment, comes to see its identity in its opposite. "Belief ... has in fact become the same thing as enlightenment."[21] Yet, while enlightenment is "satisfied," belief is "unsatisfied," for in the background is "that longing of the troubled, beshadowed spirit, mourning over the loss of its spiritual world. ... Enlightenment has on it this stain of unsatisfied longing."[22]

The two forces, Enlightenment and Belief, which began their history as opponents have, by dialectical process, come together as one, the conflict being overcome by these opposites "colliding and collapsing."[23] Each finds itself completed by the other but, "perishing through being thus completed,"[24] spirit passes on to another dialectical phase.

This dialectical action is not, of course, the whole of *Rosmersholm*, but it *is* the major spiritual movement of the play: that of Rosmer and Rebekka who, from opposite principles and identities, spiritually merge with each other until, in the final action when they must perish, it is possible for them to say "we two are one." The phase of enlightenment that succeeds their death is sketched by Hegel in his brilliant portrait of "the man of utility," whose world is drained of spiritual significance, where everything, including man, takes on utilitarian value:

As everything is useful for man, man is likewise useful too, and his characteristic function consists in making himself a member of the human herd, of use for the common good, and serviceable to all. The extent to which he looks after his own interests is the measure with which he must also serve the purpose of others, and so far as he serves their turn, he is taking care of himself: the one hand washes the other.[25]

For this stage of enlightenment, which earns Hegel's sarcasm, even religion is "profitable"—an idea that belief finds "utterly and simply revolting." This man of utility resembles Mortensgaard, and the full extent of Rosmer's degradation in the world of politics is depicted in his allowing Mortensgaard to make use of his Christian affiliations even though Rosmer has renounced them. Mortensgaard's comment treats religion precisely in the utilitarian spirit described by Hegel: "What the party really needs is Christian elements—something that everybody has to respect," although, of course, Mortensgaard is no more a Christian than Rosmer or Rebekka.

The similarities between the two texts—the section of the *Phenomenology*, "The Struggle of Enlightenment with Superstition," and *Rosmersholm*—are those of the basic conflict summarized by Hegel's title. The reader is referred to the fuller account of Hegel's chapter in Appendix II at the end of the book, where the resemblances to the play will be seen to be closer than we have been able to demonstrate here. However, the chapters in the *Phenomenology* supplied Ibsen merely with the intellectual skeleton of his play, the dialectic of thought and not the interplay of complex, suffering individuals each with his own personal history and fate, and in order to create this richer texture of dramatic conflict Ibsen loads the categories of Hegel's dialectic with a greater weight of historical, mythic, and contemporary material. First and foremost, as already indicated, we have Ibsen's perennial third-empire conflict of pagan with Christian forces: a refusal to endorse Hegel's own hard-won acceptance of the inevitability and rightness of the extinction of the pagan world and its successful sublimation into the Christian present. In Hegel's other writings, especially in the lectures on the philosophy of history, we can find sources for many of the additional layers of reality present in the play, supplementing the movement of the mind analyzed in the *Phenomenology*.

The *temporal* extensions of the realistic action and the intellectual dialectic are, we suggested, taken from two periods in European history when the central, civilizing structure of Rome suffered attack from more liberating but also more barbaric or more unscrupulous forces: the northern and Germanic inundation of a self-divided Rome at the end of the classical era; and the intellectual attack upon the Roman structure of Europe in the Age of the Enlightenment. This suggests, also, a *spatial* extension of the action into a north-south conflict, and in *Rosmersholm* this is present in Rebekka's intrusion upon Rosmersholm from northern Finnmark.

If we concede that in the realistic Cycle Ibsen continually is discovering the larger historical pattern of humanity within the microcosmic domestic pattern of his dramatic method, the parallels between the historical situation of the unhappily divided southern culture of Europe invaded by a "barbaric" and energetic northern force, and the unhappily divided *Rosmersholm* invaded by a ruthless yet energetic Rebekka

West, are striking. Finnmark is particularly appropriate for Rebekka's origins, as it has strong pagan—and therefore anti-Christian—associations and, in a drama set in Norway, it still manages to suggest a "north" to stand in contrast with the immediate scene. Rosmersholm, therefore, is analogous to Rome in the wider perspectives of human history, and I think it is possible to demonstrate that Ibsen has given to Rosmersholm qualities associated with Rome and its spirit as summarized by Hegel both in the *Phenomenology* and in the *Philosophy of History*. (In the second draft of the play there even was a military ancestor, Eilert *Hannibal* Rosmer who set up the tradition of alternating soldiers and priests, like the Caesars and Popes of Roman tradition.) The Rosmersholm tradition of patrician rule has emphasized duty, has killed joy, has been a force of oppression to its surrounding neighbors, and these details correspond very closely indeed to the judgment upon Rome and its influence on the world in German historiography. In the *Philosophy of History*, contrasting the Roman spirit with that of the Persian fullness of life and the Greek exhilaration and cheerfulness, Hegel claims that the Roman world "stifles all vitality":

> Through its being the aim of the State that the social units in their moral life should be sacrificed to it, the world is sunk in melancholy; its heart is broken, and it is all over with the natural side of the spirit, which has sunk into a feeling of unhappiness. Yet only from this feeling could arise the super-sensuous, the free spirit in Christianity.[26]

Hegel, here, seems to be echoing Herder's even more severe judgment upon Rome pronounced in the famous *Reflections on the Philosophy of the History of Mankind* (1791) where Rome is depicted as an oppressive, traditional, conservative yet divided power in the world both in its pagan and its Christian phases; its religion was "a civil and military religion"[27] and its society constantly was divided between a patrician caste and the factious plebeians. The little society of *Rosmersholm* seems similarly divided between the patricians (to which Kroll and Rosmer belong) and the plebeians such as the factious Mortensgaard who actually is called a "plebeian" by Ulrik Brendel. I think it would be possible to suggest that, in the second group of plays in the Cycle which takes up the Roman and Christian phase of the Western mind, *The Wild Duck* presents the consciousness of the Roman world from the view of the "insulted and injured" out of which the Christian communities grew, whereas *Rosmersholm*'s consciousness is that of the aristocratic and patrician point of view.

Herder describes the Roman nobility as founded on "a proud, family, civic, Roman spirit, in the first races; on which their country depended for support; and in the continued activity, the permanent stream of the same eternal state, it was transmitted from father to son."[28] This nobility sought to control the military, civic, and priestly offices and functions of Rome exactly as the Rosmer family has done, and Herder's account quoted above resembles Kroll's eulogy on the Rosmer tradition:

> KROLL: But you have a duty towards the traditions of your family, Rosmer. Remember that. Since time immemorial Rosmersholm has been like a stronghold of order and high thinking . . . of respect and esteem for all those things which are accepted and acknowledged by the best people in our society. If ever the rumour got about that you yourself had abandoned what I might call the Rosmer tradition, it would lead to disastrous and irreparable confusion.
>
> ROSMER: My dear Kroll, I cannot bring myself to see the matter in that light. To me it seems I have a bounded duty to bring a little light and happiness into those places where the Rosmers have spread gloom and oppression all these long years.[29]

In that exchange, the two views of Rome, as a force of conserving civilized values, and as a force of oppression, are succinctly presented. In the first draft of *Rosmersholm* Rosmer's "Roman" identity is more obvious in his name, Boldt-Römer. Römer is German for Roman, and close to the Norwegian equivalent, *Romer* (Roman). In both Herder's and Hegel's accounts, this patrician, superstitious, melancholy, oppressive, civilized yet divided Roman world was violently disrupted by the Germanic peoples of the north whom, however, it finally assimilated, and the description of this encounter in the *Philosophy of History* strongly resembles the encounter between Rosmersholm and Rebekka West. In both cases, after violent and murderous conflict, the forces opposing each other finally merge.

When the Germans descended from the north upon Rome they discovered a culture (and its consciousness) split in two between "increasingly rampant passions"[30] on one side, that were looked down upon "from the lofty position attained by the world of mind" on the other, and this latter seemed to deny the world of the passions "all claim and value."[31] Just such a division between a "lofty" and a sensual, passionate state of mind existed in Rosmersholm before Rebekka's arrival from the north. Rosmer reveals to Kroll how the dead Beate once would give way to "wild fits of sensual passion"[32] that so often appalled him. The northern conquerors were pagans descending upon an as yet uneasily Christianized but still patrician Rome that suffered from a "discord between the inner life of the heart and the actual world"[33] which it was the unconscious mission of the Germans to overcome by means of a process of absorbing the very spirit of the culture it had opposed—a process that is repeated in Rebekka West's gradual absorption by the Rosmersholm tradition that she set out to oppose. Rebekka's pagan qualities have been noted by Hermann J. Weigand and others. To Brendel she is an enchanting "mermaid"; to Kroll she has the power of "bewitching"; Rebekka likens herself to a sea-troll slumped over the ship of Rosmer's future. Her history, like that of the other members of the Enlightenment group, Dr. West, Brendel, and Mortensgaard, is murky and somewhat scandalous and, even more than theirs, totally outside the Christian categories. She was most likely illegitimately conceived—a possibility which raises the even more scandalous implication of incestuous relations with her father; her strong erotic appeal has "infatuated" not only Rosmer and Kroll, but Beate as well. The extreme anarchy of these sexual relations bring to mind the barbarous familial and inter-sexual attachments of pagan history—such as, for instance, the history of the Volsungs.

Rebekka's actions after her somewhat ruthless arrival at Rosmersholm display the same mixture of innocence and wickedness that Hegel sees as typical of the Germanic spirit at the time that it came into such violent contact with Rome. The contradiction in the German character was the way in which, on the one hand, the Germans could be characterized by the quality of "Heart," and, on the other, the undoubted record of savage and barbarous evil that they left behind from those early years in Rome. The Germanic idiosyncrasy of Heart can be discovered in the operation of the Germanic Will:

> Will in the case of such an idiosyncrasy is exclusively *formal* Will—its purely subjective Freedom exhibits itself as self-will. To the disposition thus designated, every particular object of attraction seems important, for "Heart" surrenders itself entirely to each; but as, on the other hand, it is not interested in the quality of such aim in the abstract, it does not become exclusively absorbed in that aim, so as to pursue it with violent and evil passion—does not go to the length of abstract vice.[34]

Such a Will, in fact, resembles that "acquisitive instinct" hurrying "from gain to gain" which Ibsen described as constituting one-half of the dialectical action of the play. Despite the fact that this northern Will does not act from violent and evil passion, the first contact between the German and Roman worlds is violent:

> In the first instance we have only vague volition, in the background of which lies the True and Infinite. The True is present only as an unsolved problem for their [the German] soul is not yet purified. A long process is required to complete this purification so as to realize concrete sprit. Religion comes forward with a challenge to the violence of the passions and rouses them to

madness. The excess of passions is aggravated by evil conscience, and heightened to an insane rage; which perhaps would not have been the case if that opposition had been absent. We behold the terrible spectacle of the most fearful extravagance of passion in the royal houses of that period.[35]

I would be the first to agree that the parallels between this history and the passionate and violent actions in the background of the subtle drama of consciousness of *Rosmersholm* are broadly suggestive rather than very definite; nevertheless they are striking, especially when one considers the further parallel that in both the historical account and in the play we are presented with a modern intellectual recollection of earlier passionate violence: a moral reexamination of the forces of the spirit in the past that have gone into the creation of the conditions of the present. Rebekka's confession to Kroll and Rosmer, in Act III, where she describes how she was self-trapped into the crime against Beate, portrays the same condition of consciousness that Hegel saw as typical of the northern or Germanic spirit:[36] of not proceeding from some abstract plan, but giving itself up wholly to its objective of the moment:

> REBEKKA (*vehemently*). But do you think I set about these things in cold blood! I was different then from what I am now, standing here talking about it. And besides, it seems to me a person can want things both ways. I wanted to get rid of Beate, one way or another. But I never really imagined it would happen. Every little step I risked, every faltering advance, I seemed to hear something call out within me: "No further. Not a step further!" And yet I could not stop. I had to venture a little bit further. . . .[37]

In Hegel's account of the encounter between the northern spirit and that of Rome, the violent actions are a necessary stage of the dialectic, part of the long process of purification of the northern spirit from its barbarous passions to the supersensuous, free spirit of Christian *love*. Rebekka, too, as she confesses, has been infected by Rosmersholm's traditions, has been, she declares, purged of passion so that gradually there has grown within her a non-sensuous love for Rosmer: a love, however, that has sapped her pagan courage and will. The Ibsen of *Emperor and Galilean* is unlikely to endorse entirely Hegel's judgment that the breaking of this will was a gain for the world-consciousness or for the individual.

The drama of intensely suffering and morally reevaluating individual psyches, in the play, is extended and enlarged in the world spirit in history. The historical drama of the violent assault upon a whole civilization, of murderous, bloody passions working out their course to a final assimilation of the culture they opposed and a final purification of consciousness and a breaking of will, might at first seem a long way from the quiet though intense drama of spiritual self-examination of Rosmer and Rebekka; but if we are sensitive to the subject matter of these self-examinations, and to the imagery in which they are expressed, we will be able to see the large, violent pattern within the smaller one.

The main drama is, of course, the modern psychological one; but the modern psyche, because it is structured from the past, and because its own logic forces it ever forward until it has encompassed its entire spiritual substance, inevitably undergoes the experience of the general mind, the evolutionary process of the race. To the objection that Ibsen, instead, found the material for *Rosmersholm* in his own experiences, in his acquaintances (such as Carl Snoilsky), one would reply that there is no quarrel between this and the idea of Ibsen structuring his dramatic dialectic upon the phase of spirit analyzed in such depth by Hegel. A modern Christian, Marxian, or Freudian might well employ a far more rigid structural principle and yet find his material in his experience of contemporary life. The Hegelian dialectic is a means of giving esthetic, historical, and philosophical *shape* to the contemporary material. The structure and story of *Rosmersholm* differ far more from Snoilsky's domestic history than they resemble it; but they closely resemble the dialectical drama of Hegel's analysis.[38] In the first draft of *Rosmersholm* the main emphasis is, not upon Rosmer's or Rebekka's personal histories, but upon the broad argument of the play. Boldt-Rømer is depicted as prey to "gloomy pietistic tendencies"; the family tradition is authoritarian, civic, and dedicated to the state, supplying it with priests and military officers. Rebekka's light metaphor is more blatantly presented, and these details clearly show that Ibsen's main preoccupations in the early stages of the play's creation were with the general, the abstract, and universal conflict, rather than with the particular human variation upon this conflict.

We have tried to show that Ibsen has shaped his dramatic structure, and chosen its details, in order to find a place in his art for the historical and universal forces that underlie the appearances of the present, and that the extraordinary and careful design of *Rosmersholm* is created to express these forces. *Rosmersholm* is not about history; the action is a contemporary one, but, to Ibsen, the present inescapably *is* history, part of a continuum from which consciousness cannot truncate itself, and any adequate theatrical consciousness must, also, be a historical consciousness. Because the historical content is so rich in its accumulations, the realistic method of the plays is bound to be highly allusive and hidden, working upon many levels at the same time. We now will attempt to show how the play manages to integrate all its levels of meaning, how the philosophic dialectic, recollecting a major historical transition within the world spirit, can be discovered within a pattern of human histories and destinies that are shaped into compelling dramatic art.

Rosmersholm, first and foremost, is a nineteenth-century drama of human histories and destinies reflecting the political, ethical, psychological, and social life of the times. This might be seen as the most important dimension of the play's existence, the one to which the dramatist gave most attention, for it is on this dimension that the play will succeed or fail in gaining a contemporary audience's attention and sympathy. It is on this ground, too, that it will most readily influence an audience.

It is not the audience's attention or sympathy in itself that is important, however, but the *adéquacy* of this attention and sympathy, and it is the adequacy of the subject matter the audience is asked to contemplate, that will test the real greatness of *Rosmersholm*, just as Ibsen is not concerned with the easy and immediate influence upon his audience that the preacher or politician seeks, but the influence within the world that will emerge from a deep and steady meditation upon a complexly wrought dramatic image. The action of the play is essential and not accidental because the spiritual dialectic it expresses is one that transcends any particular time and place. The action discovers parallels with past history and past theater: the collision between the pagan and the Christian forms of consciousness, for instance, is an archetypal conflict inherited by the modern mind and observable in the disorders of everyday life—what Freud has called the *psychopathology* of everyday life. This collision is part of the structure of our world in the human community at large and within the mind of every individual within that community.

Our immediate impression of the play, nevertheless, is one of "a story of human beings and human destiny," and a satisfactory interpretation of the play must establish how this story exists in its own right and yet how it continuously lights up the larger areas of meaning for which the structure of the play has been created. We need to question every detail, however minute, of Ibsen's realism because each detail implies a consequential choice upon Ibsen's part, a significant "moment" within the total movement. We should expect a close investigation of the play to demonstrate how the dialectic observable in the *structure* of the play is also observable in its *texture*: how the broad and emphatic conflicts that make up its general argument are more complexly and subtly continued in the smaller rhythms of imagery, character trait, factual detail, scenic metaphor, and so on. If we have correctly discerned the broad, overall dialectic of the play we should be able to understand and account for more of its details than other interpretations, while this new understanding of the subtler details also should correct and augment our grasp of the dialectical structure.

Even before the action of the play commences, we can, I think, discover a dialectical tension in the *scene* of Act I. The living room of Rosmersholm is old-fashioned, its walls hung with the portraits of past and recent ancestors: priests, officers, state officials who supply a silent but impressive chorus to the action. Through the window can be seen an avenue of *ancient* trees (as in the last act of *The Master Builder*). Everything, in fact, suggests an old, settled, traditional way of life, strongly associated with state power and state service: the church, the military, and the government. Without writing a drama of state affairs, set in the antechamber of a prince, "where man and the state make their mutual arrangements between breakfast and supper,"[39] as in German Enlightenment drama, and thus removed from the deeply intimate and personal rhythms of the individual psyche, Ibsen yet has indicated historical and political perspectives larger than the immediate action. The time is evening, perhaps also suggestive of the close of a way of life, for this evening colors a vista of ancient trees. The beautifully circular action of *Rosmersholm* begins and ends in evening, with Ibsen's usual concern with the temporal as well as spatial reality of his scene.

An opposition to this old and settled order and this emphatic sense of the end of an era also is found in visual details: those "fresh birch twigs," and the profusion of flowers (which, we will hear, are foreign to Rosmersholm) suggesting renewal, vitality, and a sense that forces associated with nature have invaded the house and are opposing its non-natural, civic, and civilized values. Such an opposition between the civic and the natural, the ordered, traditional line of ancestors and the spontaneous new life of plants and birch twigs, is a paradigm of the opposition of Latin and northern Europe, especially as those birch twigs are themselves associated with the pagan celebration of midsummer eve. The contrast between the civic Latins and the forest-dwelling Germans is at least as old as Tacitus. The flowers and birch twigs, opposing the gloom of the now darkened room, are directly associated with the northern Rebekka West as, also, is the important metaphor of light with which Rebekka will light up this darkened room.

Rebekka, therefore, brings to Rosmersholm natural, vital forces alien to its civic and traditional way of life and from this scene alone we would expect the collision in the play to be between on the one hand civilized, constraining, darkening powers, and the powers of natural energies, life and renewal, on the other; or, in Hegel's words, between Superstition and Enlightenment.

The nature of the struggle begins to become apparent in the first superstitious action described in the play: Rosmer's inability to "cross the footbridge" beneath which his wife, Beate, drowned herself, and immediately we hear from Rebekka and Mrs. Helseth of a struggle between the dead and the living. To Rebekka's enlightened view, the past is something to which the living obstinately cling; to the superstitious Mrs. Helseth, it is the past (the dead) that clings to the living. The first action, and the first dialogue, of the play hardly could set out the collision more clearly and the theme of this collision will be elaborated richly in the rest of the play, which begins with Rebekka mildly making fun of Mrs. Helseth's folk superstitions, and ends with her accepting their ground of truth. In the beginning of the play Rebekka talks of "the white horse thing" merely as something Mrs. Helseth believes; at the end of Act III she confesses to having "caught a glimpse of them" herself.

Are we to take seriously the existence of the white horses of Rosmersholm? They are one of the most frequently recurring of folk superstitions, particularly in northern countries; Tacitus, in his *Germania*, speaks of presaging horses, and other writers mention specifically white horses that appear at significant moments.[40] Their function, in *Rosmersholm*, I believe, is to indicate the area of superstition itself and its relation to the characters in the play; thus they are reference points for the audience's comprehension. In Mrs. Helseth's imagination, the white horses are unquestioned inherited beliefs; they would be totally meaningless to a Peter Mortensgaard, and perhaps, also, to Kroll. Rosmer and Rebekka are far more ambiguously related to this area of supernatural experience and superstition and much of Rebekka's militant attack upon the forces of superstition and reaction derives, we will find, from the fact that her own spirit is not free of this past. Thus we can see the white horses as attraction-repulsion points for the various psyches in the play, defining the relation of the individual to the total spiritual substance of the play. Like the Furies who appear to Orestes or the witches who appear to Macbeth, they stand for the furthest circumference of the human consciousness—the metaphysical—where image and metaphor must take over from everyday factual reality, and the form that this area of human experience takes on in *Rosmersholm*—of a primitively traditional folk myth which, nevertheless, better than anything in the play describes the strange recoil of the Past upon Rosmer and Rebekka—is an esthetically perfect choice on Ibsen's part.

The little drama of Rosmer's inability to cross the footbridge over the stream carries at least a suggestion of being unable to cross the Rubicon to achieve triumph and victory, an appropriately Roman detail for Rosmer. It was by crossing the Rubicon that Julius Caesar propelled Rome towards civil war, from which he emerged triumphant; but Rosmer finds himself unable to engage in the civil war that has broken out in his society because his own past is a Rubicon he cannot cross. Thus the expression "to cross the Rubicon" which denotes the ability to take a firm decision is here deepened and subtilized to denote a far more complex, modern confrontation—a drama in the mind and of the mind.

Rosmer's sensitivity over the footbridge is quickly contrasted with the blunt, imperceptive manner with which his more rigidly inflexible brother-in-law can cross the stream. Kroll represents a more primitive development of consciousness, one that will not venture from orthodox belief towards a more vulnerable area of enlightenment and one that, consequently, is more sure of its own moral strength. This strength, however, is illusory, for the very inflexibility of this level of intellectual consciousness prevents it from comprehending the pressures of the age, and we learn that Kroll's own household, his wife and children, already have defected to the ranks of Mortensgaard's enlightenment. Kroll has many of the characteristics of the "despot" in Hegel's belief trinity of priest, despot, and multitude. He is capable of such gestures as sternly forbidding Rosmer to cross his threshold, while crossing Rosmer's; his speeches are unyielding and authoritarian, and we learn that he is something of a tyrant in his own home and at school. He will be Rebekka's bitterest enemy and his language is the most aggressive in the play, filled with an imagery of repression and war; but the battle he wishes to fight is one that Rosmer and Rebekka already have outgrown. His aggression, therefore, is a reversion to a lower stage of spiritual conflict, an earlier phase of the dialectic. He brings to mind the martial and reactionary brutality of patrician Rome, described by Herder, and also the constantly recurring figure of reaction in Enlightenment drama, the despotic force of reaction and unenlightenment, such as the Duke of Alba in *Don Carlos* and *Egmont*. Though, in *Rosmersholm*, we witness a clash of psyches and not a clash of swords, the drama of the spirit itself, we can see in the drama of consciousness the same forces as in the conflicts of world history.

The play opens with the apparent victory of Rebekka, but will go on to show that, as yet, she hardly is conscious of the powers she is fighting against; Beate is only "greatly missed and greatly mourned" and the house of Rosmersholm is "empty" and we have the impression that the past is something dealt with and comfortably separated from

the present, a memory only. Like the references to the memory of
Beate, the references to Rebekka's past also seem innocuous, seen in
a mood of indulgent sympathy. Rebekka had come from the north with
her crippled foster-father, Dr. West, who was broken by the "terrible
sea-voyages" of the journey south. The doctor caused her some trouble
until he "gave up the struggle" (*fikk stridt ut*) and died. This history,
inserted into the story, is somewhat obtrusive and calls for interpretation,
though it functions, also, as a plausible realistic detail not seriously
eccentric to the total structure. Above all, it sets up the idea of the past
as something safe, comfortably contained in the present, calmly talked
about and even used for self-congratulation. Only on a later reading or
viewing of the play is one aware of the tremendous self-deception, the
failure to grasp realities, of the characters at this phase of the dialectic.
When Kroll explains that he remained absent from Rosmersholm in
order not to be a reminder of past unhappiness, Rosmer and Rebekka
react in the following ways:

ROSMER: How good of you to think like that. You always were considerate.
But it was quite unnecessary for you to stay away on that account. Come
along now, let us sit down on the sofa. (*They sit*) No, it really doesn't upset
me to think about Beate. We talk about her every day. We feel as though she
still belonged to the house.
KROLL: Do you really?
REBEKKA: (*Lights the lamp*). Yes, we really do.[41]

The irony, here, which is really unobtrusive on a first viewing,
depends upon a quite complex relationship between the past and
present in the minds of the three speakers, gradually to be revealed by
the play's action. But already, in that unconscious action of lighting the
lamp as the conversation turns to the presence in the house of the
dead Beate, we see a tiny foreboding of Rebekka's later more desperate
attempt to battle against the past. Rosmer's and Rebekka's easy acceptance of Beate's seeming presence in the house will later turn into their
complete helplessness before it until, in Mrs. Helseth's words, the dead
woman takes them both into the nether world. And this inability to
comprehend the presence of the past in the domestic history of Rosmersholm is paralleled by an inability to comprehend the power of the
past in the realm of ideology in which they are engaged.
The lighting of the lamp, which, of course, lightens the stage, leads
to a change of mood as the conversation turns to the outside world of
political agitation where another light, *The Beacon* (it is Rebekka who
speaks out its name), is attempting to dispel another past, the historical
and ideological past of Europe. Nothing better illustrates the complex

subtlety of Ibsen's dramatic method than the unobtrusive naturalness of this transition where the delicate use of the light symbolism opens up the dialogue to the perspectives of ideological conflict without any heavy signaling. It is just such subtlety, however, that renders it difficult to convince the skeptical of the many levels upon which Ibsen's art is operating. The account of *The Beacon's* proprietor, Mortensgaard, not only brings into the dialogue the perspectives of political and social agitation, it also continues the theme of the contrast between past and present. The dubiousness of Mortensgaard's past is openly discussed; it is part of his acknowledged identity which he has learned to adapt to his present ambitions. It thus stands in strong contrast to the far more guilty, but unacknowledged past of Rebekka which, when acknowledged, will force her to abandon her ambitions. The contrast is all the stronger because Mortensgaard's transgression was a sexual one—adultery—and Rebekka will be shown to have sinned far more gravely against sexual mores in her relations with Rosmer, Kroll, and Beate and, possibly, with her father, Dr. West. We have seen how, in *Ghosts*, Ibsen seems to agree with Plato's concept of the erotic—later acknowledged by Freud—as the fount of human culture and in *Rosmersholm* he directly links erotic rebellion and transgression with ideological rebellion. This idea of the sublimation of erotic energies into ideological, cultural energies is also a major theme of the Enlightenment dramas of Schiller, especially of the important *Don Carlos*.

The argument of the dialogue now settles upon the collision of the forces of unrest in the social and political world, and against this unrest Kroll solemnly salutes and invokes the Rosmersholm *tradition* which, with its long roll call of state servants, soldiers, and priests, has stood as a bastion of law and order. *This* past, so confidently and complacently invoked by Kroll, is, like the smaller past of Rebekka's actions in *Rosmersholm*, far more ambiguous than Kroll is capable of understanding, and it is at this point that the dialogue is interrupted by a bizarre figure from that past—Ulrik Brendel who, we learn, was chased from the house with a horsewhip by the autocratic father of Rosmer. The timing of Brendel's appearance is very important to our full understanding of the play; he appears at two dialectically critical moments, in the first and last acts, and the symmetrical relationship between these two appearances within the play's structure alerts us to the nature of the play's total rhythm. Brendel, obviously, is an aspect of Rosmer's identity, that side of his character associated with his apostasy, and I think it also is possible to see him as a variation upon Ibsen's "satanic" figure in the Cycle which continues all the way to Ulfheim in *When We Dead Awaken*. "Brendel" and Brendel's pen name, Hetman, suggest both fire

and light, archetypal metaphors of rebellion (Prometheus) and satan-
ism.⁴² The devil as an extension of the identity of the priest, an old
European tradition, is employed by Ibsen in the Manders-Engstrand,
Molvik-Relling pairs, and in Rosmersholm he appears most sympathetically, appropriate, perhaps, to Enlightenment satanism. For satanism
is the rebellious and revolutionary, as well as the tabooed, aspect of
human consciousness, frequently representing values of the past not
permitted by the present. Such was William Blake's judgment in *The
Marriage of Heaven and Hell*, where satanism represents the energies
denied by a rationalistic and moralistic culture. Satanism also represents
the debasement or frustration of these energies (e.g., joy-of-life) within
the repressive order. In the second draft of the play, the reference to
the satanic disgrace, in Brendel's account of himself, is somewhat more
obvious than in the final version. Ulrik Rosenhjelm (Brendel)—the name
recalls the pagan associations of Rosenvold, in *Ghosts*—relates that once
he had belonged to "good society, the best society . . ."

and . . . [I was] the first in that society. They threw me out because I had the
ability and courage to say and write what those fine people would rather
have had concealed. Now I no longer move in good society—except when I
enjoy my own company, alone.

In the final version Ibsen more wittily makes Brendel refer to "those
paragons of virtue who threw me out of the Debating Society." Clearly,
having been "thrown out" of a virtuous assembly is intrinsic to Brendel's
identity, and strongly suggests such archetypal figures as Hephaistos,
Lucifer, and Loki, all associated with fire. The function of such a mythic
underpinning to the character would be to encapsule, within a very small
compass, an archetypal human action—one that has been repeated in
countless cultures and will continue to be repeated independently of
the ephemeral modern character, Ulrik Brendel, who is the present vehicle
of this action. Goethe's Mephistopheles and the stage devil of older
drama might also contribute to his character and at one important point
in the play Ibsen actually supplies a quotation from *Faust*, referring to
Mephistopheles, and applies it to Brendel.⁴³

The most striking parallel, however, is between Brendel and an
extraordinary character who makes a prominent appearance in Hegel's
own text, "The Struggle between Enlightenment and Superstition," upon
which, we claim, the dialectic of *Rosmersholm* is based. In 1805, while
Hegel was at work upon the *Phenomenology*, Goethe brought out his
translation of Diderot's *Le Neveu de Rameau* (Rameau's Nephew) and
Hegel seized upon this brilliant work, seeing in its central character,
the nephew of Rameau, an exemplary expression of one aspect of the

enlightened spirit, that of the "witty insight" and its mocking relation (reminiscent of Loki) to the established order. Rather bewilderingly Hegel works Diderot's amusing and disturbing dialogue into his own difficult text.[44]

The similarities between the nephew of Rameau and Brendel are numerous and striking. There is first the overall character which, in both cases, is witty, somewhat dissolute, impoverished, brilliant yet preposterously "theatrical" in speech. He has squandered his talents yet represents, in Diderot's account, a form of revolt against the mores of his society. The nephew was a tutor and entertainer of polite society who earned "bed, board, coat, waistcoat, breeches and shoes" as the learned clown of society and in Diderot's dialogue he has been thrown out of good society for speaking his mind and has become, like Brendel, disheveled in appearance. He is very much given to picturesque oaths and exclamations, as is Brendel, and when asked why he has not produced any great work he explains how, when he had persuaded himself of his genius, he took up his pen to write but found that there was "nothing doing": "the god was absent." In almost the same words, Brendel, when asked by Rebekka about all his unwritten works, replies:

> For twenty-five years I have been like a miser sitting on his padlocked chest. And then yesterday . . . when I opened it up to get at the treasure . . . there was none. . . . The mills of time had ground it all to dust. Not a blessed thing. *Nichts.*[45]

The nephew ironically professes to admire the opportunist and sycophantic Bouret as "the greatest man in the world" for much the same reason that Brendel ironically professes to admire Mortensgaard as "the lord and master of the future" because (as in Hegel's equally ironic account of the utilitarian spirit) he can live his life without ideals. There can be no doubt that Ibsen has worked Diderot's vivid portrait of the nephew into the brilliant character of Brendel, and he would have been quick to see in the nephew an appropriate vehicle of the rebellious forces of the human consciousness.[46]

The reaction of the other characters to the news of Brendel's arrival adds further overtones to his character. Rebekka is surprised that he is still alive, Rosmer believed he was on tour with a theatrical company, while Kroll, with typical harshness, believed him to be in the workhouse (*arbeidsanstalten*)—all of these judgments suggesting a character somewhat redundant in the modern age, somewhat theatrical, and perhaps condemned to a place of hardship and disgrace. It is not difficult to see in these details light suggestions of a satanic or Mephisthophelean identity. Brendel and Mortensgaard, oddly, are the only characters described in detail in the stage directions of the play, and the description of Brendel is particularly rich:

> He is an impressive figure, with grey hair and beard, rather gaunt, but alert and vigorous. He is dressed like a common tramp. Threadbare frock coat, down at heel, no sign of a shirt. He is wearing old black gloves, and carries a soft dirty hat crumpled under his arm and a walking stick in his hand.[47]

There seems to be a discrepancy between the person and his dress, the quality of the man and the social situation from which he suffers. Everything suggests the brilliant outcast who has seen better days in society and, perhaps, in the theater. The discrepancy between intrinsic quality and outward mode of behavior and speech (which is clownishly pretentious and artificial) matches the discrepancy between essence and appearance. To his "disciple," Rosmer (Johannes), he uses the words of Christ to his favorite disciple (Johannes), ". . . you whom I have loved most" (*du, hvem jeg har elsket mest*), and his speech is interlaced with not always accurate phrases from French and German. He describes himself as a "sybarite" whose powers of artistic creation have been sealed in his private imagination only, not objectified into works of art. The element of the wastrel and squanderer corresponds to Hegel's account of the "witty insight" that was left behind by the developing dialectic of Enlightenment's struggle with Belief.

Another indication that Brendel conveys those qualities we have associated with the "satanic" and the rebellious aspect of man is his fondness for alcohol which almost always functions in Ibsen's plays, as G. Wilson Knight has pointed out, to represent a futile attempt, in a repressive world, to return to sources of joy and energy. When we think of such diverse drinkers in Ibsen's plays as Julian of Act III of *Emperor and Galilean*, Dr. Rank of *A Doll's House*, Alving and Engstrand of *Ghosts*, the ebullient Thomas Stockmann of *An Enemy of the People*, Old Ekdal and Relling of *The Wild Duck*, and Eilert Løvborg of *Hedda Gabler*, we will see the prominence and importance of this theme in Ibsen's scheme of things, and his impressive perception of more profound and more universal meanings and causes behind everyday phenomena. If we remain only at the level of the surface and accidental aspect of Brendel's character, it will be easy for us to underestimate what he stands for and the nature of the criticism of life that he represents. If we do fail to perceive this, we are bound to be puzzled by the way in which Rosmer and Rebekka take him seriously. By his very dissoluteness and fall from grace, squandering his brilliant gifts, he implies that something is radically wrong with the world of *Rosmersholm*.

Ulrik Brendel is, perhaps, Ibsen's most brilliant single character: his "wrong notes" of fulsome rhetoric, false gesturing, his general air of emotional and intellectual dissolution, the strong impression of belonging to an earlier time and place than that in which he finds himself, all build up a conceptually and theatrically rich and complex figure. In the dialectic of the play he seems like an anachronistic figure who turns up at moments of rebellion like a fighter of earlier lost causes. In good Hegelian terms he tells his audience:

> At certain recurrent intervals I am compelled to exert myself in the battle for life. That is not something I enjoy doing; . . . but . . . *enfin* . . . compelling necessity.

His identity with Rosmer is forcefully established. He was Rosmer's old tutor, planting in his pupil the seeds of rebellion that Rebekka later has nurtured into open revolt. He underscores Rosmer's moods throughout the play. In Act I, as Rosmer jubilantly announces his campaign to challenge his society, Brendel, too, optimistically announces his campaign to place his "mite on the altar of liberty." In Act IV his despairing rhetoric luridly underscores Rosmer's finer-toned revolt, giving that revolt stronger dramatic identity. He is, as it were, an extension of Rosmer, suffering in the world of action the defeat that Rosmer will experience in the world of consciousness. The identity with Rosmer is emphasized when Brendel actually borrows Rosmer's clothes in which to preach his version of the message Rosmer, too, would preach. These clothes are the outward signs of Rosmer's identity and the outermost and most conspicuous garment, the overcoat, will be pawned and will have to be redeemed by Mortensgaard who also will be concerned to redeem Rosmer's own outward appearance—his Christian identity which he has intrinsically discarded.

Rebekka describes Brendel as going off "to his great sacrificial feast" and succeeds this sombre (and somewhat Roman?) comment with, "Now we can have our refreshment." But the momentary appearance of Brendel in *Rosmersholm* now leads immediately to the revelation of Rosmer's apostasy, and it is Brendel's appearance that seems to give Rosmer the courage to speak out, as it will do, also, in the last Act. For the first time, Rosmer and Kroll face each other in open hostility and it is at this point that Kroll raises the specter of the dead Beate: a specter unexorcised from the consciousnesses of Rosmer and Rebekka. The latter is seriously unnerved and even mentions the white horse seriously, momentarily siding with the superstitious Mrs. Helseth, and she takes up the white shawl, a significantly repeated action in the play which, in its *unconscious* nature, suggests an agitation far below the surface, among the deeper forces of the spirit which are working and weaving towards Rebekka's final acceptance of the Rosmer tradition, signaled when she at last places the completed white shawl over her head for her death-marriage with Rosmer. The act closes with the extinguishing of the light.

Act I has unfolded the full conflict upon the stage and has subtly suggested the wider ideological and historical perspectives that surround the little human drama. The events in the microcosmic world of Rosmersholm begin to take on the shape of archetypal events in the evolution of human consciousness: enlightenment against traditional prejudice, pagan energies against Christian traditionalism, freedom against constraint, the power of the past against the life of the present—all these are discovered to be historical and atemporal forces operating upon contemporary life. The skill with which Ibsen has handled this vast material and shaped it into a subtle and symmetrical drama of consciousness is the result of the dramatist's life-long absorption in his vision. The mythic, historical, esthetic, and philosophical perspectives of the play—its universals—*are* discoverable by paying close but imaginative attention to the particular details of the play.

The somewhat abstract nature, and formal shapeliness, of the dialectical argument of *Rosmersholm* is a feature, also, of German Enlightenment drama from Lessing to Goethe. In Schiller, the passionate, melodramatic plot (of, for example, *Don Carlos*) is the means by which we are led to discover the highly abstract idealist argument for which the plot exists. In Lessing's *Nathan der Weise* the characters in the play clearly embody the abstract entities of the argument; while the plays of Goethe's Weimar period, *Torquato Tasso* and *Iphigenie auf Tauris*, so clearly are conceived to embody the abstract argument that they only just establish the minimum human complexity of identity necessary for dramatic faith. The great merit, as well as the great weakness, of German Enlightenment drama is the primacy it gives to the *idea* which the dramatic dialectic embodies, over the human subject, and such a disparity suggests that there is a gulf between the actual and the ideal in the enlightened consciousness that will lead to the even more pronounced division within consciousness of Romanticism. Ibsen in *Rosmersholm* has, I believe, taken up this phase of consciousness with its disparity between the actual and the ideal, has analyzed it in depth and, by better relating this condition of consciousness to plausible human experience, speech and gesture, has "corrected" its too-abstract quality. The passionate human story with its guilt and destiny is inextricably woven into the idealistic argument far more successfully than Schiller and Goethe were able to effect; but the beautiful shapeliness of the play and the themes of its ideological collision—revolution versus civilization; superstition versus enlightenment; the old order under the impact of new movements of thought and feeling—owe a great deal to the Enlightenment dramatists.

In Act II the established order strikes back at the pair who have challenged it. Rebekka's victory in getting Rosmer to defect to the ranks of the Enlightenment was a blow against the traditional order far more serious than Mortensgaard's attacks in *The Beacon*, but while *The Beacon* proceeds to probable victory the deeper and spiritually more adequate conflict in which Rosmer and Rebekka are unwittingly engaged raises powers that will defeat them. Mortensgaard's success, of course, is far less significant than Rosmer's and Rebekka's failure.

Act II opens ambiguously, the two sides of the Rosmersholm consciousness for the first time divided. Rosmer has slept well, his conscience easy now that his apostasy has been brought into the open and the path to his action within society made clear. But Rebekka, who most had wished for this, has been frightened by Kroll's reference to the dead Beate and we hear that she did not sleep until "the early hours of the morning." Ibsen's decision to change his original plan which would have delayed Rosmer's confession until the second act is superbly justified, for this act can be devoted fully to the recoil upon Rosmer and Rebekka of the full weight of the past.

Ibsen has disturbed the symmetry of this play slightly by setting this act in Rosmer's study: the only time that the action of the play leaves the living room. The study, with its books and writing table, displays the bookish resources with which these enlightened figures vainly hope to combat the darker forces of the human consciousness and the cruder world of politics. So unable to comprehend the forces within themselves, how can these two idealists hope to work upon and transform the consciousnesses of others in the way that Rosmer envisages?[48] In Act II, Rosmer's study is to be invaded by Kroll and his language of barbaric violence, by Mortensgaard with his spiritually degrading opportunistic politics, and by the ever more troubling and menacing spirit of the dead Beate. By placing the action of this act in Rosmer's study, Ibsen seems to be making a comment on the bookish resources of Rosmer's spiritual revolution, drawing attention to the lamentable inadequacy of his spiritual weapons.

G. Wilson Knight has observed that books generally come in for ironic treatment by Ibsen. Julian's development, in *Emperor and Galilean*, from the tormented and divided prophet of a new direction of spirit, to the academic reviver of a dead culture, hoping to change the world by means of books and pamphlets, can stand as an emblem of the direction of Western humanism. Mrs. Alving's book-enlightenment collapses before the life values she has offended; while Hedda Gabler's scornful indifference towards the content of Løvborg's books, for all their fame, in contrast to her intense feelings towards the *origins* of those books—in Løvborg's and Thea's relationship—provides us with a clear judgment on the value of book enlightenment or achievement. The "revolution in the human spirit" which Ibsen felt to be necessary, is unlikely to come from books, however finely written, for it is only too easy for the spirit to be bold in print and yet to evade a direct confrontation with life. One of the distinguishing features of modern bourgeois culture is the way it is continually agitated—and entertained— by bold revolutionary books that satisfy our craving for danger while keeping it safely within the realm of thought and imagination. In Rosmer's case, it is more the uncomfortable disparity between the realm of noble and lofty sentiments which he expresses, and the conditions of the actual human world with which he must engage, that provokes Ibsen's irony.

The lofty, impartial height from which Rosmer hoped to conduct his campaign to ennoble mankind is undercut from the beginning by the confession of Rebekka, his partner in this enterprise, that she has recommended Brendel to Mortensgaard from the conviction that Rosmer will need an ally in his conflict with Kroll and his friends. Kroll's appearance, soon after this, further underscores the nature of this collusion, for he brings a report of Brendel's somewhat rapid decline. This extension of Rosmer, in Rosmer's clothes, has been mixing with "the lowest company," getting drunk, abusing the company and being violently set upon. Furthermore, Brendel has pawned Rosmer's overcoat which is redeemed by Mortensgaard. This whole, somewhat comical *vignette* is a capsuled parody of Rosmer's own situation (and, perhaps, a recollection of Mephistopheles in Auerbach's Keller, in Goethe's *Faust*). As a patrician, leaguing with a "plebeian," he too will be violently set upon by men of low principle and, as Rebekka already has foreseen, will need Mortensgaard's help.

The dialogue now shifts from this contemporary, political conflict to the more disturbing moral and spiritual conflict, as Kroll once again introduces the more menacing theme of Beate. The rather lurid details of Brendel's recent actions perhaps served as a thematic preparation for the far more lurid details of Beate's history, and the reader or viewer is conscious of a sudden darkening of the texture of the play which had begun so innocently in the first act. We hear of Beate's "wild fits of sensual passion," of the "tormented and overwrought" condition in which she predicted Rosmer's apostasy, and also the startling accusation of Rosmer's adulterous relations with Rebekka. These sensational details stand out in stark contrast to the pure and higher motives that Rosmer and Rebekka profess so that their opponents, and even their "ally," Mortensgaard, can impute to their actions far different motives than the idealist ones that they profess. We are reminded of Hegel's account of the most critical stage of the opposition between Belief and Enlightenment, when Belief sees the work of Enlightenment merely as "deception and delusion," as "lying unreason and malicious intent." It is now that Kroll promises Rosmer "a fight to the death," warning him that the "fury of the storm" will break over him: images that look beyond the little provincial setting to a far more devastating conflict. As Kroll's threats reach their climax—"Now it is war to the knife"—Mortensgaard appears, making the study a battlefield between the two forces. Kroll decides to "quit the field, for the time being," leaving Rosmer and Mortensgaard in possession.

But this alliance between Rosmer and Mortensgaard hardly advances the cause espoused by Rosmer and Rebekka, for Mortensgaard now reveals the opportunism of his politics. He is willing to enlist the pastor, but not the apostate, in his cause, for it is as pastor that Rosmer is most useful to him. The intrinsic spiritual development of Rosmer is of no interest to him. "What the party needs is Christian elements—something that everybody has to respect," he tells Rosmer, and this dishonest manipulation of the public mind is the total opposite of Rosmer's envisaged aristocratic brotherhood honestly and openly striving for the highest mutual development.

In Mortensgaard Rosmer confronts a victim of that former Belief that he now has discarded, for Rosmer, as pastor, once branded Mortensgaard for an action (adultery) that, as enlightened apostate, Rosmer recognizes as not being a crime. The ironic reversal of this situation is that Mortensgaard now confronts Rosmer with a letter that accuses the ex-pastor of the selfsame crime, yet he is willing to conceal the fact in order to keep up the appearance of that Christian orthodoxy in which neither of them believes: a multiple irony typical of a complex moral texture of Ibsen's art. This letter, too, like Kroll's revelations a little earlier, brings Beate's presence menacingly on the stage, involving her passionate drama in the ideological conflict and emphasizing that the spiritual forces of Rosmer and Rebekka, for all their greater impressiveness and depth in relation to the forces around them, are barred from any future activity—at least at the level at which, alone, they can exist.

The high and noble powers affirmed by Rosmer and Rebekka are dragged lower and lower in the course of this act. Rosmer allows himself to be manipulated into dishonesty by Mortensgaard; Rebekka is discovered hiding in Rosmer's bedroom to overhear his conversation with Kroll and Morgensgaard; and the "pure and beautiful friendship" is crumbling away before the pressures, external and internal, brought to bear upon it. Rebekka is forced back more and more upon her own guilty past, while Rosmer is tormented with doubt and intimations of guilt. The two spirits that so confidently had anticipated moving outward, into the world of social and political realities, now are being driven, remorselessly and inevitably, *inward*—and this movement of each of the consciousnesses inward is, mutually, a movement away from each other. Rosmer attempts to halt this process of separation with his offer of marriage, but Rebekka's strange refusal only the more emphasizes the presence of some insurmountable cause of division. Act II ends with Rosmer, asking in bewilderment, "What . . . is . . . this?"

Act III develops the atmosphere of deviousness and division that began to emerge under the pressure of the dialectical conflict opened up in Act II. The act begins with Rebekka slyly questioning Mrs. Helseth about the letter once sent by Beate to Mortensgaard and proceeds to her listening, half-seriously only, to the housekeeper's account of the Rosmersholm history, where the children never cry and the men never laugh—a spiritual condition which, says the housekeeper, has spread like an infection to the surrounding district. This history impresses upon us Rebekka's isolation from the Rosmersholm way of life, the way in which it is opposite of all that she stands for; but, as she listens, she works upon the white shawl, a movement to which we already have been alerted as a suggestion that Rebekka is absorbing and re-creating the Rosmersholm spirit.

Deviousness, secrecy, concealed intentions now overwhelm the action. *The County Times* (*Amstidenden*), the ideological opponent of *The Beacon*, attacks Rosmer and Rebekka by means of ugly innuendo. Kroll himself arrives, but wants his visit concealed from Rosmer so that Mrs. Helseth must whisper secretively to Rebekka and Rebekka must dissemble to Rosmer. At this morally lowest point of the play Rosmer and Rebekka seem overwhelmed by the unsuspected forces, within themselves and outside, that they have raised. Rosmer exclaims that he would like to "bring a little light into all this murky nastiness" (the "light" imagery of this play is appropriately prevalent) and to realize an enlightenment vision of mankind engaged in "friendly rivalry," giving up bitter conflict and "striving on and on . . . up and up . . . ," but he falls back upon despair, tormented by a sense of guilt for Beate's death and by a total uncertainty as to his own past motives. The nature of Rosmer's despair clearly implies that the dialectic of the play is one involving somewhat abstract and universal spiritual powers. The goal of the enlightened protagonists of the play is frustrated by that contaminated (*tilsmusset*) past they have in common, for there "can be no victory for any cause that springs from guilt." This strikes us as being more valid in the realm of such universal spiritual transformations as Ibsen's third-empire vision than in the realm of actual human intercourse where total innocence is neither very likely nor very desirable. This contrast of an elusive but necessary innocence and, instead, consciousnesses weighed down by guilt, clearly points up Rebekka's situation and makes more convincing her later, self-destructive decision to confess. To be effective, a spiritual force must work in happiness upon men; but happiness is impossible when there is even the suspicion of guilt for others' suffering. Rosmer's salvation, it seems, lies in having this suspicion removed from his consciousness by Rebekka who will take the entire blame for Beate's death upon herself. Using Ibsen's own terms in his description of the play, we can set out the spiritual dilemma as follows: the enlightened spirit, wishing to work effectively upon men, finds itself checked by "these traditional doubts, traditional fears, traditional scruples"[49] that are the result of centuries of Christian consciousness. The less scrupulous, more healthy pagan "acquisitive instinct hurrying from gain to gain" in enlisting the Christian spirit to its cause, finds itself infected with conscientiousness, thus losing what Hilde Wangel will call a "robust conscience" just as the Christian partner is infected with guilt over the deeds of his pagan associate. I already have suggested this is a drama within one consciousness, and the completest depiction of this is in *Emperor and Galilean*. Constantius, the warrior-emperor of his Christian empire, is tormented by guilt over actions necessary, he feels, to maintain his power. His pagan and imperial role is infected by his Christian remorse and his Christian conscience is tormented by his imperial policies; but, worse than this, each side of this divided nature exacerbates and drives to madness the other. The Christians, including Constantius, out of their sickly consciences, commit worldly and fleshly crimes more vilely than would the pagans who felt no guilt over them; and in reaction to this, they are driven, also, to fanatic excesses of spiritual abasement and self-torture. (Halvard Solness, of *The Master Builder*, is a modern version of this character.) In Julian, the same mutual destructiveness of these dialectically *un*assimilated antinomies is even further exacerbated as the intensely subjective and Christian Julian attempts to revive and relive the unsubjective, spiritually daring life of paganism. The extremely subtle philosophical portraiture of *Emperor and Galilean* depends upon our continually detecting these ironies: of characters whose beliefs are contradictions of their natures.

This produces a psychological dualism reminiscent of Dostoevskyan fiction. The marriage of Julian, the chaste and other-worldly "pagan," with Helena, the erotically passionate "Christian," is the crowning irony of this dialectical interplay of incompatibilities.

The subtle dialectical interplay of the psyches of Rosmer and Rebekka, whereby each has "infected" the other in a form of spiritual sublimation of sexual intercourse, will fully be revealed only at the end of the play. At the present stage of the dialectic Rebekka is not consciously aware of how much of the Rosmersholm spirit she has absorbed. It is at this point that Kroll appears and presents to Rebekka her history in its ugliest and extremest light—the history of a ruthless power working without scruple or consideration upon a more sensitive *tradition.* Rosmer's and Rebekka's pasts are, says Kroll, absolutely different (*himmelvidt forskjellige*) and his version of Rebekka's past shows it to be lawless in its origins and lawless in its later history. She is, he claims, the natural daughter of Dr. West and there is a strong hint that this relationship has led to incest. She has bewitched and infatuated Beate as well as Kroll and Rosmer and her relationship with the latter needs to be, Kroll believes, "legalized." This series of sensational and lurid disclosures establishes Rebekka as something entirely alien to Rosmer and all he stands for: as alien as the world of barbaric anarchy from the world of civilized order. It is this image of herself that prompts Rebekka now to confess, to take upon herself the entire burden of blame for the savage events that led to Beate's death, and to leave Rosmersholm forever. Her confession, before both Rosmer and Kroll, brought out with such painful and reluctant effort, seems finally and forever to effect that estrangement that Kroll believes is the only relation between these two consciousnesses. In miniature, I believe, we have here a confrontation of seemingly absolute psychic opposites as must have occurred when the northern and savage hordes confronted an exhausted, Christianized Rome in which assimilation seemed totally impossible. Yet, for the future of the race, assimilation was necessary and inevitable, and the later history of the Western consciousness has recorded this. Similarly, at the time of the Enlightenment, just such a confrontation of absolute opposites, and just such a fundamental assimilation and union, took place between the consciousness of the old Roman Christian order of thought and that of the new progressive order of intellectual freedom.

For Rebekka's confession of her guilty alienation from the Rosmersholm tradition ironically has demonstrated the exact opposite: to what a great extent she has moved *towards* Rosmer's tradition, for the conscientious desire for atonement that her confession represents derives from his tradition and not from hers. Rebekka, as that confession demonstrates, has moved substantially towards the moral order of Belief and the act ends with her confessing to Mrs. Helseth that she has caught a glimpse of "the white horse of Rosmersholm," a superstition that represents an extreme expression of the Belief consciousness.

The last act closes off the vistas that were opened up so confidently in Act I, and we find the details of Act I reappearing in a darker key. Once again it is evening, "a shaded lamp" burning on the table. Rebekka now is preparing to depart from Rosmersholm in contrast to the first act where she is shown fully established in the old house. Even this flight, as she learns from Mrs. Helseth, will grotesquely be misinterpreted by the people, for the housekeeper believes that that Rosmer is getting rid of Rebekka in order to avert scandal over her pregnancy. The "pure and beautiful friendship," an unreal ideal in the human world, already is collapsing into lurid scandal that will make impossible Rosmer's role of ennobling his society in the new terms he and Rebekka once envisaged. Rebekka now is closer to the simple Mrs. Helseth than at any point in the play, and her agreement with the housekeeper that "we are only human" contrasts with the earlier idealistic ambition to create spiritual aristocrats out of humanity. Rosmer and Rebekka are forced back upon the "only human" in themselves, discarding the wider spiritual extensions that they envisaged emerging from this humanity; and both are forced to concede the defeat of the cause they served.

It is now that Rebekka completes her confession, not to explain her past but to illuminate her present condition of consciousness. When she first came to Rosmersholm she felt for Rosmer "a wild uncontrollable passion" that swept over her like a winter storm on the northern sea—a blind and unconscious passion that made her "fight to the death" with Beate. This *passion* was crushed by the alien Rosmersholm tradition which sapped her spirit and crippled her willpower. A "great transformation" took place within her, reaching to the very depths of her soul, a transformation that was the beginning of *love* (in contrast to the pagan *passion*) but it was a love which has made her "sick," has taken away her strength. For "the Rosmersholm philosophy of life ennobles . . . but it kills happiness."[50]

Though Rebekka has confessed her conversion to the Rosmersholm way of life, marriage with Rosmer is impossible, for her new spiritual condition makes her confront her past as an insurmountable barrier. Her past, which is intrinsic to her identity, is in conflict with this new identity which has dialectically developed in union with Rosmer: if the future lies with Rosmer, therefore, she only can be an alien and retarding presence, "some sea-troll slumped over the ship that is to carry [Rosmer] forward."[51] The future, however, does not belong to

Rosmer; he and Rebekka are two forces meeting only at the moment of their mutual exhaustion. Precisely because they have tested life at its most profound and essential they have pushed the terms of their existence to their furthest limits—a dialectical development typical of the Cycle. In *Rosmersholm* the abstract quality of the dialectical development imposed upon the human story is perhaps more marked than in the other plays in the Cycle, and this may in part be due to the model of the Enlightenment drama which, I believe, Ibsen was using. It is the history of a northern passionate force coming south, encountering an unhappy and divided traditional and patrician order, entering into a deadly duel with the weaker half of this order, winning, but being ennobled and purified through association with a noble but life-denying tradition. This pattern of action, which makes up the human story of *Rosmersholm*, corresponds unmistakably to Hegel's account of one of the major moments of European history in the development of the modern consciousness: the contact between the savage northern spirit and the divided and exhausted Roman world. Any analysis of the modern consciousness, if it is to be adequate, must take account of this "moment" in the life and growth of the European spirit. To relive this moment in modern terms, to discover its presence underneath the appearances of modern everyday reality, as Ibsen has done so subtly in *Rosmersholm*, is analogous to the psychoanalyst's art of discovering long-forgotten traumata in the familiar and habitual rhythms of everyday life.

The devastating return of the unsubdued past upon Rosmer and Rebekka, and their program of enlightenment, corrects the optimism with which Lessing, Schiller, and even Goethe assumed so confidently that the Past could be exorcised by the enlightened Spirit. The nebulousness of Rosmer's enlightened ambition of creating spiritual aristocrats out of men reminds one particularly of Schiller, as does the insistence upon *happiness* as an indispensable element of spiritual conversion. In Enlightenment drama the dialectic was weighted too heavily in favor of the enlightened protagonists who, even if they were defeated as in *Don Carlos* and *Egmont*, are given at least philosophical victory. (Egmont, for example, dies after receiving a reassuring visit from the spirit of Freedom.) This inevitably falsified the historical and the human situation (and Hegel would say that it falsified the truth of the Concept), for it opens the dialectic of the play to perspectives that go beyond the experience of the situation—a falsification against which Richard Wagner protested. Ibsen seems to have been acutely aware of this falsification, for in his own historical-philosophical drama, *Emperor and Galilean*, in which he claimed the critics would find the positive world view they had demanded, he is careful to leave the major quest of the play—the establishment of a third empire of spirit envisaged by Maximus—in a context of defeat and doubt rather than in a context of exultant affirmation.

Rosmer and Rebekka inhabit a particular spiritual universe, a *gestalt* of consciousness, and cannot transcend its terms; therefore they must struggle and suffer without assurance of posthumous justification and without external assurance of the authenticity and adequacy of their values and actions. That there *are* other terms than those of their particular dialectical universe, terms which give meaning to their attempts to transcend it, *we*, surveying the whole Cycle which requires this "moment," *are* aware.

The close of the play completes its dialectical development. Rosmer's Christian and Roman tradition can be convinced of Rebekka's spiritual transformation only by means of the test of *sacrifice*; the sacrifice of physical life for that of the spirit and, perhaps, of that "honor" to which the Romans sacrificed their lives. While his mind hovers fearfully over this undeclared idea, there is "a loud knock at the door," and Ulrik Brendel reappears still wearing the clothes he borrowed in Act I. This appearance of Brendel is a masterstroke of timing on Ibsen's part, and the extreme symmetry of this return of the action to the beginning produces in the viewer a "click" of recognition that a design somehow is being completed. In Act I Brendel had appeared as Rosmer was hesitating to tell Kroll of his apostasy and Brendel's rhetorically expressed rebellion gave Rosmer courage to speak out. Now it is Brendel's rhetorically expressed despair that will give Rosmer the courage to speak out his terrible, despairing request to Rebekka. It is Brendel who rhetorically depicts the extent of Rosmer's defeat by describing his own. Like Rosmer, he is bankrupt of ideals, "a king standing amid the ashes of his burnt-out palace." He has made the terrible discovery that the world does not need his form of rebellion, that he is out of date. His lurid, "satanic" rebellion is as redundant in the world of Mortensgaard, the man of utility, as Rosmer's dream of ennobling mankind. He longs only for "the great Void" (*det store ingenting*) into which the old spiritual forces will vanish.

Brendel gives voice to Rosmer's unspoken thought when he warns his old pupil not to build his hopes upon the "enchanting little mermaid," Rebekka, unless she shows herself capable of *sacrifice*. Rosmer's success is assured only on the condition:

That the woman who loves him goes out into the kitchen and gladly chops off her dainty, pink and white little-finger . . . *here*, just near the middle joint. Furthermore, that the aforesaid woman in love . . . equally gladly . . . cuts off her incomparably formed left ear. (*Lets go and turns to Rosmer*) Farewell, my conquering Johannes.[52]

This speech is, in fact, a rewording of a crucial speech in *Emperor and Galilean* and should, therefore, alert us to the wider scheme of meanings behind the action of *Rosmersholm*. At a moment of disillusion over his ambition to restore the suppressed pagan world in all its glory, Julian bitterly compares the half-hearted spirit of his pagan followers with that of his Christian opponents:

> These Galileans, I tell you, have in their hearts something I dearly wish you would strive for. You call yourselves followers of Socrates, of Plato, of Diogenes. Is there one of you who would gladly go to his death for Plato's sake? Do you think our Priscus would sacrifice his left hand for Socrates? Would Chytron let them cut off his ear for Diogenes' sake? Of course you wouldn't! I know you, you whited sepulchres! Be gone from my sight: . . . I have no use for you![53]

Julian is insisting that no spiritual persuasion can be called serious if it is not one for which men are willing to sacrifice their bodies. Without such sacrifice the spiritual cause is a mere idea in the head, not "proved upon the pulses," in Keats's phrase. Rosmer, similarly, cannot be convinced of Rebekka's conversion to his philosophy unless she shows that she adheres to it as passionately as Beate had done, to the point of death itself. This idea might strike some readers as uncomfortably, and even morbidly, uncompromising; but it is undoubtedly an element of the imagination of the author of *Brand* and *Emperor and Galilean*.

Brendel's departure into "the dark night" with the blessing, "Peace be with you," marks, I believe, in the progress of the Cycle, the end of a whole phase of Spirit: that specifically Christian concept of the universe introduced with *The Wild Duck*. The now somewhat ludicrous "satanic" figure, Brendel, precedes the pastor into the dark night, or Void, beyond the claustrophobic little scene. The suggestion that Brendel is a "satanic" figure gains in plausibility when we note an otherwise wholly inexplicable little quotation that occurs at this point. Rebekka feels that the room is now "close and sultry" and opens a window (the sound of the mill-race would be effective at this point) opening the claustrophobic room to the surrounding night. This action, with Rebekka's accompanying comment, is taken from a vivid moment in Goethe's *Faust*, Part I. Immediately after Mephistopheles and Faust have left her room, Margarete enters and exlaims, "Es ist so schwül, so dumpfig hier" ("It is so close and sultry"), and she straightway opens the window. Rebekka's words are, "Aa, hvor her er kvalmt og lummert," which is an exact translation of *schwul* and *dumpfig*. A feeling that a confined room was close and sultry would be an appropriate response to a recent visit to the room by Mephistopheles, and Ibsen can have no other reason for inserting this little episode in his play than that of creating in his audience a response of uneasiness deriving from the unconscious, or barely conscious, recollection of the episode from Goethe's play.[54]

The grave closing moments of the play beautifully and fully sound out the great themes of its argument. Rebekka reveals to Rosmer the process of her transformation by the Rosmersholm spirit and the breaking of her more ruthless will. Though each no longer can rejoin the stream of life, take part in its great events, they can between them affirm the reality of the potent spiritual union of their disparate traditions. Rosmer's "cause" stands or falls upon the proof of Rebekka's total transformation and the only proof Rebekka can give is her sacrifice of herself. Similarly, Rosmer's ability to articulate this requirement of her and his ability to accompany her, at last step on the footbridge and, by his marriage with Rebekka, dispose at last of the ghost of Beate, reveals to what an extent he, too, has absorbed her courageous will. As so often in the Cycle, therefore, their death is not a defeat but the affirmation of the reality of a spiritual action that will survive them. In the world of external action Rosmer has experienced "a dismal, pitiful defeat," and Rebekka's spirit has been broken. But this world of external action, which Mortensgaard and Kroll will inherit, was inessential in not facing up to its total spiritual substance in the way that Rosmer and Rebekka have done. *Until* this spiritual substance was faced and comprehended, the world of action was merely, in Matthew Arnold's phrase, a place where ignorant armies clash by night, where characters and conflicts, instead of being ennobled by struggle, only can deteriorate and be dragged down. The tragic logic of Ibsen's ethical world parallels that of Hegel's dialectic, in which death is the necessary condition of life: death is the dialectical consummation of a particular spiritual form which will remain incomplete, and therefore invalid, until it is thus consummated.

The death-marriage of Rosmer and Rebekka sanctifies a struggle that otherwise only could have ended in ignominious compromise: a compromise, it must be admitted, which the mass of humanity would have to make if it is to survive. The death-marriage not only esthetically satisfyingly closes the play: it also is the culmination of the play's dialectical logic which cannot be evaded in art as it can in life. The play's logic thus reproaches the unheroic compromise which common-sense reality wisely insists upon. Rosmer and Rebekka are given the dignity of spiritual forces raised to such a level that they alone can pass judgment upon themselves. "There is no judge over us," Rosmer declares, echoing the phrase of Don Caesar in Schiller's *Braut von Messina*, an "aristocratic" phrase that Hegel cites as an example of the princely hero, "subject to no external necessity of right and law."[55] As these higher characters go off to die, in the high Roman fashion, their death is absorbed in the folk consciousness of the housekeeper, Mrs. Helseth, as the death of the hero in Greek tragedy is absorbed by the chorus. Mrs. Helseth's speech, upon which the curtain falls, swiftly brings together the main themes of the play: the white horses, the shawl, symbolic of Rebekka's growing "Rosmersholm" consciousness, the foot-bridge, the stream, the "sinful" (*syndige*) lovers, and the dead woman, Beate, who takes the lovers into her world of death. This "coda" to the whole four-movement dramatic symphony complexly juxtaposes present and past, living and dead, the atavisms of the spirit that refuse to be exorcised as well as the power of the past that it is rash to forgive and forget. In this last speech, the drama of the higher spiritual powers who have courageously completed their rhythm through to death, is returned to the consciousness of common humanity which may or may not be capable of a more authentic spiritual mode of life—a nobility equal to but less guilty than that which it has witnessed, as Ibsen, in the Trondheim speech, believed the women and workingmen of the future might be. This, after all, would constitute the "use" of history for those who, like Ibsen, are too wise to ignore it.

Rosmer and Rebekka, therefore, like the protagonists of Greek tragedy, have been both the vehicles and the victims of universal forces. They join company with Orestes or Antigone. Ibsen's tragic argument has been a highly abstract one in this play as it is in the Enlightenment drama upon which it is modeled and from which it frequently quotes. This abstract quality is necessary if the play truly is to express the Enlightenment spirit; but Ibsen contrives to supply a graver, deeper dialectical rhythm and a profounder and more convincing human content than we find even in the best Enlightenment drama. The great achievement of Enlightenment drama had been that of creating a dramatic structure and rhythm in which the crisis of the play's movement was a crisis of intellectual perception, not of mere theatrical sensational-ism; but the great weakness of the form was a certain stiltedness and declamatoriness (the Weimar manner) in character, action, and dia-logue. Not only cannot Egmont and Posa talk to the groundlings as Hamlet can, they cannot talk to themselves and their intimates as Shakespeare's characters can, for the idealistic gesturing made any transition to a subtly mobile and realistic level of action and language almost as impossible as for the characters of Corneille and Racine. The true goal of Enlightenment drama probably is the perfect but ethereal form of *Torquato Tasso* and *Iphigenie auf Tauris*. *Rosmersholm*, it seems to me, is the adequate realization of the form and substance of Enlightenment drama. It dramatizes the ideological conflict—tradition and civilization versus freedom and change—through the convincing rhythms of individual psyches: it inextricably involves the passionate plot of the love story with the higher drama of ideas in conflict,[56] and, though it does possess much of Enlightenment drama's abstractness of argument—what, for instance, *are* the new ideas Rebekka and Rosmer will further, and *how* will Rosmer set about "ennobling" his fellow men?—its dramatic rhythms search out and reveal a more complex and subtle human reality. As with Enlightenment drama, the crises of the play are crises of ethical perception, of radical modifications of the intellect upon the stage, giving the actors and actresses the interesting problem of conveying inward intellectual and spiritual development and change. This inward change *can* be conveyed because it is not that of a particular psychological case history—therefore an accident or aberration—but because it is a demonstrable stage of the general mind's biography. The goal of Enlightenment drama, from Lessing to Goethe, had been no less than that ennoblement of mankind that is Rosmer's professed goal and it was an idealistic attitude that was not to survive the realities of post-Revolutionary Europe. In the biography of the human mind it is that moment when the human spirit finely but futilely sought to establish for all the highest spiritual values: of friendly rivalry, of a human nobility founded upon happiness, innocence, and mutual tolerance of difference in the common struggle toward a realm of highest values. The forces the enlightened spirit raised, pagan and Christian, were to prove too powerful and ruthless to be enlisted in its program so that the Enlightenment could not survive this recognition. *Rosmersholm* is, I believe, a supremely subtle dramatic re-creation of that experience, though also extending further back to that past of pagan-Christian conflict which the Enlightenment itself so facilely took up and reenacted. *Now*, in this doomsday sessions upon the soul of the whole Cycle, this moment is more adequately re-created and reexperienced, benefiting from the great depth of Hegel's analysis of this spiritual drama.

Rosmersholm achieves a distinction of gesture and elevation of the audience's level of interest which Enlightenment drama also sought. It is one of Ibsen's deepest and subtlest plays in its simple-looking but extremely complex dramatic rhythm and it appeals to the most discriminating esthetic taste by its grave and discreet movement, its refinement of attitude, gesture, and argument, so free of the tiresome *frissons* of plot or character revelation often considered "good theater."

It thus virtually invites the audience towards a comprehension of that aristocracy of spirit invoked in the Trondheim speech. It is an invitation that only a few are capable of accepting so that it is not surprising that, in the noisy element of modern theater and show business, the play is so rarely produced.

CHAPTER 6

Death and Transfiguration in
The Master Builder

... Therefore, to begin with, I do not as yet have full command over the images slumbering in the mine or pit of my inwardness, am not as yet able to recall them at will. No-one knows what an infinite host of images of the past slumbers in him; now and then they do indeed accidentally awake, but one cannot, as it is said, call them to mind. . . . The manner in which the images of the past lying hidden in the dark depths of our inner being become our actual possession, is that they present themselves to our intelligence in the luminous, plastic shape of an *existent* intuition of similar content, and that with the help of this *present* intuition we recognise them as intuitions we have already had.

—Hegel in *The Philosophy of Mind*, p. 205

... True sanity entails in one way or another the dissolution of the normal ego, that false self competently adjusted to our alienated social reality: the emergence of the "inner" archetypal mediators of divine power, and through this death a rebirth, and the re-establishment of a new kind of ego-functioning, the ego now being the servant of the divine, no longer its betrayer.

—R. D. Laing in *The Politics of Experience*, p. 119

The Master Builder opens the third and final group of four plays in the Cycle. In this group, the human consciousness is displayed at its highest development and operation, above the levels of the objective, ethical consciousness and the subjective, self-estranged consciousness. Instead we find an objective world responsive to and reflective of the subjective consciousness: a world of mysterious powers and forces, of actions emerging from hitherto unexplored dimensions of reality and of the mind reaching out beyond the dimensions of an inadequate common-sense reality. One might say that the *scene* of these four plays is a cosmos in search of a heroic humanity, while the *characters* of the group are a humanity, "awakening" to heroism and searching for a more adequate cosmos.

253

The alienation undergone in the second group now is to be overcome and the individual, long exiled from the objective world of Nature and Society, returns from his journey into the interior of the psyche and now will invest the recovered objective world with new meanings and values. In the *Phenomenology* this is the phase of the historical ideologies of Arts, Literatures, and Religions. J. Loewenberg has written of this phase:

> The climax of the mind's phenomenology consists in its apotheosis: the human subject of the biography becomes superhuman and puts on immortality. The apotheosized mind which is to arise is the object of worship present to the religious consciousness, appearing in the course of the immediately succeeding dialectic in progressively adequate forms.[1]

We would expect the plays dramatizing this level of human consciousness to be more metaphoric, mythopoeic, visionary, and mysterious than the plays of the two previous phases and this, I believe, *is* the experience of the reader. The memories, and the consequences, of the two earlier groups—of the ethical and the subjective conflicts within consciousness—make up much of the historical and psychological substance of the last four plays which, however, break with this legacy of guilt and error and "awaken" to spiritual freedom.

The urgent and consequential division of Time into past, present, and future clearly shapes the material and action of *The Master Builder*. The past, as always in Ibsen, is ambiguous: it is the realm of tragic loss, of hopeless nostalgia, of established repression, dead habits, and ideas, and of a paralyzing constraint upon the modern spirit's quest for spiritual freedom. At the same time, however, the past also is the realm of recollected achievement, of values tabooed by the present and of definitions of human identity more challenging than those permitted by the present. Here, memory becomes not crippling and constraining but subversive and, in the unwelcome demands it makes upon the complacent spirit, terrifying in the "awakening" it instigates. This ambiguity in the nature of the past—whether it is triumph or defeat, achievement or tragic loss, benefaction or guilt—informs the whole texture of memory in *The Master Builder*, up to and including the final fall of Solness and his release from his torturing consciousness. His attempt to be adequate to the image of the past that Hilde presents to him can be seen as paradigmatic of man's requirement to measure up to the stature of the spirit presented by history: his guilt and self-torment resemble, in "domestic" terms, the opposite lesson we learn from history, that it is a record of guilt, loss, and error.

Our first impression of the play is of its fundamental absurdity. A young woman of about twenty-three enters a middle-aged man's house with a preposterously childish story of having been promised, ten years ago to the day, a "kingdom" of which she is to be the princess: the play shows this young woman, by essentially childish stratagems—of silences, sulks, juvenile enthusiasms for the "'terribly thrilling"—gradually imposing her childish vision and desires upon the man who, like a small boy living up to a "dare," agrees to overcome his fear of heights and to climb the scaffolding of the new house he has built. The plot seems embarrassingly naive with that innocent psychopathology of so much Victorian fiction involving children where the darkest Freudian impulses emerge under the thin disguise of avuncular coziness or overstraining innocence. It seems a relatively easy task to apply the Freudian critical kit and demonstrate how Ibsen's id is showing through the naive oddness of the story he is telling us. We listen with perhaps adult irritation as these two grown-ups enthuse over a castle with a princess, trolls, good and bad devils, dreams of falling through the air, of childlike vikings engaged on adventures of pillaging and of abducting women (mere schoolboy fantasies of Scandinavian history), and so on. We hear Hilde ask, with the grave concern of a child whose heart is about to be broken, "Is it true that my master builder cannot climb as high as he builds?" and we see her excitedly clapping her hands together when, promised her castle, she exclaims, "My lovely, lovely castle—our castle in the air!" just like a little girl promised an enticing birthday present. If these are possible byways of individual psychology, we can, I think, ask why they are offered for our interest. If *The Master Builder* merely is exploring the nature of the individual human psyche, we legitimately can complain that the examples offered are at once too extravagant and too unsubtle. To supplement our psychological account of the play with a smattering of the occult or of hypnotism is only to increase our impression of the extravagant absurdity of the action—its *peculiarity*—and it is to force us to project meanings onto the text rather than permitting the meaning of the play to emerge by means of the text.

Psychological criticism finds itself embarrassedly evading the text in certain places, and overemphasizing or overelaborating it in others. The criticism that uses the play in order to speculate upon the private life of Ibsen is, of course, of even less significance.

The only serious interpretation of the play must face head-on its structure and texture, its full pattern of images and details and its major overall action. It is impossible to embark upon a serious account of the play without the firm conviction that it forms a coherent and explicable whole in which all its details, no matter how minute or

extravagant, contribute to a demonstrable intention on the part of
the playwright. We must consider *The Master Builder* a work of art
organized upon principles and subject to laws which interpretation
can discover. This means, at the outset, that we must firmly distinguish
between dramatic art and "real life." In "real life" we can, finally,
throw up our hands before the inexplicability of human motives or we
can speculate and elaborate endlessly upon them: an interesting subjective hobby which, however, has nothing to do with dramatic criticism.
In this chapter we will take *The Master Builder* as a serious work of
dramatic art, not a covert autobiography or an illustration of psychopathology in the poet or in his characters. We will take Ibsen as a serious
artist in complete control over his art and its effects so that every detail
in the play can be shown to contribute to the total intention.

Serious interpretation of *The Master Builder* is a somewhat formidable
task from the extreme complexity of Ibsen's total intention, and we
had better begin with first impressions. We are aware of an extraordinary regression into childhood on the part of the two major characters
and, furthermore, on the part of another middle-aged character, Aline
Solness, whose greatest grief seems to be the loss of "nine lovely dolls"
which, even as a married woman, she seems to have carried around (all
at once). Such a detail seems bizarre and excessive: one or two dolls
would have been more convenient. These dolls, she exclaims, were
like "little unborn children." We will notice other details of childhood
and children. There are three nurseries in each of the Solness homes;
there are the dead baby twins; there is the childish "kingdom of Orangia"
(Appelsinia) promised to the thirteen-year-old Hilde; and there is the
important theme of the collision between maturity and youth. The
theme of childhood obviously is an important part of the play's meaning:
childhood as a lost condition to be returned to by sickly adults; childhood as the victim of sick maturity; and childhood as a terrifying
challenge to the older generation clinging to life and power. When
we see the elements of childhood begin seriously to invade and disrupt
the alarmed adult world, to become powerfully subversive and even
deadly, the impression of childishness in Solness and Hilde becomes
not embarrassing but alarming. The childish fantasies of their dialogues
begin to assume the dangerous potency of adult aspirations and, far
from being an unfortunate self-betrayal by the author, flawing his
more solemn intention, must be seen as a fully controlled effect important
to his intentions. We see Solness, under Hilde's prompting, throw off
all the accumulated misery of his adulthood with its crippling complex
of sorrow, guilt, self-doubt and self-division, to become a very dangerous,
boyish figure who, after his terribly thrilling climbing of the scaffolding,

would very irresponsibly have leagued himself with a young woman who, from all appearances, seems arrested at the age of twelve to thirteen years when she first thrilled to Solness's Lysanger ascent.

The incongruity between the physical age of the pair and the childlike speeches and actions they express can, of course, be interpreted psychopathologically, though such an interpretation would be hard put to explain how such a condition should affect so many people (Solness, Hilde, Aline) at one time and place. It also would find it hard satisfactorily to explain why this condition should express itself in an imagery of kingdoms, princesses, burned-down castles, castles in the air, fair and dark devils, helpers and servers, trolls, vikings, churches, homes, twins, towers, and challenges to the creator. If Ibsen is a competent writer in control of his medium, these details must have a meaning in association. The psychopathological and the autobiographical frameworks patently are too small to account for these and the conscientious critic is forced to discover a larger one.

Hilde appears before Solness, in response to his fear of youth "knocking at the door," demanding that he honor a promise made ten years ago when she was a twelve-thirteen-year-old girl. Just before she appears, Solness has told Dr. Herdal that the tragedy from which his three-week-old sons died occurred "twelve-thirteen years ago"; thus the boys would have been twelve-thirteen years old on the day that Hilde appears, arrested at the age of twelve-thirteen. The close conjunction of these two identical figures means that Ibsen intends us to pick up the correspondence. We know that Solness feels guilty over the death of the boys for he believes his whole luck/happiness (*lykken* —a key word in the play) derived from the misfortune (*ulykken*) that led to their death. He strangely fears the young, dreading they will finish him off by pushing him out of the way; yet the houses he builds himself contain three nurseries testifying to an awareness of the claims of youth. In spite of this dread of youth, Solness responds warmly to Hilde and his dialogues with her are filled with childlike fantasies.

Solness's regression to childhood, however, is a return to strength and confidence, whereas his sickness derives from his maturity. It is when Solness becomes something like a clever boy promising to build a wonderful castle for his princess that he is able to recover a long-lost courage and confidence. The heaven that Solness and Hilde envisage clearly requires that they become as little children.

Solness's success as a builder was founded on the sacrifice of young life (the twins), upon keeping back the younger generation, and he consequently has feared retribution from youth. He therefore continues ruthlessly to suppress and hold back the aspirations of the young.

Hilde's appearance, however, convinces him that he can enlist "youth against youth" and, at first reluctantly, then enthusiastically, he accepts her youthful vision of him, established when she was a twelve-thirteen-year-old girl, and becomes a daring child again. Behaving like a young boy overcoming his fear of heights, he relives his at least half-legendary past and is destroyed, but only after bequeathing to the younger generation (Ragnar and Hilde) an image of himself doing "the impossible." While, therefore, he is the victim of the "retribution" he has feared, his death is as much a challenge as a defeat. His earlier, patronizing bestowal of a miniature kindom of Orangia on a little girl becomes, at the end of the play, a hero's attempt seriously to gain a spiritual kingdom for the new generation. It is as if Solness, by regressing to the age which his dead sons would have been on the day of Hilde's arrival, performs the childish dare they might have performed. In the transvaluing of the values that take place in the play, the term "childish" loses its pejorative connotations whereas our notions of adult wisdom and adequacy are undermined.[2]

If this regression to childhood is a major action of the play, it obviously extends beyond the circumference of individual case history, for Ibsen brings to this action an imagery and a pattern of reference that call for a more extensive interpretation. Our best procedure in finding the organizing principle behind the complex of images and references that make up the texture of the play is to start with a sure sense of its *structural* quality: to see it first as a *movement*, a succession of salient events and scenes. We then can see if this basic structure is continued and amplified in the whole *texture* of the play. There are, for instance, two main movements in the play that can be detected by close attention to the pattern of action, dialogue, and visual suggestion. The first movement is that of Solness from the imprisonment of his spirit at the opening of the play, when we see him burdened by the whole weight of the past, of guilt, jealousy, fear of retribution, self-doubt, and self-estrangement, to the condition of the ecstatic tower climber, challenging the Creator, in the last moments of the play. This startling contrast between our first and our last impressions of Solness must be an important part of Ibsen's intention.

This progressive movement of the major *character* is continued and amplified in a *scenic* progress, the three scenes representing three very different visual commentaries upon the action and creating a context which enables us to "place" the action. The scene of Act I is window-less, artificially lit, a place of work and of physical confinement. The absence of natural light, in fact, suggests a tomb-like confinement of the spirit appropriate to the action and dialogue that follows. Act II, with its glass door and bay window and its profusion of plants and flowers, visually indicates release from the confinement of Act I, a movement of the spirit outward and upward; while Act III continues this movement, the scene now becoming open-air, a veranda offering spacious vistas of old and new houses, trees, and evening sky. Any further interpretation of the play must come to terms with this striking scenic development.

The other, and contrary, major movement in the play is that of Hilde. Whereas Solness's movement is one of release and ascent, that of Hilde is of increasing confinement and of a descent into the tomb. She appears first in the play wearing "mountain-climbing clothes" (*fjelluniform*) and she wears this outfit throughout as Ibsen is careful to underscore by having Dr. Herdal comment on her dress in Act III. Hilde has descended to Solness where she is "born" as a princess in the central nursery of the house. Her innocent state of mountain freedom and ruthlessness, with which she infects Solness, gradually is overwhelmed as she takes upon herself more and more of the killing knowledge of the Solness household until, in fact, her will, *momentarily*, is broken. (Her history, in fact, closely resembles that of Rebekka West in *Rosmersholm*.) At one point, when Solness tells her that he fears retribution—a concept which is the opposite of the reckless spontaneity she represents—Hilde cries out, "Don't say those things. Do you want to kill me? Do you want to take what's even more than my life?"

The moment of her symbolic death in the play occurs at the beginning of Act III when, taking in the full import of the Solness history from the already dead Aline (Solness calls Aline a corpse chained to him), her own innocent confidence and ruthlessness are crushed. She tells Solness, when he appears immediately after her dialogue with Aline, that she has just "come from the tomb" (*gravkjeller*); in the ensuing dialogue with him she shudders as if with the cold of the tomb and at one point sinks down listlessly, her head upon the table and her eyes closed. Only when Solness returns to the pagan and viking themes of a robust conscience and the castles-in-the-air, is she revived again to be as childlike, vibrant, and eager as on her arrival. The movement given to Hilde, therefore, can be seen as that of descent, birth, death, and resurrection.[3]

Almost as important as these two movements are the *recollected* actions that emerge from the protagonists' passionate retrospections. These retrospections serve to introduce into the confined time and space of the play larger temporal and spatial perspectives, and thus are a means of further extending the play's total metaphor. We hear of the mountains from which Hilde descended, leaving her female traveling companions to proceed west. There is that winter landscape through which, Solness once anticipated, he and Aline would drive one day to find "the old robbers' castle" ablaze in the distance. There is Lysanger where Solness, at noon, triumphantly climbed his last church tower and, in a resurrection of the spirit, challenged the Creator while music came from the church-yard below and a small girl, below in that churchyard, heard "harps in the air," where Solness looked down and saw "a little devil in white" in the churchyard furiously waving a flag and became "dizzy" (*svimlende*) with the blissfully dizzy Hilde. The past action will be repeated in the final moments of the play but at the *beginning* of the play it reverses the situation of Solness and Hilde. The relation of the present condition to the recollected action can be set out by means of the following diagram:

	UPPER WORLD	
Hilde	(Tower)	Solness
(At beginning	(Mountains)	(At Lysanger
of the play)		and at end
		of the play)
Solness	(Symbolic Tomb)	Hilde
(At beginning	(Churchyard)	(At Lysanger
of the play)	NETHER WORLD	and at end
		of the play)

This height-depth pattern has obvious relevance to the "resurrection day" theme of the Lysanger ascent and Solness's and Hilde's emergence from their psychic tombs. The resurrection day theme is important to the whole of this last group of four plays which ends with a play called *When We Dead Awaken* whose central image is a statue group called "Resurrection Day." Resurrection, or spiritual awakening, in fact, is the theme not merely of the Epilogue to the Cycle, but of the whole Cycle itself. The geographical polarities of mountain height and tomb depth define the condition of spirit in Ibsen's writing at least from *Brand* onwards, and are part of his inheritance from Romantic literature.

If there is one predominant thread of imagery running through *The Master Builder*, it is that of the sun and of light. The hero's name is *Sol*-ness, and the Norwegian title of the play, *Bygmester Solness*, gives to the word *sol* full emphasis. Hilde comes from *Lys*anger (*lys* is light) where Solness ascended the tower. The movement of the play is from a con-fined, interior, windowless, and artificially lit room to the final open-air setting beneath an autumnal, sun-streaked sky. Any analysis of the play will reveal a wealth of sun and light images and references which are given full emphasis.

Also remarkable in this play is the emphasis upon "fate" and "retribution" and the somewhat associated concept of *lykke* which means both happiness and luck or fortune. This *lykke* has an attendant imagery of helpers and servers, fair and dark devils, trolls, and the agonizing sacrifices demanded by the mysterious powers. These themes are sounded too frequently and too emphatically and are too inextricably involved in the play's total texture to be dismissed merely as Solness's and Hilde's extravagant way of talking. Unless Ibsen is an extremely slipshod artist merely throwing in exotic detail, these image patterns must have a purpose which interpretation must discover. *The Master Builder*, in fact, would seem consciously to be employing details of what Northrop Frye has called the quest myth, where the hero is identified with the sun:

The sunset, autumn and death phase. Myths of fall, of the dying god, of violent death and sacrifice and of the isolation of the hero. Subordinate characters: the traitor and the siren. The archetype of tragedy and elegy.[4]

These details are present in *The Master Builder* to a remarkable extent. The hero is *Solness*, who at the opening of the play is spiritually isolated, who fears betrayal by youth and by his wife and the doctor, who encounters a siren (Hilde), who incites him to climb a tower. In the evening of the autumnal equinox (September 20) this sun-figure literally *falls* to his death. And the play is filled with an astonishingly frequent imagery of *sacrifice*. If this should sound like some sanguine sun-cult detail from *The Golden Bough*, it should be remembered that Ibsen's Germanic cultural tradition was at least as familiar with these themes as the successors of Frazer in the Anglo-Saxon world.

The imagery of sacrifice undergoes a great variety of forms and disguises. There is the sacrifice to Solness's success of Aline's old, huge "robbers' castle" with its treasures, riches, and the "nine lovely dolls." There is the consequent sacrifice of the twin boys, poisoned by the milk from the duty-conscious Aline and the sacrifice of Aline's instinct for fostering life. Aline herself has been sacrificed and is a "corpse" tied to Solness. These sacrifices, Solness believes, are the necessary price exacted by the mysterious powers of his creativity. Solness himself, however, is a sacrificial victim too, his suffering described as an open wound; and his life will culminate in a sacrificial fall from a tower.

In Act I we see Solness spiritually imprisoned or bound, tortured, yet torturing others. He tells Dr. Herdal, who is the spokesman for the rational, "realistic" vision that cannot fathom the mysterious spiritual

depths in which the Solness household is engulfed, that he accepts this
torture as reparation to his victims:

SOLNESS. I feel there's almost a kind of beneficial self-torment in letting
Aline do me an injustice.
DR. HERDAL. (*shaking his head*) I don't understand one blessed word
of this.
SOLNESS. Yes, don't you see—it's rather like making a small payment on a
boundless, incalculable debt.

The self-tormenting convolutions of psychological implication, here,
where the "beneficial *self*-torment" comes from a permitted injustice,
constituting a small payment of a debt too boundless to be calculated, is
typical of the spiritual atmosphere of this first part of the play where
the spirit seems to be strangling in its own impossibly complex dialectic.
Caught in this hopelessly sick dialectic, spirit seems to have become
antagonistic to life itself, so that the sacrifices demanded, while pro-
longing Solness's life, also increase his sickness.

Other necessary sacrifices involve old Brovik and his son Ragnar, Kaja
Fosli, those earlier rivals that Solness had to "hammer to the ground,"
as well as the two men whose deaths by falling from the tower precede
his own. Solness sees himself as in perpetual danger of being sacrificed
to the young; somewhat like the fate of the priest at Nemi at the beginning of *The Golden Bough*, his vocation seems to entail a constant
vigilance against being slain by his successor. Ragnar, he tells Hilde, will
hammer him to the ground just as he hammered Ragnar's father and
others to the ground.

In Act II Solness returns to the theme of sacrifice when he confides to
Hilde the terrible way in which his helpers and servers have aided him:

SOLNESS. If old Knut Brovik had owned the house it never would have
burned down so conveniently for him. I'm positive of that. Because he does
not know how to call on the helpers—or the servers either. (*Gets up restlessly*)
So you see, Hilde, it *is* my fault that the twins had to die. And isn't it my
fault, too, that Aline never became the woman she could have and should
have been? And wanted to be, more than anything . . .
HILDE. Yes, but if it's really these helpers and servers, then—?
SOLNESS. Who called for the helpers and servers? I did! And they came
and did what I willed. (*In rising agitation*) That's what the nice people call
"having the luck" [*lykken*]. But I can tell you what this luck feels like. It feels
as if a big piece of skin had been stripped, right here, from my chest. And
the helpers and servers go on flaying the skin off other people to patch *my*
wound. But the wound never heals—never! Oh, if you knew sometimes how
it leeches and burns.

The startling violence of the details of this speech is in key with the rest of this most violent of Ibsen's plays. Solness appears to be a sacrificial god whose pain can be appeased only by human sacrifice; and "princess" Hilde is the rescuer and auxiliary of this god. The most familiar myth of the suffering and rescued god is that of Prometheus, an archetype of Romantic literature. Prometheus, like Solness, rebelled against the Creator (Zeus), by means of fire taught man domestic industries (as Solness, by means of the fire that burned Aline's house, turned to building *homes* for human beings), and was punished by the vulture that devoured his liver as Solness has the flesh stripped from him. Hilde's rescue of this suffering figure and her leaguing with him resemble Hercules' rescue of Prometheus and suggest that Ibsen is working details of this myth into the fabric of the play.

Another prominent detail that emerges from a close investigation of the text is that of the triad. The number of times this appears in the text is remarkable and it seems a far too important structural principle to the play and to Solness's history to be dismissed. The play is in *three* acts, with *three* distinct scene changes. (Ibsen never changes his scenes without a definite purpose. *Hedda Gabler*, the play preceding this, keeps to one scene for the entire four acts.) Solness's history involves *three* houses (past, present, and future), each with *three* nurseries (implying three children, two of whom have been born and have died), *three* women (Aline, Kaja, and Hilde), *three* forms of creativity (churches, homes, castles in the air), and *three* fatal deaths from the tower. The triad, itself, is an important figure both in Hegelian philosophy and in Ibsen's major philosophical drama, *Emperor and Galilean*, with its concept of a *third* empire of the spirit sublimating both classical paganism and Christianity. And we have seen that the Cycle itself is structured upon a triadic scheme. The significance of this triadic detail will be taken up later in this study; it obviously is a detail that any adequate account of the play is forced to take into consideration.

The Master Builder opens a new section of the Cycle just as the Hegelian dialectic moves to a new phase of spirit in the *Phenomenology*, a phase involving mythic, cultic, ritualistic, and religious states of consciousness. This new section of Hegel's work begins with the religion of light and the cult of the sun: the Persian religion of Zoroastrianism whose *dualistic* nature, in Hegel's view, inaugurates the Western spirit. For the final section of the *Phenomenology*, therefore, when he is about to embark on a gigantic survey of the entire spiritual history and structure of the mind, Hegel returns to the beginning again as to the childhood of the race, but this time at the higher level of the religious consciousness. Similarly, the regression to childhood which we claim occurs in *The*

Master Builder is, essentially, to an ecstatic, mystical consciousness of worship, wonder, and the overweening elevation of the spirit represented by the "dizziness" accompanying the Lysanger ascent

The rhapsodic, fervent nature of Hilde's recollections matches the rhapsodic and fervent pages of Hegel's re-creation of the first of the Western spirit's transcendental affirmations, the Persian religion of Light.[5] The imagery of sun and light, of oracular utterances and riddles, of the ecstatic affirmation of the sun's rising and setting, recurs continually in the baffling and difficult pages in which Hegel recreates the attitudes of the religious consciousness, and these images from ancient cult, hymn, art, and ceremony signal the highest level of consciousness, as they do in the Ephesus séance of *Emperor and Galilean*, Act III. Ibsen's Julian, in fact, was a disciple of Mithraism, the Persian religion deriving from Zoroastrianism, and Maximus the Mystic, who was a Mithraic priest and martyr, is Ibsen's spokesman for the Third Empire. This religion permeated Europe, especially Germany, and had great influence upon the development of Christianity, while many of its myths parallel those of the Scandinavian Eddas, so that Persian religious concepts seem at the very foundation of the structure of the modern mind. Details from the religion of light, therefore, appropriately serve as the foundation for the play that inaugurates the last group of four plays in the Cycle which recollects the sources of the positive religions and their later life in the history of the race.

In a corresponding section of the *Philosophy of History* Hegel claims that the dynamic dualism of Light and Darkness in Persian religion began when a more vigorous spiritual race descended from the mountains upon "the dull, half-conscious brooding of Spirit" of a plains people: a detail, perhaps, behind the action of Hilde descending from the mountains upon the brooding Solness household. The warring powers of Light and Darkness are Ormazd and Ahriman, and Ormazd, "the lord of light," not only creates all that is beautiful and noble in the world: he also specifically creates a sky palace or castle in the air with solid foundations, as in Solness's and Hilde's ecstatic vision. The Persian religion, too, contains mysterious powers upon which the faithful can call, like Solness's helpers and servers.

The parallels between Ibsen's play and Hegel's account of the Persian religion, already striking enough, increase immensely in the more detailed account in the *Lectures on the Philosophy of Religion*. In this account we encounter vivid details of the sun, of light, of painful sacrifice, of the phoenix who rose up from the ashes (as Solness arose, "*svang opp*," from his fire), of the god Adonis who descends beneath the ground and is resurrected, and of the dead twins, Castor and Pollux. Hegel's account is based on the *Zend-Avesta*, the bible of the Persian religion, which contains even stronger parallels to Ibsen's play. There is first the myth of the great winter which was to destroy the earth, but which developed into a destructive fire-in-winter which destroyed the earth but restored it more beautiful than before,[6] as in the Scandinavian myth of Ragnarök. There is the sky palace, "built of heavenly substance, firmly established, with ends that lie afar, shining in its body of ruby over three thirds of the earth."[7] There are the helpers and servers, the Fravashis, or inner powers, that wait upon the faithful, and a tradition of painful sacrifice performed by the initiate into the Mithraic mysteries.[8] Two of the most prominent and beautiful hymns in the *Zend-Avesta* are devoted to two mythical figures, the maiden-goddess Anahita and the sun god, Mithra. Anahita is a goddess of waters who descends to the aid of her heroes. The hymn describing Mithra also describes the sky palace, the helpers and servers, and the tradition of painful sacrifice. It is dedicated to the nineteenth day of the month, the date upon which the action of *The Master Builder* commences; while the next day, the 20th, the date of Solness's ascent, is dedicated to victory. The hymn of the nineteenth day ends invoking the "helpers" to "come satisfied into this house; may they walk satisfied through this house."[9] And throughout the *Zend-Avesta* can be found the light-darkness, height-depth imagery so important to the metaphors and the action of *The Master Builder*.

There is also in Zoroastrianism the tradition of *three* sons of Zoroaster the tower builder: two sons will be forerunners, while the third will be the savior who will "usher in the general resurrection of the dead." The modern form of Zoroastrianism, Parsee religion, is a religion of fire and of tower structures. A number of the important details of Zoroastrian religion parallel remarkably closely the writings of Scandinavian religion and myth, parallels that were pointed out by Ibsen's famous contemporary fellow Scandinavian, Viktor Rydberg, in his audacious work on comparative religion, *Teutonic Mythology*. Novelist, poet, scholar, and anti-Christian, Rydberg, as Strindberg recounts in his autobiographical *The Son of a Servant*, had great impact upon the Scandinavian imagination, so that it is most unlikely that Ibsen was unaware of his work.[10] An important chapter of *Teutonic Mythology* discusses the Icelandic Troy saga, in which the northern gods are linked directly with Troy, joining the mythological traditions of north and south in a way that would, one imagines, greatly interest Ibsen. (The claim of a distant Trojan heritage is, of course, a commonplace in European legends of many races and countries.) Zoroaster, Rydberg demonstrated at length, is connected in mythology with the Scandinavian Odin. Zoroaster also was the legendary builder of the tower of Babel; and both Odin and

Zoroaster later were linked with Mithra. The chapter in which Rydberg discusses the connections between Zoroaster, Babel, Mithra, and Odin ends with an account of Odin sacrificing himself for mankind by climbing the tree, being pierced by a spear and *singing* runes. (Hilde insists that Solness *sang* at the top of the tower.)

Other accounts of the Odin myth were, of course, available to Ibsen and we can assume he knew of many of them. P. A. Munch, a countryman Ibsen admired, wrote a survey of Norse mythology mentioning this Trojan connection, and Snorri Sturluson's *Prose Edda* is prefaced by an account of the exodus of Odin and his companions from Troy as it was burned down—"that goodliest of homes and haunts that have ever been."[11]

The existence of links between the various mythologies, Persian, Greek, Germanic, and Christian, would be important to a poet concerned to depict the total human consciousness, in which these mythologies would have an important place; for, as Hegel wrote, in all these conceptions, "the universal god is present." Zoroaster, who had two sons, who is traditionally the architect of the *tower* of Babel (an act of rebellion against the Creator); whose religion, Parsee Zoroastrianism, requires the building of tower structures and includes, prominently, the details of fire, sun, light, a sky palace "firmly established" (this is echoed directly in Solness's promise to build his sky castle "on a firm foundation"—*med grunnmur under*) and which contains the mysterious helpers; who is linked in comparative mythology with Odin who climbed a tree and sang, with the phoenix who rose from the ashes, and so on, seems, at least, to inspire a great number of the many elusive details of the play: as, of course, he *should* if Ibsen follows Hegel in seeing the Persian religion of light as the essential foundation for the whole structure of the modern consciousness. An adequate psychoanalysis of the *Weltgeist*, even in the guise of contemporary reality, would have to start on this foundation.

We have seen that there are strong links between the southern mythological traditions of Persia and Greece (and, one should add, the Judaic-Christian myths) and those of the Germanic north, and within the texture of *The Master Builder* a number of parallels with Northern mythology patently can be detected. The dialogue, of course, repeatedly returns to viking themes in the "duets" of Solness and Hilde, and these overt Scandinavian recollections are only the most salient moments of a whole complex of such recollections.

In Wagner's *Ring* cycle Wotan (Odin) is tormented by guilt and self-doubt, due to the unscrupulous methods by which he gained the ring that gave him absolute power, a power gained at the cost of sacrificing love (a theme treated at greater length in *John Gabriel Borkman*).

Wotan fears the younger generation and the destructive Nemesis that his theft will bring upon him. Before the theft of the ring Wotan has had to wrong his wife, Fricka, goddess of the home and hearth. Grimm, in *Teutonic Mythology* (1844), shows how Fricka, who represented the highest conception of beauty, and was the goddess of growth, increase, was linked with Aphrodite, Hera, and even Mary, by various European traditions, and both as Frigg and Mary she would be the mourning mother. (Baldr, like Jesus, was to return from the underworld and usher in a general resurrection of the dead, and a regeneration of the world.) In *The Master Builder* Aline, the mourning mother, caring for plants and flowers and for fostering new life, concentrates in her modern identity many of these features.

The Solness family history, so singular when offered as typical or exemplary modern experience, does make better sense if we see it as performing the more ambitious task of discovering within the microcosm of the family history the larger history of human consciousness recorded in its mythopoeic expressions as in its cultural history. The Solness family history, and the present "plot" of the play, then can be seen as chosen by Ibsen for its capacity to contain the drama of the total consciousness of man rather than for its representativeness of a particular moment of nineteenth-century bourgeois history. Being representative of this much larger drama of the total consciousness and its history, the texture of the play is likely to be packed with innumerable references to and transformations of the major, archetypal expressions of Western consciousness. Thus, much of the oddity of the Solness family history reflects the oddity of these expressions themselves.

Wotan, in Wagner's *Ring* cycle, is placed in tragic conflict with the younger generation both of the twins, Siegmund and Sieglinde, and with Siegfried and Brunnhilde. The first drama in the cycle, *Das Rheingold*, shows us Wotan dreaming his castle into existence, to the alarm of his wife, Fricka. Wotan is called the Son of Light, must deal with fair and dark spirits, and the sun and light imagery, in contrast with an imagery of darkness, runs all through the cycle, as does an imagery of fire, its dramatic climax, perhaps, occurring in Brunnhilde's tremendous hymn of awakening, "Heil der Sol."

In *Siegfried*, Wotan, in answer to Mime's questions, tells of *three* realms beneath, on, and above the earth. In this opera, Wotan's power decisively is broken by the younger generation when Siegfried breaks Wotan's staff which is associated with the god's ability to wish or will into being those things he seeks to achieve. Grimm, in his *Teutonic Mythology*, describes at length Odin's power of creatively wishing, remarking that Odin is the personification of *wunsch* and is accompanied by wish-maidens, just as Solness's uncanny-seeming power to wish into reality what he desires is associated with such young women as the young Aline, Kaja Fosli, and Hilde Wangel. The destruction by fire of Asgard in the *Ring* and in the old accounts of Scandinavian mythology might be referred to in the destruction by fire of the old house, referred to as "that hideous old robbers' castle" by Dr. Herdal—a not inappropriate description of modern ideas of the old viking culture. There seems to be one major parallel between the *Ring* cycle and *The Master Builder* in the similarity of Brunnhilde and Hilde, which we will take up later.

Details of the Solness family history also can be related to other accounts, easily available to Ibsen, of Scandinavian lore and mythology, such as those of Grimm, Munch, and Rydberg. The tragedy in the past of the Solnesses can be summed up briefly. Solness anticipated a fire-in-winter that would destroy the old house or castle (*borgen*) and this occurred, though differently than the way he expected it to, and Solness was able to embark upon the career that made his fortune. Solness's career, therefore, begins with the destruction by fire of a "castle" and is to end with the dream of a towered castle. Aline, who could not stand the cold, contracted a fever after the fire but, from a perverse sense of duty (*plikt*) which she set above happiness, insisted on breast-feeding the twins, who died from her poisoned milk. She now is a figure of perpetual mourning, dressed always in black and reiterating the word "duty." Not long after the fire, Solness achieved his triumph at Lysanger where he set the wreath on his last (church) tower. Hearing music from the churchyard, and ecstatically challenging the Creator, he became aware of a "little devil" in white furiously waving a flag. This was Hilde born, we can say, at this moment as the parthenogenesis of his rebellion. The story, to say the least, is odd, and its oddity increases, we will see, in the many accretions it undergoes in Hilde's retelling. Even in its bare details, however, it has something of a mythic quality: both too simple and too powerful as a version of everyday experience. And it does show resemblances to Scandinavian myth.

Odin, like Zeus, is, as Grimm has shown, a sky god of the sun and of light. As the northern god of poets he is the equivalent of Apollo, and thus associated with Helios, Sol, Mithra, and Ormazd. The strange detail of the fire-in-winter, described at such length by Solness, must remind us of the great fire-in-winter, anticipated by Odin who alone knew when it would occur, the fire that was to destroy the castle Asgard in the holocaust of Ragnarök. Odin, of all northern gods, demanded, and suffered, particularly savage forms of sacrifice; some, like the horrible "spread-eagle" similar to Solness's description of the flesh torn from his breast and torn from others to patch the wound. Solness's first name, Halvard, is phonetically very similar to Odin's designation as "Allfar" (Eddic, *alföðr*), and the accounts describe him as, like Solness, possessed of thick hair and beard, a green coat, and a hat. (Solness's "grey-green coat" and "soft felt hat" are odd specifications as indications of psychological character, but become functional if Ibsen is subtly awakening a visual reference.)

After the holocaust of Ragnarök Odin was to be survived by two sons who would avenge the destruction and rebuild the world more beautifully than before. Then Baldr the beautiful would return from the nether world and a new race of man would begin. Grimm notes the parallel between Odin's sons, Vidar and Vali, and the twins, the *Dioscuri*, who appear in Hegel's account of the Persian religion of light, and Grimm relates, also, how these twins will be joined by a *third* (Baldr).[12] The myth of Baldr's death, descent in the nether world, and resurrection, fits the metaphoric action given to Hilde. In Snorri, Grimm, and Wagner we find the details of fair and dark devils or helpers. In Snorri's account, the leader of the Valkyries, Brynhildr or Hildr, appears in the same story that Ibsen dramatized earlier in his career as *The Vikings at Helgeland*. The best-known version of this story is the *Volsunga Saga*, and in Ibsen's adaptation, Hildr becomes Hjørdis and resembles Hilde of *The Master Builder* in her "robust conscience." The Brunnhilde, Brynhildr, or Hildr qualities in Hilde Wangel are not difficult to detect. Her mountain-identity, her innocent ruthlessness, her action of awakening reborn in Solness's central nursery (like Brunnhilde awakened by Siegfried and the sun [Sol]), and the ambiguity of her mission—to rouse in Solness her vision of his heroism but thereby to incite him to a heroic death— are highly suggestive of the whole ambiguity of the Valkyrie figure. (Dr. Herdal's account of how he met Hilde up in the mountains with a group of female companions, and how he and Hilde made "a lot of noise" together sounds a little like a humorous reference to *Die Walküre*!) Grimm mentions that Hildr lives "on a tower" and in one of the versions of her identity, as Veleda, he recounts, "she was believed to travel about and make visitations to houses" like the "prophesying and boon-bestowing women" who would "pass through the country knocking at the houses of those whom they would bless."[13]

It is my intention only to suggest the mythopoeic substance that Ibsen might be employing as the foundation for his portrait of the total modern consciousness from its origins to the present. The details may seen to proliferate alarmingly and many of the parallels, while being thoroughly appropriate, depend, I agree, upon the extent to which we assent to the proposition that all this substance of the mind is of great importance to Ibsen. In itself, it could not be of great importance, but as the *substratum* of the history of the culture of the West, of its Mind or Spirit, it would be indispensable. We cannot, therefore, be content merely to note exotic mythopoeic details hovering round the realistic text like decoration on bad architecture; keeping Ibsen's "third-empire" goal in mind, we have to note these details but place them in a more serious, rational, and ambitious account of the evolution of consciousness. The myths are expressions of human experience and human aspirations: experiences of loss, of terror, of hope, of dreams, of possible achievement, all of which shape the consciousness that will create and be created in turn by history. I have here merely tried to extend a little the area of relevance in Ibsen interpretation, as a preliminary for a more close analysis of the play in the pages that follow.

The many and varied mythopoeic and religious concepts it is suggested Ibsen has woven into his realistic modern drama are bound to provoke objections from a way of thought that views reality (the poet's subject) as the common-sense recording of immediate appearances truncated from other forms of consciousness separated by time or space; but from the viewpoint of the nineteenth century, and, indeed, from much contemporary literature and theory, the human consciousness exists in and is a product of a rich and even inexhaustible continuum of consciousness without temporal or spatial borders, in which alternative or "past" modes of consciousness *can*, with effort, be recalled. For Hegel, such recall, but by means of a strenuous dialectical program that takes full account of the historical and the rational process, is the *requirement* of the modern educated consciousness. It is by a similarly hard-won, rational, and dialectical process that Ibsen, in his last plays, now can inhabit a transfigured cosmos, a rich and complex universe of recovered spiritual realities and possibilities not unlike the spiritual worlds of *The Waste Land*, Pound's *Cantos*, the plays of Samuel Beckett. The realism of *The Master Builder* cannot be condemned for flouting everyday reality for it is depicting a transfigured reality, the reality we, if we were awakened, would inhabit, possessed of more dimensions of consciousness than are dreamed of by the pragmatists' philosophy. What is odd about Ibsen's method is that he attempts to reconcile this transfigured universe with his experience of living in the mundane context of modern bourgeois life: a far more ambitious and unpopular program (not unlike that of T. S. Eliot) than the creation of immediately historical and mythopoeic fictions.

In his speech at the banquet of the Norwegian League for Women's Rights, in 1898, an occasion, one imagines, when Ibsen was more than usually aware of the confrontation of his poetic vision with an urgent and contemporary moment, Ibsen defined his task as a poet as "the description of humanity" and not of eccentric individuals or of himself. The problem would be to detect the *essential* identity of humanity beneath the immediate and particular appearances it assumed. In the last four plays this essence is multidimensional and expresses itself in a language that is highly wrought, enigmatic, issuing from areas of consciousness (once objectified in cult, myth, and religious practice) not obviously related to everyday life in the present, yet essential to the highest identity of the race. The ancient mystery cults, temple worship, divine hymns (such as the *Zend-Avesta*) supremely established this identity, which then was available to the ancient tragic poets. The devout modern arrives at such a consciousness in the Mass or church service or, at present, in various "consciousness expanding" cults; but, for the most part, these are drastically separated from secular life which is indifferent to their claims. Thus the "ethical" world of objective social customs and duties and the subjective realm of individual experience are not transfigured, in typical bourgeois culture, by an overarching religious or spiritual consciousness that is the culmination of conscious life.

In *The Master Builder* this tactful separation of the practical and the spiritual which modern bourgeois culture has effected is abruptly and fearfully ended and the obstinately banal and unideal terms of modern life are gradually transfigured and become more alarming, more absurd, even more childish, than common-sense desires, so that the play most frequently is seen as a study in psychopathology. The convergence of the spiritual realm with the pragmatic is an explosive one but it is necessary for a spiritual awakening. "It is fearful to fall into the hands of the living god," and, in a way, Halvard Solness has fallen into the hands of the living god when his universe begins to demand commitments he has evaded. We clearly see this when the demand is more or less a conventional one, as in the case of Barbara Undershaft in *Major Barbara*, or Celia Coplestone in *The Cocktail Party*, for we can "place" these commitments within the available disciplines of Socialism or traditional Christianity. Halvard Solness's commitment is more difficult to grasp because Ibsen's spiritual universe is more complex than that of Bernard Shaw or of T. S. Eliot; but for Solness, too, the universe suddenly becomes dangerous, frightening, and exhilaratingly significant. *The Master Builder* is a drama of spiritual resurrection from the tomb of material everyday reality and because resurrection is a fearful thing, unwelcome to that material side of our selves that has compromised so continuously with the demands of spiritual reality that we no longer are aware of that reality, it is not surprising that this affirmative drama of spiritual renewal has been read as an object lesson in avoiding rash commitments! On this level the play is reduced to a self-congratulatory bourgeois homily on living life carefully and calculatingly, according to that "ledger" world that Hilde Wangel so scorns.

Solness has, fearfully, fallen into the hands of the living god, as did Orestes, Oedipus, Pentheus, Socrates, Jesus, and Ibsen's Julian, and though we may congratulate ourselves on avoiding their suffering, we also must confess to avoiding their significance.

Because the interplay of essence and appearance, universal and particular, is significant to Ibsen only at the point of their explosive contact which will spark off the dialectic, Ibsen, in the last plays, maintains his fine fidelity to his realistic method. It is a solid and substantial world that we are to see invaded by the living god, and we are meant to feel the full and crushing burden upon the spirit of what Wordsworth called "the weary weight / Of all this unintelligible world" before we see the burden cast aside. *The Master Builder* begins with a scene of petty confinement and intolerable servitude and ends with an audacious, open-air scene of ascent, and no interpretation of the play's ultimate meaning can run counter to this striking scenic development. It is not likely that such a scenic development is illustrating a cautionary moral parable nor a study of psychopathological breakdown. It is, on the other hand, very likely illustrating an account of *liberation* of some sort, of release from confinement.

And the rhythm of liberation is, in fact, the dominant rhythm of the play. Each of the three acts enacts a movement from entombment to emancipation so that, remarkably, the play is a threefold repetition of the same action. Each act begins with the themes of sickness, self-torture, guilt, and an agonized submersion in the Past, and each ends with a jubilant assertion of the spirit on the part of Solness and Hilde. Each act contains passionate retrospections on the same double-vision of the Past: the fire and its attendant tragedy and guilt; and the Lysanger ascent and its triumphant assertion against the Creator. Similarly, the details of the mysterious powers, of sacrifice, of the repression of the younger generation, of the kingdom and its princess, of Solness's threefold division of his career into churches, homes, and the towered castle, all appear in the dialogues of each act, though Ibsen is extraordinarily careful in preventing this repetition from being monotonous. It was, however, a very great risk to take and in taking this risk Ibsen must have felt it essential to the whole conception of the play.

The total rhythm of the play is incremental for as the main action and subject matter is repeated three times, so it gathers together more and more of the total content of the play making the last retrospections extremely rich in *leitmotiv*. These passionate retrospections of Solness, Aline, and Hilde are good examples of Ibsen's fine ability to dramatize the process of *thought*, of creating a drama of the *mind*. It is an extremely intellectualized drama and the major actions, until the final breaking free from remembrance to action in the last moments of the play, all have taken place far back in the past.

The scene in the first act of the play is windowless, artificially lit by three lamps: one centrally placed, one on the left, and one on the right of the stage. Within the inner workroom Knut and Ragnar Brovik are drawing plans; in the foreground, Kaja Fosli is writing in the ledger. The arrangement of the stage between a foreground room and an inner room recalls the stage division of *Hedda Gabler* and suggests the same phase of spiritual self-division (amply illustrated in the action and dialogue that follows) as the second group, from which this first play of the last group decisively will break away into light and air and visionary affirmation.

Solness's three human helpers all are in some way enfeebled. Knut Brovik is old and frail; Ragnar has a slight stoop; and Kaja Fosli is weak and sickly in appearance. These slave-like helpers in Solness's unambitious creativity contrast strongly with the mysterious and powerful "helpers and servers" whom Solness fears to call upon. Our first visual impression of the Solness household, then, is one of activity, but also of a lack of creative vitality. For a moment we watch these helpers silently working but suddenly old Brovik stands up with every sign of exhaustion and exclaims, "No, I can't go on much longer." These are the first words spoken in the play announcing one of its main themes: of failing powers and enforced, reluctant servitude.

Solness's relation to these workers is a mixture of despotism and dependence so that while he must retain them he yet fears and distrusts them. He needs, in particular, to keep Ragnar in his power, for Ragnar, as the younger generation, represents the force that will displace him; yet he now has only contempt for the kind of creativity Ragnar represents. As he tells Dr. Herdal:

You see, I need Ragnar—and the old man as well. He has a real knack for calculating stresses, cubic content—all that damned detail work.

Solness's contempt for "damned detail work" parallels Hilde's contempt for "ledger" work—poor Kaja's similarly calculating and detailed chore—and this contempt felt by the pair suggests the creative imagination chafing under conditions of limited imaginative and spiritual courage: that same confrontation of bourgeois pragmatic reality with the wider spiritual requirements of man that we have decided is a theme of this play, and which we find in such a contemporary of Ibsen as, for example,

Nietzsche. This conflict of imaginative vision and practical possibility, of a consciousness aware of and responsive to larger spiritual powers but inhabiting a given world of common-sense factuality, supplies the major dialectical antithesis of the play. In this opening scene we are watching the first stage of a mutual disenchantment, of a new pragmatic order chafing under the tyranny of older spiritual powers, and the older spiritual powers limited and imprisoned by the new pragmatic order. This conflict is ended when Solness dismisses his practical helpers and servers in order to meet Hilde's demand for a not-ordinary kingdom and a towered sky-castle for which damned detail work hardly can be required.

When Solness invades this scene of enfeebled workers, arriving from below, we immediately are impressed with his controlled *vitality*:

He is a middle-aged man, strong and forceful, with close-cropped hair, a dark moustache and thick eyebrows. His jacket, grey-green with wide lapels, is buttoned, with the collar turned up. On his head is a soft grey felt hat, and under his arm a couple of portfolios.

This impression of virile strength, however, is startlingly contradicted by his actions, for he immediately whispers furtively to Kaja and demonstrates to the audience the ignominious nature of his relationship with her. The rest of the action, until the arrival of Hilde, will develop an atmosphere of deceit, fear and sickness, and self-estrangement. Solness's lonely frustration and misery, however, is only the center of a general *malaise*, for everyone in the household seems to reflect something of this sickly condition and there even is an attendant doctor, baffled by the ills that plague the Solness household, to underscore the theme. William Archer commented that Solness dies of the over-great demands which Hilde makes upon his sickly conscience,[14] but since the whole household is, to some extent, "sickly," the symbolic interpretation clearly must go beyond individual case history.

Ibsen now constructs a series of episodes in order swiftly to demonstrate the effects of Solness's sickness upon others. Knut Brovik mentions that "a young couple" are anxious about the plans of their new house and Solness at first impatiently dismisses the subject until he learns that Ragnar might get the commission. This alliance of youth with youth is what the master builder most fears and we have the first clear statement of that fear. He imagines a whole league of youth actually pushing him from a narrow space that he occupies with difficulty, shouting "Give way! Give way!" (*Gi plass! gi plass!*) whereas old Brovik (like Foldal in *John Gabriel Borkmann*) is only happy in seeing the young take over. Solness, then, like any remarkable and outstanding individual of an animal or human herd, actually is resisting the order of nature in which the old must give way to the young.

An extraordinary episode follows in which the unnaturalness of Solness's relation to the young is made clear. He has taken possession of Kaja completely and is using her as a kind of fifth column, as "youth against youth," as he later believes he can enlist Hilde. He employs Kaja in order to prevent Ragnar's possible revolt and Kaja, as Rolf Fjelde points out, goes down on her knees to him "rapturously" exclaiming "Oh God! Oh God!" as if Solness *were* a god.

While we are watching Solness unscrupulously manipulating one of his victims, we see the action interrupted by another of his victims, Aline Solness. Aline, like Irene in *When We Dead Awaken*, is, essentially, dead and Solness will describe her as a corpse chained to him. She remains fixed at that moment of disaster when the old robbers' castle was destroyed though once she possessed the gift of rearing souls, of fostering life, as Solness tells Hilde. Though "thin and careworn," she shows "traces of former beauty" and is dressed perpetually in mourning black. Her voice is low and plaintive and its *leitmotiv* is the little word *"plikt"*—duty—which, as in *Ghosts*, will be used as the antithesis to the concept "joy." In the single consciousness of the play Aline would represent a lifeless mourning over the loss of a richer past—of the old spacious house and its garden, the treasures it contained, like the memory of a vanished culture. Aline mourns most of the loss of *lifeless* things and has not the slightest interest in the "new house" Solness is building, because it never will replace the vanished past. I would suggest that Aline is emblematic of a whole area of the modern consciousness: retrogressive, nostalgic, lamenting the vanished riches of the past and so incapable of *using* the past to contribute to the present and future. This was a powerful element in the imagination of Ibsen's major would-be pilgrim to the "third empire," Julian, and it was, of course, a major element in the consciousness of Ibsen's own day, as in our own.

The first appearance of Aline is linked with that of the doctor, and this first act will contain an emphatic repetition of the word "sick" (*syk*) which undergoes a great many variations. Solness's conversation with Herdal brings us to the first of the play's retrospections. He tells the doctor a "strange story" of how Kaja oddly seemed to answer in response to his own unspoken *wish* to enlist her against Ragnar's defection. His inner will was obeyed in the way that he has come to believe it will be, but its results have been perverse; in order to keep Ragnar he has had to pretend to care for Kaja, and his only pleasure in this perverse situation is the even more perverse satisfaction of experiencing the "beneficial self-torment" (*velgjørende selvpinsel*) of letting Aline do him the "injustice" of suspecting his fidelity. By thus torturing himself he feels he is paying a small amount on a "bottomless debt." Another ramification of this perversity is that now he suspects Dr. Herdal of having been enlisted by Aline to spy upon him in order to detect symptoms of "sickness" or "madness" in him: such is the extraordinary psychological texture of the Solness household which seems enveloped in clouds of mutual distrust.

From this idea of Solness as a "sick" man the dialogue shifts to that of him as a *"lykkelig"* (happy, fortunate, lucky) man. *"Lykkelig"* is richer than "happy" for it suggests "luck" or mysterious good fortune and the word later will develop these ambiguities through many repetitions in the play. Solness has a mysterious "luck" on his side which, however, exacts a fearful price of *sacrifice* from others, and in this dialogue the luck is connected directly to Aline's tragedy and the burning of the old robbers' castle. With the primitive's sense of the luck of the gods requiring constant sacrifice yet liable disastrously to turn against its possessor, Solness confesses to Herdal his fear of losing this luck by means of the young who, "shaking their fists and shouting: Give way! Give way!," will then finish him off. Again, and in the same phrase, we have that image of an alarming army of the young against whom Solness must fight his battle for survival.

Solness's first retrospection has returned to the story of the fire, and has hinted at the tragedy of Aline, twelve-thirteen years ago, the fire from which Solness "soared up" like the phoenix. Herdal remarks that Solness never had "better foundations" than now (*står visst nu så grunnmuret*)—a phrase that will reappear as the "solid foundations" of Solness and Hilde's castle in the air.

The militant army of the young, in Solness's alarmed vision, will, he believes, come "knocking at the door," and there follows that audacious stage direction of the knock on the door which, at first seeming a too blatant irony, is, on further reflection, seen to have exactly the right shock value for the audience, for we are now seeing onstage the mysterious power Solness has described: his uncanny ability to will into existence his wishes—a godlike power associated only with the highest gods: Zeus, Odin, Jahveh. The knock on the door thus is as effective as that of *Macbeth*, for it suddenly lifts the whole drama from the psychological plane upon which, up to now, it had existed, and suggests a direct intervention from the spirit world. It brings onto the stage the presence of the wonderful and awesome over which Solness's mind, in solitude, has been brooding, and the reactions of the two men to the knocking emphasize this dual nature of the reality being presented. Solness, "with a start," exclaims, "What is that?" and the pragmatic doctor sensibly replies, "Somebody's knocking."

Hilde's appearance changes decisively the whole substance of the play, lifting it from the psychological and social realms of significance and bringing to the realm of possible human action wider dimensions of significance: the endeavor in which Hedda Gabler, before her, failed. From this point on, the action will develop Solness's response to the knocking and not Dr. Herdal's, and Solness gradually will be released from the psychological brooding that has miserably confined him and his creativity, to embark with Hilde upon an exhilarating but unnerving program of ecstatic mutual myth-making, in which reality is forced to conform to the highest spiritual adequacy. This emerges most clearly in the later retrospections of Solness where, though the ground covered is the same as in the retrospection with Herdal, the *content* will be completely transformed.

Solness later will declare that he has unconsciously *willed* Hilde's arrival as, earlier, he had willed Kaja's offer to work for him. Richard Schechner, writing on the last four plays, suggests that the "unexpected visitors" in these plays "are, as Jung has it, 'personified thoughts.' They are those sectors of the hero's mind that cannot be faced directly."[15] In Wagner's *Die Walküre* there is a very similar relationship between Wotan and Brunnhilde, Brunnhilde being the embodiment of Wotan's innermost will and reconciling the god to accept the triumph of the younger generation. At one moment, Brunnhilde declares to Wotan:

> Zu Wotans Willen sprichst du,
> sagst du mir was du willst:
>   wer bin ich,
> wär ich dein Wille nicht?

(To Wotan's will you are speaking, whatever you say to me; Who am I if not your Will?)

and when Brunnhilde defies Wotan and assures the survival of the younger generation (Siegfried, son of the twins Siegmund and Sieglinde), she pleads that she obeyed the unacknowledged, *truer* part of Wotan's divided will. (*Die Walküre*, III, iii.) The highly ambiguous nature of Hilde's relation to Solness derives, in part, from her representing that which he dares not acknowledge to himself: the overreaching action that will clear the way for the younger generation by means of a splendid leave-taking.

Hilde arrives at a point when the stage light is dimmed, for Aline has turned down Kaja's lamp, perhaps subtly preparing for the displacement of that character which Hilde will effect. From the moment of Hilde's entry Solness increases in buoyancy and strength; in fact, each of Hilde's entries in the play are movements towards the liberation of Solness. Henry James finely called Hilde "the animated clock-face, as it were, of Halvard Solness's destiny,"[16] and the frightening ambiguity of his surrender to this destiny is suggested in the following exchange:

HERDAL. (*playfully, with a glance at Hilde*) . . . You read the future all right, Mr. Solness!
SOLNESS. How so?
HERDAL. Youth did come along, knocking at your door.
SOLNESS. (*buoyantly*) Yes, but that was something else completely.

Solness, in effect, refuses to see the signs and insists on interpreting them to his own advantage despite the uncanny warning behind the coincidence of the responsive knock at the door. The irony is that Hilde *does* force Solness to make way (*gi plass!*) but in the form of a splendid death that is like a brilliant setting of the sun. What will be recovered in Solness is his Promethean rebellion against the restrictive order of the universe (the Creator) and the image that he leaves to the younger generation (in Hilde's mind) is of this bid for the highest possible attainment.

Hilde arrives at a house where three nurseries are standing ready for a guest,[17] but Hilde's actions and speeches indicate that she will be no child of its present life, will not fit into it as undemandingly as Kaja had done. There is a curious little scene where she wanders about his room, her hands behind her back while he follows her with his eyes, his hands behind his back—the imitated gesture implying that already he is following her, cautiously, in spirit. She reacts scornfully to the idea that she should "write in the ledger" and her account of herself, as arriving with no trunk and no money, suggests a spirit that totally rejects the "ledger" world of careful calculation of profit and loss. The ledger world implies a finicky, bourgeois spirit, the necessary damned detail work of bourgeois life that would find towers on houses an extravagance, and castles in the air quixotic fantasies.

Hidle's audacious arrival, without money or extensive luggage, which Solness so warmly responds to, has some of the heroic individualism of the young viking hero's arrival at a foreign court willing to combat whatever evils the court is suffering from. Solness's second retrospection, this time with Hilde, turns, now, not upon loss but upon achievement: the Lysanger ascent, the last time Solness climbed a church tower. But Hilde has invested this event with a strange and fabulous content, and, between them, they build the event into a legendary happening: of

Solness ascending the Lysanger tower from a music-filled churchyard and hanging a wreath upon the tower's top while, looking below, he saw "a little devil in white" furiously waving a flag. Hilde, the little devil in the churchyard, looked upwards and heard a singing "like harps in the air" from the top of the tower and became (though she does not quite own up to it) "dizzy" (*svimlende*) with the similarly dizzy Solness. This is the beginning of a piece of mutual myth-making of an imaginative re-creation of the past which is validated only when Solness attempts to live up to it in the final moments of the play. The extraordinarily double vertical vision of Solness, above, looking down, dizzily, and hearing music from below; and Hilde, below, looking up, dizzily, and hearing music above, thus wrenching the playgoer's imagination apart, also is repeated at the end of the play as the attention is focused both on the crushed skull on the ground, signaling failure, and upon Hilde's rapturous gaze upward as she announces she heard "harps in the air," signaling triumph.

When Solness descended the tower, Hilde relates, he then did "the real thing": he greeted her as a princess, promised her a kingdom in ten years, then bent her backwards kissing her many, many times. As Hilde was then a mere "twelve-thirteen"-year-old girl the story is startling and Solness emphatically denies it; but Hilde, by a childish stratagem of sulks and offended silences, gets Solness to allow that this passionate encounter *might* have taken place. His concession, at this point, is that of an adult to a willful child, but it already is the starting point for his complete acceptance of this childish story. It is worth noting the stages of Solness's conversion to Hilde's version of the past. He first insists it was a dream in Hilde's mind. Then he suggests it was something *he*, perhaps, had secretly willed and desired. Already he has transferred the event from her mind to his own. Finally, he agrees that he moved from the desire to the action, and that he *did* in fact act as she described. Whether the encounter *did* take place "in fact" is something the audience can never be sure of, but this is less important than the process we are observing of Solness accepting and endorsing Hilde's re-creation of the past. When he accepts Hilde's version of the past and moves on to make it a reality in the present, he is laying the "solid foundation" for those visionary castles in the air that represent the widest possible liberation of the spirit. Solness's hesitant responses to Hilde's promptings can be seen as the spirit's somewhat fearful acceptance of spiritual possibilities which, however outrageous, are more liberating than modern normalcy. It is no accident that the imagery surrounding this encounter is of kingdoms and princesses: "childish" details, to the modern sense, but leading back to larger ideas of the human gesture and identity than the ideas of the ledger world. For all their childishness, then, Hilde's ideas carry the seeds of subversion for they throw into sharper relief the adult discontent with given reality. This discontent is hinted at in Solness's secret desire to build houses with towers—which we can read as the desire to extend the terms of modern creativity, or modern life, beyond the enclosed and self-justifying pragmatism of the ledger (*protokollen*) world.

The nature of both the retrospections and the aspirations of Solness and Hilde, in fact, illustrates perfectly the subversive use of the past described by a modern Hegelian, Herbert Marcuse, in *One Dimensional Man*. Contrasting the impoverished, "one-dimensional" thinking of present-day culture whose positivistic outlook has capitulated to the tyranny of established facts, to the given reality, with the older, "critical" function of reason and the imagination, Marcuse finds four major subversive devices of the older literature: memory, art, idealism, and sublimated sexuality. These are able to present to the given reality of the present requirements or values that suggest an alternative, and better, order of reality; and this, precisely, is the function of these elements in the duologues of Hilde and Solness. Both from the immediate memory of the Lysanger ascent, and from the racial memory of its archetypal overtones, Hilde brings into the Solness household dimensions of reality that reproach the petty restrictedness of the present. This memory is of an overweening work of art, a great Babel-like structure, and Hilde exclaims, remembering it, "I never dreamed that anywhere in the world there was a builder who could build a tower so high." Solness's act of climbing this tower was an example of human courage and audacity —an idealistic extension of the human gesture to the height of the sublime. And the sexuality of Hilde and Solness's relationship, their passionate encounter in the past and their present relationship, far from being a detail of sexual psychopathology, is remarkably chaste, sublimated to such a degree that Henry James assured his readers "there was nothing to prevent the play from being one to which a young lady, as they say in Paris, may properly take her mother."[18] The subversive rather than erotic nature of Solness's relationship to Hilde probably baffles and annoys modern readers more than anything else, and though there may be some consolation for the amateur Freudians in pointing out the somewhat obvious resemblances of towers to phalli, dreams of falling to orgasms, and Hilde's condition to that of arrested pubescence, it is all too obvious that Ibsen's great play, stalking bigger game, takes all this in its stride as only so much somewhat trivial detail in its total design. The main point is not that towers probably relate to phallic creativity but that, in Ibsen's play, the movement decisively is not only downwards to these origins of consciousness, but also upwards, to more alarming realities. The "kingdom" and the towered castle Solness promises to build for Hilde are dimensions of the spirit which their childish recidivism has resurrected from folk memory and re-created in dangerously idealistic terms. These idealistic lovers certainly do not envisage setting up a *ménage à trois* on the lines of Judge Brack, whose attitude to given reality is the exact opposite of the subversive: instead, like the lovers in Fitzgerald's *Omar Khayyam*, they long to shatter the order of the universe and remould it nearer to the heart's desire. Thus the function of memory in the play is not only that of passive recollection but also of idealistic *re-creation*. Hilde, with her excited vision of her master builder triumphantly descending his tower, promising her a kingdom and kissing his princess many times, reveals to Solness what the past, in its widest dimensions, *should* have been and what, if he has the courage to accept her challenge, it *was*.

The re-creation of the past in terms more adequate and more challenging, in order to transform the present reality into the means towards an idealistically envisioned future, makes up the very definite dialectic of Time—of memory, present discontent, and future aspiration—of *The Master Builder*, and is succinctly expressed at that moment when Solness at last takes up Hilde's challenge:

SOLNESS. Are you quite sure this isn't some kind of dream—some fantasy that's taken hold of you?
HILDE. (*caustically*) Meaning you didn't do it, hm?
SOLNESS. I hardly know myself. (*Dropping his voice*) But one thing I know for certain—that—
HILDE. That you—Go on!
SOLNESS. That I *ought* to have done it.
HILDE. (*exclaiming spiritedly*) *You* could never be dizzy!
SOLNESS. So we'll hang the wreath this evening—Princess Hilde.

This idea of the re-creation of the past, of transforming it from a constraining power to a force of liberation, had been a keystone of the philosophy of a thinker Ibsen admired, Friedrich Nietzsche, who was, Ibsen remarked, "too aristocratic" to be "popular in our democratic age."[19] In *Thus Spake Zarathustra*, the first three parts of which were published before Ibsen started on *The Master Builder*, and which similarly draws upon the Zoroaster/Zarathustra figure, Zarathustra claims that he has taught man the subversive re-creation of the past:

I taught them to work on the future and to redeem with their creation all that *has* been. To redeem what is past in man and to re-create all "it was" until the will says "Thus I willed it! Thus I shall will it!"—this I call redemption and this alone I taught them to call redemption.[20]

The parallel between this and Solness's response to Hilde's account of his past, "Then I ought to have done it," is even more striking if we keep in mind the way in which the localized past of ten to thirteen years, in the play, becomes suggestive of a far greater, historical past, stretching back into the legendary and mythical. Solness, singing at the top of the Lysanger tower, *"lys levende"* as Hilde describes him, already has moved beyond the common-sensical realm of everyday reality, into the legendary and archetypal, and so has Hilde, down in the churchyard with its music, hearing harps in the air and catching the eye of the dizzily high Solness. Given the surname of the ascendant Solness, it might not be inappropriate to recall a strophe from Albrecht's *Titurel*, cited by Grimm, describing the "clang of strings" when "the sun to whirling took," which Grimm relates to the legend of the Memnon statue "which at sunrise sent forth a sound like the clang of a harpstring, some say a joyful tone at the rising and a sad at the setting of the sun."[21] Ibsen quite obviously remembered and made use of this legend in *Peer Gynt*, IV, ii, where, at sunrise, Memnon's statue gives out music to the uncomprehending and pragmatic Peer,[22] who lives in a cosmos denuded of the living Past.

Certainly, if we are to attune ourselves to even only a part of Ibsen's poetry in *The Master Builder* we have to move from Dr. Herdal's understanding of the events to Solness's and Hilde's, and we ought to see that the substance of their retrospections, if it seems fantastic in terms of individual psychopathology, is not extravagant in terms of the biography of human consciousness from its mythopoeic "childhood" to its bourgeois present. The first act of *The Master Builder* decisively has moved from the terms of socio-psychological drama, which its details might have sustained and, like Solness's own last tower ascent, has started unnervingly to climb the scaffolding of another dramatic structure. The mythopoeic material, always beneath the surface of the two earlier groups of plays, now has come out into the open to become the substance of Solness's and Hilde's dialogues.

Act I ends with Hilde's establishment in the Solness household, Solness jubilantly seeing her as a recruit in his campaign of "youth against youth." The action of installing Hilde is itself significant:

MRS. SOLNESS. All right Miss Wangel, your room's all ready for you now.
HILDE. Oh, how kind of you.
SOLNESS. Nursery?
MRS. SOLNESS. Yes, the middle one . . .
SOLNESS. (*nodding to Hilde*) So Hilde sleeps in the nursery, then . . .

Like everything else in this riddling play, the detail of the *central* nursery, seemingly so unimportant to its strictly realistic intentions, is of importance to its total metaphor. Hilde, sleeping in the central nursery, is "born" in the Solness household (in Act II she describes herself as having slept like a baby in its cradle) and the odd detail of the two empty nurseries, one on each side of her, surely is meant to make us envision her as flanked by the dead twins. This fits too well within the predominantly *triadic* structure of the play to be accidental, so that Hilde becomes Solness's terrible new child appearing twelve-thirteen years after the earlier children who would themselves have been twelve-thirteen years old—the age at which Hilde first met Solness.

Act I ends ardently, in strong contrast with its enfeebled and self-torturing opening: Solness is tense but excited, Hilde rapturous. Her cry, "Oh, you beautiful big world—!" (*Men du store, deilige verden—!*) echoes the cry of Miranda, "Oh brave new world!" in another late play whose dialectic similarly is between old age and youth and of a creator's magic powers used, like those, also of the aged Oedipus, for a final supreme assertion against the whole substance of the past. True, the ardor of Solness and Hilde is built of strange materials but their affirmation is as poetically real and true as Prospero's even though Ibsen, with poignant integrity, establishes his poetic values only on a firm foundation of familiar figures and surroundings. Ibsen refuses to give "poetically" what he cannot substantiate "realistically" and this sets up a dramatic tension between the terms of recognizable modern life, with which he starts out, and the larger gestures of the spirit which, as a visionary poet, he inherits from the whole past of the race. If the gradual progress of this act has been the transfiguration of reality into a mode spiritually more adequate, the apotheosis of the human spirit attempted in the last act never loses sight of that condition of humanity and human realities upon which, alone, such an apotheosis can be established.

Act I already has presented us with the full substance of the past— the tragic loss and the triumphant achievement—upon which the whole action and dialogue of the rest of the play will be built, and the two terms, loss and achievement, are two poles between which the dialectic swings. This dual vision of the past, both as tragic waste and as spiritual triumph, is inevitable to the historical vision, and it is central to Hegel's philosophy. In a passage in *The Philosophy of Religion*, Hegel observes how Nature herself "has already made an endless number of attempts and produced a host of monstrosities: myriads of beings and various forms have issued from her which were not, however, able to continue in existence, and, besides, she did not concern herself at all with the disappearance of such forms of life."[23] After this survey of the very dialectical condition of life itself—written long before Darwin—Hegel goes on to extend this process of destruction/creation to the life of the mind and the history of mankind:

> We see the earth covered with ruins, with remains of the splendid edifices and works left by the finest nations, whose ends we recognize as having substantial value. Great natural objects and human work do indeed endure and defy time, but all that splendid national life has irrecoverably perished. We thus see how, on the one hand, petty, subordinate, even despicable designs are fulfilled, and on the other, how those which are recognized as having substantial value are frustrated. We are here certainly forced to rise to the thought of a higher determination and a higher end, when we thus lament the misfortune which has befallen so much that is of high value and mourn its disappearance. We must regard all those ends, however, as much as they interest us, as finite and subordinate and ascribe to their finitude the destruction which overtakes them.[24]

History, to Hegel's admirably tough-minded vision, is both inspiring and lamentable, subject to a process and a destiny that prohibits becoming so attached to some aspect of the past that one only can bewail its loss. In suitably reduced, "domestic" terms, this is the dual vision of the Past explored in *The Master Builder*, and Act II will develop it further. This extraordinary act is made up of three major retrospections so that the drama is given over to the consciousness struggling with its Past. Though the *scene* of this act presents us with the impression of renewal, a reawakening of powers, with its emphatic abundance of natural light streaming through the bay window and glass door and its profusion of plants and flowers (in strong contrast with the windowless, artificially lit Act I), the action nevertheless begins with the same imprisonment of consciousness within the *tragic* past. Aline, as always dressed in black, is tending the flowers, the function of caring for life contradicted by her mourning dress. The themes of sickness and death predominate in the dying and Aline darkly hints that this might not be the only death to first dialogues of this act. Ragnar appears with news that his father is occur. This death talk is momentarily lightened by a reference to Hilde who has been "up for hours" and busy, suggesting that a challenging vitality has invaded this house of sickness and gloom.

Hilde has filled a role—of being "born" into the house—for which it was waiting:

> SOLNESS. . . . So we did find use for one of the nurseries after all, Aline.
> MRS. SOLNESS. Yes, we did.
> SOLNESS. And I think that's better, really, than all of them standing empty.
> MRS. SOLNESS. You're right—that emptiness—it's horrible.

But before Hilde enters, to manifest this life renewal, Solness and Aline return the dialogue to the tragedy of the burned-down house and the dead twins. Aline sees the disaster as a "misfortune" (*ulykken*), a term that Solness, in agreement, takes up. The antithesis *lykken-ulykken* becomes a verbal pattern in this act and in itself expresses the dual nature of the past.

Solness and Aline recollect the Past guiltily and self-torturingly, displaying, at the same time, a total estrangement from each other, for each receives the other's confession of guilt with astonishment. Aline's guilt is expressed in terms of divided *duties*, a dilemma that even is developed comically in the last act. Her sense of the past as tragic loss has killed any interest in the future so that the new house (clearly a symbol of a new mode of life), which Solness has built primarily for her, is meaningless. Aline's self-reproach, that she allowed her weakness and grief to interfere with her *duties* to Solness and the twins, is made in the very terms that so drastically separate her concept of life from his. In the middle of a dialogue of guilt and remorse Solness cries out despairingly:

. . . Never a touch of the sun [*sol*straale]! Not the least glimmer of light [streif*lys*] in this house!

and the dialogue now plunges into its darkest mood, in which Solness suspects Aline of attempting to trap him into betraying symptoms of insanity and Aline recoils from him in terror. Solness describes how he feels a terrible "burden of debt" under which he must "sink," a debt that is "weighing upon" him and "pressing him down." These metaphors, with their evocation of physical torment and punishment, suggest some terrible penalty imposed upon Solness for his luck and the whole dialogue, colored by the ambiguous word "*skyld*" (debt and guilt) ends with the word "sick"—a return to the condition of the opening of the play until Solness abruptly and startlingly exclaims:

Ah, now it begins to brighten! (Naa *lys*ner det!)

as Hilde enters calling out "Good morning!" With such a definite sun-and-light imagery in the play, even the conventional greeting reveals important meaning. Hilde has slept well, like a princess and like a baby in its cradle (*vugge*), and she now relates a childish dream of falling. Solness confesses to sometimes dreaming the same dream and the two of them confide, like small children, that in these "wonderfully thrilling" dreams in which their blood runs cold, they tuck their legs up under them as they fall. The foetal cosiness of this action is thoroughly in keeping with the regression to childhood of their dialogues and, of course, it means that Hilde assumed this foetel position in a dream in which she was sleeping in a *cradle* in a *nursery*. At the same time, of course, these dreams of falling more somberly predict Solness's final fall from the tower that Hilde will urge him to climb. Thus the detail of falling combines the meanings of both birth and death—a condensed ambiguity typical of the verbal patterns of the play.

The change of tone in the play's dialogue once Hilde enters is striking. The sickly adult anguish over the past, of Solness's estranged conversation with Aline, gives way to an animated lightheartedness and a childlike exchange of confidences that poignantly emphasizes Aline's isolation from Solness's spiritual rebirth. She leaves, antagonizing Hilde with the *leitmotiv* "duty"—a word Hilde feels is like the lash of a whip. The little word *"plikt"* (duty) is used six times by Solness and Hilde in about as many lines, its "sharp and cutting" quality sounding like a flagellation Aline inflicts upon potentially joyful life.

Hilde, in spiritual affinity with Solness, speaks out the idea (that he alone should be allowed to build) that *he* secretly had been formulating "in his solitude and silence." Solness now tells Hilde to look out of the bow-window towards the new house on the right with its scaffolding, its three empty nurseries, and its tower. This "nearly finished" structure, occupying the site of the old robbers' castle, stands for an extension of creativity beyond the modest "homes" to which Solness has devoted his time since the tragedy of the fire, and it may even be that the new house stands for the play, *The Master Builder* itself, which, too, is a nearly finished structure at which the audience is looking. Immediately after indicating his future house, Solness asks Hilde to sit facing the bow-window so that she can see both the garden with its new house, and himself.

As Solness now returns to the tragic destruction of the old house we have the extraordinary visual situation of Hilde looking at Solness and the *new* house from the *present* house while he is describing the *old* house. Solness and the scene and events he is describing to Hilde thus are seen in all three time dimensions, past, present, and future. We already have had emphatically established that the new house can be seen through the bow-window, so that Hilde's comment, "Now I'm looking at both the garden and you," and Solness's direction, "Over on that ridge there, where you see the new house . . . that's where Aline and I lived in those early years. There was an old house up there then . . ." forces *us*, too, to "see" Solness in these three time dimensions.

This second retrospection in Act II returns to the subject of the fire and the death of Solness's sons who, we now learn for the first time, were twins. The story of the fire as told to Hilde is notably richer and more detailed than the versions that emerged in the dialogues with Dr. Herdal and Aline, for it is with Hilde that Solness can share the full reality of the experience. The triple time dimension in which we meditate upon the tragedy makes it an event of the present and of the future as well as of the past; in other words, we see its consequences through the time span from the distant past, the later history of Solness's career, and the effort of transcending this whole history which Hilde will urge upon Solness, for his future. Solness had feared a Nemesis from the young who were sacrificed to his career, and "Princess" Hilde, emerging from the central nursery of Solness's house which the sacrificed twins, also, should have inhabited, is surely a part of this Nemesis, however deviously it is working.

It must be conceded that the sheer amount of "fact" communicated in Solness's retrospection with Hilde makes for low-keyed drama. The stage situation is reduced to that of Hilde as mere prompter and feed to Solness's lines, and these lines, rather than setting off reverberations of action upon the stage, are delivered "straight"—as information—in the manner of Prospero's long retrospective speech to Miranda in Act I of *The Tempest*, so that we find ourselves confronted with a dramatic action and language which, though complex in terms of the information conveyed, is not complex enough as a dramatic event. What is more, though the details of Solness's history are too matter-of-fact for poetry, the facts are too odd and mysterious, too eccentric, to be easily comprehended. As in much of Shakespeare, where the verbal complexity seems excessive to the ethical or philosophical reality being established, we are made uncomfortably aware of the lack of a sufficiently compelling, counterpoising esthetic convention, such as the choral ode in Greek tragedy, to make the impact between form and content dynamically interactive and thus complexly, *dialectically*, consequential as objective art. The impression, however, of Solness immersed in a complex history and destiny, greatly suffering yet greatly creative and "lucky," does hold our attention even while it puzzles. The long retrospection which begins with the tragic fire and ends with intimations of mysterious forces, helpers, and servers, set in its triple time scale, covers, by analogy, a sweeping span of time. The old house, dark and ugly outside but comfortable within, which did not have a tower, was a primitive wooden structure. Its destruction founded Solness's career but at the expense of the young life born in it, for though the twins, being fundamentally "sound," survived the fire, they could not survive the poisoned milk of Aline who, out of *duty*, insisted upon feeding them.

The loss of the young life from the old house killed Solness's desire to build more churches, so that the Lysanger church was his last such structure and his ceremonial wreath-laying on the top of the tower, instead of being an affirmation of the god to whom the church was built, became an act of defiance against the god who could demand such sacrifice. From that moment on, Solness built no such ambitious structures: neither robbers' castles nor churches; instead, he devoted himself to building homes for people, comfortable, "sunlit" and suitable for happy families,[25] that did not seek to make man godlike and heroic (the castle) nor the adoring worshiper of a sublime god (the churches) but were concerned with making human life comfortable, enlightened, happy. The three kinds of architecture, here, are suggestive. The old wooden house, called both a "robbers' castle" and a "packing case," was hideous on the outside but comfortable within, and I think any Scandinavian would associate this wooden structure with the early, pagan and viking culture[26] whose wooden buildings were so often destroyed by fire, like Asgard itself. The next great wave of northern building genius was, precisely, that of the great church builders (for the medieval castles were, essentially, the continuation of the old pagan and warrior genius) and, like Solness who calls himself only a master builder, not an architect, the builders of the great cathedrals often were anonymous master masons. The Gothic cathedrals, with their great towers, were the major art form, the major assertion of spirit, of the northern Christian world—the one contribution, perhaps, that raised the genius of the Middle Ages to the level of artistic supremacy.[27] The third form of building, the comfortable homes, suggests a retreat both from the pagan, warrior values of the castle and the other-worldly aspirations of the cathedrals, to that comfortable, bourgeois culture of later Europe which Wagner, for one, described as so stultifying to artistic genius. There is something of the same uncomfortable drop from the master builder who entranced young Hilde with the idea that "nowhere in the world was there a builder who could build a tower so high" to the maker of homes for happy families.

Particularly odd, in Solness's narration, is the account of the twins' death. Most readers or viewers must have experienced some exasperation in learning that the twins did not die in the fire (as dramatic economy would require) but through yet a further complication, just as the fire itself broke out, not as predicted by Solness, but from another cause. Ibsen, arresting the movement of his narrative by means of these obtrusive complications, obviously is finding a place for important details of his final meaning which we should try to account for. We notice, also, the curious finality about Solness's and Aline's childlessness as in all the cases of *kindermord* to which James E. Kerans, in a fine study of *Little Eyolf*,[28] has drawn our attention. Ibsen's marriages, and their offspring, are always, I believe, metaphors for the mating (or, rather, mismating) of spiritual forces—notably pagan and Christian—whose issue, were not their pasts in some way or other disastrously compromised, would be some form of synthesis associated with Ibsen's concept of a third empire of spirit. We think of Brand and Agnes, Peer and Solveig, Julian and Helen, Alving and Helene, Rosmer and Beate (and Rebekka), Tesman and Hedda, and so on, in which the union generates antithetical forces (not, strictly, masculine and feminine) that obviously represent more in Ibsen's scheme of things than a highly pessimistic view of the marriage institution, and Solness and Aline are no exception to this pattern. The death of the twins[29] made Solness's last church something he built reluctantly, and he rebelled against the power (the Creator) who demanded such sacrifice. The most explicit example in Ibsen's writing of this sacrifice of child and wife, hollowly compensated for by a new church, is *Brand*, a play we must keep in mind if we are to understand *The Master Builder*. At this point in his narration, however, Solness does *not* reveal that he rebelled against the Creator.

To suggest that the old wooden house burned down, and that the churches and then the homes for happy families are emblematic of phases of the European consciousness (perhaps the artistic consciousness) lands us in fewer difficulties than seeing them as emblematic of phases of Ibsen's dramatic career, in which we are doomed to such speculations as "If *Catiline* and the early historical plays are the old robbers' castle, and *Brand* and *Peer Gynt* are the churches, *what* is *Love's Comedy*, or *Emperor and Galilean?*" It is better to see that Ibsen's career returns again and again to the main currents of European culture, Greek, Roman, Germanic, and Christian, and that by evoking these phases in *The Master Builder* Ibsen is bound to evoke phases of his own career as a dramatist. We then can place the Solness tragedy of loss and destruction more plausibly, for, after all, Ibsen neither lost nor destroyed his earlier work (which frequently was performed in his lifetime), whereas past cultures and the phases of consciousness they represented *were* destroyed and lost sight of in European history. The development of history, as Hegel pointed out, has entailed the destruction and loss of much that was fine, especially the *life* that did not survive the monuments. The troublesome twins might then, tentatively, be interpreted as possibilities of human consciousness (pagan and Christian, emperor and Galilean) frustrated from development beyond their promising, youthful vigor. This idea at least has the merit of appearing before, quite explicitly, in Ibsen's writing. In *Emperor and Galilean*

Julian burns his fleet and, in a feverish ecstasy, sees twin aspects of
human consciousness perishing in the fire:

Yes, the fleet is on fire! And more than the fleet is on fire. On that red
seething pyre the crucified Galilean is burning to ashes; and the earthly
Emperor is burning with the Galilean. But from the ashes shall rise . . . like
that marvelous bird . . . the god of the earth and the emperor of the spirit in
one, in *one*, in *one*.

This imagery of fire, sacrifice, and the phoenix rising from its ashes,
in a drama which, while drawing upon an immense mytho-historical,
religious, and philosophical heritage, shows its hero, Julian, moving his
capital to Antioch to be nearer Helios, the sun god, and also dreaming
of founding a kingdom of the sun, may make the suggestion that these
details reappear in *The Master Builder*—and that, therefore, the two
plays are the work of the same creative imagination—more plausible,
especially as Ibsen again and again insisted upon the importance of his
world-historical drama as a key to understanding his life's work.

Despite the terrible fire and the tragic loss Solness is, Hilde avers,
a *"lykkelig"* man—again the translation "happy" is inadequate, for
Solness takes up the word in its second meaning of good luck or fortune.
Solness's luck and happiness demanded that he pay a price, the sacrifice
of home and children. "This good luck, Hilde, it couldn't be bought for
less." The tragic loss never will be made good "in this world," Solness
tells Hilde, and when she observes that he yet continues to build nurseries, he replies:

Have you ever noticed, Hilde, how the impossible, how it seems to whisper
and call to you?
HILDE. (*reflecting*) The impossible? (*Vivaciously*) Oh yes! *You* know it too?

This is a turning point in the play and the word "impossible" (*umulig*)
now will be used with extraordinary frequency, reaching a climax of
iteration when Solness, in the last act, climbs the tower. We notice
that Hilde receives Solness's concept of "the impossible," *reflects* upon
it, thus taking it into her mind, then "vivaciously" (*livfull*) assents to it
—another of the many moments in the play when either Solness or Hilde
receives a concept from the other, takes it over, and thus spiritually
"grows" onstage, like a master and a devoted disciple. The word "impossible" is to assume such importance in the play that it must represent
an important intention on Ibsen's part; it is connected with Solness's
rebellion and with his attempted liberation, and it is sparked off by
Hilde's question about the three nurseries that Solness has built in his

home of the future as in those of the past and the present. Thematically, therefore, it is linked to the concept embodied in the persistent image of the three nurseries which, we have seen, at least suggests the "third-empire" goal of Ibsen's lifelong quest as an artist and thinker: an aspiration that might well seem a tower of Babel of the human spirit.[30]

In my copy of the Bible in Norwegian, God destroys the tower of Babel (that archetypal emblem of human rebellion or hubris) because he fears that man will find nothing *impossible* (*umulig*) to perform that he can imagine. The word for impossible (*umulig*) is the same reiterated throughout the text of *The Master Builder*, and we have seen that there was, in comparative mythology, a connection established between northern mythology and the legend of Zoroaster (Zarathustra) as the builder of the tower of Babel; that was undoubtedly one of the reasons why Nietzsche chose the Persian sage and mystic as the spokesman of his own audacious philosophy of the superhuman. The Babel myth obviously affected Ibsen's own imagination; it lies behind many of the rebellions and "ascending actions" in his plays and behind the poetic quest to raise man to the status of the demigod (the third empire). The myth is very powerfully present, for example, in that drama of spiritual pride and ascent, *Brand,* and at one important point Brand openly invokes the Babel example. The play, like *The Master Builder*, contains the metaphor of three stages of architecture. In the past was a pagan temple dating from "king Bele's days." Upon the site of this destroyed temple, next to a "great big ugly wooden shed," stands the church, built out of the spoils won by the "pious heroes" of old—the sheriff's ironic reference to the vikings. This building is pulled down to make way for Brand's new church which, however, Brand abandons as soon as it is consecrated. Brand then moves on to the inhuman architecture of the Ice Church, perhaps symbolizing the inhuman abstraction of his quest carried to its idealistic limits; for the Ice Church, not built by man, is not a structure in which man's *humanity* will be reflected. The "syllogism" of the three human structures bears some resemblance to the buildings in *The Master Builder*, and just before Brand renounces the new church the Dean reminds him of the Babel episode in biblical myth:

> Just now, I merely would recall your mind
> To that great tower of Babel, which was planned.
> —Tell me yourself how far its builders got![31]

The builders failed, the cynical Dean observes, because they became *individuals* instead of remaining a herd; and Brand's program of bringing spiritual awakening is, precisely, to attack the herd instinct and to awaken the *individual*. The Dean draws this lesson:

> When in life's struggle, God would strike a man
> He makes him first an individual.
> The Romans said He robbed him of his wits,
> But mad and singular are just the same!

(We should be alerted by this not to read the references to Solness's "madness" and "sickness" as indications of serious psychological disorder; like the abnormalities of the mystics, they more likely indicate spiritual strength.) What is more, says the Dean, such a "mad" individual is doomed to die and Brand replies to this with Hegel's paradox that death is the condition of life:

> In death I see no final overthrow.

and he continues:

> And are you, then, so perfectly convinced
> That in the end, these builders we discuss,
> With common language and united wills
> Would have succeeded in the task proposed
> And built the tower of Babel up to heaven?

to which the Dean readily agrees:

> That is the second moral in the core,
> Preserved and hidden in the fable's shell:—
> That every building planned to find its roof
> Among the stars of heaven is bound to fall.[32]

To this, Brand replies that "aspirations of the soul" (this brings to mind the "castles in the air") can, like Jacob's ladder, reach right up to heaven.[33]

The thematic parallels between this passage in *Brand* and *The Master Builder* are striking and suggest that both plays are dealing with what, for Ibsen, is the same objective reality of human consciousness: the aspiration to transcend the despotic structure of conventional reality, an aspiration which, for all the ambiguity of its self-destructive logic, contains an admirable integrity totally lacking in the "herd" that compromises, wisely, with conventional reality.

The three time dimensions surrounding Solness's dialogue with Hilde enlarge with the mythopoeic resonance of the iteration of the word "impossible" but this, for the moment, is left in abeyance as Solness returns again to the tragedy of the fire. This time, however, the tale is related in more ambitious and poetically suggestive terms. There is a "troll" in Solness[34] shaping events for him but also exacting for everything of "beauty" and "splendour" the price of human happiness (*menneskelykke*)—his own happiness and that of others, especially of Aline whose destiny should have been that of building up young souls so that they could "stand on their own, poised, in beautiful noble forms— till they'd grown into the upright human spirit." This image irresistibly recalls sculpture and thus, perhaps, an esthetic education of mankind as in Hellenic culture. This "gift" of Aline's now lies like "a charred heap of ruins" and Solness is tormented and divided as to whether he is guilty or innocent of the disaster, a doubt that Hilde sees as his "sickness." Solness's long retrospection, in which the theater audience's attention is almost intolerably strained, is now interrupted by the appearance of Ragnar and here we are given a vivid episode illustrating the consequences of Solness's inner torment upon others and upon himself, for he behaves towards Ragnar in a way that Hilde calls ugly, evil, and cruel. This episode vividly brings Solness's history up-to-date as we see it repeated in the lives of those with whom he comes into contact— especially the *young* who will have to inherit his world.

Solness justifies his actions on the grounds that he has paid a price— the price of his own inner peace—and the phrase he uses, *sjelefred*, "peace of soul," to designate the sacrifice his situation requires, is suggestive of a compact with dubious powers, like Faust's. This theme leads to the third retrospection of this act, his account of the unnerving power of *willing* that he seems to command. The retrospection begins with "a ridiculous little detail"—the "crack in the chimney" from which small sign Solness was able to predict his own success; and this little sign opens up into a vision of a winter's day, with Solness and Aline returning from a ride in a sleigh to the old house where "the people at home" would have fires blazing in the stoves ready for them. Solness and Aline would first see smoke rising up and then, pulling in at the garden gate, "there the old packing case would stand, a great mass of flames." The odd thing, however, is that Solness has described, not what actually happened but what he wrongly predicted would happen, for, to Hilde's (and the audience's) exasperation, he admits that the fire did not start from the chimney crack but from a clothes closet. This, however, is all the more disturbing for it means that the fire, not having the *likely* cause anticipated by Solness (the crack in the chimney) nevertheless *did* take place according to his desire or willing. The details of the ride through the winter landscape, the smoke in the distance, the great pillar of fire (*ildsluer*) take on the quality of legendary events—of legendary predictions fulfilled, with variations in detail, by actual history,[35] even more devastatingly than the legend predicted.

The theme now develops into the idea of the "chosen" or "special" people upon whom certain powers attend: who can "wish," "will," and "desire" something so insistently that it *must* happen. The suggestion of the occult, of magic, about this is reinforced by the qualification that this wishing and willing is obeyed by "helpers and servers" whom the chosen and special person must learn to command; it is the same problem as that of Julian and Maximus in the séance scene of *Emperor and Galilean*. The idea is one familiar to literature and to history: that the chosen hero can call upon divine or metaphysical aid or is strangely favored by "luck," "fortune," or even the *Weltgeist*. It is a metaphor for the hero's uncanny ability to operate with seemingly more than human success— to be in the right place at the right time and command events while men as gifted are helpless. In the Homeric world, it is the god who chooses and attends upon the hero, as Athene attends upon Achilles and Odysseus. Closer to Solness, is Sophocles' Oedipus at Colonus or Philoctetes whose great suffering is also the condition of more than human power, and this concept is regained by Shakespeare in Prospero, calling upon his helpers and servers. A darker version is Macbeth entrapped by the equivocal powers of darkness. These are the poetic equivalents of Hegel's belief that the world will works through the chosen hero, the Alexander, Julius Caesar, or Napoleon, and Julian's attempt to master these powers of the spirit in order to gain mastery over the objective world of historical forces is a fascinating portrait, like that of Earl Skule, of *inadequacy* in this form of mastery, despite qualities in many respects greatly superior to the successful Jovian.

The equivocal helpers and servers, fair and dark, who wait upon Solness, also exact suffering so that, as with Oedipus, Philoctetes, and even Prospero, Solness's unusual powers derive from his unusual suffering. He alone, he affirms, knows how to call upon the terrible powers, and this is known as luck (*lykken*) but, Solness cries out, this "luck" is a terrible wound which, to be assuaged, must be provided with the suffering of others. The image Solness uses is that of flesh torn from his chest; and other victims have to be flayed to patch this constant wound.[36]

At this moment, when the imagery seems to look back to primitive human sacrifice, Solness and Hilde recollect the viking age and the way in which those single-minded heroes, "light-hearted as *children*" (my italics) could so free-heartedly and without conscientious scruple give themselves up to their way of life—the strongest possible contrast to the condition of Solness. Solness had declared that there was a "troll" within him corresponding to the mysterious helpers and servers without, and that these inner forces can call upon the outer. But the outer powers, too, are double-natured and the ability to choose between them—good or ill—or to accept both obviously is connected with the problem of mastering the riddle of the self (the troll within) in order to master the powers in the world without. Solness's success was due to his ability to predict, and to call upon mysterious powers, a "luck" that had to be paid for at the price of "happiness" (*lykken* in both cases!). Divided over the ambiguity of the troll within and the powers without, Solness has developed a sickly conscience, afraid and guilty over calling upon his great forces. Hilde tells him to call on *both* kinds of "devils," the fair and the dark; a strong conscience, she insists, would dare what it most wanted. Solness, on the other hand, has seen the devastation caused by the troll within working in conjunction with the ambiguous powers, and wishes to be certain that he could call only on the *good* devils.

This dualism of good and evil, fair and dark was, for Hegel, the beginning of the spiritual life of the West, introduced into it by the Persian religion whose cosmos was divided between the god of Light (Ormazd) and the god of Darkness (Ahriman), who were also, respectively, Good and Evil. Because only from such a dualism or set of antinomies can *dialectical* evolution emerge, so the whole of Western (and modern) Consciousness is founded upon this Persian religious consciousness. This dualism was adopted by Christianity (it was alien to Hellenic and northern thought) to become the history of self-estrangement traced in the second group in Ibsen's Cycle.

Immediately after expressing his torment and uncertainty over the dual nature of the powers he wishes to call upon, Solness recollects the sagas and the vikings, light-hearted as children. Hilde urges Solness to be similarly childlike, to recognize "*all* those enchanting little devils, your friends. The blond and the black-haired, both." This regression to the childhood of the race is a return to a robustness of conscience, a capacity once again to act spontaneously, thus denying the inhibiting dualism that Solness expressed. To the excitedly responsive Solness, Hilde is like some "wild bird of the woods" hunting its prey and then, in a striking image, he declares, "You are like the dawning day. When I look at you—then it's as if I looked into the sunrise."

Like the movement of Act I, therefore, the movement of Act II is emphatically from self-estrangement, doubt, guilt, and self-torture to affirmation. The regression to a childlike consciousness and the mythohistorical recollection have become subversive of the conditions of the present, and impel Solness from thought to action. He now releases Ragnar from his servitude, giving up Kaja Fosli at the same time, and surrenders himself to the somewhat unnerving powers that Hilde has urged him to accept with a robust conscience. The Lysanger ascent is now recollected again and the theme word "impossible" forcefully used. Hilde has told Aline how she saw Solness at the tower top and Aline comments, "Yes, I've heard people talk about that. But it's so completely impossible," to which Solness replies, "forcefully," "Impossible—yes, impossible! But all the same I stood there."

The earlier tower ascent is a legend only half believed, the "impossible" that people talk about, like legends of great human achievement in the past that suggest a state of consciousness utterly different from that of the present; but Solness and Hilde take it with the utmost seriousness, the seriousness of children for whom the world is still a place of infinite possibilities for which only the most "impossible" legends of the past are the adequate premonitions. Act II, therefore, ends with another movement of the spirit *forward*, Solness declaring that if he did not act in the past as Hilde described, promising her a kingdom, calling her a princess and kissing her many times, then he *should* have done it. He now promises to hang a wreath over the new home "that will never be a home for me,"[37] and Hilde ecstatically whispers, "Terribly thrilling."

The event for which Hilde has waited ten years, of seeing Solness "great" and thus adequate to her childhood image of him, fatally *simplifies* his nature, but it is a simplification to which Solness eagerly assents for, like most romantic concepts of man, it offers a heroic dignity which a more tortuous reality denies. In Hilde's dialogue with Aline over the "impossible" we see Solness contrastingly defined by the two women: to Aline his nature is "sick" and incapable of "heights" whereas Hilde insists that "her" master builder can climb as high as he builds, meaning, presumably, that man can live his most ambitious conceptions directly as reality. Solness, deserting Aline for Hilde, accepts her concept, and the ensuing action, in Act III, proves neither woman "right" for it will be as much triumph as defeat.

This inherent ambiguity of the action of Act III is richly and vividly explored from the outset. We find, for example, a scenic extension of the partial emancipation of Act II: the setting, now, is an open-air veranda, still part of the old house, but looking across to the new which now is visible to the audience. This dialogue of old and new, age and youth, continues in the "old" trees that spread over the veranda, shading the light of the sun. Beyond the fence of the garden, in the background, is a street "with old dilapidated houses" which suggest the end of a dying era—Ibsen hardly can have any other reason for this scene direction. The time, too, suggests an end; it is evening in the autumnal equinox and the sky is streaked with the light of a setting sun. In this setting there only can be performed the "fall" of Solness but, like a sunset, it will be a splendid fall, full of light, for Solness will die only after fully summoning and asserting his complete spiritual nature. This scene of sunset, of fall, of old houses and a half-finished new house with an ambitious tower, of a great leave-taking by the hero, creates an elegiac and complex mood that recalls a passage in Nietzsche's *Thus Spake Zarathustra*:

> I want to go under; dying I want to give them my richest gifts. From the sun I learned this: when he goes down overrich. . . . Like the sun Zarathustra too wants to go under; now he sits here and waits, surrounded by broken old tablets and new tablets half-covered with writing.[38]

It is not necessary to prove that Ibsen must have read this passage; his whole endeavor, in the Cycle, placed him, like Nietzsche, in relation to the entire spiritual tradition of the West and in these last four plays, again like Nietzsche, there are intimations of new developments or possibilities for the human spirit of which, however, the present can know nothing.

The dialogue of this act, like that of the others, once again opens on the themes of gloom and distress, but this time it is Hilde, not Solness, who is the victim of the tragic past. She appears from the garden carrying "wild flowers" in a small bouquet at her breast. Aline is startled by the sight of the flowers for she has not been down into the garden for a long time and is unaware of the wild flowers growing abundantly among the bushes. When Hilde asks Aline if she does not "fly" down to the garden every day Aline takes up the pregnant little word with a "wan smile" and answers, "I don't 'fly' anywhere, not any longer." The word has the same ambiguity as in English and though the meaning "rush" or "run" is intended, the particular emphasis given to the word in the dialogue makes us consider its original meaning of flying in the aerial sense, perhaps touching off a memory of older spiritual powers; after all, we already have heard Hilde likened to a bird. The contrast between the two women is powerful: Aline, in black and wrapped in a shawl, looking over the veranda to the new house she has no desire to enter; and the audaciously homeless Hilde with her "wild flowers" and mountain-climbing clothes. The mythic implications of the young girl carrying flowers who soon will "enter the tomb," and the mourning mother, in black, whose deathly sorrow will chill Hilde to the bone, surely are very rich. As in the Proserpina myth, the confrontation of Hilde with Aline, and Hilde's temporary defeat and symbolic death suggest the most sombre expression of the dialectic of youth and age, death and renewal.

Once again we move back into the past, and in this act we will have one major retrospection from Aline and one from Solness and the substance of the past that each recollects now clearly defines their totally opposite identities—opposites that have emerged only through the agency

of Hilde. Aline recollects the fire, the death of the twins, the loss of
the house with its treasures, jewels, dresses, and the "nine lovely dolls"
that were like "unborn babies." All these objects are the *decorations*
of the spirit, like the arts, and mourning their loss more than the loss
of life is analogous to mourning the lost or ruined artifacts of past cultures
and not their vital spiritual life. For the death of the twins was, Aline
accepts, "destiny" to which she must submit and be grateful, but the
loss of the treasures and riches from the old house is inconsolable. This
retrospection, with its emphasis on duty, destiny, the dead twins "who
are so well off now," and the treasures from the past certainly bring
to mind Hegel's account of the Hellenic phase of consciousness whose
concepts were duty and destiny and whose lost artifacts often have
been mourned by the Western consciousness.[39]

By mourning the loss of these *lifeless* objects, while complacently
accepting the death of the twins, Aline betrays a deathliness at the
center of her own spirit and it is this which overwhelms Hilde. This
is a sufficiently appalling detail of individual psychology but if we are
right in seeing Ibsen's plays as microcosmic of larger spiritual realities,
it also is suggestive of a deathly quality within the Western spirit
itself. This, while admiring the past, admires only its lifeless things:
such as its art treasures, its lost masterpieces. Such a non-vital return
to the past is the opposite of Hegel's (and Ibsen's) resurrection of the
past which is concerned with the recovery of its spiritual vitality and
validity, not with its outward forms. Nietzsche's alarming resurrection
of paganism, Kierkegaard's no less alarming resurrection of primitive
Christianity correspond, one imagines, to Ibsen's idea of the way
these forces might yet create a "third empire" of spirit. Such living
forces would contrast with the lifeless records of the past so devotedly
honored in the present; Julian's mistake had been to believe that the
past *form* of paganism could be revived whereas Hegel's paradox is
that Athens had to die in order that what was vital in it should become
a living force in consciousness—a force that the continuing *form* of the
defunct culture might have obscured. To the creative spirit—Solness—
an attitude to the past such as Aline's only can be stultifying, making
her a corpse he must drag around. In Aline, therefore, even the past
achievements are deadly to the continuing life of spirit.

The effect of Aline's retrospection upon the spirit of Hilde is decisive—
a good example of Ibsen's almost unique dramaturgy of the com-
munication of consciousness onstage, the modification of one consciousness by another that makes up his subtle dialectical dramaturgy. By
the time Solness appears, Aline has drained away Hilde's vitality and
crushed her spirit and, for a moment, Hilde is similar to another

northern pagan in the Cycle, Rebekka West, whose spirit was broken by the forces of the past that she combated. When Solness appears, driving Aline away, Hilde tells him she has just "come out of the tomb" (*gravkjeller*). This is Hilde's metaphoric descent into the realm of the dead over which Aline presides and with which Solness had to live, and struggle, so long.

Hilde, now "chilled to the bone," decides to leave Solness and, having taken on the deathly knowledge of Aline, she also takes on her language. When Solness protests her leaving, she replies: "You have your duties to her. Live for those duties."

This iteration of so alien a term, so much part of the identity of Aline, indicates the temporary annihilation of Hilde and, in a reversal of roles, it is Solness who will resurrect her. In a speech bristling with mythic overtones, Solness exclaims that the powers or "devils" have killed Aline:

Yes, devils! And the troll inside me too—they've sucked all the lifeblood out of her. (*With a desperate laugh*) They did it to make me happy! Successful! And now she's dead, thanks to me. And I, alive, chained to the dead. (*In anguish*) I—I, who can't go on living without joy in life!

Here we find vampire devils who have sucked the life-blood of Aline; a wife who dies for her husband (like Alcestis); a dead wife chained to a living man, all sacrifices that suggest the artist's compact with dangerous powers. Solness's insistence that *joy* is essential to his creativity was central to Romantic and German Idealist theories of creativity. We find it in Schiller, in the famous *Ode to Joy* and philosophically formulated in his *Letters on the Esthetic Education of Mankind,* and the concept is imported into England in Coleridge's *Dejection Ode.* The theme appears again and again in Ibsen's writing, in the defeated *livsglede* (joy-of-life) of *Ghosts,* the elusive "happiness" of *Rosmersholm* and, of course, complexly modulated in *The Master Builder.* Solness sees his own creativity defeated and, for a moment, both he and Hilde seem overwhelmed by the spiritual problem they have opened up— of not daring to take hold of happiness because someone stands in the way. Solness looks forward only to a life without joy and therefore without creativity once Hilde leaves, and Ibsen marks this spiritually low point in their relationship through the visual details of Hilde sinking with her head on the table, resting on her arms and speaking "motionless, as if half-asleep." She is revived, however, when Solness, "his eyes resting on her," returns to the themes of Hilde as the bird of prey, of the viking spirit and the robust conscience. Hilde's eyes return to "their happy, sparkling look" and she and Solness now create between them a legendary "kingdom" for Princess Hilde, which possesses a castle that stands "very high up—and free on every side" from which Hilde can look out afar: a castle with an immensely high tower offering a summit vision of the works of others, builders of churches and houses.

It is not enough, I think, to call this "poetry" and thus by definition inaccessible to rational analysis, for this would be saying that it is bad poetry. The castle with the terribly high tower gives way to an even more nebulous concept, the "castle in the air," forcing us either embarrassedly to ignore the particular words of this situation, or to take them seriously. The very childishness of this imagery, we have suggested, is deliberate, and the nebulousness of the final castle in the air "with a solid foundation" must be seen as a visionary charting of an area of spirit later to be occupied—an acknowledgment of dimensions of spiritual ambition, like Nietzsche's Overman, which later must be fulfilled. Because Solness and Hilde have become like visionary children, the details of kingdom, princess, and castle are appropriate; but the "castle in the air" with "a solid foundation" is not a childish but an adult term for impossibly ambitious wishes. What we witness, then, is an activity ("dreaming castles in the air") scorned by the adult world, but now taken up with all the deadly earnestness of childhood—an attempt to do what only the innocent and childlike spirit would attempt, to find a "solid foundation" of reality for mankind's loftiest concepts and ambitions. It is such dangerous children as Solness and Hilde, with their naive faith in substantiating utopias, who create revolutions and insist on taking ideals seriously. Only a drastic regression to childhood, therefore, successfully could ignore all the considerations and objections that prevent the adult world from attempting to give a solid foundation to their castles in the air. When Solness and Hilde enthusiastically take up this term they are boldly challenging all the pejorative connotations the adult world puts on it; they justify idealism (which gives youth its poignant appeal) by enthusiastically embracing the most damaging term their enemies might use against them. The sublime childlikeness of Solness and Hilde's half-playful, half-serious language with its straining after the impossible has exactly the right mixture of the exasperating and the alarming sufficient to dispel all the worldly cynicism engendered in the reader of *Hedda Gabler*.

Solness takes leave of Hilde as the concept of the castle in the air has just tentatively been formulated, and at this moment Ragnar enters with the wreath which Hilde greets with "an outcry of joy." Rolf Fjelde has commented that the wreath is an ambiguous symbol, noting that Solness, more and more as the drama progresses, takes on the immemorial role of the sacred king whose fate it is to undergo a ritual death at the height of his powers on a marked day—here at the autumnal equinox—so that the energies of the tribe may find release and renewal, an impression that is strikingly reinforced when, in the last act the young king, Ragnar, brings to the old king, Solness, that ambiguous symbol of victory and death, the ribboned wreath.[40]

While Solness is offstage, leaving with the wreath, we hear two accounts of him that conflict with Hilde's idea of her hero. One is from Ragnar who relates to Hilde how Solness had taken possession of Kaja's mind, and when Hilde insists that this was only to keep Ragnar, the young man reflects that Solness has been *afraid* of him just as he is afraid of climbing the scaffolding of the tower which "no power on earth" (*ingen makt i verden*) would get him to perform as once he had performed at Lysanger. Hilde, "in a frenzy," cries out "I *will* see it! I *will* and I *must* see it!" On the plane of individual psychology Hilde's insistence is part of that alarming seriousness which, if it is to be hero-worship, insists on the object of its worship being a hero; as the action Hilde will wish or will into existence is a repetition of that Lysanger ascent that now has been re-created as something fabulous and wonderful, her frenzied determination is like the cry of the younger generation insisting its world be as wonderful, as fabulous, as the most marvelous accounts of the human spirit have claimed. Solness has responded to Hilde's demand that he deliver her such a "kingdom" by acknowledging the truth of her vision of the past and agreeing to act, now, like the hero of such a past, and Hilde will hear nothing against him that suggests her dream of him is greater than the reality.

Aline Solness, also, with her terror of Solness's being so "mad" as to attempt the ascent, endangers Hilde's vision of him. Aline leaves Hilde with the task of dissuading Solness; she herself is somewhat comically torn between duty and duty. She should stand by Solness and prevent him risking his life; at the same time she should welcome the ladies just now arriving. As she explains, exposing the absurdity of a life lived by the concept "duty," "When you have duties in so many directions, then—." Solness is seen approaching and, as previously in this act, Aline runs from a confrontation, almost emblematic of Duty fleeing from Joy-of-Life! Hilde is standing on the veranda as Solness approaches, and he ascends to her from the garden—an action that I think Ibsen intends as a recollection of their earlier vision of the master builder ascending to his princess on the tower: the veranda, at least sets Hilde above him, awaiting his approach, and his ascent to her will be an affirmation of their mutual vision.

Before this vision is decisively reaffirmed, Solness once again recollects the past, but this time its triumphant content will be asserted and the guilt and loss, in which he had been imprisoned until the arrival of Hilde, finally discarded. This second retrospection of Act III is a *redemption* of the past and the action that Ibsen creates, of the master builder ascending to his princess and recollecting the past in order finally to transcend it, drawing upon its positive, subversive content for the substance of a future action, is the consummation of all the tortured dialectic that preceded it.

Solness's ascent to the veranda occurs after he has eliminated one by one the various constricting elements of his consciousness. Old Brovik, Ragnar, Kaja, and Aline now have been discarded for a spiritual freedom and affirmation of which the tower climbing is the symbol. Now, it is only the master builder, ascending to share his vision with his "princess," and it is from this visionary freedom that he now surveys his past. For this reason, this last retrospection is a complete transformation of the past, is the most visionary in the play, and is presented as a confrontation between human and divine creativity. Hilde, earlier, had imagined standing on the tower's balcony and looking over the entire creativity of man—those who build churches and those who build homes. Solness now ascends to his princess and gives her just such a panoramic history of his past church and house building.

Aline's retrospection with Hilde had drawn upon the ethical, duty-conscious, and fatalistic attitude Hegel saw as typical of the pagan Hellenic mind. In the *Phenomenology* the overthrow of this phase of spirit made possible the subjective, Christian phase of spirit in self-estrangement and the elaborately complex cultural and psychological life it generated. From the destruction of Aline's old house issued the career of the master builder, and the whole character of Solness, as this retrospection will make clear, is one of Christian self-estrangement and self-division.

Innocently exclaiming that he was "afraid" Hilde's summons came from Aline, Solness now has to justify to Hilde, who seizes upon this word, his fear of climbing the scaffolding, and his explanation recollects Christian history. He is afraid of "retribution" from God and to explain this he recollects his whole life. He came from "a pious home" and believed building churches the noblest thing he could choose to do; so he built "poor country churches" feeling "He" would be pleased with his work because this creativity was used entirely for the honor and glory of God and not of man. Like Brand and the early Christians, Solness at this stage believed that man's life should be spent in adequate God worship and not in the creation of human happiness and honor. In order that Solness would more adequately build to the honor of

God He destroyed Solness's home and children, also ensuring that Solness became a complete master in his field.

The idea that the service of God requires complete abandonment of human happiness by self-renunciation and the renunciation of the world is opposite of the pagan view of life in which the best way of serving the divine purpose is the arduous seeking after *human* perfection: of beauty, knowledge, power, and the creation of "beautiful noble forms." The difficult and demanding god of Solness also had created a "troll" within him to revel/rampage (*romstere*) as it willed and had at the same time surrounded him, outside, with a world of good and bad devils: an eminently Christian soul in a Christian cosmos, self-divided and inhabiting a world itself divided into good and evil. But then, says Solness, he did the "impossible" by climbing "straight up to a great height" and directly challenging the Mighty One (*mektige*) by crying:

Hear me, thou mighty one! From this day on, I'll be a free creator—free in my own realm as you in yours.

And this was the "singing" that Hilde heard "in the air." Solness, after this rebellion, gave himself up to working on behalf of man, not of God, of building "homes for human beings," not temples that only a divinity can inhabit, but this whole new direction has exhausted itself in disillusion, for building homes, merely, is a worthless activity. But his career, he declares to Hilde, is only just beginning and he now will build the only things in which human beings can find *happiness* (*lykke*)—castles in the air.

In this extraordinary retrospection, delivered as a kind of *apologia pro vita sua* just before he rouses himself for his supreme reassertion of his spirit, Solness covers his entire *triumphant* life span, beginning with the boy emerging from the pious home and ending with the affirmation of the Lysanger rebellion; the themes of loss and guilt now are totally discarded from the past and we are impressed with the image of a tremendous creativity, chafing under the restrictions of building mere houses, yet having broken with the world view that once built soaring churches. It is, in essence, the condition of the modern thinker, especially of the nineteenth-century one who, though breaking with the old sustaining ideology of Christianity, discovered the bourgeois materialist ideology to be an intolerable confinement. The resolve to build "castles in the air," in which alone, says Solness, man can be happy, patently implies that only the highest and most ambitious realms of thought or imagination, too ambitious to be realized as mere material edifices (i.e., systems), can satisfy man's aspirations to godhead. Both the old robbers' *castle* (the emperor nature?) and the great towered churches (the Galilean?), though more adequate than the homes for happy families, were, as dwellings for the *whole* human spirit, inadequate; but the sky castle with the tower combines emperor and Galilean, pagan and Christian, body and spirit. The fairy-tale visionary quality of the towered castle is perfectly right for the visionary quality of Ibsen's own concept of "the third empire" which must remain a distant goal ecstatically and poetically affirmed and striven for, but not presented as an actual, tangible life style. Nor is this a weakness of Ibsen's concept, for it is only the impossible goals that are worth striving for, goals like truth and freedom that never will be absolutely won, and, in fact, would prove unbearable if they were! Tangible, possible goals, on the other hand, are not the province of the poet, but of the social reformer who is less interested in the generation of new ideas (the growth of consciousness) than in the just government of the *status quo*:[41] the just distribution of its material resources, and the extension of its rights and duties.

In this last dialogue with Hilde, which almost is a musical duet, regression to childhood and archetypal recollection have recovered and reinstated man's rebellion against an imprisoning and constricting universe or world order, which the great myths of rebellion—Babel, Prometheus, Faust—expressed. Solness has resurrected the essential in his past and has discarded the spiritually constricting—the deadly nostalgia for the past, of Aline, and Solness's own guilty and jealous relationship to the past and present shown in his dealings with Aline, the Broviks, and Kaja Fosli. The past now stands as a single, simple challenging act of rebellion and triumph which Hilde, in order to be convinced of her master builder's resurrection, wants to see repeated. All the tortuous progress of the play, its continual reversions back into the past (like the flashbacks of modern films), its obscure texture of fires, winter landscapes, trolls, cracks in chimneys, nine dolls, towers, twins, vikings, sun, light, autumn, etc., etc., creating just that surrounding medium of opacity and obscurity which the workings of human history have wrapped around consciousness, was like the heavy bank of cloud through which the sun figure, Solness, now emerges in splendid light and freedom. Hilde has freed him from his mind-forged manacles as Hercules struck the chains from the bound Prometheus and now their ecstatic duet explicitly challenges God and once more claims the realm of the superhuman for human creativity:

HILDE. . . . Just once more, master builder! Do the impossible again!
SOLNESS. (*looking deep into her eyes*) If I did try it, Hilde, I'd stand up there and talk to Him the same as before.

HILDE. (*with mounting excitement*) What would you say to him?

SOLNESS. I'd say to him: hear me, almighty lord, you must now judge me as you think fit. But from now on I intend to build only what is most beautiful in the world.

HILDE. (*ecstatic*) Yes—yes—yes!

SOLNESS. —build it together with a princess that I love—

HILDE. Yes, tell him that! Tell him that!

SOLNESS. Yes. And then I'll say to him: Now I'm going down to throw my arms around her and kiss her—

HILDE. —many times! Say that!

SOLNESS. —many many times, I'll say . . .

In this duet Solness and Hilde assert as a goal for the future what had been claimed half-fabulously, for the past, the semimythic conception thus taking on the reality of a serious project. The childlikeness of the conception—the climbing of a tower, the triumphant descent, the kissing of a "princess," the gift to her of a sky palace—is all the more emphasized at the end of the duet when Hilde claps her hands together like a little girl exclaiming, "Oh, master builder, my beautiful, beautiful castle. Our sky castle!" This first play of the last group has returned to the very origins of consciousness, the infant (the twins and Hilde in her "cradle"), and the child has purified that consciousness from the accumulated sicknesses of adulthood and has allowed it combatively and buoyantly to take on the future:[42] a future that will more somberly be explored in the plays that follow, for if Solness and Hilde resurrect the spirit "before the Fall" *Little Eyolf* presents us with a profoundly post-lapsarian world.

The Lysanger action will be repeated in other details. There will be music on the ground, again, this time from "the band of the builders' union," a fine conscientious banality on Ibsen's part, for *this* master builder insists upon the most solid foundation of reality even for his most poetic flights.

The final action, of Solness's ascent of the tower watched by the terrified Aline, the puzzled doctor, the cynical young Ragnar, the enthusiastic ladies, and the ecstatic Hilde is scored for every level of emotional response and, with the accumulated memories that we now bring to this action, makes up one of the richest of Ibsen's *ensembles*. The dramatic method, here, is at its most audacious, deliberately courting disaster, and it *can* be questioned, I think, whether Ibsen successfully escapes the danger of a too great incongruity between the rich *meanings* now inhering in the stage situation and the *means* by which they are conveyed. Solness, climbing the house tower, generates what must strike us as excessive emotions and wonder from the onstage spectators. They react as if they are watching a marvel; and when

Ragnar tells us that all the young architectural students have come expressly to watch and crow over Solness's inability to climb his own tower, we find it hard to credit such malice in that profession, or, given the malice, that it could be satisfied merely by evidence of vertigo in their oppressor. In his attempt to give to Solness's ascent the largest possible meaning and greatest intensity of emotion at the same time, Ibsen has been forced into implausibility—an implausibility, however, due to the rigorous honesty of his method. This implausibility becomes most evident when the key word "impossible" powerfully reappears. We are reminded, by the word, of such an epic rebellion as the Tower of Babel, but also we are uncomfortably reminded that there is nothing wondrously impossible about climbing a practical tower even if the climber suffers from a fear of heights:

HILDE. All these ten years I've seen him like this. How strong he stands! Terribly thrilling, after all. Look at him! Now he's hanging the wreath on the vane!

RAGNAR. I feel that I'm seeing something here that's—that's impossible.

HILDE. Yes, it's the impossible, now, that he's doing. (*With the inscrutable look in her eyes*) Do you see anyone up there with him?

RAGNAR. There's nobody else.

HILDE. Yes, there's someone he's struggling with.

RAGNAR. You're mistaken.

HILDE. You don't hear singing in the air, either . . . ? I hear the singing—a tremendous music. (*Crying out in wild exultation*) Look, look! he's waved his hat! He's waving to us down here! Oh, wave, wave back up to him again—because now, now it is fulfilled! (*Snatches the white shawl from the doctor, waves it and calls out*) Hurray for master builder Solness!

It is impossible not to admire the integrity with which Ibsen insists on establishing even his most visionary intentions upon a very firmly rendered reality, setting up an urgent dialectical interplay between the realm of spirit and the realm of material reality; but so intense is this dialectical interplay, at this moment, that one wonders if the two terms, the visionary and the everyday, do not defeat each other in their struggle.[43] If they do, it is an honorable defeat, more so than the less problematic successes of Expressionist mysticism on the one hand, or of spiritually unillumined realism on the other. Nevertheless, even the audience's uneasiness at the strain imposed here upon the realistic method helps to underscore the play's argument which *is* that of the difficult, dangerous, and perhaps even "impossible" transcendence of given reality which continually must be undertaken by the human spirit.

The biblical phrase "For now, it is fulfilled" is the *consummatum est* motif which Inga-Stina Ewbank has shown as a *leitmotiv* in Ibsen's writing occurring when the human spirit is lured or tempted towards the superhuman;[44] but we have seen how the whole texture of the play brings to this phrase more than merely a somewhat solemn echo of the supreme *moment* in Christian history. Implied in the phrase is an eternally repeated human action of transcendence, conveyed in the myths, legends, and histories of culture after culture up to the present so that, however much the outward forms of this action may have changed as, for instance, in the bourgeois industrial culture of Ibsen's own age, the mythic expressions of the actions remain true to human experience.

Had Solness succeeded in descending the tower after challenging "the mighty one," he and Hilde would, presumably, have gone "beyond good and evil" to a life and a creativity consonant with the idea of the "third empire." To postulate such a conclusion, however, is to see how the play *only* could end with Solness's death, for such a third empire hardly can be delivered onstage by the dramatist. In the form of the visionary towered castle it can be a fruitful lure and temptation to the human spirit, a metaphor for the reaching after the superhuman, like W. B. Yeats's fabulous Byzantium or Nietzsche's Overman. The whole action of the play has been Solness's gradual preparation to live up to this ideal—to discard that from the past that would be a barrier, and to recover that from the past that can serve as an example and precedent—and if the result is an action that, in its final moments, reveals an uncomfortable strain between the worlds of everyday and of symbolic reality, that, in itself, gives the play, and Ibsen's whole method, its distinction.

Aline "falls" at the same time as Solness (who is the *third* to fall from his tower) and this is, *visually*, her "death" also. The crowd registers horror, but the play ends, nevertheless, on a note of "hushed, dazed triumph" as Hilde exclaims:

But he went straight to the top. And I heard harps in the air. (*Swings the shawl up overhead and cries with wild emotion*) My, my master builder.

The crowd's cry of horror and Hilde's cry of triumph, Hilde's last words that force our attention from the broken defeated *body* on the ground to the triumphant *spirit* at the top of the tower, wrench our attention violently between the ideas of defeat and victory, flesh and spirit, maintaining a rich ambiguity, and preventing us from seeing Solness's fall merely as a negative defeat. Solness, at the cost of his body's crucifixion, has affirmed the spirit's willingness to take on the great gesture, to summon up all that is most alarming and challenging (and vital) in its past and with this childlike but sublime and subversive spiritual content to attempt "the impossible" against the conditions of the present. As far back as *Peer Gynt* Ibsen had shown that to be *sub*-human, to be a "troll," was to be content with the motto "To thyself, be sufficient," whereas to be *human* was to adopt the motto "To thyself be true." Truth to the highest human identity means striving beyond sufficiency to one's present, *given* identity; and it is precisely the unreachable, impossible goals that strain humanity to this truth. The frustrated attempt to gain an impossible third empire of spirit does, nevertheless, affirm the potent existence of such a goal, and the last words of the play, Hilde's cry, "*My, my master builder*," imply that Solness's final, heroic identity has been taken over, absorbed by the younger generation, i.e., by the future. Like the guilty elders of Shakespeare's last plays the older figures in Ibsen's last four plays wrestle with and overcome these ghosts and devils from the past and thus, hopefully, hand onto the younger generation a future purged and purified of the old dialectic of evil and guilt; but in addition to this, Solness hands on an example of spiritual heroism.

The foregoing analysis has discussed *The Master Builder* in a context of meanings not usually associated with Ibsen's realistic method, meanings that have been assumed to belong only to that embarrassing oddity, *Emperor and Galilean*, whose centrality to the author's life work, insisted upon by Ibsen, has been so confidently discounted. Ibsen's dramatic method, we are insisting, involves a mediation between the world of everyday appearances—the subject of most contemporary realism—and the world of universals which include mytho-historical, religious, and philosophical dimensions of reality.

The dimensions of reality implicated in the structure and texture of *The Master Builder* involve every area of reality. On the physical, pre-biological level is the rhythm of the sun's rising and setting, the rhythm of eternally repeated death and resurrection in which the sun must go down in evening to rise in the morning, the year's decline in autumn to revive in spring. On the biological level is the life of the organism, the conflict of the generations, where the old must give way to the younger, where the death of the individual is the condition of life for the group—a situation against which the highly developed human consciousness, like Solness, vainly protests. The recovery of such a rhythm in the form of modern realism is one of Ibsen's most significant achievements in this play (and those that follow), for it returns to the affirmative nature of tragedy in which we are brought to recognize and acknowledge a cosmic Necessity as disconcerting but as implacable as that of the Oedipus plays.

Associated with the cosmic and biological rhythms of the play is its archetypal, mythopoeic story in which we recognize the "wasteland" theme of great energies atrophied, frustrated, and sick which are rescued, in a reversal of the Sleeping Beauty fable, by the princess who enters Solness's enchanted household and dispels its complex, accumulated spells and so restores fertility to the tribe. (The theme of childlessness, of conflict with "the younger generation" and of the imprisonment of the young lovers, Ragnar and Kaja.) Generated from such an archetypal theme are myths of sacrifice, loss, the suffering god, and great legendary triumphs on behalf of man as in the myths of Prometheus, Odin, the Tower of Babel, and Christ.

Moving beyond the mythopoeic realm into the conscious creations of literature we are reminded of such great expiatory reconciliations with the past as *Oedipus at Colonus*, *Philoctetes*, Shakespeare's last plays, or Goethe's *Faust*. In the clash of the generations is implied, I think, the clash of world orders, where older forms of human consciousness or spirit must give way, splendidly, to the new, just as Ibsen himself believed the age in which he lived marked the closure of a whole world order and that in its place "something new is in the process of being born."

These huge layers of reality beneath the surface realism of the play, physical, biological, archetypal, mythopoeic, historical, esthetic, religious, and philosophical, all express themselves through a story recognizably of Ibsen's own time in which a modern bourgeois hero is brought to face the fact that his "time is up" and that he either must deliver the fabulous kingdom of "castles in the air" or die splendidly. We are shown that even in the reduced world of modern bourgeois culture the mind still can conceive castles in the air, although the body—and maybe the will—is weak. Our comfortable contemporary culture, therefore, is brought, abruptly, face to face with precisely the type of heroic and idealistic challenge it was designed to evade, and it is this which makes the realism of *The Master Builder* so discomforting, even embarrassing, to the Worldly Wisemen of this culture who, like Judge Brack, insist that people do not do such things. The legendary and fabulous, the heroic and impractical terms of Solness's and Hilde's dialogues, refusing thoroughly to face or even keep to "the facts," in fact to continually and absurdly attempt to transcend "the facts" in order to reach to more adequate areas of spiritual reality, are bound to irritate those for whom the given facts make up the only viable system of reality.

Does, then *The Master Builder* hold the mirror up to Nature? Is Ibsen actually saying that the bizarre history of the Solness household is typical of his age? Odd though it seems, the answer is yes. (An atypical, eccentric story would have no more interest for us than a freak show.) The play is an investigation into human consciousness: its past, its present, its possible future. It searches out the darker and more savage areas of consciousness and its energies and frustrations, recorded in myth, legend, literature, and history, energies and frustrations that often are too conveniently disregarded by the present; and it reintegrates these into an image of the reality—even the psychopathology—of everyday life so that we are startled to discover that behind the local identity of a contemporary architect is a long evolutionary line leading back to the very origins—and beyond—of consciousness. The Solness household appears so eccentric, therefore, precisely because it has become, untypically, the vehicle of universal human consciousness in the same way that the archetypal family histories of Greek tragedy would seem eccentric as accounts of particular families. *The Master Builder*, therefore, like the other plays in the Cycle, is not "fictional" in the way of much nineteenth-century fiction, in which the author invents a story which attempts to *simulate* the realities of everyday life; it is fictional in the great tradition of Western literature in which details are created to conform to a thoroughly *objective analysis* of a very complex reality. An art form in which invention is subordinated to analysis, in which all the details of the fiction stand in strict relation to a distinct account of the nature of reality (in which category we also must put most Greek tragedy, *The Divine Comedy, The Faerie Queene, Paradise Lost, Pilgrim's Progress, Faust, Ulysses, Finnegans Wake*, the plays of T. S. Eliot, and the work of Samuel Beckett), obviously does not permit us the pleasures of subjective musings on the nature of the fictions and their "characters"; instead we have to construct an interpretative method which will better be able to *locate* Ibsen's meanings and intentions within a structure of reality which we plausibly can claim Ibsen conceived.

This is not the same thing as making everything in Ibsen remind one of something else, and it is for this reason that we cannot have recourse to Jungian, Freudian, or Marxian structures of reality. Our method must be to return to Ibsen's own age and to understand the nature of its thinking, to pay attention to Ibsen's own pronouncements and, above all, to continue to return to the plays themselves both individually and as a Cycle and to better inhabit Ibsen's world, understand its logic. Nothing could be more fallacious than the belief that, armed only with twentieth-century, post-Freudian (or Marxian) common sense—in other words, with the limitations of our own particular world view—we are at all equipped to understand Ibsen's art. We must inhabit a larger universe, psychologically, morally, historically, and esthetically. The foregoing analysis of *The Master Builder* is an attempt to suggest the nature of the spiritual universe Ibsen inhabited and which he made the subject of his art; and though some readers may feel I have gone "too far," I am, on the contrary, conscious of having explored only a fragment of its total, audacious intention. *The Master Builder* presents us with expanding circumferences of meaning and an adequate interpretation of the play would have to encompass them all, from an old poet's meeting with a young girl one summer at Gossenssass, to the most far-reaching speculations on the destiny of the world soul, dreaming on things to come.

Epilogue

We have described Ibsen's Cycle of realistic plays as a single, massive artistic conception, perhaps the greatest single achievement of the nineteenth-century tradition of apocalyptic artists and thinkers. Everything we know of Ibsen's own life accords with this idea. A lifetime of poverty, exile, obloquy, and loneliness hardly is the prerequisite for the modest exercises in conventional or unconventional bourgeois moralism so often attributed to his realistic art. The insistence that Ibsen's concerns are miniscule, his learning irrelevant, his intellectual comprehension narrow and shallow, and his imagination timid has served the cause of those who would not be attracted to the intellectual and esthetic disciplines required to interpret a more ambitious poet. Ibsen still is one of the few really major artists for whom very modest critical and intellectual attainments are considered sufficient for adequate interpretation. We hope that we have demonstrated that it is possible to interpret Ibsen both in the widest-ranging and yet most closely accurate terms: that close and deep analysis of his marvelous dramatic structures reveals an art of profound and sublime meditation upon life. It is true that we have very categorically specified what we feel to be the total intention of the realistic Cycle, but we believe that this demonstrably increases rather than diminishes the idea of the full range and complexity of his art.

We have paid a great deal of attention to the imaginative and intellectual implications of Ibsen's art, but we have all the time attempted to keep in mind that we are discussing dramatic art works, organized as plays and only completed as performances in a theater. Drama always has been an ambiguous art form and the right of individual plays to qualify as drama is contested by those who, on the one side, might deny its *literary* adequacy as a work of art and those who, on the other, may contest its theatrical viability. It is not difficult to claim the widest range of implications for a realistic novel such as *The Magic Mountain* or *Ulysses;* it is far more difficult to insist that at least as wide a range of implications inhere within the realistic struc-

312

ture and texture of Ibsen's Cycle, for the dramatist is not permitted the devices the novelist enjoys whereby he can obtrude his intentions in his work. Furthermore, the drama must ensure that its viability with the public be established on a first night before a relatively uninformed audience that does not enjoy the novel-reader's privilege of being able slowly to meditate upon the text before him. Ibsen's plays triumphantly demonstrated their capacity to excite, agitate, and enthrall first-night audiences, so that the interpreter now can proceed beyond this dimension of their existence to those dimensions which place the Cycle with major works of literature. The director who would present an Ibsen play today still must rediscover that quality of immediate urgency that will make the play a compelling experience for a modern audience; but in an age in which the particular conventions of Ibsen's art have been superseded he will want to know what in that art is of sufficiently enduring importance to warrant revival—in other words, he will want to understand the universal vision which that art is serving. The idea of Ibsen's art that I have set out, of the recovery of archetypal identities, of the dialectical subversion of repressive and inadequate reality for a more essential reality, and of a vision of everyday reality as complexly textured with the Past, is, I believe, a compelling one, and one that a modern director can work with in order to make the experience of watching an Ibsen play a form of revelation.

Theatrical effectiveness and immediately communicable meaning by means of the melodramatic devices of the nineteenth-century theater is what *Ghosts* has in common with *The Second Mrs. Tanqueray.* Ibsen, however, obstinately remains with us in spite of still fashionable denigrations of his art, whereas Arthur Wing Pinero is a mere curiosity of dramatic history, and this suggests that the most essential thing for us to get clear is in what consists the immense *difference* between the two dramatists. *The Second Mrs. Tanqueray* quite obviously is a meretriciously sensationalist work, whereas *Ghosts,* for all its awkwardness, is an authentic masterpiece, one of the major works of world drama which our theater will be all the poorer for not reviving. The difference between Ibsen's and Pinero's plays lies in the nature of the Idea each embodies *and* the adequacy of the human and esthetic embodiment, and any attempt adequately to perform *Ghosts* must come to see that, for all the superficial similarity of theatric method, the means of production that are suitable to *The Second Mrs. Tanqueray* are unsuitable to *Ghosts.* Simply because of its greater achievement, *Ghosts* presents the theater with more of a problem than does Pinero's play.

Since the demise of Greek tragedy the theater of the Western world
has never been able to establish a theatrical occasion that in itself
makes the greatness of the play indistinguishable from the greatness of
its conventional form (Lionel Abel has coined the word "metatheatre"
for this situation) and this has led often to the odd fact that many a
dramatic masterpiece has an embarrassingly similar form, content, and
method to a patently inferior and meretricious work. *Hamlet* has a
great deal in common with *The Spanish Tragedy, Don Carlos* with
the worst Sturm and Drang bombast. The purpose of Ibsen's realistic
plays might be the awakening of us dead to spiritual truth and freedom,
but their form and method is embarrassingly similar to the conventional
plays of moral and psychological sensationalism of his—and our—day.
Among contemporary dramatists Samuel Beckett most clearly has
recognized this dilemma by deliberately incorporating the most banal
of theatrical conventions—that of the music-hall comedian—into his
philosophical drama. It is all the more important for the interpreter of
Ibsen, therefore, while conceding the extent to which Ibsen's dramatic
method resembles that of the boulevard theater of his times, to be
able to demonstrate the immense disparity in achievement between
them. Ibsen has raised his art to the point where his achievement in
the drama arrives at the same level of distinction and adequacy as the
finest achievements in literature, by giving significant form to significant
content. Henry Arthur Jones and Arthur Wing Pinero are as capable as
Ibsen of pulling off the exciting theatrical effects of nineteenth-century
theater—they probably pull off more, in fact; but they are incapable of
pulling them off to sufficiently distinguished purpose, whereas Ibsen's
great purpose can make us overlook that he is pulling off theatrical
effects at all.

Dramatic art without intellectual content probably is more deadly
than academic art (closet drama) without theatrical life, for at least
the latter is the failure of good or misconceived intentions—greatly
preferable to the success of bad intentions. It is recorded that one
Athenian dramatist, on meeting a rival who won the dramatic prize
by base means, asked him, "Tell me, when you beat me, do you blush?"
The modern theatrical profession is far too brazen to blush—it
probably does not realize there is anything to blush about—and one only
keeps patience with the theater, frankly, for the rare epiphanies that
occur and raise it from a bawdyhouse to a temple of the Holy Ghost:
the moment when one sees an Idea take on palpable esthetic reality,
as in an attempted adequate production of *Oedipus the King, The
Tempest,* or *Rosmersholm.* It is these epiphanies that make one enjoy
all the frank chicaneries of this illusionist art.

Ibsen was more than a man of the theater, yet it is just as true to say that his vision could be embodied only in the theater. It is remarkable to what an extent he became, so early, exclusively a poet of the theater at a time when the theater in Europe did not engage the attention of major European writers to an exclusive degree. Both Chekhov and Strindberg wrote major non-theatrical works, as did Ibsen's fellow countryman, Bjørnson. I think this is an important point, for it suggests that Ibsen had an idea of the theater that he spent a lifetime in realizing, and that he made his theatrical art totally adequate to his vision of life. That vision, we have seen, was profoundly historicist, and was bound up with a messianic purpose—not untypical of his age—of contributing to a revolution within the spirit of mankind. Henry James remarked that Ibsen's characters are too concerned with learning to live to be able to *play* with life, and though this overstates the case—for there is "play" in the esthetic beauty of his structures— it does indicate the presence, in Ibsen's art, of a massive act of the Will, an element present, also, in his formidable life of isolation and commitment. This total subordination of himself to his art makes him the least approachable of the nineteenth-century giants; he loses himself in his art as Hegel insisted the philosopher must lose himself in the Concept. The key to Ibsen's conception of himself as the dramatist of his age lies, I think, in the idea of Alienation.

The problem of History and the problem of Alienation both occur at the same time in European culture; it is therefore no accident that the philosopher of History, Hegel, also is the philosopher of Alienation. In post-Revolutionary Europe, in the age of Romanticism, human consciousness confronts a world that is the negation of a full and free development of the consciousness, and must "negate the negation" in order to rediscover itself in the world. The unfree and repressive Present that denies the development of a full humanity is a historically determined one and can be overcome only by an understanding of History in the fullest sense. Archetypal memory becomes a means both of understanding the conditions that have produced alienation, and of recovering lost human identity by restoring to humanity dimensions of spirit not immediately discoverable within the structure of the Present. In Ibsen's drama Memory is liberating inasmuch as it makes the individual adequate to his fate. It does not insure the individual against tragedy—quite the reverse—but the action of the individual collecting—or recollecting—himself before his fate, whether it is the painful fate of a Mrs. Alving, or the unnervingly enigmatic fate of master builder Solness, is a positive and affirmative gesture for all its tragic outcome.

Neither Hegel nor Ibsen sees the overcoming of alienation as the means by which to realize a utopia free from tragedy. Rather, it raises the consciousness of individuals so that, paradoxically, they are more vulnerable to genuinely tragic experience. Charles Rosen, in a review of M. H. Abrams's *Natural Supernaturalism: Tradition and Revolution in Romantic Literature,* notes the "Romantic metaphors of alienation of man from nature, of man from himself." He continues:

The marriage of nature to the mind of man is a metaphor for the overcoming of this inner and outer division. The most persistent metaphors Abrams finds is that of the "circuitous journey," the vision of a regained paradise, a return through alienation to an original state of "organic" unity, now made transcendent by incorporating and resolving the contradictory forces of the journey itself. The circle is therefore generally a spiral, a return to the same point on a higher level. As the mature mind, in Wordsworth, returns to the child's unconscious acceptance of the world, now transformed by experience, so Hegel's spirit in reaching absolute consciousness attains the static condition, the complete repose of pure undifferentiated, unalienated being.[1]

The scale of the alienation—the entire structure of subjective and objective reality—means that the circuitous journey for the consciousness awakened to a realization of its condition will be long and arduous before it can be overcome and this, I believe, accounts for the complexity and scale of Ibsen's Cycle. But because consciousness—or Spirit—continuously is working upon and within this huge and minutely detailed structure of reality, so this structure continuously is undergoing "epiphanies" in which repressive reality is illuminated by recovered spiritual content. Such epiphanies occur in Wordsworth's *The Prelude* where the world of Nature becomes transfigured with spiritual meaning and where, elsewhere, the most humble characters, the Leech-gatherer, the Idiot Boy, the Sailor's Mother, become the unexpected vehicles of profound spiritual insight. More surprising and more consequential is the occurrence of these epiphanies in the seemingly despiritualized realities of Ibsen's Norway or James Joyce's Dublin. It is a profound Hegelian paradox that after the spiritual has been lost in its various modes as a vital function of a given human culture, it can be regained, in its totality, by the artist or thinker who rediscovers it everywhere in the present. The overcoming of alienation by the recovery of the total human spirit within the conditions of the Present is the redemption (or "awakening") of both the individual and the world.

Lionel Trilling describes the function of the epiphany in Wordsworth and Joyce in terms that apply equally to Ibsen, noting that

... the increasing concern with the actual, with the substance of life in all its ordinariness and lack of elevation, was not directed to practicality alone. It also made the ground of a new, or rediscovered, kind of spiritual experience. To emphasize the intractable material necessity of common life and what this implies of life's wonderlessness is to make all the more wonderful such moments of transcendence as may now and then occur. This, it will be recognized, is the basis of Joyce's conception of the "epiphany," literally a "showing forth." The assumption of the epiphany is that human existence is in largest part compounded of the dullness and triviality of its routine, devitalized or paralysed by habit and the weight of necessity, and that what is occasionally shown forth, although it is not divinity as the traditional Christian meaning of the word would propose, is nevertheless appropriate to the idea of divinity: it is what we call spirit. Often what is disclosed is spirit in its very negation, as it has been diminished and immobilized by daily life. But there are times when the sudden disclosure transfigures the dull and ordinary, suffusing it with significance.[2]

It would be worth considering to what extent this discovery of spirit within the "ordinary" and "trivial" is an attempt, in fact, to overcome the Christian dualism between sacral and secular and to re-create the numinous world of paganism: in other words, for man to overcome the Fall by *his own* imaginative and intellectual awakening. Some such audacious endeavor has been noted by commentators of Hegel (and of Goethe) and is thoroughly in accord with the most ambitious program of Romanticism. The sacral now is seen to be the human: Ibsen's world becomes numinous, reveals its universal (divine) powers only insofar as the *human* spirit extends itself into the objective world.

Ibsen's concept of the epiphany differs from that of Joyce, I think, in one important respect. It has been observed that the Romantic movement was the culmination of the Protestant spirit: that many Romantic and Revolutionary ideas of the later eighteenth and the nineteenth centuries took up again tendencies within the seventeenth-century Protestant movement. (Wordsworth's affinity with Henry Vaughan is well known to students of English literature.) Ibsen is, I believe, the great dramatist of the Protestant spirit as Shakespeare is of the Catholic. (Of course, in both cases, this is a matter of spiritual affinity, not of doctrinal allegiance.) The major difference between the two spiritual persuasions is of that between, on the one hand, an emphasis upon the "objective" world whose sacral character is revealed through Order, ceremony, ritual, tradition, through "show" (the Catholic) and, on the other, an emphasis upon the inward, the authentic, the individual, where the sacral depends upon the awakened subjectivity, and which will emphasize the Will, and the beneficent restlessness of the unhappy consciousness struggling for authenticity and freedom. It probably is no accident that James Joyce, whose imagination remained Catholic, although he greatly admired Ibsen, did not conceive of life in terms of dramatic and dialectical confrontation, but preferred the form of the novel, in which his imagination could explore the *given* structure of reality and all its spiritual hierarchies. The Protestant dramatist (Samuel Beckett is another example) will move away from the elaborate, the outward, the rhetorical to a concern with inward processes of consciousness whose deepest and most significant moments might well be a half-finished sentence, an exclamation, or a "pause" in which the consciousness is reflecting upon itself. Such drama is much less "quotable" than, say, Shakespearean drama so that it is difficult for the interpreter of Ibsen to demonstrate that his dramatic universe is as deep and as extensive as Shakespeare's.

It is the easiest thing in the world for denigrators of Ibsen to take a speech from, for example, *Macbeth*, set it beside a speech in, say, *Rosmersholm,* and show that Ibsen's language totally lacks the rich complexity of Shakespeare's. This demonstration would be false, however, for, in Ibsen's realism, language is not serving the same function as in Shakespeare, and one could equally as unfairly take a sequence of action in *Rosmersholm*, point out the subtle and complex modifications of consciousness in Rosmer, Rebekka, and Kroll, and ask, rhetorically, where, in all Shakespeare, is to be found such complex Jamesian art. The poetry of the Protestant consciousness distrusts verbal adornment and rhetoric and the delight in verbal playfulness of a Shakespeare or James Joyce; instead, it searches for authenticity of expression and gesture, and it is here that Realism itself comes into its own. Realism becomes a tremendously difficult *esthetic* discipline, an esthetic of authenticity, particularly when, as in Ibsen and Samuel Beckett, it is wedded to an obsession with Form. Both the concern with formal beauty and purity, and the concern with authenticity of expression and gesture, will lead, also, to an emphasis upon economy of expression—an emphasis taken to its extreme in the later works of Beckett.

The obsession with Form and the obsession with authenticity sharpen the artist's eye for the inauthentic, and in Ibsen there is, in contrast to his figures who are struggling towards truth and freedom, a vivid gallery of inauthentic types and of false and inauthentic actions and speeches. This requires from the reader or viewer of Ibsen's plays a great degree of sophistication in detecting the plausible-seeming deceptions of the spirit. It leads to an art of Irony, in which the artist and his audience share a sense of the gross disparity between being and appearance, spiritual expression and the actual truth. Irony is almost impossible without a concern for Form, so that we find the ironist, from Sophocles to Samuel Beckett, passionately concerned with Form which is, as it were, a spiritual elegance, the artist's reproach to an everyday reality so indifferent to the disparity between being and appearance.

Form might be called the Logic of Art and this again would suggest an affinity with Protestantism (Luther admired Occam) which was impatient with the more easygoing Catholic acceptance of contradictions within its system. By imposing upon life experience a logic of Form that life is indifferent to, the artist makes it acceptable to the discriminating spirit. The great works of ironic art, *Oedipus the King*, Jane Austen's *Emma*, Ibsen's plays, the finest novels of Joseph Conrad, and the plays of Samuel Beckett, contrast, by their elegant frugality, with the richly expansive and life-celebratory art of, e.g., Chaucer, Rabelais, Shakespeare, and James Joyce. There is, for instance, very little irony in Shakespeare, for Shakespeare is too naively immersed in his comic or tragic situations to impose upon them the perspectives of strict Form. Shakespeare's Form, it has been said again and again, is "organic," working outward from within. The Greek contentment with the very rigid disciplines of three actors, a chorus, and the unchanging Form of Tragedy, delighting in the great difficulty of making these frugal terms contain everything, is totally alien to the Elizabethan who changes his scenes, adds and drops characters at will, often forgets quite important details and so allows contradictions, allowing himself to be dictated entirely to by the needs of the situation he is dramatizing. In ironic art the spectator must all the time be aware of the formal nature of the work, for it is this form that permits ironic detachment as well as implication in the events. In the supreme works of ironic art this does not result in a cold remoteness from the events but, on the contrary, a painfully heightened awareness of their import.

It is his ironic sense of form that gives to Ibsen's art its great complexity, its capacity to include the greatest implications by means of his frugal terms. The ironic vision is, basically, a fatalist one, and one realizes that in Greek tragedy and in all formal drama, the form of the play is its "fate," for its end is formally determined from the beginning. The passionately suffering actors "realize" the esthetically perfect Idea of the play. The deep paradox of formal drama, that its intellectually perfect Idea is realized by passionately suffering individuals, is also the paradox of Hegel's philosophy, which sees the entire history of the world as an Idea being realized by millions of passionately suffering individuals, a Greek tragedy on a cosmic scale. This is the only bearable form of fatalism: fate as esthetically and logically realized Form, applicable only so long as we are aware of the artistic structure. We can *enjoy* the suffering of Oedipus because we take pleasure in the ironic conjunction of formal perfection and chaotic reality: of blindly willed and arbitrary actions building up a logically inevitable fate. We permit the logical fatalism of this play, or of *Rosmersholm*, because we are pleased to see chaotically tragic experience being responsive to the decorum of formal intelligence. It overcomes the negation of human consciousness that the world continually is threatening, for the developed human consciousness, from mythic to scientific thought, is the imposition of Form upon experience.

This conjunction of concern with Form, with Irony, and the Protestant spirit might at first seem unusual but I think it holds, for the creation of Form is an "inward" requirement of the spirit rather than a response to the given world. Bernard Shaw remarked that Shakespeare's genius was not universal for there was one area of life wholly closed to him, that area of inward exaltation that we find in Bunyan's *Pilgrim's Progress*. Shaw noted that Shakespeare never could have written, "And Fearful went over the river singing." Sophocles knew of this experience, for both his Antigone and his old Oedipus are responsive to this inner world and can lose the outer world by allegiance to this invisible value. This vision returns to drama first, I think, with Schiller, where Nature and History are being remolded by the poet to conform to his idealist radicalism. In two plays, *Brand* and *Peer Gynt*, Ibsen examines first the idealist imperative taken to a disastrous extreme, then the equally disastrous loss of this inner vision. The perfected form of a play is the outward manifestation of this inward exaltation, the firm means by which the most terrible experience can be contemplated and controlled.

The ironic *structure* of *Ghosts*, for example, is more important to its total meaning than the particular events dramatized within the structure. The structure is in itself an *action*. Mrs. Alving has tried to reconstruct reality and the identity of her husband, from her own one-sided vision, but, as she acts, so reality, and the identity of Alving, are being reconstructed inevitably and in opposition to her endeavor, revealing the true structure of reality which she, both consciously and unconsciously, has concealed. The Hellenic archetypes which the dialectic of the play discovers within the events of the Alving life history are as fictional as Helene's fiction of her husband; but these archetypes create a *truer* fiction, one that is more adequate to the universal realities behind the appearances. Mircea Eliade, in *Cosmos and History*, notes that the folk consciousness always re-creates personal experience in terms of archetypal and mythic experience, so that events even within the memory of a people might be totally transformed to accord with archetypal models, their *historical* reality being considered irrelevant. Thus the popular imagination returns phenomenal experience to traditional patterns and models, and much the same purpose seems to lie behind the tendency of many modern writers to return modern everyday experience to archetypal models. Much of the power of *Ghosts* derives from this emergence of universal or archetypal realities through the seemingly everyday facts; a form of *redemption* of reality is occurring, in which the accidental and arbitrary is revealed to be fated and inevitable—to reveal Form, in other words. The debate as to whether tragic fate can operate by means of so contingent (and curable) a device as syphilis is wholly irrelevant. It is not the capacity of syphilis to destroy that is the tragic circumstance, but the capacity of any set of modern circumstances to reveal, under analysis, the inescapable archetypal conditions of Greek tragedy. As with *Oedipus The King*, *Ghosts* is not a tragedy of painful but avoidable *actions*, but of painful and (to the highest spirit) unavoidable *knowledge*. Mrs. Alving is tragic because, like Oedipus, she stubbornly pushes forward to inevitable tragic insight, because she possesses, like Oedipus, the qualities of courage and of intellect that make her capable of tragic experience. And the Form of the play, like that of Sophocles' play, is a "syllogism" that is completed by Helene's questing intellect. To be strictly accurate, it is completed by the rising Sun which, on one hand, is pure indifferent materialism and cosmic mechanism, signifying the different relative positions of two planets; but which, on the other, is just as much pure Spirit, the law of *livsglede*—joy-of-*life*—which has been so intensely and painfully localized in the little drawing room but now is seen to be extended into the cosmos itself.

The endeavor behind *Ghosts* and the other plays in the Cycle is the very sane one of rejoining the individual and fragmented modern consciousness to more universal concepts of reality and of human identity. Even the concept of an Absolute Spirit as the completed realm of human consciousness and Reason, which drew upon Hegel so much ironic commentary, now seems far saner than the disastrously inadequate Absolutes that have agitated the modern world: materialist, economic, racial, national, political, or metaphysical, each a partial aspect of reality that sets up to be the Whole.

There is a great deal more initial excitement in trying to make a partial vision do service for the Whole; one thinks of Dostoevsky's morbidly intense art, but classic art is that which, in Matthew Arnold's phrase, "sees life steadily and sees it whole." From *Brand* onwards, Ibsen's concern is with the totality of human experience rather than with fervent adherence to any one part of it, and the complete Cycle is an astonishing achievement on the dramatist's part in entering with so much sympathy and dramatic urgency into dramas of the human spirit that would have to be explored and then embodied in art form. One can see why Ibsen declared that everything that he had written he had lived through *inwardly*, and that each new poem or play was the means for his own spiritual emancipation and purification, for each new play was as much an act of discovery and of unexpected recognition as of expression of personal past experience. It would be an act of fusing his consciousness with archetypal human consciousness, as well as rescuing this archetypal content from Oblivion by reestablishing it within the texture of the Present.

The Past confronts human identity with the greatest threat for it is in Time that identity is in danger of being utterly dissolved and annihilated in a mere succession of seconds or moments each one utterly beyond recall. Yet, paradoxically, it only is in Time that identity can be established, for if we have no extension in Time we have no identity whatsoever. Man grows, evolves, in Time from embryo to adult and his culture tells him that his larger identity as "Man" has evolved in pre-historical and historical time. This time sequence also creates the sequence of events which, when acknowledged, become one's "fate." Memory, the means by which one's identity is rescued from oblivion, also is the means by which one's fate is clarified as Form. Ibsen's mnemonic drama is a continuing process of salvaging identity, Form, from the fluid process of Time. Time does not simply surround and erode identity as in Chekhov: it also is a repository of forgotten or repressed identity which can (and indeed must) be fatefully rescued and acknowledged. There is thus a dialectical interplay between human consciousness and Time, an equally balanced combat, in Ibsen's drama, that we do not find in Chekhov's.

In fact I believe Ibsen's art best can be understood as the art of dramatic Time, in which human consciousness battles for authentic and freely functioning identity, employing subversive Memory to salvage the tabooed or forgotten past, to combat the alienated present, and to create authentic possibilities for the future. In the Cycle as a whole, this memory gradually expands from the immediate, the individual, and the social into the archetypal, filling the space of the cosmos with human consciousness. There also is in Ibsen, however, and in contrast to Hegel, a poignant sense of the possible impermanence of the whole endeavor: how it might, without vigilant action, be swallowed up in the "Gulfo Placido" of all-surrounding, non-human Time and Space, so that at the end of the Cycle, Rubek and Maia "hear the silence."

The terror of non-identity, of loss of human identity, is, I believe,

Ibsen's "heart of darkness." It is sounded fully in *Peer Gynt,* and in the Cycle itself the most terrible play, *Ghosts,* has, as its horrible climax, not physical death but *mental* death, the collapse of the *mind,* of mere animal survival and the loss of human, that is, dialectically struggling, consciousness. Suffering, struggle, conflict, all these are seen as the necessary and even healthy disquietude of the life of spirit; the most terrible condition is the loss of these for that condition of mental stasis or self-annihilation that actually is the goal of certain spiritual traditions.

This indicates how fully Ibsen assented to Hegel's concept of human identity as the Will's commitment to action and knowledge, and how far he was from the Schopenhauerean attitude which, while according Will so important a role in his philosophy, was hostile to its operations. It is the decisive operation of the Will, in Ibsen's dramas, which gives them their strong dynamism which, when joined to his fatalistic formalism, can seem melodramatic to modern audiences. Events are moved to such consequential effects, and end in such ironic inevitability, that we may protest this is not "true to life." The point is, of course, "true to *what* life?" The everyday life of most of us, it is true, is never raised to alarming and consequential coherence, where the trivial and inessential fall away as we move into a clearer and more demanding dialectic; but even today, the life of the modern rebel, or the individual brought to tragic awareness, or the individual who responds to a "'call" that transfigures the nature of his world, experiences that fateful acceleration of dramatic rhythm that we find in Ibsen's drama. It might be that the comparative lack of a more "contemplative" rhythm and vision is a defect in Ibsen's art; his realistic plays seem like *Antigone* without the chorus, as Chekhov's plays, by contrast, seem like the chorus without Antigone. This is to overstate both cases, though Francis Fergusson makes much the same point in his *An Idea of the Theatre,* but it does suggest that in content as well as form, modern drama, by its own honest reflection of the modern condition, has not been able to return to the integrated vision of Greek tragedy.

To understand Ibsen's dramatic method, and to see in what way it is not melodramatic, it will pay, I think, to see its origins in German Enlightenment drama, especially the drama of Schiller, whose shapely structures are dialectically animated by crises of intellectual perception, self-awareness, and dynamic spiritual growth. To see Schiller as attempting to revive Shakespearean drama for his own age is to misconceive his endeavor and to see his art as overstrained compared to Shakespeare's. But Schiller is dramatizing a wholly different idea of the human condition than the Elizabethan idea: one in which, as in much Romantic literature, man can remake himself in Time, can become an agent of historical forces, and transform himself and his world from a fallen to a free and creative condition. This idea obviously is located in the liberal idealism of Schiller's middle-class culture, struggling to evolve its own world of liberated human consciousness. Ibsen, at the end of this tradition, is the poet of a middle class that has had to learn to see itself no longer as the mere victim, but as the agent, of injustice. The noble bourgeois victims of Lessing's *Emilie Galotti* or Schiller's *Wilhelm Tell* were to become the betrayers of the revolutions of 1848 and the bloody suppressers of the Communards of 1871, while the ardent idealism of the early years of middle-class advance lost itself in the complacent materialism of the later nineteenth century. Edmund Wilson has pointed out that both Flaubert and Ibsen, such thoroughgoing and disenchanted realists, remained, at bottom, Romantics. Schiller and Ibsen are the two great dramatists of Romantic bourgeois idealism, at the beginning and the end of this movement. Both are dramatists of dynamic Time. Schiller confidently organizes human history into an affirmative dialectic animated by such great and semi-mythic archetypes as the Promethean Posa; the tragic Wotan-like Phillip; the blind incarnation of the death of the Spirit, the Grand Inquisitor; such figureheads of Passion and of Power, Mary and Elizabeth; and even the idea of Nature as dramatic character, in *Wilhelm Tell*.

It was Schiller's particular genius to be able to create archetypes, who have all the vivid immensity of mythic figures, out of the characters and events of history by investing them with ideological significance and setting them in stark dialectical conflict. This same dramatic method lies beneath the reduced realistic world of Ibsen's plays, though now handled with perhaps more self-knowledge, subtlety, and irony, if with less immediately compelling power. To the reader accustomed to the "epic" quality of Shakespearean drama with its contrapuntal method of parallel subplots, Schiller's dialectical dramas can seem melodramatic until one discovers their ideological base and their beautifully formal shapes. The dialectical drama that emerges with Schiller and continues through Kleist, Buechner, Hebbel, Ibsen, and Shaw, structures the world in terms of crises of ethical and philosophical perception, and these plays lose their power if they are reduced merely to psychological drama. They are plays that conceive human actors as vehicles of ideological forces; they concretize, in human and dramatic terms, as conflicts lived through and suffered, concepts that remain remote abstractions in more pragmatic realistic plays. For this reason, the characters do not *discuss* ideas so much as *embody* them—this is true even of Shaw at his best.

It requires the greatest tact in the interpreter or director to demonstrate in what way an Ibsen play concretizes, through passionate individual and subjective action, the finely controlled objective "argument." As both the human and the ideological issues are equally compelling, the right kind of production is problematical, but this is inevitable to any complex drama, and the problem is worth solving. The collapse of Osvald Alving, the death of Hedvig, or the death of Solness, are poignant "existential" experiences for the playgoer, but they also should be moments that clarify the nature of the reality the play is revealing.

It is his ultimate control over the deeply explored human and ideological realities he is presenting that gives Ibsen's art, in the realistic Cycle, its classic status. It makes Ibsen (the "Sphinx of the North") less accessible than the more sensational artists of universal or existential themes (one need only compare the puzzling difficulty of such a play as *The Master Builder* with the thematically similar but much more simple *The King Must Die* of Ionesco) but it assures him of that hard-won *distinction* that will continue to attract the more thoughtful and perceptive readers and playgoers as, in the early years of the Ibsen controversy in Europe, the best spirits *were* attracted to him. One should remember that Ibsen's most perceptive admirers were men such as Henry James, Bernard Shaw, James Joyce, Rainer Maria Rilke, Hugo von Hoffmansthal, Thomas Hardy, Thomas Mann, E. M. Forster, and so on, men who were not likely to be attracted merely by a trenchant social and psychological writer of excellent dramatic technique, but, rather, by a visionary writer whose art was seen as an exciting continuation of the highest tradition of European literature. We have insisted upon the Hegelian underpinning to the realistic Cycle because we feel that a recognition of this will help to confirm our appreciation of the great scale and complexity of its art, but this should be only the beginning, not the end, of our revaluation of that art. The Hegelian world view set up the tremendous difficulties which Ibsen forced his creativity to confront (for difficulty is what the best art is all about) but the structure of the *Phenomenology* is no more Ibsen's Cycle than the hurdles on a track are the race that has just been won. In the same way, *Oedipus the King* cannot be reduced to the mythic tradition it is transforming, nor can Shakespeare's plays be reduced to their sources.

The most recent Shakespeare interpretation, for example, is insisting that it is false to reduce Shakespeare's art to dramatized explications of an Elizabethan world view but this interpretation still would not wish to return to the innocent days when this world view was not recognized as relevant to Shakespeare's dramatic structures (in this sense, at least, Hegel's concept of the advance of knowledge is relevant). Similarly, the superb human, ideological, and formal content of Ibsen's art in the individual plays and in the whole Cycle has all the inexhausti-bility and continuously new relevance of the best art and will continue to give rise to new and exciting interpretation long after its Hegelian substance has been absorbed and "put in its place."

Ghosts

Hegel's analysis of the dialectical evolution of the Ethical World takes us through the emerging ethical laws of man vs. woman (*A Doll's House*) the living vs. the dead (*Ghosts*), and the individual versus the community in an action where two brothers contend for control of the community (*An Enemy of the People*). The account of the Ethical World draws its illustrations from the life of the Greek city-state, and the dialectical conflicts of this society (which, for Hegel, will be repeated in every ethical society) are best exemplified, for Hegel, by the actions of Greek drama.

Hegel's text is difficult going but is so provocative and so compressed that it might be as well to quote an excerpt from the section (pp. 466–92) that has especial relevance to *Ghosts*. The reader then will be able to judge for himself the extent to which Hegel's text calls to mind the argument of Ibsen's play. The important thing to bear in mind is that the parallels between Hegel's text and Ibsen's play, if sometimes they seem obscure or tenuous, are maintained consistently, *in sequence*, for the whole of Ibsen's account of Spirit and Ibsen's Cycle of twelve plays. It is the theme of this study, however, that Ibsen's relation to Hegel's text is all the time imaginative, independent, and often critical and that the correspondences often are ironic and even parodic.

Immediately preceding the passage quoted below, Hegel describes how, under the concept of *Duty* in the ethical society, the individual inevitably is forced into a one-sided ethical action which, from the *other*, violated side, becomes a crime. It is only through such crime, however, that the nature of the *whole* structure of the ethical society can emerge:

Ethical self-consciousness now comes to find in its deed the full explicit meaning of concrete real action as much when it followed divine law as when it followed human. The law manifest to it is, in the essential reality, bound up with its opposite; the essential reality is unity of both; but the deed has merely carried out one as against the other. But being bound up with this other in the inner reality, the fulfillment of the one calls forth the other, in the shape of something which, having been violated and now become hostile, demands revenge—an attitude which the deed has made it take up. In the case of action, only one phase of the decision is in general in evidence. The decision, however, is inherently something negative, which plants an "other" in opposition to it, something foreign to the decision, which is clear knowledge. Actual reality, therefore, keeps concealed within itself this other aspect alien to clear knowledge, and does not show itself to consciousness as it fully and truly is [an und für sich]. In the story of Oedipus the son does not see his own father in the person of the man who has insulted and whom he strikes to death, nor his mother in the queen whom he makes his wife. In this way a hidden power shunning the light of day waylays the ethical consciousness, a power which bursts forth only after the deed is done, and seizes the doer in the act. For the completed deed is the removal of the opposition between the knowing self and the reality over against it. The ethical consciousness cannot disclaim the crime and its guilt. The deed consists in setting in motion what was unmoved, and in bringing out what in the first instance lay shut up as a mere possibility, and thereby linking on the unconscious to the conscious, the non-existent to the existent. In this truth, therefore, the deed comes to the light;—it is something in which a conscious element is bound up with what is unconscious, what is peculiarly one's own with what is alien and external:— it is an essential reality divided in sunder, whose other aspect consciousness experiences and also finds to be its own aspect, but as a power violated by its own doing, and roused to hostility against it.

It may well be that the right, which kept itself in reserve, is not in its peculiar form present to the consciousness of the doer, but is merely implicit, present in the subjective inward guilt of the decision and the action. But the ethical consciousness is more complete, its guilt purer, if it knows beforehand the law and the power which it opposes, if it takes them to be sheer violence and wrong, to be a contingency in the ethical life, and, wittingly, like Antigone, commits the crime. The deed, when accomplished, transforms its point of view; the very performance of it eo ipso expresses that what is ethical has to be actual; for the realization of the purpose is the very purpose of acting. Acting expresses precisely the unity of reality and the substance; it expresses the fact that actuality is not an accident for the essential element, but that, in union with that element, it is given to no right which is not true right. On account of this actuality and on account of its deed ethical consciousness must acknowledge its opposite as its own actuality; it must acknowledge its guilt.

> Because of our sufferings we acknowledge we have erred.[1]

To acknowledge this is expressly to indicate that the severance between ethical purpose and actuality has been done away; it means the return to the ethical frame of mind which knows that nothing counts but right. Thereby, however, the agent surrenders his character and the reality of his self, and has utterly collapsed. His being lies in belonging to his ethical law, as his substance; in acknowledging the opposite law, however, he has ceased to find his substance in this law; and instead of reality this has become an unreality, a mere sentiment, a frame of mind. The substance no doubt appears as the "pathic" element in the individuality, and the individuality appears as the factor which animates the substance, and hence stands above it. But the substance is a "pathic" element which is at the same time his character; the ethical individuality is directly and inherently one with this its universal, exists in it alone, and is incapable of surviving the destruction which this ethical power suffers at the hands of its opposite.

Rosmersholm

In "The Struggle between Enlightenment and Superstition" which occupies pages 559–98 of *The Phenomenology of Mind* (if we include the related chapters on "'Enlightenment" and "The Truth of Enlightenment"), Hegel's analysis of spirit is concerned with the phase of consciousness whose most exemplary manifestation was the battle of the *philosophes* with the orthodox structure of Roman Christian orthodoxy —the period immediately preceding the French Revolution. The struggle, however, is one that mind always will have to undergo and therefore can be found taking place in the present where life or consciousness at this level is still experienced. Enlightenment's attack upon Roman orthodox belief, especially the sensuous objects of that belief, corresponds somewhat to earlier and more violent attacks upon the "Roman" structure of Europe, the attack of the Lutheran Reformation and that of the inundation of an uneasily Christianized and exhausted Rome by the Germanic tribes. What all these very different movements have in common is the breakdown of a hierarchic, traditional, authoritarian, civilizing, law-giving structure, dominating the temporal and spritual worlds, by a free, even anarchic, reckless and unscrupulous force of violent change. The smash-up of patrician and classical Rome; the breakdown of the Papal domination of an increasingly nationalistic Europe; and the overthrow of traditional and authoritarian structures of thought by the new spirit of inquiry in the eighteenth century, all present us with the collision of two forces, one of which is settled, even *petrified* (Christ's pun on Peter's name contains an unwelcome meaning!) in the past and tradition, the other, "hurrying from conquest to conquest," is urgent, fluid, headstrong, and destructive.

The movements and countermovements of the spirit in the age of the *philosophes* that Hegel analyzes is undramatic but a dramatically possible collision can be detected. If we were to set out Hegel's argument as a cast of characters it would appear as follows:

Enlightenment (Pure Insight)

(a) From a somewhat irresponsible "witty insight" to the concept of ultimate reality as "a great Void." (Ulrik Brendel.)

(b) Enlightenment as shallow utilitarianism. (Mortensgaard.)

(c) Enlightenment discovering its true nature to be that (Belief) which it had fiercely opposed. (Rebekka.)

Superstition (Belief)

(a) The naive consciousness of the multitude. (Mrs. Helseth.)

(b) Belief totally hostile to enlightenment, seeing its motives only as malicious and deceitful. (Kroll.)

(c) Belief discovering its true nature to be its opposite and perishing with this union. (Rosmer.)

In a somewhat rare reference to the historical background of his analysis Hegel at one point sees the ranks of Belief as composed of the priesthood, the despot, and the superstitious multitude, identities which are worked into those of Rosmer, Kroll, and Mrs. Helseth. Ibsen, however, has somewhat altered Hegel's analysis. Hegel had described how Enlightenment wished to free the multitude from the powers both of the despot and the superstition-encouraging priest, and it was upon the consciousness of the multitude that Enlightenment primarily was concerned to work:

The insight that is without will [i.e., objective purpose] and without individualized isolated self-existence, the notion of rational self-consciousness, which has its existence in the total conscious area, but is not yet there in the fullness of its true meaning. Since, however, pure insight rescues this genuinely honest form of insight, with its naive simplicity of nature [i.e., the multitude] from prejudices and errors, it wrests from the hands of bad intention [i.e., the priesthood] the effective realization of its powers of deception, for whose realm the incoherent and undeveloped [*begrifflos*] consciousness of the general area provides the basis and raw material, while the self-existence of each power finds its substance in the simple consciousness. (562–63)

This is the action with which Rebekka, long ago, started out, when Rosmer was merely a means to further the new ideas, and when she was prepared to "use" him to spread these new ideas in opposition to the orthodox powers that stood in the way of the multitude's enlightenment. *Rosmersholm* opens, however, with Rebekka and Rosmer (no longer a minister) working in unison, and so ripe for Ibsen's perennial confrontation of pagan and Christian forces in consciousness—a unison that does not contradict Hegel's analysis but represents, rather, a late stage of it. Thus the earlier phases of the dialectic would be *recollected*.

Enlightenment, in Hegel's account, infiltrates itself into the culture it will influence, like "a scent" (563) or an "infection" subtly achieving its destructive work until consciousness is at last aroused, but too late. Before consciousness is aware, the old idol is overthrown and all that is left is the dead form of the spirit's previous state (565). However, Enlightenment's victory over belief is hollow, for its whole nature is to work negatively and, since it recognizes no reality outside itself, its activity also must negate *itself* (565).

As insight, therefore, it passes into the negative of pure insight, it becomes untruth and unreason; and as intention it passes into the negative of pure intention, becomes a lie and sordid impurity of purpose. (565)

The dilemma of the spirit that Hegel indicates here does seem to be that in which Rebekka finds herself after the achievement of all she has worked for. In setting up the conditions by which she can free Rosmer and freely associate with him, she has created the very opposite of this pure freedom; she has indeed negated herself by converting what seemed pure intention into "a lie and sordid impurity of purpose." This, however, merely is a stage in Enlightenment's evolution which will lead to a new insight:

The complete attainment of insight, therefore, has the sense of a process of coming to know that content as its own, which was to begin with opposite of itself. Its result, however, will be thereby neither the reestablishment of the errors it fights with, nor merely the original notion, but an insight which knows the absolute negation of itself to be its own proper reality, to be itself, or an insight which is its self-understanding notion. (566)

Hegel then proceeds to recapitulate the stages of Enlightenment's struggle with Belief from the viewpoint of Belief, which sees the activities of Enlightenment as "destructive negation," "simply lying unreason and malicious intent" (567), phrases that call to mind Kroll's attitude to Rebekka. There follows an account of the various positions Belief and Enlightenment go through until we arrive at Enlightenment's concept of Absolute Being (ultimate reality) as "the great void" (580), a phrase used with great emphasis and significance by Brendel (*det store ingenting*). In the place of this great void Enlightenment sets up as positive truth "sense certainty" which, in a further clever and subtle analysis, Hegel shows to correspond, essentially, to Belief's insight, for Enlightenment's Absolute Matter turns out to be identical with Belief's concept of Absolute Spirit.

The discovery of the identity of the two opposing life principles, Belief and Enlightenment, is the highest reach of this dialectical

movement or phase of consciousness; but Hegel goes on to trace a
further (lower) development from this dialectical collision: the emergence of a utilitarianism that is shallowly untroubled by the terms of
Belief and Enlightenment at their gravest and which, therefore, can
operate a spiritually denuded world.

At the higher level, Belief as well as Enlightenment sees the Absolute
as "merely the empty void" (588), "it is a sheer longing." (Brendel's
words are, "I am homesick for the great void."—"*Jeg har fått hjemve
efter det store ingenting.*")

Belief in this manner has in fact become the same thing as enlightenment—
the conscious attitude of relating a finite that inherently exists to an unknown
and unknowable Absolute without predicates; the difference is merely that the
one is enlightenment satisfied, while belief is enlightenment unsatisfied. (589)

(The footnote to the Baillie translation notes, here, "i.e. the contrast
between Belief and Enlightenment becomes a contrast inside enlightenment itself." Thus it is that the *enlightened* pair only, Rosmer and
Rebekka, carry this level of the play's dialectical evolution.) Hegel
continues:

It will be seen whether enlightenment can continue in its state of satisfaction;
that longing of the troubled, beshadowed spirit, mourning over the loss of
its spiritual world, lies in the background. Enlightenment has on it this stain
of unsatisfied longing . . ." (589)

One of the images that recurs throughout Hegel's argument is that
of "the dull, silent, unconscious working and weaving of the spirit at
the loom of its own being, to which belief, as we saw, sank back when
it lost all distinction and content" (590). By means of this "working and
weaving" (591) of Spirit the two sides of the opposition within
Enlightenment, of Belief's concept of absolute being as pure thought
and Enlightenment's concept of absolute being as pure matter, arrive at
a confrontation that can be transcended only by these opposites "colliding and collapsing" (596). Belief now finds in pure insight (Enlightenment) "the moment that makes it complete; but, *perishing through being
thus completed,*" it is superseded by the next stage of spirit, that of
utilitarianism, which inhabits the drastically reduced terms of the next
phase of consciousness.

The meaning of Hegel's argument is more difficult than its *movement*,
for it is based upon historical and cultural examples that Hegel rarely
reveals. The movement clearly describes two phases of self-consciousness at first diametrically opposed as Belief and Enlightenment, arriving, by dialectical interchange, at a single identity but perishing at that

moment, to be superseded by a newer, shallower phase of Spirit which, as Brendel remarks, is able to live life without ideals and thus has become the inheritor of the future. This is, in fact, the dialectical movement of *Rosmersholm* however much Ibsen might have fleshed out this bare spiritual skeleton with vivid human detail. That intriguing and repeated image of "the working and weaving of the spirit," that Hegel employs, does seem to be caught up by Ibsen in the significant working upon the white shawl which Rebekka almost unconsciously performs. The importance of some such action to Ibsen's whole conception of the play can be seen in the very first drafts where Rebekka is shown working with a sewing machine.

The final phase of this dialectic, of a culture drained of spiritual significance, of a world of "things" of pure utility without distracting spiritual content (where even such a spiritual concept as religion has become a "thing" to be utilized) marks the need, in fact, for a spiritual crisis, even of life and death, and it is this development which follows in the next section, "Absolute Freedom and Terror," upon which the dialectic of *The Lady from the Sea* is structured.

Professor Loewenberg has offered an illuminating account of the difficult section "The Struggle between Enlightenment and Superstition," emphasizing the highly *militant* nature of the conflict from both sides, Belief and Enlightenment. Enlightenment begins its campaign, much as Rebekka begins in the Rosmer household, in order to end an unhappy division within consciousness:

Who can be true to his inner and deeper self as long as he is made to conform to the artificial code governing life in a cultural society? The more perfect the conformity, the greater the pathos of separation between conventional speech and uninhibited thought, between proper conduct and intellectual rebelliousness. Such pathetic division, experienced by a mind whose self-alienation has for its concomitant no strong feeling of revulsion, must needs breed hypocrisy and cynicism.

But how ignominious a conformity radically disavowed by mental reservations! This situation it is which forms the content of an insight arising within a cultural society when here and there some individuals definitely feel the antithesis of outer conformity and inner revolt to be intolerable. But this insight, still inert and personal, does not go beyond intention to clarify and resolve the antithesis by articulate thought. The intention must come to animate an active crusade against all the irrational tendencies over or dormant in a state of culture. Only when the diffusion of effort to challenge everywhere the presence of the irrational becomes actual and effective, may pure insight be said to have made its appearance. (231–32)

This appearance, however, as Loewenberg goes on to show, is only the first stage of a dialectic in which the forces of Belief will rally, while those of Enlightenment will reveal fundamental contradictions. Enlightenment enters upon an "incessant struggle" with "what it comes to view as offences to reason and truth," and these take on the identities of priesthood, despot, and human gullibility (233).

There must be a preliminary phase during which the work of enlightenment must be done by stealth. Reason's light cannot appear everywhere at the same time, its rays now falling on this obscure region, now on that. . . . Sooner or later, however, the pervasive influence of enlightenment becomes generally apparent, foreshadowing the imminence of the struggle to come. And once the strife takes place, the disaster threatening all beliefs can no longer be averted. Forced to be on the defensive, they are called upon to give proof of their credibility. (234)

Now, however, the struggle becomes more fierce because "beliefs, fighting with their own weapons, enter the battle for the preservation of their own autonomous and inalienable rights. Militancy engenders militancy, and belief and insight now become gravely involved in open warfare" (235). This, it seems to me, well describes the terms and the nature of the conflict in *Rosmersholm*: of Kroll, fighting with his own powerful weapons against Rosmer and Rebekka, especially by raising the specter of Beate. The process whereby, through the mutual examinations undergone in the conflict, Belief and Enlightenment at their most advanced recognize their affinity and even identity— the recognition that makes the death marriage of Rosmer and Rebekka possible—is described by Loewenberg as follows:

The insight that initially appears pure—an intellectual vision purged of belief —becomes in the course of the dialectic transformed into a species of belief. Assuming the shape of a discursive philosophy, enlightenment comes to embrace within its purview issues relating to religion and metaphysics and ethics, its determinate position constituting a synthesis of agnosticism and materialism and utilitarianism. What actually develops is a clash of opposed beliefs, each involving the insight proper to it. Hegel hints that the contending claims resemble in essence the incompatible laws central in the *Antigone*; in obvious allusion to the tragedy, he speaks of one claim as possessing a "divine right" and of the other as enjoying but a "human right." (243)

The very great depth at which Ibsen explores the clash between Civilization and Revolution in *Rosmersholm* brings his dramatic argument remarkably close to Freud's analyses of civilization whose achievements are won at the cost of the instincts and their happiness. "The Rosmersholm way of life ennobles, but it kills happiness," Rebekka declares, and we remember that it killed Beate, whose name *means* "happiness." In his account of Freud in *Eros and Civilization*, Herbert Marcuse observes:

Freud's metapsychology is an ever-renewed attempt to uncover, and to question, the terrible necessity of the inner connection between civilization and barbarism, progress and suffering, freedom and unhappiness—a connection which reveals itself ultimately as that between Eros and Thanatos. Freud questions culture not from a romanticist or utopian point of view, but on the ground of the suffering and misery which its implementation involves. Cultural freedom thus appears in the light of unfreedom, and cultural progress in the light of constraint. Culture is not thereby refuted: unfreedom and constraint are the price that must be paid.

But as Freud exposes their scope and their depth, he upholds the tabooed aspirations of humanity: the claim for the state where freedom and necessity coincide. Whatever liberty exists in the realm of the developed consciousness, and in the world it has created, is only derivative, compromised freedom, gained at the expense of the full satisfaction of needs. And in so far as the full satisfaction is happiness, freedom in civilization is essentially antagonistic to happiness: it involves the repressive modification (sublimation) of happiness. Conversely, the unconscious, the deepest and oldest layer of the mental personality, is the drive for integral gratification, which is absence of want and repression. (18)

Ibsen himself, as we saw, described the conflict of *Rosmersholm* as that between the moral consciousness, with its roots deep in tradition and the past, and the "acquisitive instinct" hurrying from conquest to conquest, and it is not difficult to translate Freud's "gratification" into Ibsen's "conquest." There also are two kinds of past in Ibsen's account of his play: the past of civilization and valid tradition, and the past of the acquisitive instinct which, as *instinct*, would be one of the oldest attributes of the human psyche. For someone of such a historical cast of imagination as Ibsen, it would not be far-fetched to see tradition and order symbolized by Roman and Roman-Christian authority, nor to see the "acquisitive instinct" (Ibsen, of course, does not mean the instinct to acquire money!) hurrying to control more and more of its world, in *pagan* terms.

Marcuse describes how Freud has outlined the structure of the modern mind in terms of a past-conditioned situation:

According to Freud's conception the equation of freedom and happiness, tabooed by the conscious, is upheld by the unconscious. Its truth, although repelled by consciousness, continues to haunt the mind; it preserves the memory of past stages of individual development at which integral gratification is obtained. And the past continues to claim the future: it generates the wish that the paradise be recreated on the basis of the achievements of civilization. (17–18)

The chapter in *Eros and Civilization* titled "The Dialectic of Civilization" (pp. 71–96) brings us close to the center of the dialectic of

Rosmersholm whose *Hegelian* argument, we already have seen, accounts for those aspects that remind us of Freud. The most important problem in the evolution of culture, Freud believed, was the sense of guilt, for the price exacted by the progress of civilization required "the forfeiting of happiness through the heightening of the sense of guilt" (p. 71). The suppressed and submerged instincts upon which civilization is built break out into the complex ills of modern society. Civilization, founded upon a primal act of tribal aggression (the sons killing the father), later imposes taboos and restrictions to prevent further expressions of aggressive instincts. Guilt and remorse are the tools of this repression which ultimately create a tension that leads to a struggle between Eros and Thanatos, the pleasure principle against the death instinct. The sense of guilt required for the maintenance of civilization becomes so great that "individuals can hardly support" it (p. 73). Marcuse observes that Freud's belief in the supremacy of civilization and its right to preserve itself by suppression, conflicts with his own theory of the instincts which

impelled him to go further and to unfold the entire fatality and futility of this dynamic. Strengthened defense against aggression is necessary; but in order to be effective the defense against enlarged aggression would have to strengthen the sex instincts, for only a strong Eros can effectively "bind" the destructive instincts. And this is precisely what *the developed civilization is incapable of doing* because it depends for its very existence on extended and intensified regimentation and control. The chain of inhibitions and deflections of instinctual aims cannot be broken. "Our civilization is, generally speaking, founded on the suppression of instincts." (73–74)

I believe this argument illuminates the dialectic of *Rosmersholm* and allows us to visualize its opposition of civilizing, constraining, repressive forces, associated with Rosmersholm, and the forces of liberation, sexuality, happiness, associated with Rebekka. The tensions Freud exposes within civilization were, in fact, detected by the dramatists of the German Enlightenment. The collision between the instinct for freedom and gratification and the requirements of law, order, and civilized decorum (the reality principle) are dramatized clearly in Goethe's *Torquato Tasso*, where the *tradition* of the court of Ferrara, strict in maintaining order and punishing transgression, is invoked by Antonio Montecatino in much the way that Kroll invokes the similarly strict Rosmersholm tradition. This conflict, too, is the constant theme of Schiller's writings where the concern for Joy and Freedom nevertheless recognizes the difficulty of placing these instincts and aspirations within the context of an educative civilization. Schiller's final repudiation of the Kantian concept of the moral law, which depended upon the self-repression of the individual instinctual life, was approved of by Hegel. Schiller develops this theme most fully in the *Letters on the Aesthetic Education of Mankind* and it is likely that Freud inherited more of this tradition than he was aware. Freud's account of the tensions within the individual psyche are explicable, as in Hegel, only in relation to the universal history of the race, and this idea was explored thoroughly by the German tradition of letters from the time of the Enlightenment to the modern age. No doubt this is why the arguments of such writings by Freud as *Thoughts on War and Death* or *Civilization and Its Discontents* remind us again and again of Enlightenment texts. Herbert Marcuse discusses the Freudian theses in relation to Enlightenment writing, especially the writing of Schiller, in his chapter "The Aesthetic Dimension" (pp. 156–79) in *Eros and Civilization*, in which the reader will find much that will bring to mind the themes of *Rosmersholm*.

The Master Builder

Hilde's fateful journey from the mountains to the Solness household may seem a long way from the God as Light section of Hegel's *Phenomenology*, but the omnipresent sun-and-light imagery of the play *does* correspond to the first recollected "positive religion" in the great celebration of the religious consciousness which reconciles the Objective World and the Subjective, overcoming their alienation and reintegrating the human spirit in its cosmos. Hegel sees the Persian religion of light—Zoroastrianism—as the very foundation of modern man's spiritual evolution: the point at which spirit decisively breaks with the Asiatic religious consciousnesses and, by means of a significant *dualism* (between Light and Darkness, Day and Night, Good and Evil), inaugurates the dialectical evolution of the Western spirit. It is essential, therefore, that this religion of light should be first in the procession or parade of spiritual idols that makes up the *Götter-dämmerung* of the last sections of the *Phenomenology* and of Ibsen's last four plays. The spiritual progress from the religion of light to the fully revealed religion of Christianity is, for Hegel, a progress towards greater and greater concretion and anthropomorphism: from the nebulous quality of light and darkness, to pantheism, where spiritual concepts take on plant and animal forms, to the phase of religious consciousness where man works upon the mineral substance of the earth investing it with spiritual significance in abstract forms until, finally, in the religion of Art, the human spirit shapes, first animal, then fully human forms of divinity. The next phase after this is the divinity appearing as a man among men (Jesus), a phase that lies outside the province of art. Once again the reader must be warned that, for Hegel, this is not necessarily a *historical* sequence, but a *logical* one which history happens to illustrate. The spiritual progress of this sequence matches the similar progress in the last four plays in the Cycle from sunset to sunrise, from spiritual "tomb" to "resurrection day."

339

In his account of the Religion of Light, Hegel very imaginatively recollects, without actually naming, the *Zend-Avesta*. The account of spiritual identity emerging through a struggle between darkness and light with its attendant imagery of the rising and setting sun, of fire and of the "sublime" but vague determinations embodied by spirit in this phase have general relevance to the action and imagery of *The Master Builder* but lack the particularity of correspondence we can find between the Hegelian text and the earlier plays in Ibsen's Cycle. The figure of the sunrise and of spiritual activity associated with the activity of the sun recurs in the pages following the God as Light section, for we have noted that Hegel's procedure in this last section is no longer linear but contrapuntal. Discussing the religious phases of oracle, cult, and tragedy, Hegel describes the oracular affirmations of the religious consciousness (in which there is a dichotomy between the human consciousness and God) in terms themselves oracular, for, as Loewenberg notes, Hegel's method throughout the *Phenomenology* is mimetic, histrionic:

> Thus the universal spirit of the Sunrise, which has not yet particularized its existence, utters about the Absolute equally simple and universal statements, whose substantial content is sublime in the simplicity of its truth, but at the same time appears, because of this universality, trivial to the self-consciousness developing further.
>
> The further developed self, which advances to being distinctively *for* itself, rises above the pure "pathos" of (unconscious) substance, gets the mastery over the objectivity of the Light of the Rising Sun, and knows that simplicity of truth to be the inherent reality [*das Ansichseyende*] which does not possess the form of contingent existence through the utterance of an alien self, but is the pure and unwritten law of the gods, a law that "lives for ever, and no man knows what time it came." (718)

This passage describes two kinds of self-consciousness; one, at a more primitive, "trivial" (childish?) phase of sublimity, uttering universals which, to the reflection of a later and more developed (adult?) self-consciousness, will *appear* trivial. This later, further-developed self-consciousness arrives at a "mastery" over the concept of the sun-divinity (once merely trivially and childishly adored) and perceives the inherent reality (the "law") of that earlier more simply perceived truth. The final sentence is, of course, a quotation from the *Antigone*. The style of the passage is much too obscure—in Hegel's obscurest manner—confidently for one to supply a gloss, but the two phases of development in consciousness do correspond to the two clear phases of Hilde and Solness's recollections, in which the *childish* Hilde, in rapt adoration of the ascending Solness at Lysanger, established a vision of him which is reestablished, at a more mature and adequate level in her adulthood, when that action of the ascending sun-figure is repeated. The *earlier* experience was linked with a promised kingdom of Orangia (*Appelsinia*) which Hilde later explicitly rejects as trivial or childish, while the later ascent is performed in order to gain a more audaciously and more maturely developed version of that kingdom where Hilde will be the princess in the tower to whom Solness will ascend. Hilde's final cry, in the play, "*My, my* master builder" implies a taking possession by her of Solness, a union of her consciousness with his.

The figure of the Sun reappears powerfully in the chapter "The Living Work of Art" where the Absolute Being takes on the identity of a *nation* "whose self is acknowledged as living in its substance." Hegel clearly has in mind the Greek city-state. This also is the phase of the godlike man—the athlete—"the highest bodily representation of what the essential Being of the nation is" (obviously a reference to the Pindaric odes). The self-consciousness turns from the ceremonial cult and from the religion of art, "as also does the god that has entered into self-consciousness as into its place of habitation":

This place is, by itself, the night of mere "substance," or its pure individuality; but no longer the strained and striving individuality of the artist, which has not yet reconciled itself with its essential Being that is striving to become objective; it is the night (substance) satisfied, having its "pathos" within it and in want of nothing, because it comes back from intuition, from objectivity which is overcome and superseded.

This pathos is, by itself, the Being of the Rising Sun, a Being, however, which has now "set" and disappeared within itself, and has its own "setting," self-consciousness, within it, and so contains existence and reality. (726)

Before leaving the phase of the "cult" Hegel recollects the beliefs and mysteries of the Greek cults in which the god is sacrificed and devoured and in which the spirit of the earth is divided between a feminine principle, "the nursing mother," and a masculine principle, "the self-driving force of self-conscious existence." In the cults of devouring the gods in the form of food and drink, "that orient Light of the world is discovered for what it really is: Enjoyment is the Mystery of its being." Hegel then describes the "cult" in a passage which resurrects an extraordinary wealth of mythic details:

What has thus been, through the cult, revealed to self-conscious spirit within itself, is simple absolute Being; and this has been revealed partly as the process of passing out of its dark night of concealment up to the level of consciousness, to be there its silently nurturing substance; partly, however, as the process of losing itself again in nether darkness, in the self, and of waiting above with the silent yearning of motherhood. The more conspicuous moving impulse, however, is the variously named "Light" of the Rising Sun and its tumult of heaving life, which, having likewise desisted from its abstract state of being, has first embodied itself in objective existence in the fruits of the earth [Demeter] and then, surrendering itself to self-consciousness [the mysteries of Bacchus and Dionysus], attained there to its proper realization; and now it curvets and careers about in the guise of excited, fervid women [the Dionysiac maenads], the unrestrained revel of nature in self-conscious form. (727)

This extraordinary passage which, while describing the advance of consciousness at the religious level, once again makes the ancient Greek consciousness dance and revel in the reader's imagination, is itself a good example of that modern action of *recollection* around which the whole *Phenomenology* is structured. The mythic figures of Proserpina (losing herself in nether darkness), Demeter (the mourning mother), the Rising sun, Dionysos, and his ecstatic women followers, all are worked into Hegel's text and, I believe, also are worked into Ibsen's text in *The Master Builder*. The major correspondence between Ibsen's play as Hegel's text, however, occurs with the "God as Light" chapter of the *Phenomenology* which, because it is brief, and is a good example of Hegel's extremely difficult but always provocative procedure, I will quote in its entirety.

GOD AS LIGHT

Spirit, as the absolute Being, which is self-consciousness—or the self-conscious absolute Being, which is all truth and knows all reality as itself—is, to begin with, merely its notion and principle in contrast to the reality which it gives itself in the process of its conscious activity. And this notion is, as contrasted with the clear daylight of that explicit development, the darkness and night of its inner life; in contrast to the existence of its various moments as independent forms or shapes, this notion is the creative secret of its birth. This secret has its revelation within itself; for existence has its necessary place in this notion, because this notion is spirit knowing itself, and thus possesses in its own nature the moment of being consciousness and of presenting itself objectively. We have here the pure ego, which in its externalization, in itself *qua* universal object, has the certainty of self; in other words, this object is, for the ego, the interfusion of all thought and all reality.

When the first and immediate cleavage is made within self-knowing Absolute Spirit, its shape assumes that character which belongs to immediate consciousness or to sense-certainty. [For Hegel the first phase and very origin of the evolution of consciousness.] It beholds itself in the form of *being*; but not being in the sense of what is without spirit, containing only the contingent qualities of sensation—the kind of being that belongs to sense-certainty. Its being is filled with the content of spirit. It also includes within it the form which we found in the case of immediate self-consciousness, the form of lord and master, in regard to the self-consciousness of spirit which retreats from its object. [I.e., thus this first phase of the religious consciousness returns to the first phases of consciousness (sense certainty) and of self-consciousness (the dialectic of master and slave).]

This being, having as its content the notion of spirit, is, then, the shape of spirit in relation simply to itself—the form of having no special shape at all. In virtue of this characteristic, this shape is the pure, all containing, all suffusing Light of the Sunrise, which preserves itself in its formless indeterminate substantiality. Its counterpart, its otherness, is the equally simple negative—Darkness. The process of its own externalization, its creations in the unresisting element of its counterpart, are bursts of Light. At the same time in their ultimate simplicity they are its way of becoming something for itself, and its return from its objective existence, and shapes itself as the diverse forms of nature. But the essential simplicity of thought rambles and roves about inconstant and inconsistent, enlarges its bounds to measureless extent, and its beauty heightened to splendour is lost in its sublimity.

The content which this state of pure being involves, its perceptive activity, is, therefore, an unreal by-play on this substance which merely rises, without setting into itself to become subject and secure firmly its distinctions through the self. Its determinations are merely attributes, which do not succeed in attaining independence; they remain merely names of the One, called by many names. This One is clothed with the manifold powers of existence and with the shapes of reality, as with the soulless, selfless ornament; they are merely messengers of its mighty power, claiming no will of their own, visions of its glory, voices in its praise.

This revel of heaving life must, however, assume the character of distinctive self-existence, and give enduring substance to its fleeting shapes. Immediate being, in which it places itself over against its own consciousness, is itself the negative destructive agency which dissolves its distinctions. It is thus in truth the Self; and spirit therefore passes on to know itself in the form of self. Pure Light scatters its simplicity as an infinity of separate forms, and presents itself as an offering to self-existence, that the individual may take sustainment to itself from its substance.

In the *Lectures on the Philosophy of History,* Zoroastrianism, the *first* of the Western religions, precedes the religions of India, Egypt, and Greece (the sequence is, of course, "logical," not chronological), and from Zoroastrianism sprang the religion that set up the strongest challenge to Christianity, Mithraism, which also was a cult of the sun god. One disciple of Mithraism was Julian, the hero of Ibsen's major "world-historical drama," and Julian dies trying to gain Persia, home of the sun religion. Ibsen gives the dying Julian the final words, "Oh sun, sun, why did you betray me." Ibsen's prophet of the third empire, Maximus of Ephesus, was a famed disciple and martyr of Mithraism, and initiated Julian in its mysteries, and Mithraism was most widespread among the Germanic peoples in the Middle Ages, many of its myths directly paralleling those of the Scandinavian Eddas. The religion of Light, claims Hegel, constitutes strictly the beginning of World History; for the grand interest of Spirit in History, is to attain an unlimited immanence of subjectivity—by an absolute antithesis to attain complete harmony.

The action of regression to infancy or childhood, which we suggested takes place in *The Master Builder*, would, therefore, be suitable if we see the play inaugurating the last phase of the Cycle where we rise to the level of the religious consciousness but at the same time return to its origins: a level of consciousness which, whatever its chronological appearance in the world, fittingly synthesizes and supersedes the spirit of the objective world of customary institutions and conventions and the subjective world cut off from (alienated from) the objective world and from Nature. After a great deal of initial hostility, Ibsen interpreters now are conceding the possibility that Ibsen is employing mythopoeic methods in his realistic plays, and especially in the last plays. It should be no cause for dismay that we now can see these methods as wholly serious and part of a concern to render the totality of human experience and identity, not merely exotic or entertaining fragments of it.

Notes and References

Introduction

1. *Scandinavian Studies*, 34/1962, pp. 245–57.
2. *The Reader's Encyclopedia of World Drama*, ed. John Gassner and Edward Quinn, New York, 1969, pp. 440–41.
3. Imre Madách, *The Tragedy of Man* (tr., J. C. W. Horne), Corvina Press, Budapest, 1963, p. 200.
4. In the same spirit Ibsen declared that after his own age had passed away, "poetry, philosophy and religion will fuse together to form a new category and a new power in life, of which however we who are now alive are incapable of forming any clear impression."
5. *Introduction to the Reading of Hegel*, Basic Books, N.Y., 1969, p. 133.
6. Cf. Karl R. Popper, *The Open Society and its Enemies*, Vol. II.
7. *Breve fra Henrik Ibsen*, I. Indledning, p. 15, Gyldendalske Boghandel, København og Kristiania, 1904.
8. *Ibsen: Letters and Speeches*, ed. Evert Sprinchorn, Hill & Wang, 1964, p. 98.
9. Ernst Cassirer remarks that a recent historian raised the question "whether the struggle of the Russians and the invading Germans in 1943 was not, at bottom, a conflict between the Left and the Right wings of Hegel's school." (*The Myth of the State*, Yale University Press, 1946, p. 248.)
10. Johann Gottfried von Herder, *Reflections on the Philosophy of the History of Mankind*, Chicago, 1968, p. 6.
11. Henry James, *The Scenic Art*, Hill & Wang, 1947, pp. 252–53.

Chapter One

1. Preface to *The Philosophy of Right*, Berlin, 1820.
2. *Either/Or* II.19, Doubleday (Anchor), New York, 1959.
3. "The Metaphoric Structure of 'The Wild Duck'" in *Contemporary Approaches to Ibsen*, Oslo, 1966, pp. 72–95.
4. *Ibsen: Letters and Speeches*, ed. Evert Sprinchorn, Hill & Wang, 1964, p. 330.
5. *The Flower and the Castle*, Maurice Valency, Universal Library, 1966, p. 234.
6. Such things, of course, *have* occurred in literature, in Dante's incorporation of Thomism, the neo-Platonist poets' use of their master's vision, Spenser's systematic use of Aristotle, and so on.

7. Without overstraining the significance of a single short conjunction, we may note, in response to the claim that Ibsen was Kierkegaardian, that this title's *and* implies a challenge to the Kierkegaardian *or—Emperor or Galilean*.

8. *Letters and Speeches*, p. 137.

9. *Phenomenology*, p. 456.

10. Ibsen probably employed the first part of the *Phenomenology* in *Emperor and Galilean*, especially in the section "Julian Among the Philosophers."

11. Harald Höffding, *A History of Modern Philosophy*, II, 178, Dover, 1955.

12. *Phen.*, p. 89.

13. G. W. F. Hegel, *The Phenomenology of Mind*, tr. J. B. Baillie, Translator's Introduction, p. 54. George Allen & Unwin, revised edition, London, 1931.

14. *Phil. Hist.*, p. 79. Hegel's idea of the structure of the mind as containing within itself all its prior phases of existence is probably the single most important contribution of this philosophy to modern literature and thought— at least of as much consequence as the famed dialectic. We find this structure of the mind reappearing in the second part of Goethe's *Faust* (written long after the *Phenomenology*), in Wagner's theory and practice, in Ibsen's Cycle, in T. S. Eliot's concept of Tradition, Joyce's archetypal and mythic recollection (and that of Thomas Mann)—in fact it is *the* major development of modern culture. It is present in the psychoanalytic theory of Freud and in the concept of the Collective Unconscious of Jung. In *Civilization and Its Discontents* Freud hesitantly offers what he feels is a startling and novel idea: "that in mental life nothing which once has been formed can perish—that everything is somehow preserved and that in suitable circumstances (when for instance, regression goes back far enough) it can once more be brought to life." (Tr. James Strachey, Norton, 1962, p. 16.) Freud has in mind not merely the individual but the *general* mind which still contains its earliest cultural traumata, e.g., the primal father-slaying that has begotten a continuing tragic dialectic of repression and attempted liberation creating the complex ills of modern life—an idea very close to Ibsen's detection of archetypal conflicts beneath the disorder of modern everyday life. Freud suggests we envision the structure of the mind as if it were the city of Rome in which, instead of one building superseding another, built on the ruins of its predecessor, *all* the buildings of Rome still stood intact in their original places, from the earliest tribal settlement to the most recent structure. This impossible condition is, however, the condition of the mind, suggests Freud: "The fact remains that only in the mind is such preservation of all the earlier stages alongside of the final form possible." This idea of the mind has powerfully been reformulated by the neo-Marxist philosopher Leszek Kolakowski: "An understanding of the totality of culture, after all, presupposes an understanding of the genesis of its particulars. Even in our most banal gestures there are vague recollections of the origins of human culture just as in our bodies we find traces of our ancestor the lemur, our ancestor the fish, and our ancestor the starfish. Each of us is therefore an individual being and at the same time a member of a species whenever we dream, shoot during a war, make love, write learned treatises, babble away when soused, or go to striptease shows. A genetic and structural understanding of the unity of all these modes of behavior is tantamount to an understanding of our humanity, in other words it is the proper goal of

philosophical anthropology. The multi-storied layers of our psychic structure have different degrees of mobility like the different layers of oceanic water; yet those plainly visible undulating motions of the surface are ultimately determined by the whole of that stratification and thus at first glance seem to be the work of capricious chance." ("An Epistemology of Striptease," *Tri-Quarterly*, 22, Northwestern University Press, Fall, 1971.) Since 1966 I have continually suggested that Ibsen's art is responsive to this idea of culture and have found that this idea generates hostility and derision among traditional Ibsen scholars. Yet it is an idea absolutely central to modern European art and thought since the time of Hegel, and is considered the most valid way of understanding Wagner, Thomas Mann, James Joyce, W. B. Yeats, T. S. Eliot, Ezra Pound, Samuel Beckett, et al. The idea of the burden of the past, in fact, has been present to the European imagination since the time of the Greek tragedians. Hegel's great revolution was to locate this structure of the past within the human psyche, and to insist that its recovery was essential to the truth and freedom of the modern consciousness.

15. *Eros and Civilization*, Vintage Books, 1955, p. 106.

16. *Ibid.*, p. 212.

17. *Hegel, Texts and Commentary*, tr. and ed. Walter Kaufmann, Doubleday, 1965, pp. 389–90.

18. Hegel's difficult concept of the Past and Present coexisting with the Future and constituting a completed, atemporal reality or identity—(the Concept or *Begriff*)—might be easier to grasp if we consider an analogy from art. Michelangelo's Sistine Chapel fresco depicts the totality of Christian history from Creation to Judgment Day. From one point of view this is a clear chronological and historical sequence, from the innocently awakening Adam to the guilty souls contemplating damnation or salvation, at the end. From this point of view the history exhibits a strong dialectical aspect: Creation; Fall; Expulsion and Wandering; Crucifixion and Salvation—a violent travail of the Spirit in Time. But from another point of view there is no temporal succession at all, for all this is an atemporal, static design in the mind of God and the viewer of the frescoes. Fall, Desolation, Crucifixion coexist side by side as necessarily complementary to the idea of the Whole. And this, in fact, *is* how Hegel describes his account of the travail of spirit in and out of Time. He sees it as like a post-by-post journey of a stagecoach, thus emphasizing its chronological succession; yet, at the end of the *Phenomenology* he describes the whole ghostly succession of spiritual dramas as "a gallery of spiritual shapes (*Geistern*) or pictures," thus suggesting its atemporal, static nature. These two aspects of spirit's journey may be recollected in Ibsen's *When We Dead Awaken* where Rubek and Maia remember the station-by-station train journey that has brought them to this last stop of their mutual journey: and where, later, Maia confides to Ulfheim that Rubek's castle contained a gallery with pictures or ghosts (petrified shapes) all around its walls. Thus, in Ibsen's Cycle, as in Hegel's *Phenomenology* and Dante's *Divine Comedy* we have the paradox that the arduous and painful spiritual journey continually must be undertaken, and yet that it is eternally completed.

19. It is interesting to reflect that the condition of the modern hero in the actual world is similar to Julian's. A great revolutionary leader—a "hero" such as Lenin or Mao—is expected to understand his world theoretically as well as to change it practically by his actions. He must not only act, but act from

"correct theory" in order to ensure that his actions are those the nature of reality requires. The volumes of writings left by Lenin, and the ideological disputes entered into by revolutionary leaders, would have astonished such successful but non-"intellectual" world conquerors and shapers as Alexander, Julius Caesar, and Napoleon. The portrait of the tortured intellectual, Julian, vainly fighting the world spirit with pen and sword, stands out strikingly from the portrait gallery of earlier heroes in history and drama. Yet the alternative to the tortured intellectual hero is the more alarming unintellectual hero appealing below complex Reason to such "ideas" as blood, race, soil, the mystique of a Führer. The denigration of Critical Reason, documented brilliantly by Herbert Marcuse in *Reason and Revolution*, has many adherents in the tradition of modern letters. In T. S. Eliot's *Murder in the Cathedral* we come upon the concept of the Saint as Führer, for that play derides the whole realm of the rational and historical world, and declares a mysterious, non-rational bond between the saint-leader and the simple folk for whom historical and rational processes are manifest irrelevancies and absurdities. After this, Ibsen's problems and difficulties in *Emperor and Galilean* appear to us all the more poignant and attractive. A fine and complex contrast between the burdened consciousness and the "brutal" consciousness appears in the Rubek-Ulfheim pair in *When We Dead Awaken*.

20. *Hegel: A Re-Interpretation. Texts and Commentary*, p. 437.

21. *Ibid.*, pp. 406–408.

22. *Hegel's Phenomenology: Dialogues on the Life of Mind*, Open Court Publishing Co., 1965, p. 17.

23. *Ibid.*, p. 19.

24. One should remember, however, Ibsen's judgment on this tradition in the unflattering figure of Mr. Cotton in *Peer Gynt*.

25. *Ibsen: The Intellectual Background*, Cambridge, 1946, p. 142.

26. I have quoted this passage from the only available English translation of Brandes's lecture, that by Evert Sprinchorn in Eric Bentley's *The Theory of the Modern Stage*, Penguin Books, 1968, pp. 383–97.

27. *Op. cit.*, p. 151. (Maybe the date of Downs' useful book, 1946, explains its tendency to play down the influence of German thought on Ibsen's art.)

28. *Ibid.*, p. 385.

29. *Ibid.*

30. *Op. cit.*, II, p. 396 (see Hegel's whole argument, pp. 388–401).

31. The reader will perceive how closely this description fits such modern exiles as Ibsen, Joyce, Eliot, Pound, and Beckett.

32. *Hegel: A Re-Interpretation*, Doubleday, 1965, p. 116.

33. The program of the Cycle, and even its triadic structure, calls to mind Dante's program in *The Divine Comedy*, and M. C. Bradbrook, for one, has noted the similarity of temperament and situation between the two poets, exiled from their homelands, and yet writing of nothing else, as Joyce was to write of nothing but Dublin while drawing upon the entirety of history. The combination, in the Cycle, of Greek dramatic form with Dantean cyclical and triadic form *might* be a conscious pagan-Christian synthesis on Ibsen's part. The passionate dialectical drama, engaged like Hellenic art with the life of *this* world, might then be "sublimated" within the timeless design of the triadic Cycle in which the passionate individuals, so self-absorbed, are all elements

of the eternally repeating design. This would be an appropriate Prelude to the art of the "third empire."

34. The original title of Dante's work, *Commedia Dantis Aligherii, Florentini natione, non moribus*, insists that the *Commedia* is Dante's *own* drama, both as individual Florentine and as universal Christian man.

35. *Letters and Speeches*, p. 114.

36. *Ibid.*

37. *Ibid.*, p. 187. In the original the last two lines more strongly state: "To be a writer is to hold Judgment Day over oneself" which may echo Schiller's "Das Weltgeschichte is das Weltgericht." (The world's history is the world's court of justice.)

38. Cf. Ivan Soll, *An Introduction to Hegel's Metaphysics*, University of Chicago Press, 1969, pp. 73–75.

Chapter Two

1. It is just such a total unfolding of spirit through Time that Hegel's system sets out. In the *Phenomenology* we find the whole system capsuled in embryonic form. From thence Hegel proceeds to trace the unfolding of spiritual reality as Logical Idea, as Space (Nature) and Time (History), and as Spirit (Art, Religion and Philosophy). In the *Lectures on the Philosophy of History* we see Spirit unfold itself as events in the historical world. In the *Lectures on the Philosophy of Fine Art* we see this progress in terms of evolving art forms and artistic expressions; and there are similar lectures in the *Philosophy of Religion* and *The History of Philosophy*. Hegel himself outlines the path he believes a modern poet should take in terms very similar to those I am claiming apply to Ibsen's intentions. The recovery of the past, Hegel notes, is one of the fundamental actions of Art itself. It is to the poet's advantage to draw upon the material of the past, where the content of Spirit is more readily discernible in concrete form and where the merely accidental and contingent has been replaced by the essential and universal; but the poet, too, Hegel warns, belongs to his own generation and it is to his own generation's ethical customs, modes of conception, and intellectual outlook that he should address himself. (*Phil. Fine Art*, I, 356–57.) The modern poet should make himself familiar with the "historical content of a former mythology and all that is most strange to ourselves in earlier conditions of state life and national custom," and, indeed, Hegel reminds us, it is just this acquaintance with the mythology, art, literature, *cultus*, and usages of antiquity that is the starting point of the present system of education, something that is the possession of every schoolboy. (*Ibid.*, 367.) Not only this conventional lore, but even the Indian, Egyptian, and Scandinavian mythologies might, Hegel suggests, one day be a part of our intimate inheritance, for "in the religious conceptions of all these peoples the Universal God is present." (*Ibid.*) Hegel nevertheless warns the poet that he is not writing for an audience of university professors, but for his own people, and that *direct* representations of ancient mythological figures leave the modern audience cold. The modern writer should strive to make his work intelligible upon its face "without any one having to undertake first a circuitous route of extensive historical investigation. For Art is not addressed to a small and select circle of the privileged few, but to the nation at large." (*Ibid.*, 369.) Such art works "must be clear to our-

selves as representations of our century and our own people, so that we may be able to find ourselves entirely at home in it, and not have before us a world foreign to that we live in." (*Ibid.*, 370.) Hegel is not advocating modern realism, but his call for an art responsive to the total past yet intelligible on its surface to the present age clearly looks forward to Ibsen's method in the Cycle, and to much later European realism.

2. *Ibsen: Four Major Plays*, tr. Rolf Fjelde, N.A.L. (Signet), 1965, p. xix.

3. *To the Finland Station*, Doubleday (Anchor), 1953, pp. 189–90.

4. "Who can fail to see in Zola's epic the tendency to symbol and myth that gives his characters their over-life-size air? That Second Empire Astarte, Nana, is she not symbol and myth? Where does she get her name? It sounds like the babbling of primitive man. Nana was the cognomen of the Babylonian Ishtar: did Zola know that? So much the more remarkable and significant if he did not." Thomas Mann, "Suffering and Greatness of Richard Wagner," *Essays*, Vintage Books (Random House), 1957, p. 199.

5. Lessing's *Hamburg Dramaturgy*, with its rejection of French "rules" and its return to a reinterpretation of Aristotle (and Shakespeare), is paradigmatic of the whole movement.

6. The breakdown of the Enlightenment concept of an international community of Reason, with its very ahistorical bias and its emphasis upon universal humanity, saw the emergence of nationalism in the nineteenth century, with its profound grasp of ethnic and historical development, of the "inward" life of nations and individuals, together with a disturbing indifference to the old concept of the community of Reason. It was Hegel's great merit to reassert this concept after absorbing the great change. Of course, such historical events as the Revolution and the Napoleonic reshaping of Europe had their great effect (Hegel completed the *Phenomenology* while Napoleon, nearby, was fighting the battle of Jena) and all helped to destroy the optimistic Enlightenment faith in Reason's ability bloodlessly to transform man and his world almost outside of Time and its processes.

7. Cf. *The Survival of the Pagan Gods*, Jean Seznec, Harper, 1961.

8. *Wagner on Music and Drama*, ed. Goldman and Sprinchorn, Dutton, 1964, p. 91.

9. One is reminded of those ecstatic passages in Wordsworth in which the poet loses his identity and sees "into the heart of things," a renewing of energies not unlike the individual recharging his psychic batteries.

10. *The Birth of Tragedy*, tr. Francis Golffing, N.Y., 1956, pp. 56–57.

11. *Ibid.*, pp. 136–37.

12. *The Drama Review* (T-42), New York, Winter, 1968, pp. 44–46.

13. *Ibid.*, pp. 45–46. I have used my own translation of this text, but refer the reader to Mr. Fjelde's. I have retained certain images and phrases not necessary to Mr. Fjelde's argument, but useful to my own.

14. *Ibid.*, pp. 44–45.

15. *Ibid.* (The contrasting modes of "naive" and "sentimental" poetry set out in Schiller's famous essay seem to be reconciled in Ibsen's program of reflection and spontaneity.)

16. *Phen.*, pp. 89–91.

17. *Ibid.*

18. *Ibid.*

19. *Ibid.* My italics.

20. *Phil. Fine Art*, IV, 209.

21. *Ibid.*, I, 13. It is Hegel's argument that a *reflective* culture such as the modern world is one in which "we adhere strictly to general points of view and regulate particular matters in consonance with them, so that universal forms, laws, duties, rights and maxims hold valid as the determining basis of our life and the force within of main importance. What is demanded for artistic interest as also for artistic creation is, speaking in general terms, a vital energy, in which the universal is not present as law and maxim, but is operative in union with the soul and emotions, just as, also, in the imagination, what is universal and rational is enclosed only as brought into unity with a concrete sensuous phenomenon. For this reason the present time is not, if we review its conditions in their widest range, favorable to art." (I, 12–13.) Herbert Read, in *Art and Society*, comments that this passage "shows how rightly Hegel, almost alone among philosophers, understood the nature of art," though Read is concerned to refute Hegel's conclusions.

22 *Phil. Fine Art*, II, 396.

23. *Oxford Ibsen*, IV, 607–608.

24. Morse Peckham, in *Man's Rage for Chaos*, remarks that the generation of "Wright, of Schönberg, of Picasso, of Stein, of Joyce, . . . involved a thorough stylistic break in the continuity of their respective artistic styles such as European culture had never seen." (P. 14.)

25. It is worth reflecting that the founder of modern psychoanalysis, Sigmund Freud, saw in the individual case history a microcosm of universal human history, so that the individual life history realized a fate intrinsic both to the individual and to the species.

26. Ibsen very likely was aware of the pun on *spiritus* (Spirit) as semen, familiar to the Elizabethans as in Shakespeare's "The expence of spirit in a waste of shame / Is lust in action. . . ."

27. Pp. 121–22.

28. *Collected Works of Henrik Ibsen* (Archer, tr.), N.Y., 1923, XI, 453.

29. Alexandre Kojeve suggests the "end of history" signaled by the close of the *Phenomenology* is the appearance of Man as an animal again. (P. 159.)

30. Helmut Motekat, "Hegel and Heine" in *A Hegel Symposium*, Austin, Texas, 1962, p. 78.

Heine's warning is remarkably similar to that given by Ibsen in Act III of *Brand*, where Ibsen sets the lonely integrity of the priest's spiritual struggle against the hordes of animalic and monstrous forces that are ever waiting (like the Powers of Darkness in *Macbeth*), to take over the human kingdom:

GERD: "Have you heard? The Priest's absconded!"
From the hills and from the barrows
Swarm troll-shapes and apparitions,
Dark and hideous, large and small.
Ugh! how viciously they strike
Almost tearing out my eye;
Now they've taken half my soul. . . .

. . . Listen! all the bells together
Are ringing down the wild, bare heaths.
What congregations now assemble

Traveling down *that* chapel way!
Can you see the trolls in thousands
The priest's power once kept in the sea-depths?
Can you see the thousand dwarf-folk?
Until now they lay fast-buried
With the priest's seal heavy on them.
Sea and grave no longer hold them:
Out they're swarming, cold and clammy,
Troll-babes, seeming dead, rise, snarling,
Rolling back the rocks behind them
Screaming, "Hear us, mother, father,"
And *human* parents give them answer!
The parishioner now walks among them
As any father among his sons
And women press these risen corpses
Against their breasts and give them suck . . .

In this nightmare, the landscape itself bursts open and swarms of hideous and monstrous figures, lying dormant and uneasily subdued by Brand's unwearying battle with the trolls that infest the mind and heart, take possession of the human community, just as any modern nation might find itself unlearning the lessons of centuries of civilization and returning to brutality. There could be no more powerful image of Ibsen's belief (similar to Hegel's) in the desperate necessity for humanity to struggle to create and to maintain its highest identity and to subdue the monsters of its own unexamined impulses. It shows, also, how, for Ibsen, the "mythical" and the subconscious, while being essential aspects of our full psychic life, which therefore must be acknowledged and integrated into the life of Reason, can, if unacknowledged, break out into the psychopathology of everyday life and into the mass neuroses that threaten our entire human community.

31. W. Kaufmann, *Hegel: A Re-Interpretation*, p. 454.
32. *Collected Works* (Archer, tr.), XI, 244.
33. *Ibid.*
34. *The Poet in the Theatre*, Hill & Wang, 1960, p. 12.

Chapter Three

1. Ibsen remarked that the times of day and night affect the speech and behavior of characters so that the dialogue in his plays would be different for morning, afternoon, or night. Hegel, discussing the effects of Nature on the human mind, makes the same point: "We are attuned to different moods in the morning and evening. In the morning we are more seriously disposed, mind is still more in identity with itself and Nature. The day belongs to opposition, to work. In the evening, reflection and fancy predominate. . . ." (*Philosophy of Mind*, Oxford, 1971, p. 39.) It might repay investigating Ibsen's dialogue to discover this temporal condition and atmosphere.
2. *Letters and Speeches*, p. 237.
3. *Ibid.*, p. 343.
4. It would be true to the Hegelian vision, as well as, I think, to our experience of Ibsen's art, to see the Cycle as one great conceptual *movement*,

made up of progressively smaller movements (dialectical actions): that of each group of plays, of each play within the group, of the movements of each Act and the dialectical actions within each Act.

5. There are, in fact, accounts of the plays that see them as a subjective, personal, even autobiographical *progression* on Ibsen's part, his personal outgrowing of the earlier stages through belated self-knowledge, disillusionment, and so on. It certainly represents no diminution of Ibsen's stature as an artist to see him, at this stage of his career, fully in control of this progression. Indeed, it might well be the formidable *greatness* of his artistic intentions that will dismay and alienate those readers who are more at ease with a smaller artistic intention.

6. This world of Objective Spirit, of an external condition of spiritual tyranny, can, I think, be seen as equivalent to the "emperor" realm of Ibsen's dualism of emperor and Galilean, just as the Subjective Spirit corresponds to the Galilean. Human truth and freedom, therefore, require the individual's discovering of his truth and freedom within his external world of rights and duties *and* within his internal world of subjective repression. The "third empire of spirit" would emerge from the transcendence of both.

7. An obviously analogous dialectical situation is the Marxian one in which the successful capitalist, professing to serve the cause of individual enterprise (at the expense of other individuals) actually is preparing the economic conditions under which, alone, Socialism will emerge. J. M. Findlay summarizes the dialectic of this phase of spirit in terms that closely parallel the dialectic of *The Pillars of Society*. "The cult of the Matter-on-hand, is therefore, yet another case of that self-absorbed high-mindedness. . . . Not only was it the typical vice of German Romanticism, but we may identify it as the vice of the American business executive, the disinterestedly frightful Nazi, or the pure practitioner of scholarship or research. . . . Hegel points out, however, that the 'truth' of all this disinterested 'honesty' is to be *not* as honest as it seems: to do something merely in order to try to do it, is in a sense not honestly to try to do it at all. A society of high-minded 'players of the game' is, in a sense, a society of cheats: they *appear* to need each other's help and co-operation, but they are each really putting on an independent show, and are indifferent or hostile to such help. The premature arrival of the rescue party spoils the 'last stand.' " (*Hegel: A Reassessment*, p. 111.) This last situation brings to mind the comic dismay of Bernick's friends when actually called upon to serve the community as they profess to do.

8. The "unexpected visitor" who arrives from about ten years previously, forcing a drastic reappraisal of a decade of life, appears in many plays in the Cycle; but the opening figures Lona, Gregers, and Hilde are by far the most consequential.

9. The coffin-ships are a subtler symbolic device than they have been given credit for. They not only supply an analogue to the social situation (their disrepair and patchwork covering resembling the philosophic and moral lack of integrity in society) but at the same time they are a shocking manifestation of what such a society is capable of when its only motives are the greedy self-interest of individuals.

10. Bernick is amazed to discover that Lona Hessel's motives were "not hatred, then? Not revenge?"

11. Ivan Soll, *An Introduction to Hegel's Metaphysics*, Chicago, 1969, p. 73, also pp. 44–46.

12. Loewenberg, p. 189.

13. *Phen.*, pp. 440–53.

14. *Ibid.*

15. *Ibid.*, pp. 457–82.

16. *Ibid.*, pp. 483–92.

17. *Ibid.*, pp. 493–506.

18. *Ibid.*, p. 443.

19. *Ibid.*

20. "Intelligent, veritable (*wesentlich*) well-doing is, however, in its richest and most important form the intelligent universal action of the state—an action compared with which the action of a particular individual as such is something altogether so trifling that it hardly is worth talking about. The action of the state is in this connection of such great weight and strength that if the action of the individual were to oppose it, and either sought to be straightway and deliberately (*für sich*) criminal, or out of love for another wanted to cheat the universal out of the right and claim which it has upon him, such action would be useless and would inevitably be annihilated. Hence all that well-doing, which lies in sentiment and feeling, can mean is an action wholly and solely particular, a help at need, which is as contingent as it is momentary. Chance determines not merely its occasion, but also whether it is a 'work' at all, whether it is not at once dissipated again, and whether it does not itself really turn to evil." (*Ibid.*, p. 444.)

21. Loewenberg, p. 186.

22. While possibly not endorsing Voltaire's observation that Christianity's main contributions to the world were theology and venereal disease, Ibsen's picture of this historically evolved society is extremely somber in its life-destructive aspects: from the coffin-ships in which the pious social pillars would have sacrificed human life, the devastation of instinctual life in Rank and Osvald, and the polluted streams of *An Enemy of the People*. "Society" in this account is an agent of Death.

23. For Hegel, the result of the process of testing laws so that they hold good "as an activity inside consciousness" (*Phen.*, 450) is the creation of a higher spiritual phase of self-consciousness. The process of testing laws, too, results in the emergence of universal laws independent of the will of given individuals: "The pure and absolute will of all which takes the form of immediate existence." (*Phen.*, 451.) In the actions of the Greek tragedies that underlie Hegel's text, the particular and selfish conflicts of, e.g., Clytemnestra and Agamemnon give way to the unselfish, truly ethical action of an Orestes reluctantly obeying the will of Apollo, and, finally, the action of the enlightened democratic court passing impartial judgment on the whole substance of the earlier conflict.

24. Unless we accept such a dialectical development linking all the plays, it is difficult to understand why Ibsen required—as he did—that the plays be read in the order in which they were written.

25. Accounts of the play that see *Ghosts* as a demonstration to the critics of *A Doll's House* of Nora's *not* leaving home and husband miss the point. Torvald Helmer is no philandering Captain Alving but the very pillar of society Helene Alving admires. Nor is Helene's fault her returning to Alving

at Manders's insistence. As the play makes clear, it is Helene's allegiance to a life-denying pietism which despises Eros that has to be punished by the forces of Eros and Dionysos.

26. Rørlund sees the operation of providence in Bernick's refusal to allow the railway to come into the town: but when the businessmen decide to bring the railway in, and claim "providence" arranged the terrain for this purpose, Rørlund eagerly assents to this explanation. Rørlund's universal reason, because it shelters itself from dialectical conflict, is both everywhere and nowhere.

27. *Nyt Tidsskrift*, 1883. Quoted by Michael Meyer in his biography of Ibsen. Ibsen's comment to Brandes that Raphael's art did not move him because Raphael's people "belong to a period before the fall of man" insists that if Hellenism is to be revived it must work upon a post-lapsarian world. Julian believed the Fall could be undone (in Hegel's account the Fall *is* the loss of the Hellenic world), and so his Greek revival pedantically missed the subversive dynamism of the Greek spirit.

28. *Oxford Ibsen*, VI, p. 15.

29. This observation very obviously has relevance to the figure of Aline Solness in *The Master Builder*, and in my analysis of that play I interpret the character of Aline (who mourns the loss of "nine lovely dolls") as analogous in its situation to an arrested Hellenism or paganism unable to advance within the changing consciousness of the world.

30. Thus Hegel completely anticipates Nietzsche's description of Christianity as a "slave's religion" but, in contrast to Nietzsche, sees this development of consciousness as profoundly *necessary*.

31. In the *Philosophy of Fine Art* Hegel notes how this new development of consciousness "appears on the prosaic ground of rational discussion and from thence is within the soul and its religious emotions, mainly by means of miracle, martyrdoms, and so on, carried into the world of subjective knowledge." (II, 265.)

32. Hamlet's comment "I could be bounded in a nutshell, and count myself king of infinite space, but that I have bad dreams" perfectly expresses this subjective vision in which a potentially extravagant subjectivism is thwarted by subjective suffering!

33. Readers may object that this gives a too *positive* interpretation to Hedvig's admittedly ambiguous death. Gregers Werle brings into the Cycle the Christian requirements of self-sacrifice; and it is only in this group that we encounter *suicide* as a gesture of consciousness—the suicides of Hedvig, Rosmer, Rebekka, and Hedda Gabler. In the first and last groups the deaths are not strictly suicides. Osvald would prefer to live healthily, Rank cannot help but die, and Nora retreats from suicide. The deaths of the last group are the results of pushing *life* to its limits.

34. The somewhat unconvincing ending of this play may be deliberate on Ibsen's part. Hegel, too, faithfully "mimes" this Kantian moment (the Categorical Imperative) in the history of consciousness, though his whole philosophy protests against it.

35. Hegel himself is an inveterate and ingenious punster but *his* puns, like Ibsen's, are, I think, the thinker's indication of a rationality even in the accidents of language. Certainly, as a professional in this sport, he can be allowed a certain disdain at the superstitious Roman method!

36. J. B. Baillie writes of this dialectical development, which applies particularly to the action of *The Wild Duck*: "The process of spirit in this second stage [the first stage, that dramatized by Ibsen in the first four plays, is "the realization of the objective social order in and through individuals"] assumes from the start a conscious contrast between the individual spirit and a universal spiritual whole, a contrast which, while profound, the individual seeks to remove, because the universality of spiritual existence which he seeks to attain is implicitly involved in his very being as a spiritual entity. His spiritual life seems, to begin with, rent in twain, so complete is the sense of the opposition of these factors constituting his life. His true life, his objective embodiment, seems outside him altogether and yet is felt to be his own self. He seems 'estranged' from his complete self, and the estrangement seems his own doing, because the substance from which he is cut off is felt to be his own. The contrast is the deepest that spirit can possibly experience, just because spirit is and knows itself to be self-contained and self-complete, 'the only reality.' The contrast can only be moved by effort and struggle, for the individual spirit has to create or recreate for itself and by its own activity a universal objective spiritual realm, which it implies and in which alone it can be free and feel itself at home. The struggle spirit goes through is thus the greatest in the whole range of its experience, for the opposition to be overcome is the greatest that exists. Since its aim is to achieve the highest for itself, nothing sacred can be allowed to stand in its way. It will make any sacrifice, and, if necessary, produce the direst spiritual disaster, a spiritual 'reign of terror' to accomplish its result."

37. *Ibsen: A Collection of Critical Essays*, ed. Rolf Fjelde, N.Y., 1965, p. 121.

38. Ibsen, we are told, modeled Hedvig upon his recollection of his sister, of the same name, and his reason for this might well have been that Hedvig Ibsen was to become a very devout Christian. But one cannot help noticing that in Rembrandt's great painting "The Night Watch" a dramatic flood of light falls upon a young girl caught up in the darkness and confusion. Ibsen, himself a painter, must have known of this most famous of paintings and he may have wished to catch some of its feeling in his own great work.

39. I know that this might seem too much "*galskap*" for some readers to swallow and that readers might prefer a much more cautious approach such as "Possible Shakespearean Details in *The Wild Duck*"; but then Ibsen is not writing for an academic audience and to savor his full *galskap* we should throw away academic good taste and caution. Being outraged by Ibsen's intentions is a more lively reaction than one usually encounters in accounts of his art. We should keep in mind that, for all the grandeur of his dramatic vision, Ibsen's plays also are outrageous *fun*, like Samuel Beckett's.

40. The similarity between *The Wild Duck* and *Hamlet*, in case the reader attributes all the above *galskap* merely to the present writer, has been noted by Sidney Mendel in "The Revolt against the Father: The Adolescent Hero in Hamlet and The Wild Duck," *Essays in Criticism*, Oxford, 1964, pp. 171–78. Mendel, however, fails to see the quite conscious and slyly comic parody that Ibsen is performing on Shakespeare's plays.

41. The vexed question of Ibsen's reading (about which astonishingly little is known) must remain a question for the present. Ibsen scholars have been eager to see Kierkegaardian influence, despite Ibsen's explicit disclaimer, and

reluctant to see Hegelian influence, despite Ibsen's explicit admiration for Hegel. I would agree that Ibsen's disclaimers should be taken cautiously; but is it then good logic, after seeing influences where he denies them, to deny the influences that Ibsen *does* imply?

42. Accounts of the neo-paganism of Enlightenment thinkers and movements are too well-known to need detailing here. Of especial interest is that this later intellectual war against "Rome" is a sublimation of the earlier physical struggle.

43. Richard Wagner describes the two spiritual traditions and their function in a new spiritual revolution in terms very similar to Ibsen's "third-empire" concept: "The free Greek, who set himself on the very pinnacle of Nature, could procreate art from very joy in manhood: the Christian, who impartially cast both Nature and himself aside, could only sacrifice to his god on the altar of renunciation: he durst not bring his actions or his work as offering, but he believed he must seek His favour by abstinence from all self-prompted venture." In Wagner's third empire, "Jesus would show us that we are all alike men and brothers; while Apollo would have stamped this mighty bond of brotherhood with the seal of strength and beauty, and led mankind from doubt of its worth to consciousness of its highest godlike height." *Wagner on Music and Drama*, pp. 60–63, p. 69.

44. *Phen.*, pp. 604–605.

45. *Ibid.*

46. The English translator of *The Lady from the Sea*, J. W. McFarlane, in fact draws attention to the Kantian nature of the play's resolution: Ellida's final decision, McFarlane writes, "is in the Kantian sense, a sublime act; her 'freedom with responsibility' a kind of popular paraphrase of the Categorical Imperative." (*Oxford Ibsen*, VIII, 9.)

47. *Phen.*, p. 607. For an excellent account of Hegel's treatment of the French Revolution and its Kantian aftermath, see Jean Hyppolite, *Studies on Marx and Hegel*, Basic Books, N.Y., 1969, pp. 35–69.

48. Loewenberg, p. 259.

49. Rolf Fjelde, "The Dimensions of Ibsen's Dramatic World," *Contemporary Approaches to Ibsen*, II, 1971.

50. Wagner's intensely Romantic hero puts in a nominal appearance in *The Wild Duck* but, it seems to me, he is much more a presence behind the identity of the Stranger. Wagner's hero arrived in a ship which had the mysterious quality of suddenly appearing without warning. We hear that the English ship on which the Stranger arrives has the same odd quality: ". . . she slips in, you know, between the islands. There's no sign of her—then, suddenly, there she is."

51. A quotation from Henry James, who remarks that "one winces considerably" from these characters in a play that "might have sprung from the fancy of Hawthorne, but the atmosphere is the hard light of Ibsen."

52. In the little notebook whose entries mostly refer to *Hedda Gabler* Ibsen's very first note is, "My dramatic theories developed for the French, Translation of the acting style as of the language—etc.—" This proves nothing, but the conjunction is appropriate. (Cf. *Oxford Ibsen*, VII, 480.)

53. The "thesis-plays" of Augier and Dumas *fils*, however, are hardly much above the Scribean level and those who see these writers as anticipating Ibsen's methods and themes show they are wholly unaware of the nature

of Ibsen's art. For Augier and Dumas *fils* want all that Scribe wants *plus* a good conscience—a luxury Scribe modestly forewent! The "abuses" they attack are all correctible without any fluttering in the dovecotes of the bourgeoisie.

54. *Oxford Ibsen*, VII, 490.

55. A subtle detail often missed by readers is Tesman's cowardice over the hat, for it is *he* who placed it on the chair, not Aunt Julie; yet he permits his poor aunt to take the entire blame!

56. *Letters and Speeches*, p. 299.

57. The nature of this pagan group is made more complex from the Apollo-Dionysos dualism of Nietzsche's famous work on tragedy. Hedda and Diana, both associated with pistols and shootings, resemble the divine siblings Apollo/Artemis (Diana) both armed with a bow with which they killed *children* (Niobe's). Løvborg, with his drinking, vine leaves, and the dismemberment of his book (pieced together at the end of the play) is obviously Dionysiac. Ibsen knew Nietzsche before beginning *Hedda Gabler*, for he wrote congratulating Georg Brandes on his lectures on the philosopher, and it is most likely Ibsen would have read *The Birth of Tragedy* (1872). Nietzsche's preface to that book insisted it was about scholarship and contrasts the "Alexandrian" scholar (frightfully like Tesman) with the inspired scholar (similar to Løvborg). Apollo, in Nietzsche's scheme, is the god of Order, Beauty, Illusion, and Dionysos of irrational, wild, and uncontrollable reality. Apollo is half-fascinated, half-repelled by Dionysos but finds he cannot live without him. Dionysos's orgiastic rites contrast with Apollo's military-like rigidity, yet it is from the union of Apollo-Dionysos that, alone, tragic art is born. Hedda's military background, her austere control, her reaching for an illusion of beauty and her loathing for all that is "sordid and ugly," including sickness and death, her attachment to music (which is an Apollonian *and* a Dionysiac art), together with the nature of her relationship to Løvborg, strongly suggest that she was conceived as representative of the Apollonian vision as it was reduced in the modern world, and I refer the reader to Nietzsche's great work in order to gain an idea of the nature of the play's implications. Hedda shoots herself when her last *illusion* is destroyed, and as she is about to die she plays "a *wild* dance melody" suggestive of the Dionysian spirit that she has as last the courage to absorb for tragedy.

58. The relationship between Julian and Agathon, in *Emperor and Galilean*, strongly resembles that of Hedda/Thea: in Julian's easy domination of his Christian friend, his intellectual superiority, the slight element of "homosexuality" in his attraction for Agathon: "How thick and glossy your hair has grown. So curly, too . . ." which reminds us of Hedda's irritated fascination with Thea's hair.

59. "At this point, then, Spirit knows its principles, the universal element of its actions. But this work of Thought, being universal, is at the same time different in form from the particular, real work, and from the concrete life which brings the work about. When this point is attained, we have both a real and an ideal existence. If, for example, we want to gain a general representation of the Greeks and their life, we find it in Sophocles and Aristophanes, in Thucydides and Plato. In these individuals the Greek spirit grasped itself in thought and representation. This is its deeper satisfaction, its consummation; but it is at the same time ideal and different from its active reality." (*Reason in History*, Library of Liberal Arts, p. 92.)

60. Presumably the backward movement of the line as it loops to make the knot represents, in Hegel's image, the retrogressive actions necessary to a full dialectical action. As the knot is completed the line loops forward again but retains the backward action of the knotting. Hegel's images do have this very healthy substantiality.

61. Very much like Wordsworth, Hegel (and Ibsen) insists that the microcosm, man, fully exists only as he extends himself (his Reason) into the macrocosm, Nature: that there is in the human spirit an affinity with and responsiveness to the cosmos. For Wordsworth the "mind of Man" can be emotionally and mystically attuned to the "Spirit of the Universe": for Hegel this is the goal of a fully developed Reason (which *includes* the mystical). Rolf Fjelde observes: "Only for ordinary consciousness, i.e. mind in its most primitive state of awareness, is the cosmos separated into a self here and an object world there. For the most evolved form of Consciousness, that which Hegel designates as Reason, the inner and the outer spheres of action are perceived as innately one continuum, obeying the identical laws, or dialectics, of behaviour." ("Dimensions of Ibsen's Dramatic World, p. 58. in *Contemporary Approaches to Ibsen*, Vol. II, Oslo, 1971.)

62. Professor Loewenberg describes the arrival of the religious consciousness in the *Phenomenology* as follows: "On the one hand, religion exemplifies the final and over-arching form of consciousness to which all the preceding forms are ancillary, and on the other, it represents more than a form of consciousness terminating man's dialectical odyssey—it serves as a bridge that leads to the conception of absolute spirit free from myth and allegory. Looking before and after, as it were, the religious consciousness moves from lower to higher expressions until it reaches the stage that marks its transformation into a consciousness purely speculative. For the consciousness distinctly religious is cosmic in sweep; it appears on the scene only when the whole is envisaged in its wholeness." (*Op. cit.*, p. 291.)

63. Hegel has in mind the Indian religions.

64. *Phen.*, p. 702.

65. *Ibid.*, pp. 702–703.

66 Jacob Grimm, *Teutonic Mythology*, III, 996–97 (also p. 1099 for the "evil eye" detail).

67. This is pointed out by J. C. Kerons, who also draws attention to the irrevocability of the child deaths in Ibsen's plays: that the parents seem denied any possibility of making up this loss in the future, which alerts us to the *thematic* nature of this detail.

68. Hegel describes the mineral forms as related to spirit as to the "light" that "throws its significance on them." *Phen.*, p. 704.

69. The original, *skinndøde*, is untranslatable. It can mean "as if dead," or "suffocated" and so struggling to come to the air. Rolf Fjelde translates the word as "unconscious" which is preferable to Archer, though this speech must be counted one of Archer's successes. The original condenses many levels of meaning in its packed syntax.

70. Archer, tr., XI, 318.

71. *Teutonic Mythology*, II, 795.

72. *Phen.*, p. 707.

73. Archer, tr., XI, 337.

74. There is a passage in Herbert Marcuse's *Eros and Civilization* that, I

think, illuminates the argument built into the structure of *When We Dead Awaken* in which the artist's activity inescapably involves him in guilt against life and freedom. Marcuse describes the impossible dilemma of art which esthetically shapes the memory "of the liberation that failed, of the promise that was betrayed. Under the rules of the performance principle, art opposes to institutionalized repression the 'image of man as a free subject,' but in a state of unfreedom art can sustain the image of freedom only in the negation of unfreedom. Since the awakening of the consciousness of freedom, there is no genuine work of art that does not reveal the archetypal content: the negation of unfreedom. . . . As aesthetic phenomenon, the critical function of art to form vitiates the negation of unfreedom in art. Aristotle's proposition of the cathartic effect of art epitomizes the dual function of art: both to oppose and to reconcile; both to indict and to acquit; both to recall the repressed and to repress it again—purified." *Eros and Civilization*, Basic Books, p. 131.

75. Archer, tr., XI, 418.

76. *Ibid.*

77. *Ibid.*, p. 419.

78. *Ibid.*, pp. 441–42.

79. *Phen.*, p. 807.

80. A note to an earlier draft of the play goes, "In this country it is only the mountains which give an echo, not the people."

81. Ibsen employs *both* Norwegian words for the devil: *fanden* and *dævel.* He also tells the Inspector to go to hell!

82. *Larousse Encyclopedia of Mythology*, p. 221. See also Erik Østerud's vauable account "Naar Vi Døde Vaagner paa Mytologisk Bakgrunn," *Ibsen Aarbok,* 1963–1964.

83. The name Maia also calls to mind Schopenhauer's Maya, who represents everything of the natural world, of the senses, of ego, eros, and amor. To be caught in the veil of Maya is to be the uncultured, unphilosophical individual, trapped in Plato's Cave of Shadows and tied to the shifting values of the senses which produce only the illusions of reality. From helplessness before the veil of Maya comes all wrongdoing and guilt.

84. *Teutonic Mythology*, III, 968.

85. Archer, tr., XI, 453.

86. Hegel's dialectical philosophy is far more dramatic than it seems.

Chapter Four

1. *Larousse Encyclopedia of Mythology*, London, 1959, pp. 5–7.

2. *Phen.*, pp. 484–92.

3. Archer, tr., XII, 186. In a play resurrecting the Hellenic spirit, may not Ibsen, here, be recollecting the Greek practice of exposing sickly offspring?

4. G. Wilson Knight, *Henrik Ibsen*, Grove Press, 1962, p. 51.

5. Letter to Sophus Scharndorph, Jan. 6, 1882.

6. Archer, tr., XII, 185.

7. *Ibid.*, p. 186.

8. It is not too much to say that Ibsen, in choosing to be a *dramatist*, and not, for instance, a priest or a theologian, is taking upon himself a very definite commitment to certain spiritual and esthetic values: he is attempting by his example and his art to reestablish these Hellenic values in his world.

9. Loewenberg, p. 198.

10. *Ibid.*, p. 200.

11. *Phen.*, p. 488. (This brings to mind the nature of Osvald's collapse: escaping the dialectical conflict of both his parents only by escaping from consciousness altogether!)

12. *Ibsen: Four Major Plays*, Vol. II, tr. Rolf Fjelde, p. 105.

13. Loewenberg, p. 200.

14. *Phen.*, p. 481.

15. *Ibid.*

16. *Ibid.*, p. 484.

17. *Ibid.*

18. *Ibid.*, p. 485.

19. *Ibid.*, p. 486.

20. *Ibid.*, p. 490. My italics.

21. *Ibid.*, p. 491.

22. *Ibid.*, p. 492.

23. Malachi 4:1–6.

24. *The Libation Bearers*, pp. 980–86, University of Chicago Press.

25. It is remarkable that Strindberg, in *The Father*—a play written to a great extent in "refutation" of the imagined tendency of *Ghosts* to make Alving guilty—also should draw directly upon the Agamemnon story, by direct quotation, and by translating the "net" that enmeshed Agamemnon into the straightjacket forced upon the Captain. The "net" in *Ghosts* is the whole web of duties and life denial spun around the young Lieutenant Alving.

26. There is an ambiguity, here, though, for Osvald is physically afflicted in the *brain*, the result of which is the disintegration of his mind and his art. Nevertheless, Osvald obviously represents the intellectual sublimation of his father's *livsglede* as Regine represents its physical manifestation.

27. It is likely that the phrase *aandelige strømninger* is a recollection of Georg Brandes's famous work, *Main Streams [Hovedstrømninger] of Nineteenth Century Literature*.

28. With this in mind, such details as Manders's umbrella, cautiously staving off the rain as he also avoids facing the reckoning, and Osvald's "reckless" rushing out in the rain without a hat, at least provoke thought! The ambiguity of *regne*, for rain, making up accounts, and judgment, is exploited in the play.

29. I have retained the words Kammerherre and Kammerherrinne from the Norwegian as Ibsen obviously intends us to note the echo, here.

30. *Teutonic Mythology*, I, 241.

31. *Ibid.*, II, 447.

32. *Ibid.*, III, 994.

33. *Ibid.*

34. And, perhaps, even his surname, Engstrand? It is, of course, very dangerous for a non-Norwegian to see meanings in Norwegian names: but a portmanteau pun on *Eng -el* (angel) and *strand* (wrecked, as in the English stranded) at least fits the first name, Jakob!

35. Whether the devil was known as "Old Nick" in Europe as in England is not known to the present writer; but Bishop Nicholas foretells that whenever there is ill-doing in Norway, it is a sure sign that he is around. Old Nick could not say more!

36. Phillippians 3:2.

37. A good account of the nineteenth-century attack on Pauline Christianity in the name of a reviving Hellenism can be found in Gilbert Highet's *The Classical Tradition* (New York, 1957), especially the chapter "Parnassus and Anti-Christ." In Ibsen's own lifetime a fellow countryman wrote a book entitled *Krist eller Ibsen* (Christ or Ibsen)!

38. Apart from the Tiresias-Oedipus confrontation, Manders's outburst irresistibly calls to mind the magnificent confrontation of Philip and the Grand Inquisitor in Schiller's *Don Carlos* where a great traditional, but blind, authority is set against a struggling intellectual enightenment.

39. Sigmund Freud, *Three Essays on the Theory of Sexuality*. Preface to the Fourth Edition, Vienna, May 1920. Avon Books, New York, 1965 (ed. John Strachey), p. xix.

40. *Teutonic Mythology*, II, 442–43. It is essentially these free spirits whose passing is regretted by the Wife of Bath in her Tale. Her lament that where, once, they were to be numerously found one now only can find Christian friars is an early symptom of the condition analysed by *Ghosts*!

41. Though, undoubtedly, they *have*, in this play! Helene, as the Hellenic and Christianized partner of the northern *Alving* brings to mind accounts of the Christianizing of the North, as in Grimm's Introduction (Vol. I) to *Teutonic Mythology* and the account in the *Prose Edda*, known to Ibsen, of how the northern gods themselves came from Troy (setting up a Hellenic-Scandinavian link). Helene's arrival at Rosenvold, already attached to Manders (the Church), her flight after a brief period of marriage, her return and conquest of her husband and his estate, could be a capsuled version of the history of Christianity in the North—it fits Grimm's account. I believe it *is* Ibsen's practice to find the large historical action within the local contemporary action; nor is this method unusual in the fiction of the nineteenth century: it is to a great extent employed by Thomas Hardy, for example.

42. Once again, one must accept Ibsen's insistence on the central importance of *Emperor and Galilean* to an understanding of his whole work, even if we are forced to go against accepted Ibsen commentary. The writer of *Emperor and Galilean* is not likely to share Helene's attitude towards Alving's sexual peccadillos. After all, Alving's pursuit of the maid implies that Helene was far from adequate as a sexual partner, as we would expect of a pupil of Pastor Manders!

43. Mrs. Inga-Stina Ewbank has a perceptive account of this episode in the anthology *Contemporary Approaches to Ibsen*, Oslo, 1966, p. 106.

44. Bjørnson wrote from Paris on its immorality, from which Norway was free. His remarks far outdo Pastor Manders' denunciations. Norway, and its literature, continually was invoked as a pure and wholesome antidote to the moral sickness of Europe, both by the unhappy Europeans themselves and by the Norwegians. (Cf. Robert Buchanan's eulogy of Bjørnson in the middle of his own battle with "the fleshly school of poetry" of Rossetti and Swinburne. *Contemporary Review*, No. 20, 1871.)

45. *Ibsen: Four Major Plays*, Vol. II, p. 88 (tr. Rolf Fjelde), New American Library (Signet), 1970.

46. In the essay *Joyce and Ibsen's Naturalism*.

47. The wine, brought up from the cellar, and resurrecting this sunlight and happiness, is similar to Keats's famous vintage "Cool'd a long age in the

deep delved earth" (and thus literally buried like a corpse) and resurrecting, in Keats's imagination, the vanished "dance, and Provençal song, and sun-burned mirth" (*Ode to a Nightingale*).

48. The particular emphasis given to the fact that the orphanage is uninsured (Manders' exclamation, "And no insurance!" is the curtain of Act II) is also emphatically prepared for in a quite lengthy discussion on the merits of insurance. "Insurance" suggests a faith in the avoidability of *tragedy*: the discussion draws attention to the hypocrisy of Manders, who insures his *private* goods but not this exemplary *public* asset; insurance, too, might characterize the lack of genuine concern with the permanent value of the actions by which Helene builds up the false image of Alving: the memorial is concerned only to whitewash the Past, not lay foundations for the Future.

49. Alving's titles, we notice, increase in earthly importance as he declines intrinsically. His highest peak is as Lieutenant; as Captain he graces the fraudulent memorial; but his grandest title, *Kammerherre* (Chamberlain), to which Johanna and Regine are attached, is reserved for the sailor's home, a point missed in most translations.

50. *Contemporary Approaches to Ibsen*, p. 102.

51. Osvald's spiritual/mental destruction (*aandelige nedbrudd*) of course, reminds us of the Furies that afflicted Orestes; but in the wider dialectic of the play that looks back to *Emperor and Galilean*, Osvald, as the younger generation, would represent the modern spirit itself which, deriving from a broken, defeated paganism and a life-denying Paulism, is destined only for collapse. Any renewal or "third empire" must return to the more vital sources of both traditions—a theme typical of nineteenth-century writers and thinkers.

52. This is very similar to William Blake's symbols of the Imagination's concepts of God, undergoing recurring cycles from babe to senility in his Prophetic Books.

53. *Brand*, my translation.

54. "Achilles *begins* the Greek world, and his antitype Alexander concludes it: and these youths not only supply a picture of the fairest kind in their own persons, but at the same time afford a complete and perfect type of Hellenic existence." (*Philosophy of History*, p. 273.)

The Germanic world, similarly, saw its past in terms of warrior heroes: Wagner's Siegfried and Ibsen's Sigurd are not dissimilar to the Greek Achilles.

55. *Ibid.*, p. 233.

56. Ibsen once wrote to Brandes: "Raphael's art has never really moved me. His people belong to a period before the fall of man." (*Letters and Speeches*, p. 86.)

57. "The mounting sun dispels all magic and bids the spirits back to their subterranean abodes." (Grimm, III, 720.)

58. Letter to Bjørnson, Rome, January 28, 1865. (*Letters and Speeches*, p. 39.)

Chapter Five

1. *Letters and Speeches*, p. 249.
2. *Ibid.*, pp. 264–65.
3. *Ibid.*
4. G. Bell, London, 1904, p. 25.

5. Maurice Valency has noted how the symbolism of *Rosmersholm* resembles that of the *Schicksalstragödie* developed by Schiller. (Cf. *The Flower and the Castle*, New York, 1966, p. 178.)

6. *Oxford Ibsen*, VI, 13.

7. J. N. Findlay, *Hegel: A Re-examination*, p. 95.

8. Ibsen, in fact, excised the *one* definite "proposition"—Brendel's belated concept of land reform, anticipated by Henry George—that appeared in an early draft of the play. In fact, in the entire Cycle, it would be difficult to find a play serving a *cause*: rather the issues raised serve to indicate areas, or functions, of Spirit or Consciousness, being illustrations, in appropriate order, of the total activity of the human spirit which is the complete subject of the Cycle.

9. Herbert Edwards, "Henry James and Ibsen," *American Literature* (May 1952), pp. 208–23.

10. *Oxford Ibsen*, IV, 60.

11. *Ibid.*, VI, 349.

12. *Ibid.* This is the essence of Schiller's program of lifting man from the "sensuous" sphere of his own baser impulses and the unjust power structure of the state (which represents the sensuous or natural man forming by force a repressive structure to serve dominant interests) to the "moral" sphere where, as in Kant's moral system, each individual freely assents to the creation of moral universals in which he will find his own highest interest. Schiller's program is best outlined in his *Letters on the Aesthetic Education of Mankind*.

13. *Ibid.*, 399.

14. Ibsen has been careful to establish these identities. Rosmer is an ex-priest, Kroll is shown to be despotic both as school headmaster and in his domestic life, and Mrs. Helseth is made to articulate the opinions and superstitions of the folk consciousness.

15. A summary of Hegel's account of this dialectic can be found in Appendix II at the end of the book.

16. *Phen.*, pp. 562–63.

17. *Ibid.*, p. 565.

18. *Ibid.*, p. 566.

19. *Ibid.*, p. 567.

20. *Ibid.*, p. 580.

21. *Ibid.*, p. 589.

22. *Ibid.*

23. *Ibid.*, p. 596.

24. *Ibid.*

25. *Ibid.*, pp. 579–80.

26. *Phil. Hist.*, p. 278.

27. Johann Gottfried von Herder, *Reflections on the Philosophy of the History of Mankind*. Ed. Frank E. Manuel. University of Chicago Press, 1968, p. 235.

28. *Ibid.*, p. 233.

29. *Oxford Ibsen*, VI, 328–29.

30. *Phil. Hist.*, p. 335.

31. *Ibid.* Hegel obviously is referring to Stoicism, and its attitude towards the world of the passions.

32. *Oxford Ibsen*, VI, 324.

33. *Phil. Hist.*, p. 335.

34. *Ibid.*, p. 351.

35. *Ibid.*, p. 354.

36. Bernard Shaw, in *The Quintessence of Ibsenism*, contrasted Rebekka's *northern* passion with the southern type of passion.

37. *Oxford Ibsen*, VI, 363.

38. If one studies Ibsen's drafts, one sees how he begins with the more abstract dialectic, often very broadly rendered, rather than with the human drama or with vivid character traits, and that only after this dialectical argument has been realized does he go on to "the more energetic individualization of the characters and their methods of expression." (Ibsen, *Letters and Speeches*, p. 232.)

39. Richard Wagner's sarcastic judgment.

40. Cf. *Teutonic Mythology*, II, 655–64.

41. *Oxford Ibsen*, VI, 299.

42. Hegel retells the satanic myth in philosophic terms in the *Phenomenology*: ". . . it was the very first-born Son of Light (Lucifer) who, by becoming self-concentrated, fell, but that in his place another was at once created." (P. 771.)

43. See p. 186

44. His first appearance in Hegel's text actually occurs a little before the chapter, "The Struggle between Enlightenment and Superstition," and this may explain why Brendel first appears in a sketch for *The Wild Duck*. The continual foreshadowings of characters and themes in sketches for a play, who turn up in the next play, which we find in Ibsen, suggests the dialectical continuity of the Cycle, similar to that of the *Phenomenology*.

45. *Oxford Ibsen*, VI, 325.

46. Diderot's character, in fact, brings to mind the intellectual rebels, forced into clowning in the presence of established powers in the history of Europe, so movingly honored by Jules Michelet in his *The History of the French Revolution*. It was these clowns, Rabelais, Molière, Voltaire, writes Michelet, who alone were carrying the values of Liberty, Justice, Truth, Reason.

47. *Oxford Ibsen*, VI, 306.

48. This, it seems to me, is the problem of Enlightenment drama itself, whose heroes, Nathan, Posa, even Egmont and Clara, fervently exhort others to the highest levels of noble conduct, friendly rivalry, and idealist activity while at the same time refusing to engage with the most complex and intractable areas of human nature.

49. An important part of Ibsen's meaning is lost here. Rebekka mentions the "*Slekts*tvil, *slekts*angst, *slekts*krupler" that Rosmer suffers from. These are doubts and fears and scruples in the blood, in the race, or the lineage to which Rosmer belongs: something below rational confrontation with which, nevertheless, the enlightened spirit must engage. In the life of the human race, they are the "trolls" that infest the mind and heart, or the ghosts that still return and walk again among us (*gengangere*).

50. *Oxford Ibsen*, VI, 370–71. (Rosmersholm's tradition has killed Beate, whose name means "happiness.")

51. *Ibid.*, p. 379.

52. *Ibid.*, p. 371.

53. *Ibid.*, IV, 438.

54. I believe the texture of Ibsen's plays is interwoven with innumerable such verbal and visual quotations or memories from the storehouse of Western culture in order continually to awaken in his audiences the richest possible responses. If nine-tenths of our psychic life is, like the iceberg, beneath the conscious surface, a buried storehouse of archetypal images and memories, the poet continually has to "awaken" this submerged life. It only *then* can serve a liberating function and not an imprisoning one.

55. *Hegel on Tragedy*, p. 107.

56. A major problem for Enlightenment dramatists. Carlos and Elizabeth, Egmont and Clara, even Thoas and Iphigenia have almost perceptibly to "shift gear" from the romantic plot to the ideological plot.

Chapter Six

All excerpts from *The Master Builder* are taken from the translation by Rolf Fjelde in *Four Major Plays*, I, N.A.L., 1965.

1. Loewenberg, p. 291.

2. An excellent account of the importance of the child motif in Ibsen's plays can be found in J. C. Kerans' "Kindermord and Will in *Little Eyolf*" in *Modern Drama*, eds. Travis Bogard and William I. Oliver, New York, 1965.

3. The parallel with Strindberg's Daughter of Indra in *A Dream Play* (1907) is very striking.

4. Northrop Frye, *Fables of Identity*, Harcourt Brace & World, 1963, p. 16.

5. A fuller account of Hegel's argument and its sources can be found in Appendix III.

6. *The Zend-Avesta*, Part I, *The Vendidad*, O.U.P., 1880, I, 10–11.

7. *Ibid.*, II, 180–81.

8. *Ibid.* p. 180.

9. *Ibid.*, p. 151.

10. Halvdan Koht mentions that Rydberg recorded a friend's comment on Ibsen's explanation of the basic idea of *Emperor and Galilean*: "Jag har icke hört Ibsen tala dumheter mer än den gängen" (I've not heard Ibsen speak foolishly except on that occasion). But *Emperor and Galilean* is thoroughly in the spirit of Rydberg's own thinking.

11. Snorri Sturluson, *The Prose Edda*, tr. R. A. G. Brodeur, N.Y., 1929, p. 6.

12. Grimm, I, 120, and II, 823. Cf. also Viktor Rydberg, *Teutonic Mythology*, tr. Rasmus B. Anderson, London, 1889, pp. 56–64.

13. Grimm, I, 403.

14. William Archer, *Playmaking*, Dover Publications, 1960, p. 234.

15. Richard Schechner, *The Unexpected Visitors in Ibsen's Late Plays* in the anthology, *Ibsen: A Collection of Critical Essays*, ed. Rolf Fjelde, Prentice-Hall, Inc., 1965.

16. Henry James, *The Scenic Art*, Hill & Wang, N.Y., 1948, p. 259.

17. *Four Major Plays*, p. 326.

18. *The Scenic Art*, p. 259.

19. Halvdan Koht, *Henrik Ibsen* (Ny, omarbeidd utgave), Oslo, 1954, II, 261.

20. Friedrich Niezsche, *Collected Works*, XI, 34–42 (ed. Oscar Levy), N.Y., 1964. (I have chosen Kaufmann's translation from *The Portable Nietzsche*.)

21. Grimm, II, 742.

22. It is tempting to see Peer as the pragmatic critic unable to hear the music of Ibsen's text!

23. *A Hegel Symposium*, p. 101.

24. *Ibid.*

25. The old reading of *The Master Builder*, which saw the old robbers' castle as Ibsen's heroic plays, the churches as *Brand* and *Peer Gynt* (with an embarrassing omission of Ibsen's major work, *Emperor and Galilean*), also decided, by some astonishingly optimistic calculation, that the grim demolition pieces from *The Pillars of Society* to *Hedda Gabler* were Solness's sunlit homes for happy families! Reading *The Master Builder* as an allegory of Ibsen's career is as trivializing as it is unrewarding: but it is still the accepted reading encountered in most criticisms pro *and* contra Ibsen.

26. Even Norwegian stave churches have somewhat frightening old pagan carvings on the *outside*.

27. The most frequent myth surrounding the construction of these great cathedrals, which seemed audacious examples of human hubris, is that the master builder climbed and fell from his highest tower—a sacrifice, perhaps, that reconciled the Christian community to such proud human structures.

28. *Modern Drama: Essays in Criticism*, Bogard and Oliver, pp. 192–208.

29. Another detail, both historical and mythical, associated with buildings, is the sacrifice of children whose bodies were buried in the foundations. As with the death of the builder from the tower, this sacrifice below, in the foundations, expresses the idea that human achievement must be paid for by human sacrifice.

30. Reinhold Niebuhr, in his chapter "The Tower of Babel" in *Beyond Tragedy*, has observed that any culture, ideology, or creed is a "tower of Babel": an attempt by humanity to gain godhood. Though climbing a prosaic church (or house) tower is no intrinsically superhuman feat, Ibsen invests Solness's act with overtones of the superhuman: the challenge to the Creator, the harps in the air.

31. *Brand*, tr. Gathorne Hardy, London, 1966, p. 131.

32. *Ibid.*

33. *Ibid.*, pp. 171–72.

34. This resembles the "daimon" of Socrates which, in the accounts of both Hegel and Nietzsche, was to destroy Hellenic culture and prepare the way for the self-estrangement of Christianity by detaching the individual from the sustaining, educative *polis* which had sought to create "beautiful noble forms" from its humanity.

35. This *is* an uncanny aspect of many early legends, such as the anticipated destruction of the Scandinavian pagan world by fire and its regeneration by new gods, which Christians were able to employ to their own ends; or the odd fatalism of the Aztecs whose legends anticipated the return of a white god (bearded) at about the time that Cortes and his Spaniards arrived. The Old Testament, of course, is the most familiar example of much prophecy later fulfilled, not entirely to the satisfaction of the prophets' people.

36. In addition to the suffering of Prometheus, mythology supplies us with that of Odin who was pierced by a spear as he hung upon the tree and sang

runes. To commemorate this suffering the vikings sacrificed their victims by a particularly savage form of torture and death—the "spread-eagle"—and northern mythology and history contain the tradition of the old leader sacrificed for the well-being of the tribe, in identity with the suffering of Odin. Odin also was credited with the gift of reading the future, a gift shared by certain young women associated with him. The Christian community, of course, commemorated, by fast, penance, flagellation, and *autos da fé* (burning of heretics) the suffering of their god: as savage a god as the gods of the Aztecs who also demanded human sacrifice. In a world that still sacrifices its young to its gods (its "ideals" or even its "interests") and still sacrifices its leaders on occasion, it would be difficult to find Ibsen's subject eccentric: particularly as the *scale* of our savagery has kept pace with the scale of our powers, while gaining nothing in psychological dignity or mastery.

37. The new house will never be a home for Solness, presumably because if he had survived his ascent of the tower he would have broken with Aline and joined Hilde; but the statement also predicts Solness's death.

38. *Complete Works*, XI, 242.

39. A passage so rich in historical overtones is bound to prompt speculation. Are the "nine lovely dolls" the Muses, as Dr. Alex Bolckman suggests?—suitably "unborn children" for the Muses are precedent to the art forms they represent.

40. *Four Major Plays*, I, xxxii.

41. This idealistic attitude towards reality is found again and again in Ibsen's correspondence. ". . . the only think I love about liberty is the struggle for it; I care nothing for the possession of it." (Letter to Georg Brandes, Dec. 20, 1870.) "I shall never agree to making liberty synonymous with political liberty. What you call liberty, I call liberties; and what I call the struggle for liberty is nothing but the steady, vital growth and pursuit of the very *conception* of liberty." (Feb. 16, 1871.)

42. Is it possible that the last four plays present, in sequence, *a development of consciousness* at the religious or ideological level? Thus, *The Master Builder* recovers the childlike consciousness; *Little Eyolf* records its death in the world of warring sexual-parental conflict; *John Gabriel Borkmann* rescues the youthful or adolescent consciousness from the parental quarrel; while *When We Dead Awaken* recovers the fully awakened adult consciousness. This at least would conform to the progressive nature of this group, from depths to heights, evening to dawn.

43. One is uncomfortably reminded of the *Punch* parody in which the hero is Dr. Herdal, frightened of taking his own medicine until, at last summoning resolution, he swallows a spoonful with an audible gulp while Hilde exclaims she hears harps in the air.

44. *Contemporary Approaches to Ibsen*, I, pp. 104–105.

Epilogue

1. *The New York Review of Books*, Vol. XX, No. 10, p. 12, June 14, 1973.
2. *Sincerity and Authenticity*, Harvard University Press, 1972, p. 89.

Appendix I

1. An adaptation from *Antigone*, 926. J. B. Baillie's footnote.

Selected Bibliography

The following is not a traditional "Ibsen Bibliography" but a selection of books with relevance to the theme of this book.

ABRAMS, M. H. *The Mirror and the Lamp*. Oxford University Press, Inc., 1953.
————. *Natural Supernaturalism, Tradition and Revolution in Nineteenth Century Literature*. W. W. Norton & Company, Inc., 1971.
AESCHYLUS. *The Libation Bearers*. University of Chicago Press.
ARCHER, WILLIAM (ed.). *The Collected Works of Henrik Ibsen*, Vols. I–XIII. Scribners, New York, 1917.
ARCHER, WILLIAM. *Playmaking*. Dover Publications, New York, 1960.
————. *The Old Drama and the New*. Heinemann, London, 1923.
BENTLEY, ERIC. *The Playwright as Thinker*. New York, 1955.
————. (ed.). *The Theory of the Modern Stage*. Penguin Books, 1968.
BUCHANAN, ROBERT. "The Fleshly School of Poetry." *Contemporary Review*, Nr. 20, 1871.
BURKE, KENNETH. *A Grammar of Motives*. Prentice-Hall, Inc., 1945.
DIDEROT, DENNIS. *Le Neveu de Rameau*.
DOWNS, B. W. *Ibsen: The Intellectual Background*. Cambridge, 1946.
EWBANK, INGA-STINA. "Ibsen's Dramatic Language" in *Contemporary Approaches to Ibsen*. Universitetsforlaget, Oslo, 1966.
FERGUSSON, FRANCIS. *The Idea of a Theatre*. Princeton, 1949.
FINDLAY, J. N. *Hegel: A Re-examination*. The Macmillan Co., 1958.
FJELDE, ROLF. *Ibsen: Four Major Plays*, Vols. I & II. New American Library (Signet edition), 1965 & 1970.
————. "Peer Gynt: Naturalism and the Dissolving Self." *The Drama Review* (T-42), Winter 1968, New York.
————. "The Dimensions of Ibsen's Realism." *Contemporary Approaches to Ibsen*, Vol. II. Oslo, 1971.
————. (ed.). *Ibsen: A Collection of Critical Essays*. Prentice-Hall, Inc., New York, 1965.
FREUD, SIGMUND. *Civilization and Its Discontents*. Translated by James Strachey. W. W. Norton & Co., Inc., 1962.
FRYE, NORTHROP. *Anatomy of Criticism*. Princeton University Press, 1957.
————. *Fables of Identity*. Harcourt, Brace & World, 1963.
GRIMM, JACOB. *Teutonic Mythology*, Vols. I–IV. Translated by James Steven Stallybrass. George Bell & Sons 1883–1888, reprinted by Dover Publications, New York, 1966.

HEGEL, G. W. F. *Phänomenologie des Geistes.* Verlag von Felix Meiner, Hamburg.

————. *The Phenomenology of Mind,* tr. J. B. Baillie. Revised Second Edition. George Allen & Unwin, 1949.

————. *The Philosophy of Fine Art,* tr. F. P. B. Osmaston. G. Bell & Sons, Ltd., London, 1920.

————. *The Philosophy of History,* tr. Sibrée. Dover Publications, New York, 1956.

————. *The Philosophy of Religion.* The Humanities Press, N.Y., 1962.

HERDER, JOHANN GOTTFRIED VON. *Reflections on the Philosophy of the History of Mankind,* ed. Frank E. Manuel. University of Chicago Press, 1968.

HIGHET, GILBERT. *The Classical Tradition.* New York, 1957.

IBSEN, HENRIK. *Efterladte Skrifter* I–III, ed. Halvdan Koht & Julius Elias. Christiania & Copenhagen, 1909.

————. *Letters and Speeches,* ed. Evert Sprinchorn. New York, 1964.

————. *Samlede Verker.* Hundreaarsutgave, I–XXI, ed. Halvdan Koht, Francis Bull, and Didrik Arup Seip. Oslo, 1928–1958.

————. *Collected Works,* Vols. I–XIII, ed. W. Archer. N.Y., 1917.

————. *The Oxford Ibsen,* Vols. I–VII, ed. J. W. McFarlane. Oxford University Press.

————. *Four Major Plays,* Vol. I–II. Translated by Rolf Fjelde. New American Library (Signet), N.Y.

————. "Professor Welhaven on Paludan-Müller's Mythological Poems," tr. Rolf Fjelde. *The Drama Review* (T-42), New York, Winter, 1968.

IBSEN, BERGLIOT. *The Three Ibsens,* tr. Gerik Schjeldrup. London, 1951.

JAMES, HENRY. *The Scenic Art.* Hill & Wang, N.Y., 1948.

KAUFMANN, WALTER. *Hegel: A Re-Interpretation, Texts & Commentary.* Doubleday & Co., N.Y., 1965.

KERANS, J. C. "Kindermord & Will in 'Little Eyolf.'" *Modern Drama,* ed. Travis Bogard & William I. Oliver. N.Y., 1965.

KIERKEGAARD, SØREN. *Either/Or,* I–II, tr. Walter Lowrie. Doubleday, N.Y., 1959.

KNIGHT, G. WILSON. *Henrik Ibsen.* Oliver & Boyd, Edinburgh, 1962. & Grove Press, Inc. (Random House), 1962.

KOJEVE, ALEXSANDRE. *Introduction to the Reading of Hegel.* Basic Books, N.Y., 1969.

KOLAKOWSKI, LESZEK. "An Epistemology of the Striptease." *Tri-Quarterly,* Northwestern University Press, Fall, 1971.

LESSING, G. E. *The Hamburg Dramaturgy.* Dover Publications, N.Y., 1962.

LOEWENBERG, J. L. *Hegel's Phenomenology, Dialogues on the Life of Mind.* Open Court Pub. Co., 1965.

MADACH, IMRE. *The Tragedy of Man,* tr. J. C. W. Horne. Corvina Press, Budapest, 1963.

MANN, THOMAS. *Essays.* Alfred A. Knopf, 1957.

MARCUSE, HERBERT. *Eros and Civilization.* Beacon Press, Boston, 1955.

————. *Reason and Revolution.* Humanities Press, Inc., 1954.

————. *Negations.* Beacon Press, 1968.

————. *One-Dimensional Man.* Beacon Press, 1964.

NICOLL, ALLARDYCE. *A History of the English Drama,* Vol. V, 1850–1900. Cambridge, 1959.

NIETZSCHE, FRIEDRICH. *Collected Works*, ed. Oscar Levy. N.Y., 1964.

NORDAU, MAX. *Degeneration*. Heinemann, 1895.

NORTHAM, J. D. *Ibsen's Dramatic Method*. Faber & Faber, Ltd., London, 1953.

PEACOCK, RONALD. *The Poet in the Theatre*. Hill & Wang, 1960.

POPPER, KARL R. *The Open Society and Its Enemies*, Vol. II. Princeton, 1966.

READ, HERBERT. *Art and Society*. Schocken, N.Y.

RYDBERG, VIKTOR. *Teutonic Mythology*, tr. Rasmus B. Anderson. London, 1889.

SCHECHNER, RICHARD. "The Unexpected Visitors in Ibsen's Last Plays," in *Ibsen: A Collection of Critical Essays*, ed. Fjelde.

SCHILLER, FRIEDRICH VON. *On Naive and Sentimental Poetry*. Ungar, 1966.

————. *Letters on the Aesthetic Education of Mankind*. Ungar, 1965.

SHAW, GEORGE BERNARD. *The Quintessence of Ibsenism*. 3rd. ed. London, 1922.

SOLL, IVAN. *An Introduction to Hegel's Metaphysics*. Chicago, 1969.

STURLUSON, SNORRI. *The Prose Edda*, ed. Arthur G. Brodeur. N.Y., 1929.

TRILLING, LIONEL. *Sincerity and Authenticity*. Harvard, 1972.

VALENCY, MAURICE. *The Flower and the Castle*. The Macmillan Co., 1963.

WAGNER, RICHARD. *Wagner on Music and Drama*, ed. Goldman and Sprinchorn. Dutton, 1964.

WILSON, EDMUND B. *To the Finland Station*. Doubleday, 1953.

YEATS, W. B. *Plays and Controversies*. The Macmillan Co., 1923.

Index